FUNDAMENTALS
OF
BOTANY

FUNDAMENTALS
OF
BOTANY

By

C. STUART GAGER

WITH 437 ILLUSTRATIONS

GYAN

Published by

Gyan Publishing House
5, Ansari Road
Daryaganj, New Delhi-110002
Phone: 011-47034999, 9811692060
E-mail: books@gyanbooks.com

Distribution Network
gyanbooks.com
India, USA, Canada, UK, Australia, France

ISBN : 978-81-212-6330-6 (PB)
First Published, 1916

2nd Impression 2022

Printed at: Gyan Press, Delhi.

FUNDAMENTALS OF BOTANY
Author: C. STUART GAGER

THE LARGEST AND OLDEST LIVING THING

The General Sherman "big tree" (*Sequoia gigantea*). This tree was 2,000 yrs. old when Christ was born. At the time of the Trojan wars and the Exodus of the Hebrews from Egypt, under the leadership of Moses, the tree was a sapling 20–30 ft. high. It has been alive during all of mediæval and modern history. Its height is 279.9 ft., circumference of the trunk at the base 102.8 ft., greatest diameter 36.5 ft., diameter 100 ft. from the ground 17.7 ft. Note that its lowest branches are at about the level of the tops of the conifers surrounding it. (Photo by Pillsbury.)

(*Frontispiece*)

FUNDAMENTALS
OF
BOTANY

BY

C. STUART GAGER

WITH 437 ILLUSTRATIONS

1916

TO

M. K. G.

AND

L. J. P.

PREFACE

An introductory course of study in botany should do at least six things for the student:

1. Teach him the fundamental elementary facts concerning plant life.

2. Acquaint him with the broad, illuminating generalizations, and with the theories and working hypotheses which have been formulated on the solid basis of observed fact. An intelligent comprehension of these fundamental concepts is far more important for purposes of general culture and a liberal education, and also for more advanced study, than an intimate acquaintance with the facts alone on which the generalizations are based.

3. Familiarize him with the methods of thought and work by means of which the science has been and is being advanced.

4. Give him some acquaintance with the great names in the history of the science, so that he may view our present body of knowledge in true perspective. The student should be made to realize that what we now know was not obtained "ready made," but only by painstaking investigation and search. Therefore, brief references are made in the following pages to a number of pioneers in the unexplored fields of botanical discovery. From an educational point of view it is quite as important to understand that our present body of knowledge has been a gradual

possession of the human race, and to know how we came to acquire it, as to possess the information which is our rich heritage.

5. Impress upon him the present limitations of our knowledge, and acquaint him with some of the more important problems awaiting solution.

6. Enlist his interest in the science by so presenting it as to make him sense its importance and value to human life in general, and to his own life in particular, and thereby stimulate him to pursue the study further, and, may be, to the point of making his own original contributions. A class that is properly taught can never inquire, at the end of the course, "What is the use of knowing all that?"

Outside of technical and professional schools, no introductory course in any subject should ever be planned or presented on the supposition that its main purpose is to pave the way for more advanced courses. The main function of all introductory courses is, as the name implies, to introduce the pupil to a new realm of thought, to acquaint him with a possible new interest in life. If he be led to discover himself in this new realm—well and good; if not—well and good also; he will find himself elsewhere, but will always be enriched and liberalized from the widening of his mental horizon by contact with another discipline than his major interest in life.

In presenting an elementary course, the aim should not be to make the subject simple—to remove all difficulties—but to make it really interesting, that is, significant to the pupil in his own life, and to make it as rich as possible as a revelation of those broad basic principles which are fundamental to all true culture, but which are to be amplified and more deeply investigated only in more advanced courses. The presentation should be made as simple as possible, consistent with the realization of these aims.

From the standpoint of pure science, the most fundamental problem of botany is that of the development of the individual plant; the ultimate problem that of the development of the kingdom of plants. In other words the foundation and the ultimate goal are, respectively, ontogeny (life-history of the individual) and phylogeny (life-history of the race).

Ontogeny is fundamental because without a knowledge of its processes the processes of phylogeny cannot be comprehended. Phylogeny is the ultimate problem because its complete solution involves an orderly description of all the phenomena of plant life, and their relation to each other.

Thanks to the nature-study movement, most students have nowadays acquired some knowledge of the parts and a few of the functions of a flowering plant before they take up the study of formal botany; for such, Chapter II will serve only as a timely review; for others, as an essential preparation for the subsequent chapters of Part I.

From an educational point of view, the most rapid progress and the most substantial results are to be obtained by an order of topics so arranged that each will throw the greatest amount of light on those that follow. It is also an immense gain for the pupil to be introduced to the broad generalizations of the science by being led to meet them for the first time in that type where their concrete embodiment is most clearly defined and most easily discerned. In the author's mind, acceptance of these two postulates points unmistakably to the fern as, *par excellence*, the best plant with which to begin the study of life-histories. A successful teacher of zoology once declared that frogs were created for the express purpose of serving as the introductory type in the study of that science; as strong a claim may be made for the fern in botany.

Such concepts as alternation of generations, sexual *vs.* asexual reproduction, fertilization, heredity, adjustment to environment, life-cycle are nowhere more clearly illustrated than in the fern; the essence of them all may be clearly comprehended by anyone who has carefully studied its life-history. And with what a rich equipment may the life-histories of all other forms, both higher and lower, be then undertaken! As Athene sprang full armed from the imperial head of Zeus, so, from a study of the fern, do all the essentials of alternation, sex, life-cycle, et cetera, leap clearly defined into the mind of the beginning student, there to remain throughout the course, illuminating all subsequent studies of life-histories.

During the past fifteen or twenty years it has been the general, if not universal, custom to study in the laboratory the same forms as those treated in the text. Part II of the present book has been planned with the idea of having, for the most part, different sets of forms discussed in the laboratory and the lecture room. This plan not only gives the pupil acquaintance with a wider range of types, but also tends to insure greater independence in the laboratory work. It has been tacitly assumed that, in connection with the use of this text, substantially the same classic types will be studied in the laboratory as have formed the basis of laboratory work for two decades. They are not only types for which material may be obtained with comparative ease in quantity, but also forms which have been demonstrated by twenty years of trial to possess large teaching value. Thus, for example, we have Ascophyllum Sphagnum, Anthoceros, Cycas, and Erythronium in the text, to be supplemented by Fucus, Polytrichum, Marchantia, Zamia, and Trillium in the laboratory. By this plan the laboratory work can never degenerate into merely having the student pretend to "verify" the statements in the text.

It is anticipated that a laboratory guide, planned to accompany this text and carry out the idea just outlined, may soon become available.

In the matter of illustrations, the author has been most fortunate in being able to command the services of Miss Maud H. Purdy for the preparation of all original drawings, and of Mr. Louis Buhle, photographer at the Brooklyn Botanic Garden, in making most of the photographic negatives and prints not otherwise acknowledged in the legends. For those so acknowledged the author expresses here his best thanks to authors and publishers who have freely granted permission to reproduce copyrighted as well as uncopyrighted illustrations. The collections of living plants, photographs, and drawings at the Brooklyn Botanic Garden have been freely at the disposal of the author, and grateful recognition is here made to that institution for the exceptional opportunities which it has afforded.

Special appreciation is here recorded for permission from Prof. David M. Mottier and Prof. Harlan H. York to reproduce, in advance of their own publication, Figs. 8 and 263, respectively.

Specifically, acknowledgment is made to authors and publishers, for permission to reproduce illustrations as follows: Prof. W. L. Bray and the New York State College of Forestry (Syracuse University), Fig. 266; Dr. N. L. Britton and Charles Scribner's Sons, Figs. 341 and 379; Prof. D. H. Campbell and The Macmillan Co., Figs. 275, 283, 140, 141, and 146; Prof. F. E. Clements and Henry Holt and Co., Fig. 27; Mr. Frederick V. Coville and the U. S. Department of Agriculture, Division of Publications, Fig. 336; Prof. H. H. Dixon and The Macmillan Co., Fig. 35; Doubleday Page & Co., Fig. 225; Prof. H. Garman and the Kentucky Agric. Exp. Station, Fig. 228; Prof. William F. Ganong and Henry Holt and Co., Fig. 69; Prof. Patrick Geddes and John Murray, Fig. 240; Geological Survey of Ohio, Fig. 581; Prof. W. D. Hoyt and the Bureau of Fisheries, Washington, D. C., Fig. 177; the Ohio Geological Survey, Fig. 412; Prof. A. C. Seward and The Cambridge University Press (London), Figs. 413 and 414; Prof. D. H. Scott and A. & C. Black, Figs. 415 and 418; Dr. Albert Schneider and Willard N. Clute & Co., Fig. 238; Prof. Hugo de Vries and The Open Court Publishing Co., Figs. 401 and 402; Prof. G. R. Wieland and the Carnegie Institution of Washington, Figs. 421–427; Prof. S. W. Williston, Fig. 432.

The conception of diagramning life-cycles, as in Figs. 321, 329, and others, appears to have originated with Prof. John H. Schaffner, of Ohio State University. These diagrams possess admirable teaching value.

It is a pleasure for the author to acknowledge a large indebtedness to his colleagues on the staff of the Brooklyn Botanic Garden, and especially to Dr. E. W. Olive, whose careful and critical reading of the entire manuscript and proof has robbed the reviewer of much that would have been rightfully his, and has added much of fundamental value. Special acknowledgment is made of Dr. Olive's interest and assistance in supervising the preparation of the drawing for Fig. 198, on the wheat rust, and for supplying the microscopical preparations from which a number of illustrations have been made, as indicated in the legends.

A similar valuable service was rendered by Dr. O. E. White in reading and discussing the manuscript and proof of Chapters XXXII–XXXVIII, and in reading all of the galley proof and part of the page proof; and by Mr. Norman Taylor, in reading manuscript and proof of Chapters XXVII–XXX.

The author is indebted to Prof. E. C. Jeffrey, of Harvard University, and Prof. E. W. Berry, of the Johns Hopkins University, for suggestions and criticisms in connection with the genealogical trees (Figs. 433 and 434), and especially to Prof. G. R. Wieland, of Yale University, who critically read the manuscript of Chapters XXXVII and XXXVIII, and to whose stimulating comments is due much of whatever value these chapters may possess.

For any imperfections and inaccuracies, of whatever sort, in the subject matter, the author alone is responsible.

C. Stuart Gager.

Brooklyn Botanic Garden.
July 19, 1916.

CONTENTS

PART I

INTRODUCTION

PART II

THE VEGETATIVE FUNCTIONS OF PLANTS

PART III

STRUCTURE AND LIFE HISTORIES

PART I

INTRODUCTION

CHAPTER I

FUNDAMENTAL NOTIONS

1. What is Botany?—The names of most sciences merely tell what they are about. Thus the term zoology (from the Greek, *zoon*, animal, + *logos*, discourse) indicates the study of animals, geology the study of the earth, mineralogy the study of minerals. A similar name for the study of plants would be *phytology*, from the Greek *phyton* (φυτόν), a plant, and this word is, indeed, sometimes used. But the generally accepted name, *botany*, tells more than *what* the science is about; it points back to *why* mankind ever came to study plants. The reason was because plants are so intimately and fundamentally related to our own lives that it becomes, not only interesting, but absolutely essential to know about them, and understand them.

The word botany comes from a Greek word, *bosko* (βόσκω), meaning, "I eat." Botany, then, was originally the science of things good to eat, and the term recognizes the fact that for all of our food we are either directly or indirectly dependent upon plants. The earliest "botanical" interests were naturally in plants as food. But it must have been discovered early in the history of mankind that some plants were not only not good to eat, but positively poisonous, causing sickness or even death; while others produced marked physiological effects, acting some on one part of the body, some on another, like medicine, and thus was early developed the study of plants in order to ascertain their medicinal properties, and their value in the treatment of diseases. This interest is still reflected in the Spanish name for a drug store—*botica.*

2. Relation of Plants to Man.—Thus we see that the primary reason for our being interested in plants at all was because they are intimately related to our physical existence and well-being. As civilization advanced, other uses for plants and plant products were discovered, and thus other reasons for being interested in them. They furnish all the wood of the world, and one has only to consider for a moment how absolutely dependent we are on wood, to realize still more vividly the intimate relation between the life of plants and that of man himself. Our houses and furniture are of wood, our food (the product of plants) is shipped in wooden boxes, crates, and barrels, over rails supported by wooden ties; most of the paper in use is made of wood pulp, and innumerable articles in daily use—lead pencils, tool handles, many musical instruments, *et cetera*—are made largely of wood. Surely, it would be rather strange if we did not have some interest, at least, in objects so closely related to our daily lives, our welfare, and our happiness.

3. Relation of Botany to Other Sciences.—It is not possible to study any one science in disregard of all the others. Plants are related not only to man, but to the air and soil in which they live; their life processes are chemical or physical in nature; they are distributed in space over the earth's surface, and in time, in the layers of rocks of various geological ages; and so the study of botany touches meteorology, chemistry, physics, geography, climatology, geology, the science of soils, and other branches of science.

4. Biology.—The science which deals with life in general is *biology*, and all the sciences which deal with living things are *biological sciences*. Zoology, human anatomy and physiology, bacteriology, and botany are some (but not all) of the biological sciences, and they are all more or less closely related to each other. There is no hard and fast boundary line between any of the sciences; they represent, rather, different points of view of nature. But it is convenient to subdivide our knowledge more or less arbitrarily for purposes of study.

5. Systematic Botany.—Just as the various "sciences" or "knowledges" represent different points of view of nature, so each science may have subdivisions, representing different points of view of its phenomena. The study of plants for the primary purpose of ascertaining their genetic relationships is *systematic botany*. The ultimate aim of this study is to disclose the course of the evolution of the plant kingdom; this aim can never be fully realized, because most of the necessary data have been lost forever in the course of the geological evolution of the earth. Systematic botany includes:

(*a*) *Classification*, or the arrangement of the various

kinds of plants according to some system (whence the term, systematic).

(*b*) *Taxonomy*, or the principles of classification, based upon the facts observed and their interpretation.

(*c*) *Nomenclature*, the principles and rules adopted for the formation and assignment of plant names.

6. Morphology.—If, in our study, our attention is centered chiefly on *structure and form*, our point of view is that of *morphology*, and we recognize external and internal anatomy, microscopic anatomy (*histology*), comparative morphology, experimental morphology (which attempts to ascertain, by experiment; the causes of form and structure), *embryology* (the study of embryos), and other subdivisions.

7. Physiology.—If we are interested primarily in what the various parts of the plant are *doing*, rather than in their form and structure, our point of view is that of *physiology*. We shall find, as we study, that the facts of form cannot be understood or explained except in the light of the physiological work of the given part; and conversely, that physiological work cannot be explained unless the structure is also understood.

8. Ecology.—Every plant lives in a certain place, with certain external surroundings; in other words it has a home, or, as we usually say, a habitat or *environment*. In order to live and keep healthy the plant must be favorably adjusted to the various features (*factors*) of its environment—the range of temperature, amount of light and moisture, components of the soil, the earth's attraction (gravity), and surrounding animals and other plants. *The science of the relation of living things to their environment is Ecology.*

9. Plant Geography.—The study of the present distribution of plants over the earth's surface, and of the causes and consequences of this distribution, is *plant geography* (sometimes called *phytogeography*).

10. Fossil Botany.—The oldest known rocks contain the remains of plants that lived thousands—probably millions—of years ago. These remains often, though not always, of stone, are *fossils*, and their study constitutes the study of *fossil botany*, or *paleobotany*. This study is not only interesting in itself, throwing much light upon our knowledge of plants, but is also of great value to the geologist, often helping him to interpret correctly the rock-layer, and to decide to what geological age it belongs. By means of fossils, we may also learn much of the climate of past ages, and the great changes that have since taken place. Thus, when we find fossil remains of tropical plants, such as palms, in the rocks of the present arctic regions, we know that there must have been a tropical climate in that latitude at the time the plants, now fossils, were living and growing there.

11. Educational Value of Botany.—From the preceding paragraphs it is evident that a study of plants will not only give us valuable information that may be used to advantage in every day life, but that it will give us a broader outlook than we might otherwise obtain over the past and present of the world in which we live; it may not only suggest to us the vocation we would prefer to follow, but may give us a breadth of view and a wealth of ideas that will help to increase both our usefulness and happiness.

12. Plan of Study.—We shall first review the structure of a familiar type of plant, and then make an elementary study of the fundamental life-processes involved in the nutrition and growth of the individual. The second part of the book will be devoted to studying the various kinds of plants, and the different ways in which they solve the same life problems of nutrition and reproduction.

CHAPTER II

THE PARTS OF A FLOWERING PLANT

13. Fundamental Terms.—The plants with which we are most familiar (flowering plants) are composed of various parts, such as leaves, roots, tendrils; and each

FIG. 1.—A cactus plant (*Rhipsalis pachyptera*) with leafless stem. The branches are flattened, thus exposing more green tissue to the light in the absence of leaves.

part has its special work to perform. The various parts of a plant having their own special work are called *organs*, and the special work of an organ is its *function*. Since they are composed of organs plants (and animals also) are said to be *organized*, and are called *organisms*. For a similar reason, the kingdom of living things is called the *organic kingdom*, or the organic world.

FIG. 2.—Kohlrabi, showing the stem modified as an organ for the storage of food, and a well developed tap-root.

14. Root and Shoot.—Everyone knows that the plants with which we are best acquainted have roots in the ground, and a stem with leafy branches above ground. It is well, however, to recall this elementary knowledge and to get clear ideas of these commonly recognized parts. The botanist recognizes leaves as merely appendages of the stem or branches, and branches as merely subdivisions of the stem. Stems may or may not have branches (Figs.

FIG. 3.—Fibrous roots on cutting of sugar cane.

1 and 305). The stem, with its branches and leaves, constitutes the *shoot*. The shoot, therefore, is all the plant except the roots. In broad outline, the structure of any common plant is made up as follows:

Plant body
- Root (with or without branches)
- Shoot
  - Stem (with or without branches)
  - Leaves

15. The Root.—When a plant has more than one root, there may be a main or *tap-root* with branches (Fig. 2), or there may be no clearly recognized main root, but numerous roots of equal value, each attached directly to the stem (Fig. 3). The root-system frequently subdi-

FIG. 4.—Aerial fibrous roots of the royal palm.

vides into smaller and smaller branches or rootlets, and these may *ramify* (branch and spread) extensively in all directions. Roots never bear leaves, but the surface of the finer, active roots is covered, for a short distance back from the tip with innumerable fine hair-like outgrowths, *root-hairs* (Fig. 36).

16. The Functions of Roots.—The functions of roots all have to do with maintaining the life of the individual plant to which they belong, either by holding the plant

FIG. 5.—Portion of root-system of a yellow birch (*Betula lutea*), showing roots serving to anchor the plant to the substratum.

firmly fixed in the ground (*anchorage*) (Figs. 4 and 5), where food elements are abundant, by taking in these food elements from the substratum (*absorption*), or by storing up, for future use, food that has been made by the plant.

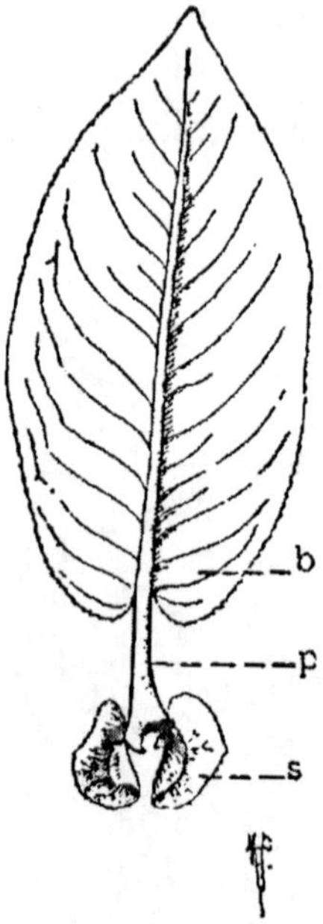

FIG. 6.

FIG. 6.—Leaf of a willow (*Salix sp.*). *b*, blade; *p*, petiole; *s*, stipules.

FIG. 7.—Diagram to show the essential parts of a "flowering" plant. *t.r.*, tap-root; *b.r.*, branch root; *cot.* seed-leaf (cotyledon); *i*, internode; *a.l*, leaf-axil; *n*, node; *a.b*, axillary bud; *r*, receptacle of floral organs; *ca*, calyx; *per*, perianth; *co*, corolla; *st*, stamens (androecium); *pi*, pistil (gynoecium).

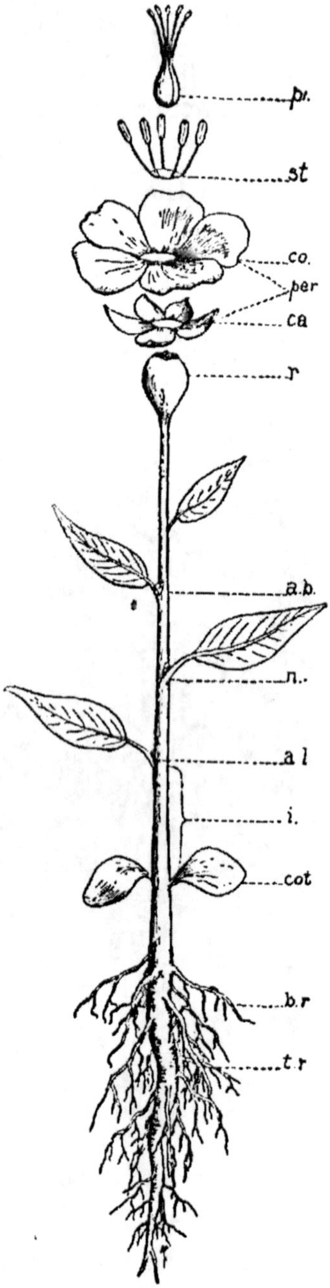

FIG. 7.

17. The Shoot.—As stated above, the shoot is composed of a branched or an unbranched stem, usually, but not always, bearing leaves (Figs. 1 and 57). The leaves are commonly composed of a flat, expanded, and usually green part (the *blade*), which may or may not be borne on a leaf-stalk (*petiole*). The portion of the leaf attached to the stem is the *leaf-base*, the edge of the blade is the *margin*, the tip of the blade is the *apex*, and the portion of the blade attached to the petiole is the *base of the blade* (Fig. 6). These parts may be tabulated as follows:

- Shoot
  - Stem
  - Branches
  - Leaves
    - Blade
      - Apex
      - Margin
      - Base of the blade
      - Veins
    - Petiole
    - Leaf-base
    - Stipules

The main functions of leaves are: (1) to elaborate plant food in the presence of sunlight; (2) to help regulate the water content of the plant. In these two functions lies the significance of the fact that the leaf-blade is flat, expanded, thin, and green. This will be explained in Chapters IV and VII. Leaves also have other important functions, to be mentioned later.

The branches serve to support the leaves, to hold them up into the light and air, and to connect them with the root-system.

18. The Flower.—The interpretation of the flower is not essential at this point, and is reserved for a future chapter (Chapter XXIX), when it may be better understood. It is sufficient here to state that the chief function of the flower is the production of seed.

The essential parts of a flowering plant are shown in the diagram (Fig. 7).

CHAPTER III

THE CELL

19. Historical.—The advancement of our knowledge of nature has often depended upon the invention of some new instrument that made possible observations that could not have been made without its aid. The balance did this for chemistry, the telescope for astronomy, the thermometer for medicine. The possibilities for understanding plant life were more than doubled by the invention of the compound microscope. By its aid the study of the finer internal structure of plants was made possible.

20. Robert Hooke.—One of the earliest to employ the microscope in this way was Robert Hooke (1635–1703) of England. He was at first interested in demonstrating the powers of the microscope on various objects. Among them he tried thin sections of cork, and found the cork to be composed of little compartments, which he called cells, since they roughly resembled the cells of a honeycomb. Marcello Malpighi (1674), an Italian, and Nehemiah Grew, an Englishman (1682), greatly extended the microscopic study of plants, adding so much to our knowledge that they are now often referred to as the fathers of plant anatomy.

21. Protoplasm.—At first the attention of botanists was devoted almost exclusively to the *walls* of these cell-like compartments, and to their shape and arrangement.

The walls were considered the important feature, and the term cell meant the space enclosed by the wall. All this was very natural, for botanists had quite generally, up to this time, devoted their best energies to studying the form and structure of plants, paying relatively little attention to their life functions, or physiology. Gradually, however, it came to be recognized that the really important part was the substance that filled the little compartments in all living *tissues*.[1] It finally came to be understood that this is the only living substance in plants (and in animals as well), and that the cell-walls, and in fact the entire organism, are built up by the activity of this remarkable substance. It was first called by several different names, but Hugo Von Mohl, a noted German botanist, called it *protoplasm*,[2] considering it as the first organic substance formed from the inorganic materials taken in by the plant. This name was generally adopted by both botanists and zoologists.

22. The Cell-theory.—The idea that all living things are composed of cells, that the cell is the unit of plant and animal structure, and that the essential thing about the cell is the protoplasm, was elaborated by Schleiden (1838) (for plants) and by Schwann (1839) (for animals), and was accepted as generally correct by all students of plants and animals. This doctrine became known as the cell-theory of Schleiden and Schwann. *The term cell is now used in biology chiefly to designate the protoplasm comprised within the cell-wall.* A cell, then, is not a compartment containing something, but is a structural unit of living

[1] An intimately connected layer, group, or body of similar cells, all having like functions, is a *tissue*.

[2] Greek *protos* (first) + *plasma* (thing formed).

matter. Many biologists now use the term *protoplast* (instead of cell) to designate the units of protoplasm.

23. Structure of the Cell.—Painstaking microscopic study of cells has revealed the fact that they have a wonderfully beautiful and complex structure (Figs. 8 and 9). The protoplast is composed of two clearly defined parts, a denser, more or less globular portion, the *nucleus*, surrounded by *cytoplasm* (*i.e.*, cell-plasm). Nucleus and

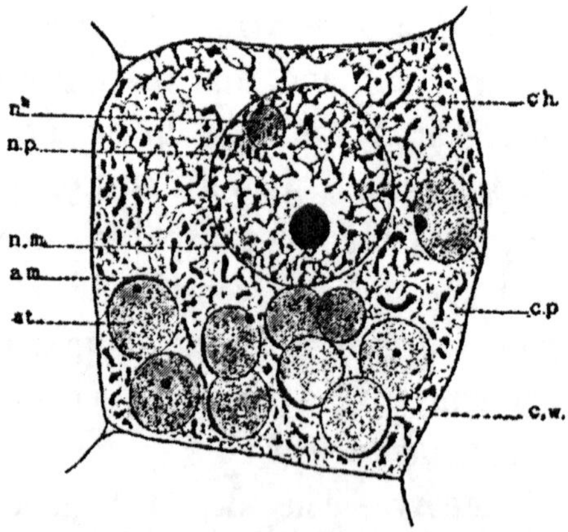

FIG. 8.—Cross-section of a cell from the root of a marrow-fat pea. *n*", nucleolus; *n.p* nucleoplasm; *n.m*, nuclear membrane; *a.m*, starch-forming plastid; *st*, starch grain; *c.w*, cell-wall; *c.p*, cytoplasm; *ch*, chondriosomes; they are scattered throughout the cytoplasm. (After D. M. Mottier.)

cytoplasm together constitute protoplasm. The nucleus was discovered by Robert Brown, in 1831. The substance of the nucleus is designated *nucleoplasm*, and there is generally a still denser body in the nucleus—the *nucleolus* (plural, *nucleoli*). Sometimes there is more than one nucleolus within the nucleus. The most important chemical substance in the nucleus is *chromatin*, a very complex *protein*, rich in phosphorus. The name chromatin refers to the dense color it acquires when treated with certain stains. The cytoplasm of many, possibly of all, plant cells contains, scattered through it, numerous tiny, deeply staining granules, called *chondriosomes.*

(*a*) The cytoplasm appears net-like, or *reticular,* in structure, and the spaces between the meshes are *vacuoles.* Each vacuole is filled with an aqueous solution of various

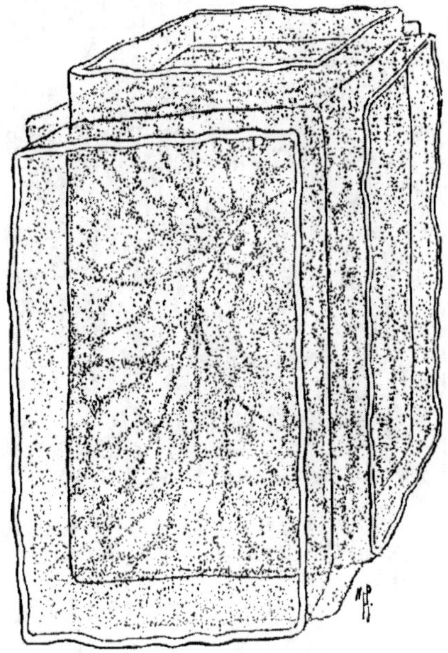

FIG. 9.—Diagram of a plant cell in perspective, with portions of adjacent cells. Note the nucleus. The lighter areas are vacuoles in the cytoplasm.

substances, known as the *cell-sap.* Insoluble solids of various nature, such as crystals and starch grains, commonly occur in the vacuoles.

(*b*) At every free surface, such as the outer surface and the walls of the vacuoles, the cytoplasm is specially organized into a *limiting membrane* (or plasma-membrane). The structure of this membrane is not well understood, although it is one of the most important parts, and much study is now being given to it, in an endeavor to understand it better.

FIG. 10.—Robert Brown (1773-1858). One of the greatest of English botanists. He discovered the nucleus in cells, and also the gymnospermy of Conifers and Cycads.

(*c*) The structural elements of a cell may be concisely tabulated as follows:

Cell
- Nucleus (nucleoplasm)
  - Nuclear membrane
  - Nucleolus
- Cytoplasm
  - Limiting membrane
  - Vacuoles
  - Vacuolar membranes
  - Cell-sap
  - Other contents (inclusions)
- Cell-wall

(*d*) Quite commonly, in plants, adjacent protoplasts are joined together by strands of cytoplasm passing through minute pores in the cell-wall.

24. Peculiar Properties of Protoplasm.—More is known of the structure of protoplasm than is indicated above, but a more detailed treatment is reserved until Chapter X. Quite as important as the structure of protoplasm are the physiological or functional characteristics, or properties, that distinguish it from every other known substance. The most significant and wonderful of these is its ability to reproduce itself. By the vital activities of animals and plants, their living substance undergoes a continual destruction, which is accompanied by continual construction. Parts which are destroyed are constantly replaced, and new protoplasm is continually being formed. No other known substance can do this. If a crystal, for example, of salt, is suspended in a saturated solution of salt in water, some of the salt particles in solution will attach themselves to the crystal in a regular manner, so as to enlarge it, while preserving its characteristic shape. But here, as is readily recognized, the crystal itself is entirely inactive. It does not change another kind of matter into salt, but merely serves as a center of deposit for more salt. Protoplasm, on the other hand, entirely alters the nature of the substances which enter into it, and recombines them into a substance like itself, with entirely new properties—in fact converts the non-living into the living.

25. Secretions.—In the course of its continual destruction and reconstruction, protoplasm gives off or *secretes* other substances, unlike itself and unlike the material of which it was formed; these are called *secretions.* Such is the origin of the cell-wall. It is secreted by the protoplast which it encloses. Sugar (as in the sugar-cane), starch (as in corn and nearly all plants), fats (as in Brazil nuts), and green coloring matter and other pigments, are among the substances secreted by protoplasm.

26. Complexity of the Cell.—A recent writer, after describing the minute details of cell-structure, states that, "The vital processes exhibited by a cell indicate a complexity of organization and a minuteness in the details of its mechanism which transcend our comprehension and baffle the human imagination, to the same extent as do the immensities of the stellar universe."

27. Value of the Cell-theory.—It is hardly possible to overestimate the value of the cell-theory to botany, and to all biological science. By means of it we are led to see that all the vital activities of any living thing have their seat in the protoplasts of the individual cells. If a plant or an animal grows, it does so because the individual cells of its body multiply and grow; if it respires, it is because every living cell of its body respires; if a wound heals, it is because the adjacent cells reproduce themselves and form new tissue to replace that destroyed by the wound; sickness results because certain cells behave abnormally, or perform their normal functions out of place; reproduction is the setting free by an organism of one or more of its cells, which become the starting point of a new individual. In fact, all that a plant or animal dose, physiologically speaking, is the sum total of what the cells that compose it do. Thus the cell-theory gives us a necessary, basic idea of all life-processes.

PART II

THE VEGETATIVE FUNCTIONS OF PLANTS

CHAPTER IV

LOSS OF WATER

28. Plants are Alive.—The most fundamental conception of a plant is that it is alive, just as truly and in the same sense as is any animal. Therefore it takes in water and food, respires, grows, moves, responds when stimulated, reproduces, grows old, and dies. We are so accustomed to associate life with activity that one who, for example, views a large tree, especially in winter, stripped of its leaves, and apparently motionless, except when swayed by the wind, is not always conscious of the fact that the tree really is alive. A study of plants, however, teaches us the fallacy of the idea that life is always associated with evident motion.

29. Kinds of Vital Activity.—Everything a plant does affects either one of two things—either (1) the maintenance of the individual, or (2) the perpetuation of the race to which that individual belongs. These two classes of functions are known, respectively, as (1) vegetative and (2) reproductive. This and the next five chapters will deal with the vegetative functions of plants.

30. Loss of Water Demonstrated.—If a leafy branch, cut from any plant, is laid aside for a time it will, as is well known, become wilted. Potted plants, if not kept

FIG. 11.—A fern (*Cyrtomium falcatum*), well watered and turgid. (Cf. Fig. 12).

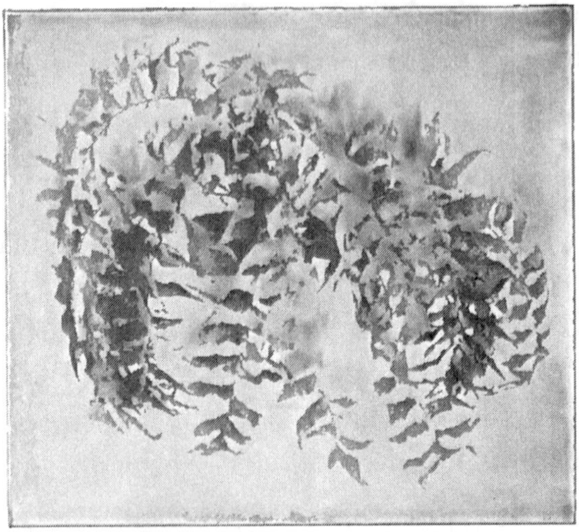

FIG. 12.—A fern (*Cyrtomium falcatum*), deprived of water for 48 hours. The same plant as shown in Fig. 11.

well watered, and plants growing out of doors, if not supplied with sufficient rain, will also wilt (Figs. 11 and 12).

FIG. 13.—Experiment to illustrate transpiration. The flower pot, covered with sheet oil-cloth, is placed under a glass bell-jar near a window at the right. The condition at the beginning is shown in jar at left; jar in middle after 3 hours. Inner surface of jar, on the side facing the light only, covered with a film of moisture condensed from water-vapor transpired by the plant; jar at right, after 24 hours; the entire inner surface of jar is covered with the film of condensed moisture.

Some plants wilt much more readily than others, but in all cases the wilting is due to the fact that water is being continually given off by the plant. This may be easily demonstrated by placing a living plant, or a few fresh

FIG. 14.—*Aster sp.*, showing transition from petiolate, through petiolate-stipulate, to sessile leaves. Note the elongation of the lower petioles, thus bringing the blade out to better light exposure.

leaves of any convenient plant, under a bell-jar or a tumbler, whose inner surface is first known to be perfectly dry. As a check or control on the experiment a second bell-jar should be placed beside the first one, but without any plant or leaves under it. The inner surface of the jar will soon become clouded by a thin film of moisture, and within a very short time, this moisture will begin to collect in drops (Fig. 13).

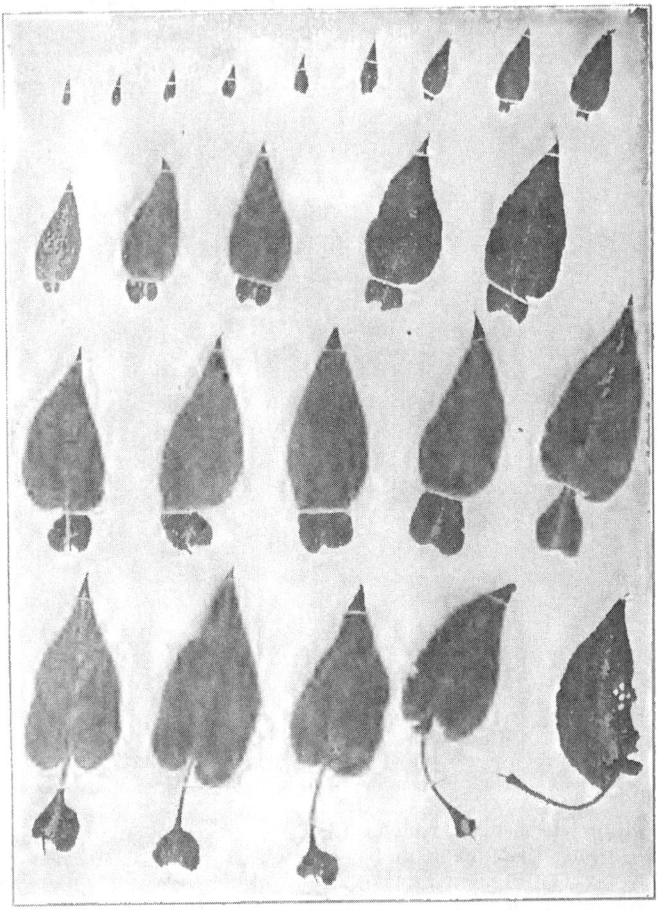

FIG. 15.—*Aster sp.* Series of leaves, all from one plant, showing gradual transition from petiolate (lower right hand specimen) to sessile leaf.

The surface of the control jar will remain perfectly dry. If the experiment is set in the sun, the result will be greatly hastened. This loss of water *from within* living plants is called *transpiration,* in recognition of the fact that the moisture must pass through the epidermis.

31. Function and Structure.—As stated in Chapter I, the function of an organ cannot be intelligently discussed unless its structure is understood, and *vice versa,* the structure of any part is without meaning, except as

FIG. 16.—Leaf of a banana (*Musa sapientum*), showing enormous development of the blade, and also how easily a leaf-blade may be torn in the absence of a marginal vein. This leaf-blade (*i.e.* without the petiole) measured over 15 ft. long and 3 ft. wide, thus exposing over 45 sq. ft. of green tissue to the light.

viewed in the light of its function. Therefore, if we wish to understand transpiration and the other functions of leaves, we must first ascertain their structure. This has significance for us only in the light of their physiological work.

32. External Anatomy of a Leaf.—We have seen (Chapter II) that the three main parts of a leaf are the blade, petiole and leaf-base. These parts may manifest every conceivable variation as to shape and size, and bear every relation to each other as to proportion. The petiole

FIG. 17.—Leaf of Hercules club (*Aralia spinosa*), partly thrice compound. The leaf-blade measured 15 in. wide at the base, and 12 in. long.

may be more or less shortened, or it may be entirely wanting so as to make the leaf-blade *sessile* (seated) on the stem (Figs. 14 and 15). The blade may be greatly enlarged (Fig. 16), or more or less branched (Fig. 17), or it may be greatly reduced, or even entirely wanting. In the latter case, the

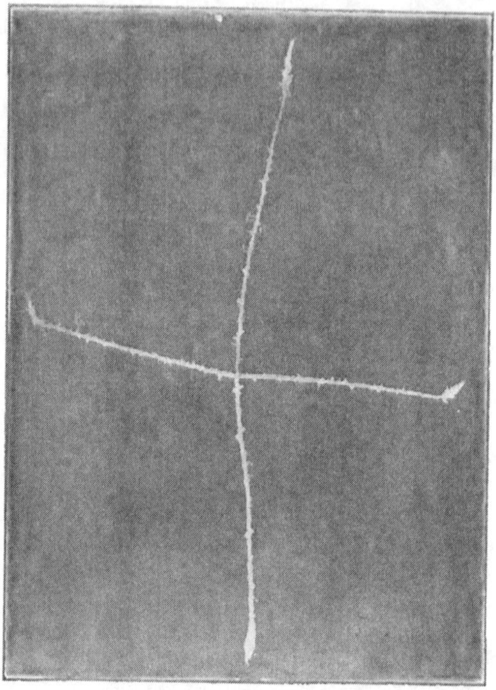

FIG. 18.—New Zealand raspberry (*Rubus australis*). The lower portion is the petiole; the blade is reduced to three spiny veins slightly expanded at the tip.

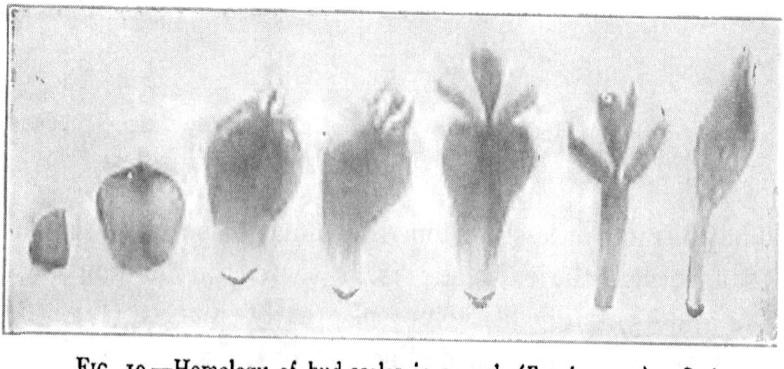

FIG. 19.—Homology of bud-scales in an ash (*Fraxinus sp.*). Series showing gradual transition from outer bud-scale (at left) to unexpanded foliage leaf (at right). The outer bud-scale is morphologically a leaf-base.

petiole may take on the character of the blade, and perform all its functions, as in the case of various acacias. In certain

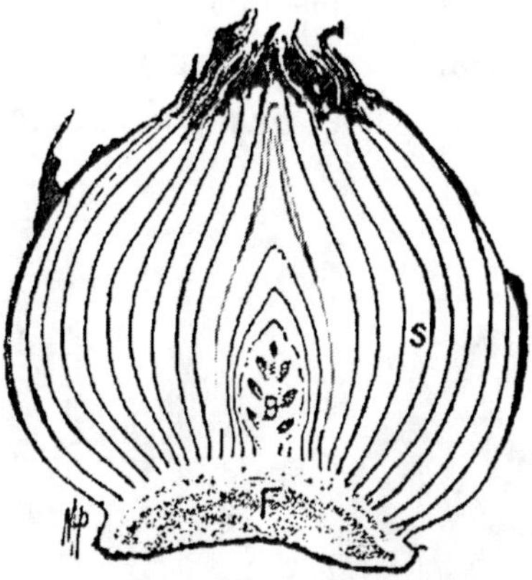

FIG. 20.—Tulip bulb; longitudinal section. *F*, solid stem; *B*, flower bud; *S*, leaf-bases serving as bud-scales, and also for the storage of plant food.

leaves nothing remains but base, petiole, larger veins, and the *tips* of the blade, as in the New Zealand raspberry

FIG. 21.—Buds of the tulip-tree (*Liriodendron tulipifera*), showing stipules as bud-scales.

(Fig. 18). In some plants, as for example, the grasses (Fig. 22), there is no distinction between petiole and blade.

Leaves may be so altered as to cease to be foliage leaves, and serve, for example, as bud-scales (Fig. 19), or other organs. In some bud-scales both petiole and blade may be wanting, the leaf-base alone serving as the scale (Fig, 20). Again, the bud-scale may consist chiefly of petiole.

FIG. 22.—Various types of leaf-blade.

or of blade, or (as in the tulip-tree) of stipules only (Fig. 21). Variations of leaves are illustrated in Fig. 22.

It is not essential here to endeavor to frame a definition of a leaf, though this would be a profitable exercise for the reader. The main thing is to emphasize the fact that the leaf is an exceedingly plastic organ, that is, appearing in many forms and disguises, and readily adjusting itself to wide variations in its surroundings. By virtue of this characteristic, it helps to enable the plant as a whole to become adapted to its surroundings. For the present purpose, we are primarily interested in leaves as foliage.

33. Internal Anatomy of the Leaf-blade.—If we take any convenient foliage-leaf, such as, for example, a leaf

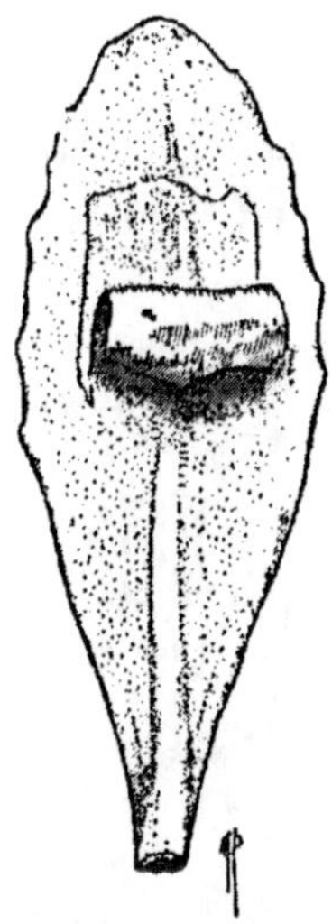

FIG. 23.—Leaf of a live-for-ever (*Sedum sp.*), with a portion of the epidermis peeled back. Underneath the epidermis is the mesophyll.

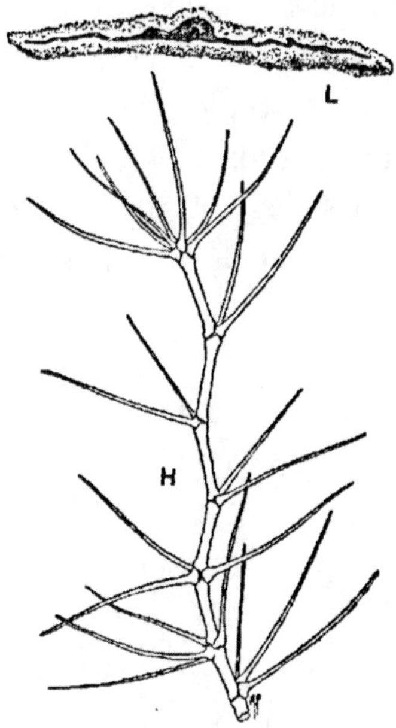

FIG. 24.—Mullein (*Verbascum Thapsus*). *L*, cross-section of leaf-blade, showing relative thickness of layer of epidermal hairs; *H*, a single hair from a leaf (greatly magnified).

of the common lilac, we may readily demonstrate, with the aid of a scalpel or sharp knife, that the surfaces of the blade are covered with a thin skin or *epidermis*, which may be peeled off (Fig. 23), disclosing the mid-leaf substance (*mesophyll*), lying between the upper and the lower epidermis. In many leaves (for example, those of the great mullein), there are numerous more or less prominent "hairs," which are outgrowths of the epidermis, and readily come away with it when it is peeled off (Fig. 24). We notice that the veins of the leaf appear to be imbedded in the mesophyll, and that they lie somewhat nearer the lower than the upper surface. The lower surface is also seen to be usually of a lighter green color than the upper, and the lower epidermis may be peeled off more readily than the upper. The explanation of these facts is found in the microscopic structure (histology) of the mesophyll, soon to be studied.

34. Histology of the Leaf-epidermis.—When a small portion of the lower epidermis is examined under the

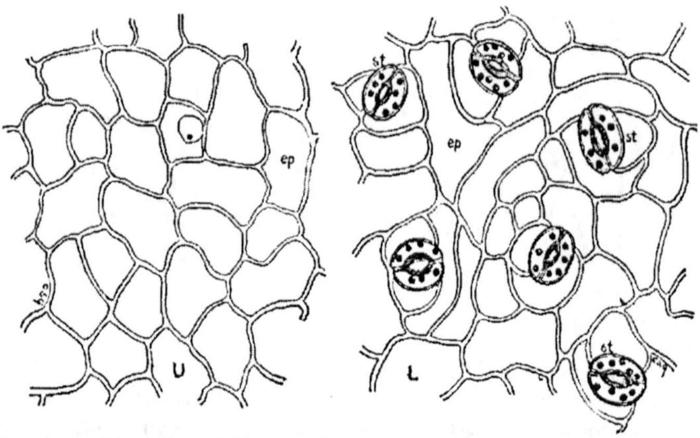

FIG. 25.—Lizard's tail (*Saururus cernuus*). Portions of leaf-epidermis; *U*, upper epidermis; *L*, lower epidermis; *ep*, epidermal cell; *st*, guard-cells of the stomata. (Camera lucida drawing.)

microscope it is seen to be composed of larger cells, irregular in shape, and of smaller cells, usually somewhat half-moon shaped, occurring in pairs, and the pairs irregularly distributed at frequent intervals among the larger cells (Fig. 25). The latter possess no green coloring matter, but the smaller cells contain numerous green bodies. The green substance is *chlorophyll* (leaf-green), and the separate green particles are *chlorophyll-bodies*, or *chloroplasts*. Between each pair of smaller cells is a tiny hole or *stoma* (from a Greek word meaning mouth or opening), and the two cells are the *guard-cells* of the *stoma* (plural, *stomata*) (Fig. 26).

The structure of the upper epidermis of the same leaf (Fig. 23) is seen to be quite similar to that of the lower,

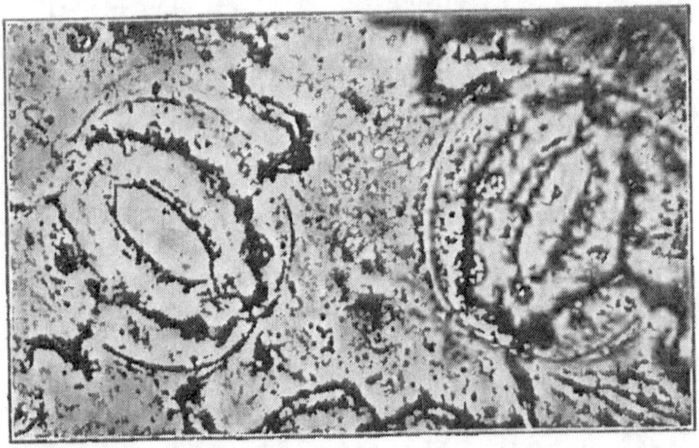

FIG. 26.—Photomicrograph of stomata from a leaf of *Verbena ciliata*, showing their condition at 9 A.M. (After Lloyd.)

except that in most plants there are fewer stomata in the upper than in the lower epidermis. In some leaves (*e.g.*, barberry, osage orange, lilac) there are no stomata in the upper epidermis; while in other plants, such as, for example, the water-lily whose leaves float on water, there are stomata in the upper epidermis but none in the lower.

35. Microscopic Structure in Cross-section.—Since all objects examined with the aid of a microscope are observed with transmitted light, that is, by light that passes through them to the eye,[1] in order to examine opaque objects, sections of them must be cut, thin enough to be readily transparent. The conditions of observation are also much simplified by this means.

Thin cross-sections of leaves, that is, sections cut at right angles to the surface, are readily made with a sharp

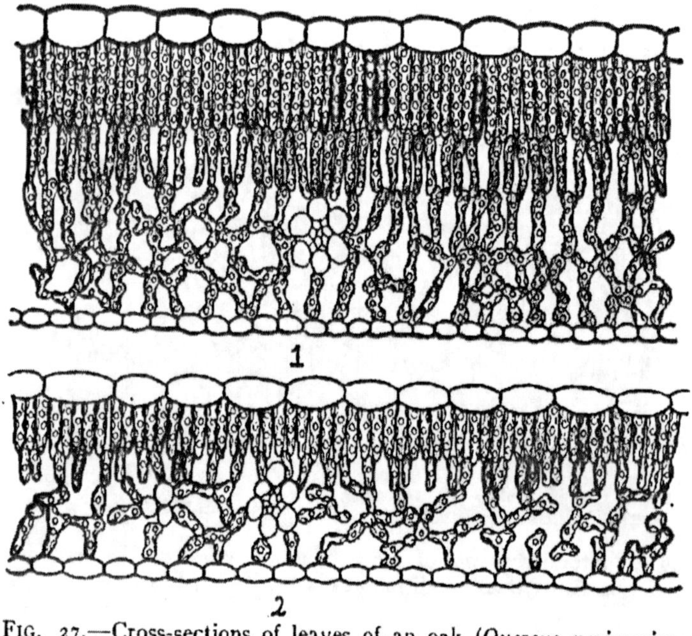

FIG. 27.—Cross-sections of leaves of an oak (*Quercus novimexicana*), showing the effect of different light conditions on the internal anatomy. 1, from leaf growing in sunlight; 2, from leaf growing in the shade. (After Clements.)

razor. When examined with the microscope, such sections disclose a structure similar to that illustrated in Fig. 27. The epidermis, both upper and lower, is seen to consist of a single layer of cells. The free surface of the outer cell-wall is coated with a layer of a wax-like substance,

[1] Objects examined with the unaided eye are observed with light *reflected* from their surface to the eye.

known as *cuticle*. The *mesophyll*, or leaf-parenchyma, has two well-defined regions. In the portion next the upper epidermis the cells are elongated, and arranged close together at right angles to the epidermis. This portion is the *palisade* layer. In the other portion of the mesophyll the cells are of irregular shapes, and loosely arranged, with *intercellular spaces*. Commonly, also, the palisade cells contain more, and more deeply colored, chlorophyll grains than do the cells of the spongy parenchyma. The above facts make it clear why the upper surface of leaves is darker green than the lower surface. Cross-sections of veins are also seen, imbedded in the spongy parenchyma. Details of their structure need not be considered here. The absence of chlorophyll from the epidermal cells (except the guard-cells) may also be noted.

36. Stomata and Guard-cells.—In the lower epidermis, sections of the stomata are found, and it is readily seen that the stomata are tiny holes or pores through the epidermis, connecting the intercellular spaces with the outside air. The guard-cells are so constructed that under changing conditions of light and moisture they may become more or less turgid. When they become more turgid, they are more convex, and thus enlarge the diameter of the stoma; when less turgid, they become less convex and this diminishes the size of the opening, and in certain cases may even close it completely. By these changes the passage of water-vapor or other gases through the stomata may be either facilitated or retarded.

37. Structure of the Petiole.—The main function of the petiole is to hold the leaf-blade well exposed to light, while, at the same time, keeping it connected with the stem. It will have been noted already that the veins converge at the base of the blade (Fig. 22). They may be traced from this point, through the petiole, into the branch. The veins are composed of *fibers* and *vessels*,

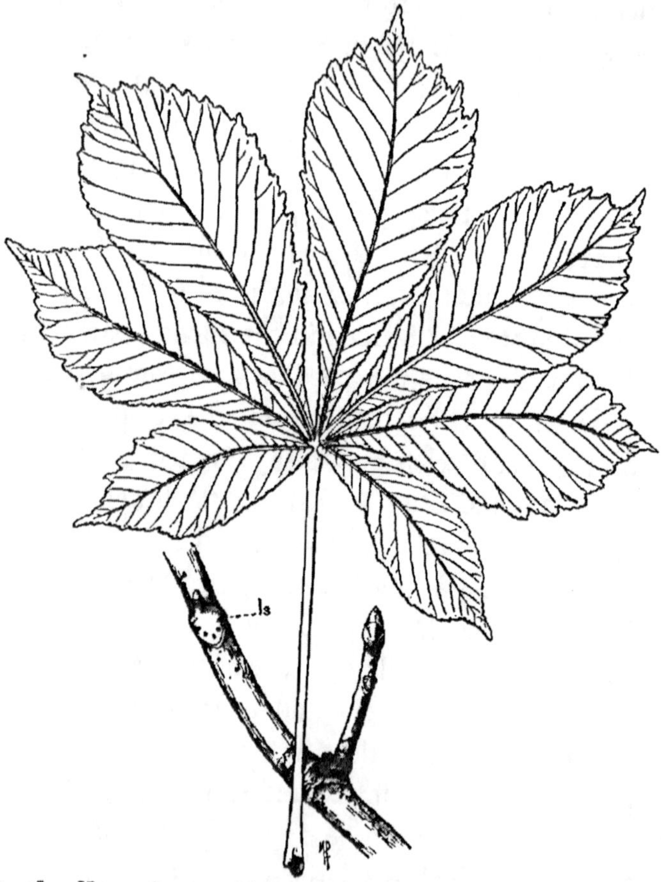

FIG. 28.—Horse-chestnut (*Aesculus Hippocastanum*). *ls*, leaf-scar, showing scars of seven fibro-vascular bundles, corresponding, in number, to the seven leaflets of the compound leaf, formerly attached at *ls*. The leaf is drawn to a smaller scale than the branch.

closely associated, and are, therefore, called *fibro-vascular bundles*. A cross-section of the petiole of a horse-chestnut leaf, for example, shows one fibro-vascular bundle for each leaflet of the compound blade (Fig. 28); each of the seven bundles extends out into the blade as the prominent *mid-vein* of a leaflet. In a common "trick" of childhood, the epidermis of the petiole of the common, broad-leaved plantain is broken by sharply bending the petiole, or by carefully cutting with a knife. The petiole may then be carefully pulled apart, so as to disclose the fibro-vascular bundles without breaking them (Fig. 29). These bundles are the channels through which liquids pass between the leaf-blade and the branch.

FIG. 29.—Leaf of plantain (*Plantago*), with the petiole stretched lengthwise from a transverse cut, showing the fibro-vascular bundles that continue up into the five main veins of the leaf-blade.

38. Transpiration.—In order to understand transpiration, we should have in mind a clear picture of the conditions within a leaf.[1] Because of moisture in the cells, the cell-walls are saturated. From their moist surfaces water is continually evaporating into the intercellular spaces (Fig. 27), so that the air in those spaces is always nearly *saturated;* that is, it holds nearly as much water as possible in the form of vapor. From the intercellular spaces the vapor diffuses out through the stomata, and passes off into the air. If the outer air is also very humid, as frequently near the ground after sunset, the

[1] While loss of water is not confined to leaves, they are the chief organs of transpiration, and if we understand the process in them, we shall understand it elsewhere.

vapor from within the leaves may not be able readily to pass off, and will accumulate in drops on the surface of the leaves, forming dew. The passing off of water is not confined to the stomata (*stomatal transpiration*), but may take place through portions of the epidermis where there are no stomata, the water passing through the cuticle (*cuticular transpiration*).

39. Control of Transpiration.—The rate of transpiration is controlled by both external and internal factors. If

FIG. 30.—*Gasteria nigricans*. Succulent leaves, with thick cuticle serving for the storage of water.

the outer air is very humid, water cannot evaporate into it as rapidly as when it is less humid. On humid days, therefore, transpiration will be diminished. It is in recognition of this fact that gardeners, in "wetting down" a plant house, do not confine the water to the plants, but thoroughly wet the walks and walls so as to maintain a favorable humidity of the air.

Naturally, anything that tends to increase humidity will retard transpiration. If the air in the vicinity of foliage is quiet, its humidity will increase owing to the

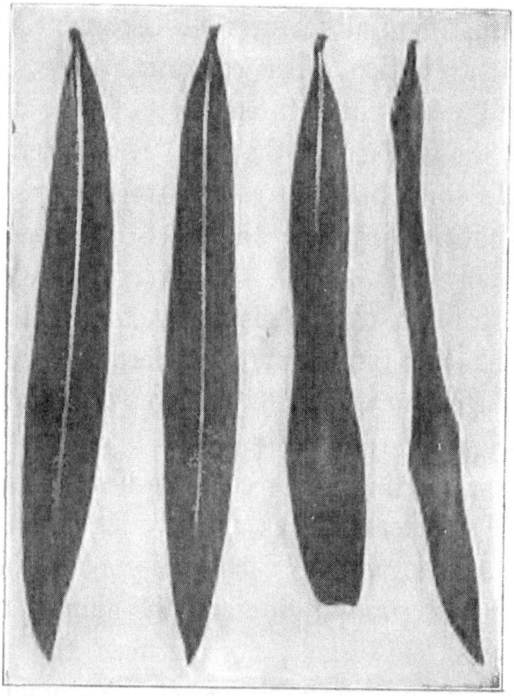

FIG. 31.—Transpiration from four leaves of oleander. At the left, both sides coated with cocoa butter; next, under surface, only, coated; next, upper surface, only, coated; right, uncoated. All exposed for the same length of time.

water-vapor from the leaves, but when the wind blows, fresh portions of less humid air are continually brought into contact with the plants, and transpiration becomes more rapid. This is why a plant or a bouquet, being carried from one place to another, will keep fresh longer if wrapped with paper.

Warm air can contain more water-vapor in a given space than colder air. For this reason, other things being equal, plants on which the sun is shining will transpire more rapidly than those in the shade, or than on a cool, cloudy day. Florists take advantage of this fact by keeping cut flowers in a place artificially cooled by ice.

Certain structural features of the plant operate to reduce transpiration. The epidermal hairs, as for example on the mullein leaf, tend to retain the more humid air near the surface of the leaf, even when the wind blows. In some plants (*e.g.*, the tropical gasterias, Fig. 30) the cuticle is greatly thickened, so that water can pass off only very slowly. The very curling of leaves, when they begin to wilt, also tends to reduce transpiration by reducing the amount of surface exposed (Fig. 31). The arrangement of leaves in a compact rosette accomplishes the same result (Fig. 32).

Evidence obtained by recent studies of transpiration in several different species of flowering plants indicates that there is no necessary nor uniform relation between the amount of transpiration and the number of stomata per unit of leaf-surface, nor between the amount of transpiration and the total area of the stomata. These studies indicate that, contrary to our earlier conceptions, the amount of transpiration is probably regulated by a complex of several factors, among which the stomata are less important than was formerly supposed.

40. Advantages of Transpiration.—It might seem, at first thought, that the loss of water by transpiration is a disadvantage to plants. Of course this would be the case were it not possible for the roots to take in water as fast as it is lost. When this is not possible, transpiration becomes a real source of danger to the plant. Indirectly, however, transpiration performs a great service, for it aids in, and is probably one of the chief causes of, the ascent of liquids taken in from the soil. Were water never given off, it would not be possible for tissues,

FIG. 32.—*Sempervivum tabulæforme.* The arrangement of the leaves in a compact rosette, the hairs on their margins, their thick cuticle, and other characters, make the plant xerophytic or drought-resistant.

already turgid, to receive a fresh supply, and, since all the elements of plant-food can be carried through the plant only in solution, the importance of this point can hardly be overestimated.

The manner in which transpiration may facilitate the passage of liquids through the stem may be illustrated by a very simple experiment. A small leafy branch of any plant (a branch of some evergreen is excellent to

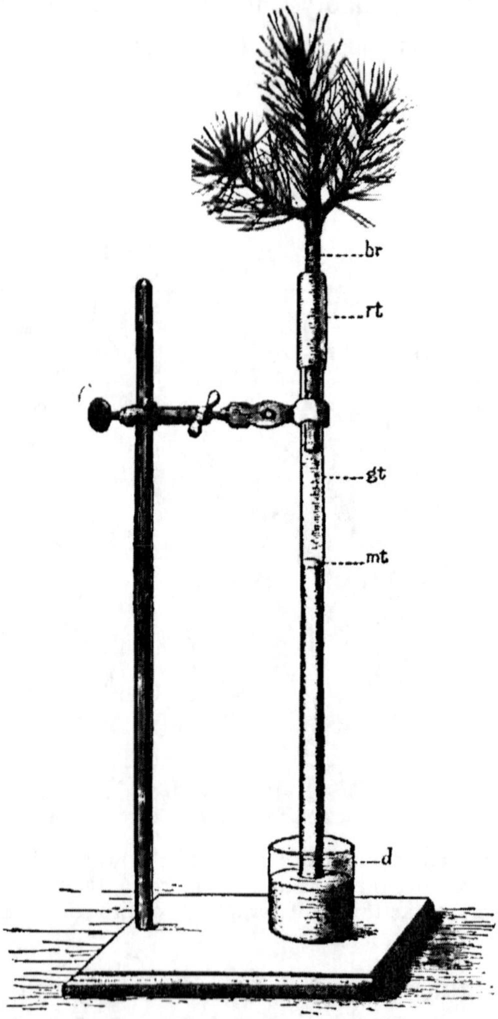

FIG. 33.—Experiment to illustrate the so-called "lifting power" of transpiration. *d*, dish of mercury; *mt*, surface of mercury column that has risen in the glass tube, *gt*; *rt*, rubber tube; *br*. branch of a pine tree, whose leaves are transpiring.

use) is inserted in the end of a piece of glass tubing about 3 feet long. The joint between the glass and the branch should be made perfectly air-tight by means of a piece of rubber tubing, about 1 inch long, extending over the end of the glass tube. Fill the glass tube with water, then invert it, and place the lower end in a dish of mercury, having care that the water remains up in the tube far enough to cover the end of the branch (Fig. 33). As transpiration proceeds, the pressure of the atmosphere will force the mercury up the glass tube as rapidly as the water passes into the plant. This experiment is sometimes said to illustrate the "lifting power" of transpiration, but from the explanation here given, it is seen that the mercury is not lifted, but pushed up the tube by the pressure of the outside air. This experiment should not be regarded as illustrating more that it really does; it does not, for example, explain the rise of sap in plants.

41. Ascent of Sap.—It is a well-known fact that, although living leaves deprived of water merely become wilted, dead leaves eventually dry up; they cannot supply themselves with water, although evaporation is taking place from their surfaces, and although the stem to which they are attached is abundantly supplied. We must conclude, therefore, that merely physical forces (imbibition and evaporation) are not sufficient to account for the rise of liquids in stems. Recent experiments indicate that, in this connection, much importance should be attached to the secretion of substances by the leaf—a physiological process.

We are familiar with such action in the secretion of nectar by the nectar-glands of flowers (Fig. 34). Some leaves (*e.g.*, *Colocasia antiquorum*) also secrete water so rapidly that it falls in drops from their tips. It is probable that, in transpiration, the protoplasm in the mesophyll cells of leaves first secretes a solution to the outer surface of the cells, and that this solution becomes concentrated by evaporation of the liquid solvent into the intercellular spaces. The concentrated solution, then, by osmotic action, causes more water to be withdrawn from the interior of the cells, and these, in turn, are

FIG. 34.—Petal of crown imperial (*Fritillaria imperialis*), showing the remarkably large drop of nectar (*n*), secreted by the nectar gland near the base of the petal.

replenished from the fibro-vascular bundles. On account of the *tensile strength* of the water column in these bundles the water is raised as rapidly as it is transpired from the leaves.

Thus, while the physical processes of osmosis and transpiration may be factors in causing the ascent of sap, the physiological process of secretion is also of very great importance. Moreover, on this basis we are able to account for the ascent of sap in submerged aquatic plants, like eel-grass, pond-weed, and others, where transpiration is not possible. In fact it may be shown, experimentally, that a leafy branch can raise water through

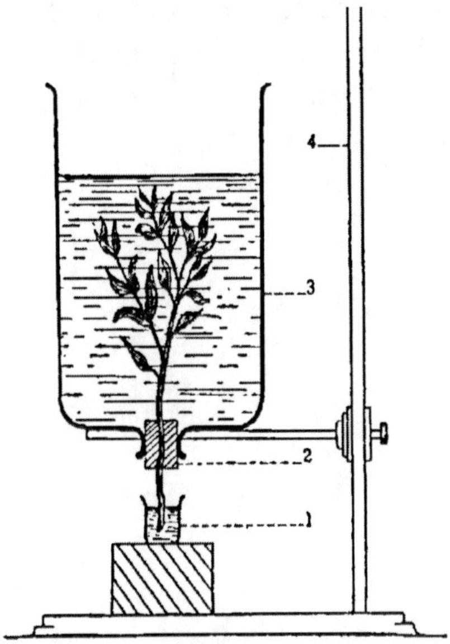

FIG. 35.—Experiment to show that secretory action in the cells of a leaf are able to cause the rise of liquid in a branch, when evaporation from the leaf-surfaces is impossible. 1, Beaker containing solution of eosin; 2, cork; 3, inverted glass bell-jar containing water; 4, iron support. In this experiment the eosin rose rapidly in the branch. (Modified from H. H. Dixon.)

the fibro-vascular bundles, even when submerged. The apparatus is set up as shown in Fig. 35, where the leafy branch, immersed in water in an inverted glass bell-jar, has the cut end of the stem in a solution of eosin or red ink. Under these conditions only secretion can operate to withdraw water from the fibro-vascular bundles, and yet the eosin will rise in the branch and into the leaves.

From this and other experiments (not described here) it is evident that the withdrawal of water from the fibro-vascular bundles in the stem by the combined action of secretion, osmosis, and transpiration may account for the ascent of sap, even to the tops of very tall trees and vines. These processes are able to raise the water column on account of its great tensile strength, by which it does not separate, although gravity pulls down on its lower end, and the physiological processes in the leaves result in a pull at its upper end.

CHAPTER V

ABSORPTION OF WATER

42. Importance of Water.—Everyone knows that plants must have a suitable amount of water in order to live and keep healthy. Deprived of water they wilt, and finally die. If they are given too much water they also suffer. The water serves many purposes. In the first place, it is needed to keep the protoplasm sufficiently moist. Protoplasm may keep alive though very dry, as in the case of dry seeds, but in order to be most active it must have enough water to keep it in a semi-fluid condition. In the second place, were it not for water, no food materials could reach the protoplasts, for there are, in general, no openings in the cell-walls large enough for solid matter to pass through. Therefore, all substances must reach the protoplasts in aqueous solution. Again, water is necessary in the transportation of materials from one part of a plant to another; and finally, it is necessary in order to keep plants from wilting, for no plant can live if it is permanently wilted.

43. Relative Water Requirement.—The amount of water required by various kinds of plants in order to reach maturity and produce seeds varies greatly. It depends in part upon the weather conditions (*e.g.*, sunshine, wind, humidity, and other factors), in part upon food supply, and in part upon the species or variety of plant. Some species are so constructed that they conserve more of the water taken in than do other species. The two extremes in this respect are desert plants, such as cacti, sage-brush, and euphorbias, and water-loving plants, such as water-lilies, ferns, touch-me-not or jewel-weed, and cucurbits like pumpkin and squash. A convenient method of measuring these differences is to compare the weight of water absorbed with the weight of dry matter produced. This ratio is known as the *relative water requirement* of the plant. Thus, if a given plant, during its growth, has taken in 100 pounds of water, and the solid matter produced, when dried out to a constant weight in a drying oven, weighs 2 pounds, the relative water requirement is (100 : 2) 50.

44. Government Experiments.—In experiments conducted for the United States Department of Agriculture, for the purpose of ascertaining the relative water requirements of various plants, it was found that the weight of water taken in by hubbard squash plants amounted in some cases to over 6,000 times the weight of the fruit, and to over 900 times the weight of the total dry substance, not including the roots. Other ratios, in round numbers, were ascertained, as follows:

TABLE I.—WATER REQUIREMENTS OF PLANTS

Plant	Water requirement based on	
	Grain	Dry matter
Rye	1,800	496
Rice	....	744
Flax	2,800	900
Cucumber	1,600	891
Sunflower	6,400	705
Purslane	....	300

45. Importance of Root-hairs.—In Chapter II attention was called to the root-hairs. Their chief function is the absorption of water and dissolved substances from the soil. This may be demonstrated by a very simple experiment. If a young seedling of bean, corn, or any other plant growing in soil, is pulled up, care being taken not to loosen the dirt from the roots, then properly transplanted in another place, and well watered, it will continue to grow, having suffered no apparent injury. If another seedling, of about the same size and vigor is pulled up, and the soil removed from the roots by means of the fingers, some of the very delicate root-hairs will be torn off with the soil, and many others will dry up owing to too prolonged exposure to the air. If this seedling is then transplanted, it will recover with difficulty, or it will wilt and die, even though well watered, showing in a very clear manner the inability of a plant to take in water when deprived of its root-hairs.

46. Location of Root-hairs.—Root-hairs for study may be easily secured by germinating seeds in a moist chamber, formed by inverting a flower pot over a saucer of water. Small seeds, such as flax or white mustard, will readily adhere to the moistened inner surface of the inverted flower pot. Within 24 to 36 hours the roots will have developed to a length of several millimeters, and the root-hairs will appear as a delicate white "fuzz," near the end of the root, but not extending clear to the tip (Fig. 36). On older roots it may be seen that the root-hairs are confined to a relatively short zone, only a few millimeters long. The hairs nearer the root-tip are shorter than those further back, indicating that they are younger.

The tip of the root is covered by a *root-cap* (Fig. 37), composed of cells that serve to protect the delicate tip as it grows through the soil. In some cases, as in the

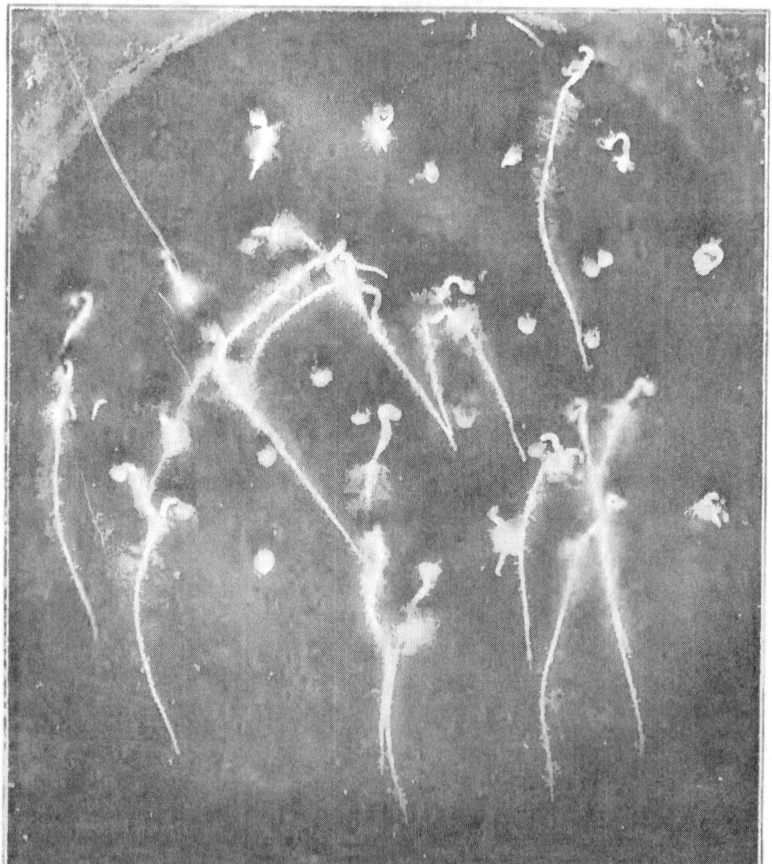

FIG. 36.—Germinating seeds of white mustard, showing development of root-hairs.

water-hyacinth (Figs. 38 and 39), the root-cap is so well developed that it may be easily seen with the naked eye, and quite readily removed and replaced. Root-hairs are never found on the region covered by the root-cap.

47. Structure of Root-hairs.—The structure of root-hairs, and their relation to the root as a whole, are illustrated in Figs. 40 and 41. It is seen at once that they are epidermal cells, elongated at right angles to the surface of the root, forming a thread-like sac, closed at both

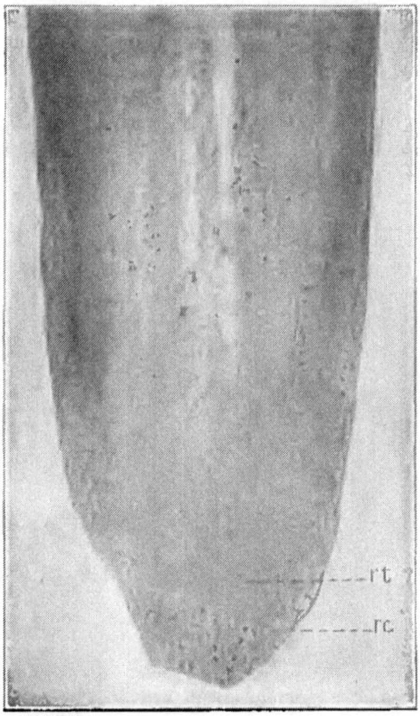

FIG. 37.—Jack-in-the-pulpit (*Arisæma triphyllum*). Longitudinal section through a root. *rt*, root-tip; *rc*, root-cap. (After F. L. Pickett.)

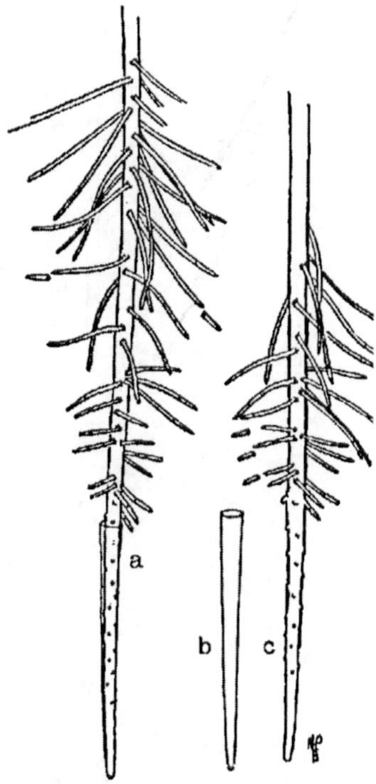

FIG. 38.—Roots of the water-hyacinth (*Eichornia crassipes* Solms), showing removable root-caps; *b*, root-cap removed from *c*.

ends. The typical cell-structure is readily recognized—cytoplasm, nucleus, vacuoles, sometimes merged into one large vacuole, cell-sap, and finally the cell-wall. It has recently been shown that the cell-wall is composed of an inner layer of cellulose and an outer layer of calcium pectate.

48. Relation between Root-hairs and Soil.—If young, active roots are removed from the soil, thoroughly rinsed in water, and examined with a compound microscope at the zone of root-hairs, it will be seen that tiny particles of soil have adhered so closely to the cell-wall of

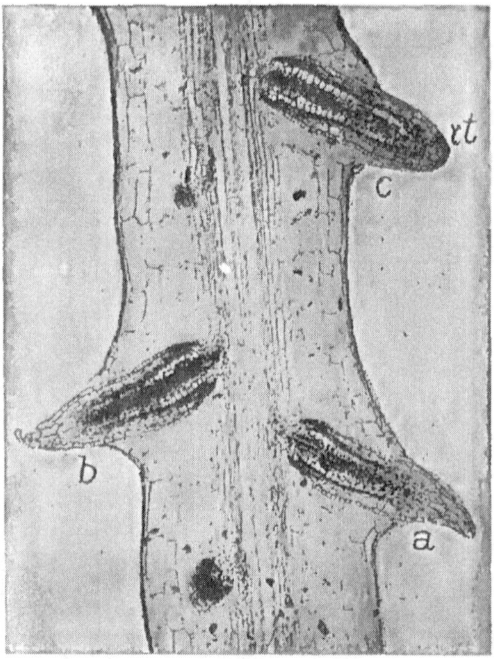

FIG. 39.—Water-hyacinth (*Eichornia crassipes*). Photomicrograph of a longitudinal section of a root, showing the mode of origin of lateral roots (*i.e.* endogenous). *a*, *b*, *c*, lateral roots; *r. t*, root-cap.

the hair that they were not washed off; in fact, they cannot be removed without tearing the hair. They appear to be imbedded in the cell-wall (Fig. 42), and are firmly held by pectin mucilage, resulting from a transformation of the outer membrane of calcium pectate. Since pectin is a water-loving colloid its importance here is recognized at once, in connection with the absorption of liquids by the root-hairs.

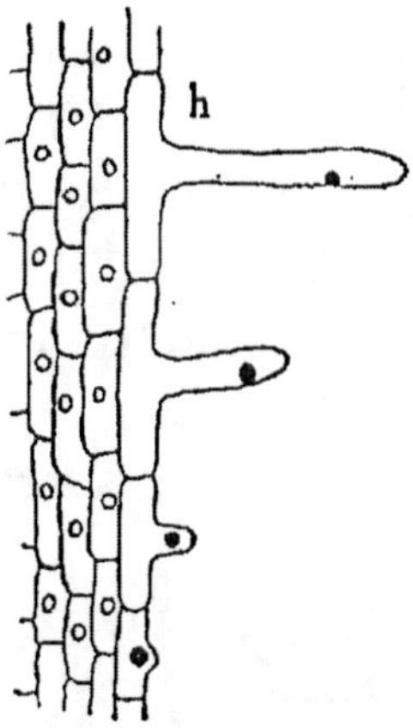

FIG. 40.—Diagram showing relation of root-hairs to adjacent cells of the root. *h*, the oldest of the four hairs shown, and furthest from the root-tip.

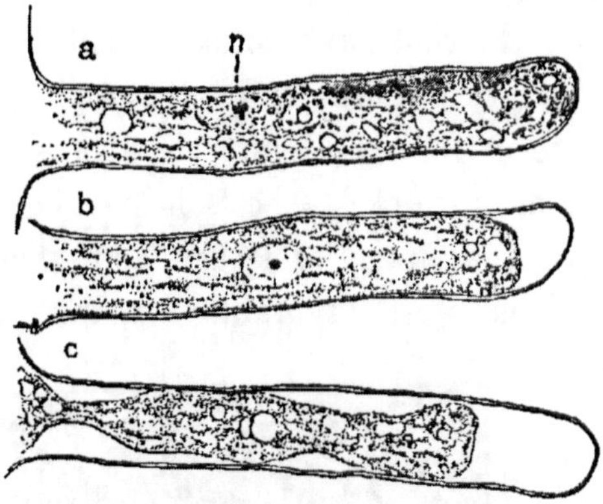

FIG. 41.—Root-hairs from the root of a mustard seedling. *a*, In state of turgor; *b*, beginning of plasmolysis after immersion in weak salt-solution; *c*, later stage of plasmolysis; *n*, nucleus.

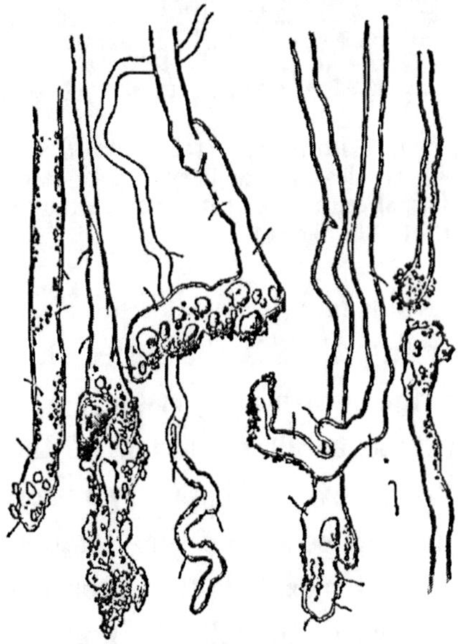

FIG. 42.—Root-hairs, with soil-particles adhering. (After Sachs.)

49. Relation between the Water and the Soil.—Fig. 43 is a diagram, showing on a greatly enlarged scale, how the root-hairs lie in the soil, and the condition of the soil most desirable for the well-being of the plant. It is seen from the figure that the soil is not compact, but open or porous, the soil particles being separated by spaces as large or larger than themselves. Under conditions most favorable for the plant, the spaces are

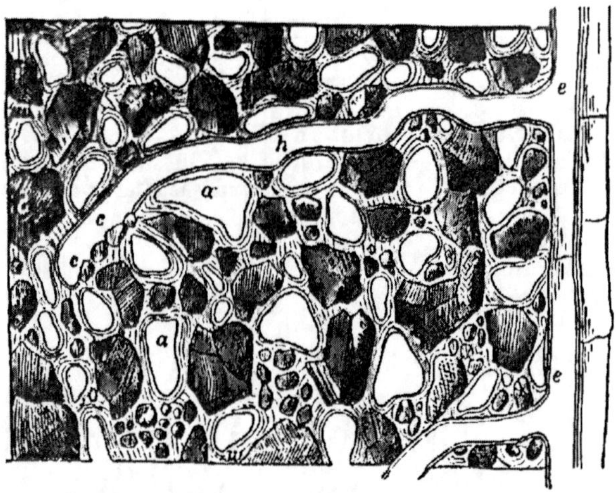

FIG. 43.—Diagram to illustrate a root-hair (*h*) in the soil, and its relation to the soil-particles, the capillary film of water (*w*), and the air spaces (*a*); *e*, epidermal cell of the root, of which the root-hair is an outgrowth, or branch. (After Sachs.)

filled with air, while each particle of soil is surrounded by a thin film of water. This is the water that supplies the plant through the root-hairs. As fast as removed it is replenished by the capillary action of the soil. Roots will continue to remove the capillary water from the soil until a point is reached where the attraction of the soil-particles for the water exceeds the absorbing power of the root-hairs; then the plant will wilt unless more water is added. *Plants cannot absorb all the water from the soil.*

50. Advantage of the Air Spaces.—Living roots, like everything else alive, need fresh air for respiration. If the spaces between the soil particles were filled with water, the air would be driven out, and the root-hairs could not respire. They would soon cease to function at all, and ultimately the whole plant would die. Thus it is seen that plants may have too much water, as well as too little. Farmers' crops (notably corn) often suffer from this cause, as well as from drought. When the soil contains too much water the leaves will commonly turn yellow and die. In order to understand how the soil-water passes into root-hairs, it is necessary to understand the physical actions of *diffusion* and *osmosis*.

51. Diffusion of Gases.—If a bottle of musk, or other perfume, is opened in one corner of a room, free from all air currents, a person standing some distance away could, in time, detect the odor. Now the only way we can smell a substance is to have one or more particles of that substance, in gaseous form, touch the olfactory surfaces of the nose. Therefore, in the case of the musk, tiny invisible particles must have left the surface of the substance, passed up through the neck of the bottle, out into the room, and travelled (though without any air currents) to the person detecting the odor. This illustrates *diffusion of gases*.

52. Diffusion of Liquids.—If a small quantity of sugar could be deposited, through a glass tube, at the bottom of a tall tumbler filled with water, the sugar would first dissolve, and the water near the bottom would become sweet. If we carefully avoided stirring the water, and if all currents in the liquid were avoided, nevertheless, within a short time the water on the surface would taste sweet, showing that some of the dissolved sugar had passed, *by its own motion*, up through the mass of the water to the top. This simple experiment illustrates *diffusion of liquids*. The dissolved sugar behaves in a manner quite similar to that of the gaseous "odor" of the musk.

53. Osmosis.—If, now, the denser sugar solution in the bottom of the tumbler were separated from the less dense water above by a porous membrane, such as a piece of bladder or parchment, the diffusion would take place through the porous membrane, and the water above would soon become sweet, as in the previous case. In other words, it is possible to have diffusion through a membrane. *Diffusion through a membrane is osmosis.*

The conditions realized in the experiment described above are a denser liquid (in the bottom of the tumbler), separated from a less dense liquid (at the top of the tumbler) by a porous membrane. Moreover, not only would the sugar solution pass up through the membrane, but the water above would pass in the opposite direction, and more rapidly than the sugar solution. This would continue until the solution was of the same density (equal amounts of sugar in equal amounts of water) on both sides of the membrane. Thus the action of osmosis may be stated as follows:

When two fluids (liquids or gases) of different densities are separated by a porous membrane, diffusion through the membrane will take place until equilibrium results. The diffusion will be more rapid from the less dense to the more dense fluid.

Or, again, osmosis may be defined as *the interchange of two fluids of different densities when separated by a porous membrane.*

54. Demonstration of Osmosis.—The contents of a hen's egg are enclosed by a porous membrane closely appressed to the inside of the shell, except at the large end of the egg. At this end the shell, as may readily be seen, is more porous than elsewhere, so that air readily enters, pressing the membrane in, and forming an air-chamber between it and the shell. With a sharp-pointed knife the shell may here be punctured, and with the aid of small scissors, removed so as to make an opening from ½ to ¾ inch in diameter. The greatest care must be taken not

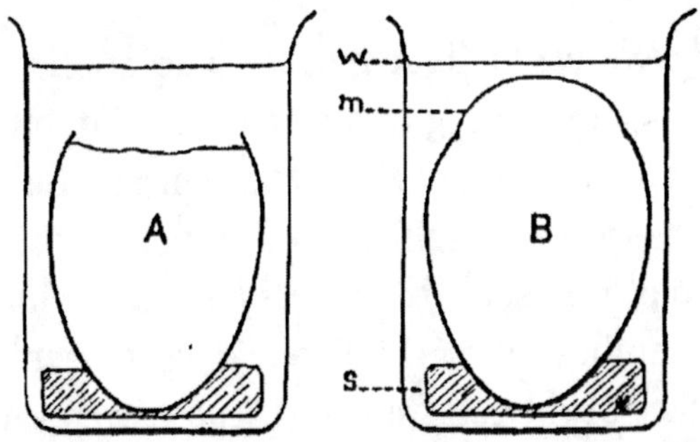

FIG. 44.—Experiment with an egg to demonstrate osmosis. *A*, at the beginning; *B*, about one hour later; *w*, water surface; *s*, support; *m*, egg-membrane.

to puncture the membrane, which at this region, lies concave (Fig. 44).

The contents of the egg are the yolk, the "white" (albumen), and an aqueous solution of various salts, which permeates the yolk and the "white." If, now, the egg is placed upright in a glass of water, so as to be completely covered by the water, we shall have realized the conditions for osmosis, the two liquids being the water outside and the aqueous solution inside the egg. Within a short time the less dense water will have passed through the membrane so much more rapidly than the dissolved salts pass out, that the membrane will begin to bulge, becoming convex and in a state of tension. This condition is known as *turgor*, and the membrane is said to be *turgid*. The turgor is the result of the *osmotic pressure* of the solution within. If osmosis is allowed to continue after this condition is realized, the osmotic pressure will rupture the membrane, and allow the contents of the egg to escape. It is partly the osmotic pressure of the substances in solution in the cell-sap that keeps the lining layer of cytoplasm closely appressed to the cell-wall of the root-hair, and other cells.

55. Application to Root-hairs.—The application of the experiment with the egg to root-hairs in the soil is obvious. The cell-sap in the vacuole is the denser liquid, the soil-water (a very weak solution of various substances dissolved from the soil) is the less dense, while the two limiting membranes of the layer of cytoplasm lining the inner surface of the cell-wall constitute two porous osmotic membranes. Under normal conditions an interchange (osmosis) begins between the cell-sap and the soil-solution. The latter soaks[1] through the thin cell-wall, passes by osmosis through the outer limiting membrane, diffuses through the lining layer of cytoplasm until it reaches the inner limiting membrane, through which it passes by osmosis into the vacuole, and becomes a part of the cell-sap. This process is sometimes referred to as *endosmosis* (osmosis from without in). In reverse order, minute traces of various substances pass out, by exosmosis. Doubtless the dissolved substances that enter the cell from without are in part altered, chemically, as they

[1] It is not necessary, here, to attempt to explain this process of soaking (*imbibition*), in the terms of physics.

diffuse through the cytoplasm between the two limiting or surface membranes.

56. Plasmolysis.—If the closed sac, formed by the porous membrane, contains the less dense, instead of the more dense liquid, then the reverse of turgor will take place, and the sac will collapse. This may be easily demonstrated under the microscope by irrigating root-hairs, or other plant cells, with solutions more dense than the cell-sap. For example, the root-hairs shown in Fig. 41, mounted in water on a glass slide, under a cover-glass, were found, by microscopic examination, to be turgid. Then they were irrigated with a 5 per cent. solution of common table salt. This solution is denser than the cell-sap of the root-hairs, so that exosmosis was more rapid than endosmosis, and cell-sap was withdrawn from the vacuoles faster than liquid entered from without. The salt-solution having soaked through the cell-wall, passed with difficulty through the limiting membrane of the cytoplasm, and thus began to exert an osmotic pressure from without, which loosened the protoplasm (*plasmolysis*[1]), and caused it to collapse. When this results, the cell is then said to be *plasmolyzed.*

57. Importance of Osmosis.—No physical phenomenon is more important than osmosis. Upon it depends the life and death of every living thing. By it, not only do plants take in necessary substances from the soil, but all the food assimilated by man and the lower animals passes into their cells. It has been demonstrated that the maintenance of turgidity is necessary in order that cells may continue to perform their normal functions. In a state of plasmolysis they cannot do so. This is illustrated in a

[1] From the Greek, *plasma* + *luein*, to loose, or set free.

simple manner by the well-known fact that, if a quantity of salt is placed on the soil around a plant, the plant will soon die. The reason is now obvious.

58. Rigidity.—Attention has been called to the fact that water serves as the vehicle by which substances in the soil are carried into the roots and transported to all parts of the plant. But the water serves another use in helping to keep the parts of the plant rigid, and thus maintaining their form. This service is accomplished chiefly by means of the osmotic pressure which obtains in every individual cell. If every cell is turgid, tissues as a whole, and the organs of which they form a part will be rigid. This may be easily demonstrated by plasmolyzing the cells in a piece of rigid plant tissue, and then restoring their turgor.

A fresh piece of a beet or turnip, about 2 inches long, ½ inch wide, and ¼ inch thick will be found to be quite rigid, so that it cannot be easily bent without breaking. If the piece is now placed in a 5 per cent. solution of table salt for 10 or 15 minutes or longer, it will be found to have lost its rigidity, and may be bent nearly double without breaking. The salt-solution as we know, caused the plasmolysis, and consequent loss of turgor of every cell, and so the entire tissue became flabby.

CHAPTER VI

THE PATH OF LIQUIDS IN THE PLANT

59. The Problem Stated.—We have seen that plants are continually losing water by transpiration, chiefly from the leaves, and making good the loss by absorption through the roots. The question now arises as to how the water passes through the stem to the leaves. Does it pass through the entire tissue of the stem, or is it confined to definite regions or channels?

60. Demonstration of Channels.—It will be easy to solve our problem experimentally by placing various stems or branches in liquid containing some coloring substance which will stain the tissues through which it passes. Common red ink may be used for this. Into water, colored with red ink, may be placed young seedling corn plants, stalks of celery, seedlings of castor-oil plants, leaves of plantain and lily, parsnips with a portion of the small end cut away, or any other available material. After the stems have been allowed to stand in the ink solution over night, they should be thoroughly rinsed, to remove the stain from the surface, and then examined by cutting off a small portion of the submerged buds. It will be clearly seen that the red coloring matter is not deposited throughout the tissue, but is confined to clearly marked channels—the *fibro-vascular bundles*. These bundles will be found to be distributed differently according to the kind of plant or its age, or both. Two general types of distribution will be recognized, represented respectively by the corn or the lily, and by the castor-oil plant or the parsnip.

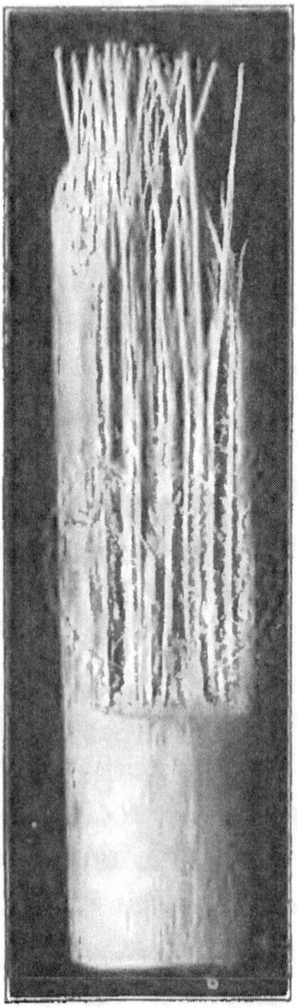

FIG. 45.—Fibro-vascular bundles in a corn stalk (*Zea Mays*).

61. Internal Structure of the Corn Stem.—In the corn stalk, the fibro-vascular bundles are distributed thickly and *irregularly* through the fundamental tissue (parenchyma) of the stem (Fig. 45). They are somewhat more numerous near the outer *rind*. A longitudinal section shows the bundles in side view, extending through the stem. The corn stalk represents a type of structure (*monocotyledonous*) common to all grasses[1] and closely related plants, and often, though misleadingly, called *endogenous*. In growth, the new tissue originates (with few exceptions, *e.g.*, *Yucca*) only at the tip of the stem. As a rule, growth in thickness results only by the enlargement of cells already formed, without involving the formation of new ones.

62. Internal Structure of the Castor-oil Plant Stem.—A type of structure quite different from that of the corn stalk is illustrated in the stem of the castor-oil plant (Fig. 46). Here the fibro-vascular bundles (in the young stem) are

[1] The Indian corn (maize) belongs to the family of Grasses (Gramineæ).

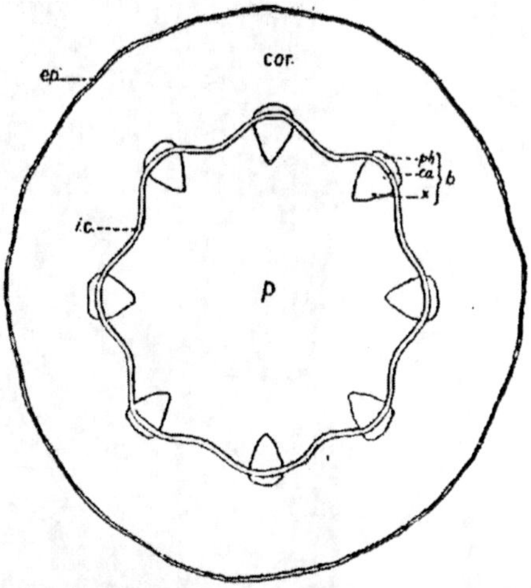

FIG. 46.—Diagram showing tissue-systems in young stem of castor-oil plant (*Ricinus communis*), as seen in cross-section. *ep*, epidermis; *cor*, cortex; *p*, pith or medulla; *b*, fibro-vascular bundle; *ph*, phlœm; *ca*, cambium; *x*, xylem; *ic*, interfascicular cambium.

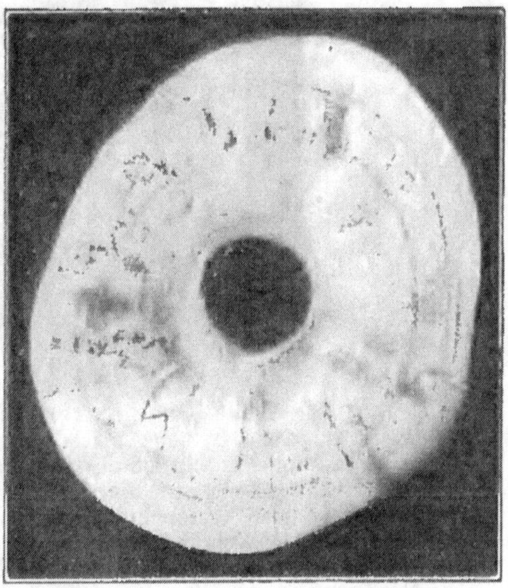

FIG. 47.—Castor-oil plant (*Ricinus communis*). Cross-section of the stem of a plant about two years old.

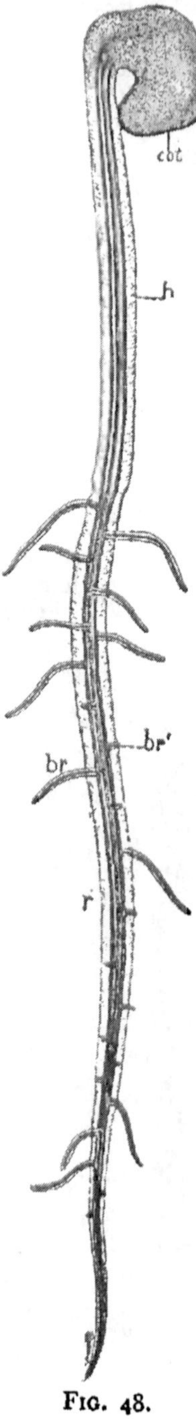

FIG. 48.

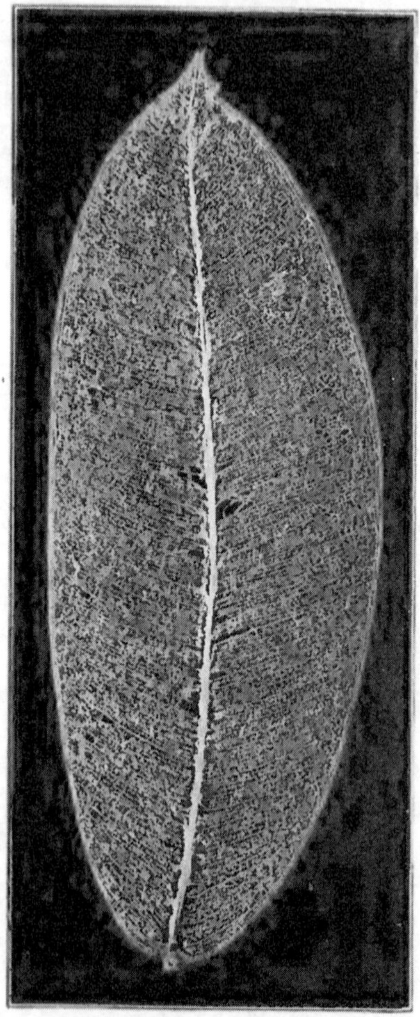

FIG. 49.

FIG. 48.—White lupine (*Lupinus albus*). Made semi-transparent by being placed for several hours in a weak aqueous solution of potassium hydroxide. After this treatment the fibro-vascular system may be clearly seen (through the surrounding tissues) by transmitted light. *cot*, cotyledons; *h*, hypocotyl; *r*, main root; *br*, *br*[1], branch roots of different ages. Note the endogenous origin of the branch roots.

FIG. 49.—The system of leaf-veins in a leaf of the common rubber-plant (*Ficus elastica*). The veins are connected with the root by means of the vascular bundles extending through the stem and roots.

distributed quite *regularly* in a circle, surrounding the central pith (*medulla*). This central tissue extends out between the fibro-vascular bundles, forming the pith-rays, or *medullary rays*. The tissue outside the zone of bundles is the *cortex*.

In older stems of this type the bundles increase in number until a nearly continuous cylinder of vascular tissue results (Fig. 47), broken only by numerous thin medullary rays. In cross-sectional view this cylinder, of course, appears as a circle. Stems having this arrangement of tissues grow by the formation of cylinders of new tissue, *outside* of, and surrounding the older woody tissue. On this account they are called *exogenous* (outside growing) stems, or, preferably, *dicotyledonous* stems.

63. Extension of Vascular Tissue into the Roots and Leaves.—As shown in Fig. 48, the vascular bundles of the stem continue down into the roots, branching out into the smallest rootlets, and connecting with the tissue which lies next to the epidermis with its root-hairs. Thus it is seen that there is an unbroken connection of vascular tissue from the roots to the leaves. Root-hairs and leaf-veins (Figs. 49 and 50) are the opposite extremities of this system, which serves for the conduction of liquids through the plant.

64. Structure of the Fibro-vascular Bundles.—When cross-sections of the bundles of the type shown in the castor-oil plant are examined under the microscope, they appear somewhat wedge-shaped, with the smaller end pointing toward the center of the stem (Fig. 51). Three well-defined regions may be clearly distinguished, as follows:

1. The *xylem*, at the pointed end of the bundle, and

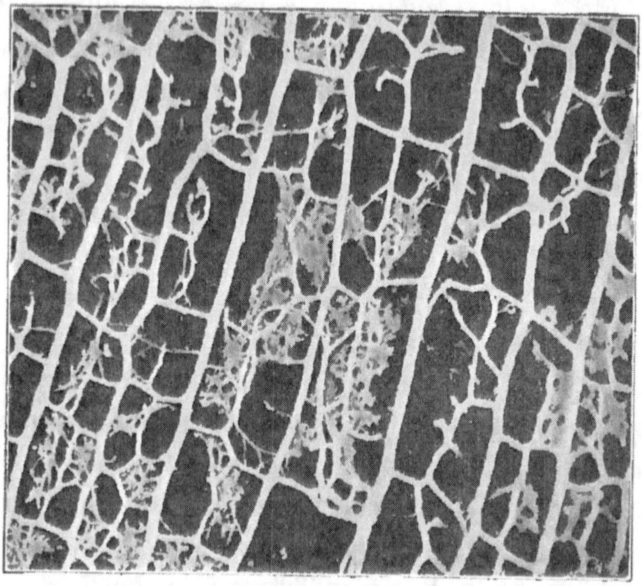

FIG. 50.—Photomicrograph of a portion of the system of veins in a leaf of the rubber-plant (*Ficus elastica*). Enlarged about six times from a portion of Fig. 49.

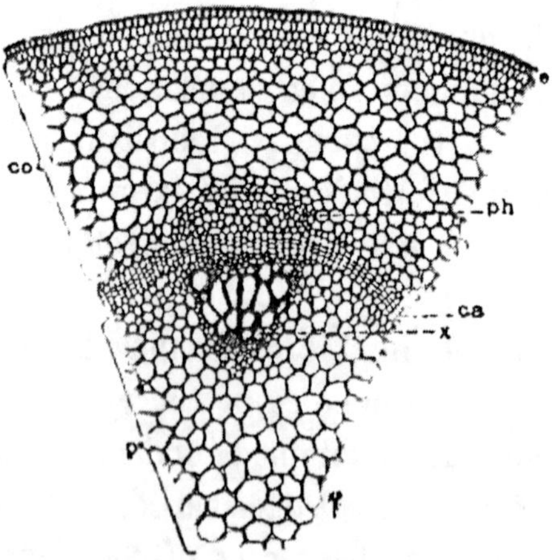

FIG. 51.—The castor-oil plant (*Ricinus communis*). Portion of cross-section of young stem. *co*, Cortex; *p*, pith or medulla; *e*, epidermis; *ph*, phlœm; *ca*, cambium; *x*, xylem. The last three elements compose the fibro-vascular bundle, the cambium being continuous from bundle to bundle; the portion between the bundles is called interfascicular cambium.

occupying most of its area. The cell-walls of the xylem are thicker than those of the other cells of the bundle, and have begun to be transformed into wood, hence the name xylem. 2. The *phloem*, at the opposite, or blunt end of the bundle. The phloem forms part of the bark. 3. The *cambium*, between the xylem and phloem, composed of extremely thin-walled cells, and the narrowest of the three regions. The cambium is embryonic tissue, with its cells in a state of active division. The new cells formed next the xylem soon become transformed into xylem-cells; those formed next the phloem, into new phloem. The cambium itself persists throughout the life of the plant. It is perpetual embryonic tissue, never becoming entirely transformed, but giving rise to new cells on either side so long as the plant remains alive. A strand of cambium extending between the bundles (*inter-fascicular cambium*) gives rise to new bundles, as well as to new fundamental tissue. In time the bundles increase in thickness, and become so numerous and close together that there is an almost continuous cylinder of wood inside the cambium, and a cylinder of phloem and other tissues outside the cambium.

65. Passage of Liquids through the Stem.—The water and dissolved mineral substances, taken in by the root-hairs, pass up through the xylem to the leaves, while the plant-food, manufactured in the leaves, passes down through the phloem, and is distributed to all living tissues. The liquids passing through the stem are popularly called "sap."

66. Economic Value of Maple Sap.—In the case of the sugar-maple, a very sweet sap flows in unusually large quantities during the early spring period of alternate thawing and freezing. During this season, in many parts of the country, it is customary to "tap" the trees, by boring a small hole into the trunk far enough to enter the wood, and then insert a wooden or metal "spiggot" or spout, through which the sap flows out and is caught in pails. It is then "boiled down," either in the sugar bush or in the house, until the water has passed off in large quantities as steam, leaving a thickened maple syrup in the kettle or evaporating pan. If the boiling is continued the syrup, when cooled, becomes maple sugar. The saps of the sugar-cane and of the sugar-beet are, as is well known, the source of the ordinary sugars of commerce.

CHAPTER VII

NUTRITION

67. Organic and Inorganic.—All substances belong to either one or the other of two classes of matter—organic or inorganic. Organic substances are, for the most part, those which compose the bodies of animals or plants, past or present, or which have been, or may be, formed by the life-processes of living things. The possibility of synthesizing certain organic compounds (hydrocarbons) artificially in the laboratory has broken down the hard and fast distinction, formerly recognized, between organic and inorganic substances. Bone, flesh, shells, bark, wood, leaves, gums and resins formed by plants, coal, sugar, flour, starch, cellulose, plant and animal juices, and all protoplasm represent organic substances. Inorganic substances are those which have never been incorporated into the bodies of plants or animals, or if so, have since lost all evidence of that fact. Water, salt, iron, oxygen, carbon, glass, sulphur, air, represent inorganic substances. Sometimes the line is hard to draw. Thus a piece of wood or of bone converted into charcoal may, if carefully handled, retain unmistakable traces of having formed a part of the body of an animal or a plant, but if the piece is ground in a mortar, a fine powder may result, that has lost all trace of its organic origin. Ordinarily, however, the two kinds of matter are easily distinguished, either by their structure or their known origin. So clearly distinct and unlike are they, that one entire branch of the science of chemistry, organic chemistry, is devoted to a study of organic substances, all of which are compounds of carbon. Inorganic chemistry is concerned with all other substances.

68. Nutrition of Plants and Animals.—The foods of every living thing—those substances which, by digestion and assimilation, can be incorporated into the structure

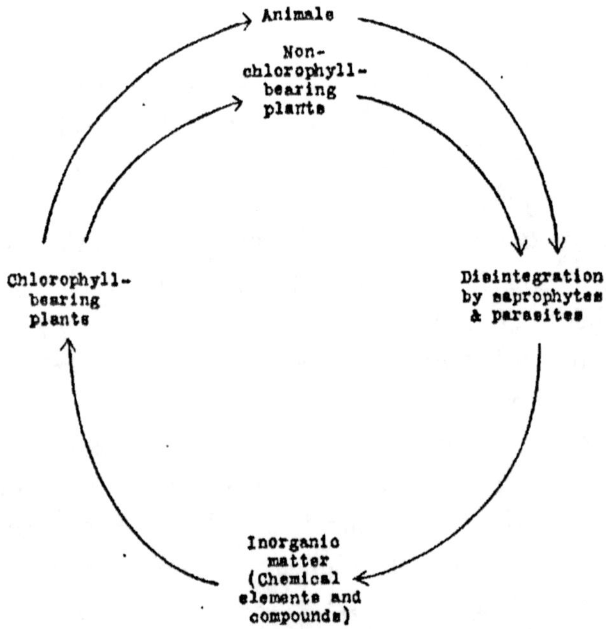

FIG. 52.—The organic cycle.

of the living body as a part of it—are all organic. In this respect animals and plants are alike; they both require organic substances as food. Thus it is evident that there must be a continual formation of organic compounds out of inorganic in order to maintain the food supply of the world. As we shall soon learn, this is the great and fundamental rôle of green plants in the world's economy—to elaborate organic compounds for food out of inorganic "raw materials." With a very few exceptions among the bacteria, plants that are not green (such as toad-stools, molds, and other fungi), and most animals cannot do this. Therefore we are wholly dependent upon green plants for the food supply of the world. Animals and non-green plants live, either directly or indirectly, upon green plants.

The bodies of all living things are constantly giving off inorganic compounds (such, for example, as the carbon dioxide given off in respiration, and the water in transpiration), and after death all bodies are (by the action of bacteria) gradually broken up into inorganic substances. Thus, we see, there is a kind of perpetual cycle, or circulation, from one realm to the other, as indicated in the diagram (Fig. 52).

69. Kinds of Foods.—When we examine the bodies of plants we find that the foods elaborated are stored in various organs or tissues. These foods all belong to one of three classes of substances, viz., *carbohydrates*, represented by starch, sugars, and cellulose; *proteins*, represented by protoplasm itself, the gluten of wheat, and other substances; and *fats*, represented by the various oils, such, for example, as olive and cotton-seed oil.

70. Chemical Composition of These Foods.—A chemical examination of carbohydrates reveals the fact that they are composed of the elements, carbon, hydrogen, and oxygen, the two latter occurring in the same proportion as in water, namely, two parts of hydrogen to one of water (H_2O). Fats contain the same elements, only in different proportions, while proteins, in addition to carbon, oxygen, and hydrogen, always contain nitrogen. Other substances almost universally found in plants are calcium, potassium, magnesium, phosphorus, sulphur, iron, and chlorine. Calcium is not necessary for all fungi (*e.g.*, not for *Aspergillus niger*), nor for all algæ. Three main problems now confront us:

1. What is the source of these food elements?

2. Where, in the plant, are they elaborated into plant food?

3. How is the process accomplished?

71. Source of the Food Elements.—Since most plants are fixed for life to a certain spot they must obtain their food elements from their immediate surroundings; they cannot, like animals, go in search of them. The carbon and oxygen are obtained chiefly from the air, where the carbon appears, in combination with oxygen, as carbon dioxide. Free oxygen (as well as in combination with carbon) is also obtained from the air. About four-fifths of the air is nitrogen, and one might naturally infer that the plant could obtain an abundant supply from that source. We shall learn later, however, that most plants cannot utilize the free nitrogen of the air, but must have it supplied in chemical combination with other elements, in the form of nitrates. These are obtained from the soil. The calcium, potassium, magnesium, phosphorus, sulphur, and iron are also obtained from the soil in the form of soluble salts, such as phosphates, nitrates, sulphates, and carbonates. The hydrogen is obtained chiefly from water (H_2O).

72. Seat of Elaboration of Carbohydrates.—Careful and thorough studies have established, beyond all doubt, the fact that the *inorganic food elements are combined to form carbohydrates only in the green cells of plants*, either in leaves, stems, or other parts. This is one of the most fundamental facts in all science. Among those

Fig. 53.—Jan Ingen-Housz (1730–1799). He was the first to recognize the difference between photosynthesis and respiration in plants.

Fig. 54.—Joseph Priestley (1733–1804). He discovered oxygen, and made pioneer studies of the function of chlorophyll.

entitled to credit for this discovery may be mentioned Jan Ingen-Housz (1730–1799), a Dutch physician, and Jean Senebier (1742–1809) and Nicolas Théodore de Saussure (1767–1845), two Frenchmen. Joseph Priestley an Englishman, also contributed to this work, both

FIG. 55.—Leaves of the tulip tree (*Liriodendron tulipifera*). At left, from a large mature tree; at right, from a young sapling. Average sized leaves were chosen from each tree. Greatly reduced.

directly and indirectly, by his discovery, in 1774, of the gas oxygen, and his experiments on the purification of the air by green plants.

73. The Significance of Leaves.—While the formation of carbohydrate food may take place in any cell containing the green substance, *chlorophyll* (leaf-green), the chief organs for this work are the leaves. This explains many facts about leaves—*e.g.*, why they are green, why they are thin and usually broad, why they are often much larger in young, rapidly growing plants that need much nourishment, than in mature plants (Fig. 55), why they occur at or very near the tips of the branches, where they are well exposed to light (Figs. 56 and 57). *There is no more important fact in botany, nor indeed in all natural science, than that all the food of the world is primarily manufactured in the chlorophyll-containing cells of plants.*

74. Importance of Sunlight.—Plants and plant parts grown in the dark are, with rare exceptions, never green. This means that sunlight is necessary in order to make chlorophyll. But green plants cannot elaborate food in the dark. This means that sunlight is necessary, not alone for the formation of chlorophyll, but for food making as well. Non-green tissues, even in sunlight, cannot manufacture food; for this process both chlorophyll and sunlight are necessary. The green cell has often been likened to a factory; the chlorophyll is the machinery, the sunlight is the energy, while the product of the factory is the manufactured food.

75. Details of the Process.—The manufacture of carbohydrates involves three essential steps:

1. Taking in the raw materials (water and carbon dioxide).
2. Recombining these parts into carbohydrates.
3. Giving off the waste material (chiefly oxygen).

Taking in the Raw Materials.—We have seen in Chapter IV that the air spaces between the green cells of a leaf are in direct connection with the outside air through the stomata. In the presence of sunlight the formation of carbohydrates begins in the green cells. This uses up the carbon dioxide in the cells, and the supply is renewed from the intercellular spaces. The gas passes through the cell-walls and the layer of protoplasm in solution in

FIG. 56.—A tree (hornbeam), seen from "outside," showing the dense foliage at or near the tips of the branches. The same tree as in Fig. 57.

water. This results in reducing the amount (and thus the pressure) of this gas in the intercellular spaces, and as a result more carbon dioxide passes by diffusion through the stomata to the intercellular spaces. Thus, as fast as the gas is used the supply is renewed from without.

76. Photosynthesis.—Within the cell, the carbon dioxide and water (or simple combinations of these) are finally, *by a series of steps*, recombined by the chlorophyll in the presence of sunlight, into a carbohydrate—probably some form of sugar. *It is this series of steps that is called photosynthesis.*[1] Not all of the oxygen contained in the water (H_2O) and carbon dioxide (CO_2) used, enters into the composition of the carbohydrate. The unused portion is set free, and is either utilized in other processes,

FIG. 57.—A tree (hornbeam), seen from among the branches (as the squirrel sees it), showing absence of leaves except at or near the tips of the branches. The same tree as in Fig. 56.

or diffuses out through the stomata to the surrounding air. Thus, the taking in of carbon dioxide and the giving off of oxygen are outward indications that photosynthesis is going on inside the green cells.

77. Starch-making.—The sugar made by photosynthesis is soluble in the cell-sap, and if it were not removed

[1] The word means combining (*synthesis*) in the presence of, or by means of, light (*photos*).

from the solution, at least as fast as it was made, it would accumulate and thus interfere with the manufacture of more sugar. Some of it is removed at once, either by nourishing the protoplasm of the cell where it was made, or by being *translocated* to other parts of the plant. But some of the sugar is removed *from solution* by being

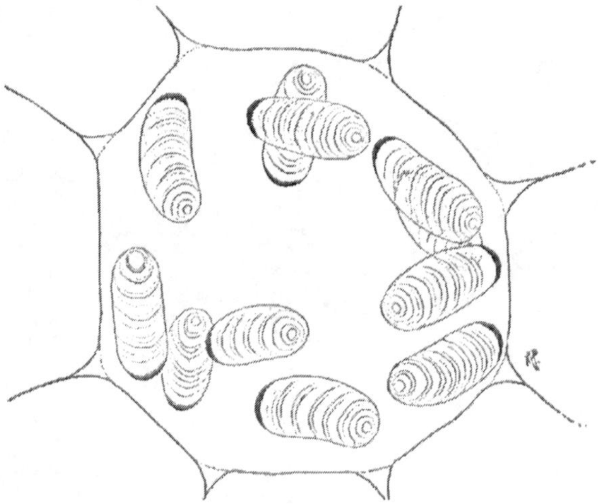

FIG. 58.—Cell of *Pellionia Daveauana*, showing starch-grains. The black, crescent-shaped body on the end of each grain is the *amyloplast*. Greatly enlarged. (Cf. Figs. 8 and 59.)

converted into starch, a substance not soluble in water. Thus the accumulation of starch in a leaf or other green tissue indicates that photosynthesis is in progress, and that the resulting carbohydrate is or has been formed faster than translocated. The conversion of sugar to starch is accomplished by certain plastids in the cell (Figs. 8 and 58).

78. Enzymes.—For a long time it has been known that during photosynthesis plants take in carbon dioxide and water and give off oxygen, but the intermediate steps have never been clearly understood. The appearance of starch in green tissues is an evidence that photosynthesis has taken place, but it was early recognized that starch was not the first organic substance to be formed. It is now known that some of the various steps in the process are accomplished by means of certain substances called *enzymes*, formed in every cell. Enzymes have the remarkable power of transforming other substances, without being thereby used up or permanently changed themselves. They belong to the class of substances known as *ferments*, but their real nature and mode of action are not well understood. Each enzyme is commonly named from the particular substance in the transformation of which it takes part, and this name usually ends with the termination, *-ase*. Thus we have *oxidase*, which acts upon substances to oxidize them, *maltase*, which acts upon maltose (a form of sugar), *protease*, which acts upon protein, and so on.

79. The Steps in Starch-formation.—Careful experiments have suggested that the first step in the formation of starch may be the interaction of water and carbon dioxide, under the agency of an oxidase, resulting eventually in formaldehyde (CH_2O). The subsequent steps may be something as follows:

2. Condensation of the formaldehyde molecules into a simple sugar, dextrose ($C_6H_{12}O_6$), by *aldehydase*.

3. Transformation of dextrose into a more complex sugar, maltose, by *maltase*.

4. The changing of maltose into dextrine by *dextrinase*.

5. The conversion of dextrin into soluble starch (amylum) by *amylase*.

6. The conversion of soluble starch into insoluble starch by yet another ferment or enzyme, *coagulase*.

Other analyses of the process of photosynthesis have been suggested, and it is possible that the one outlined above may become more or less modified in the light of future experiments.

80. Storage of Food.—As stated above, some of the food elaborated in the leaves is transferred to various

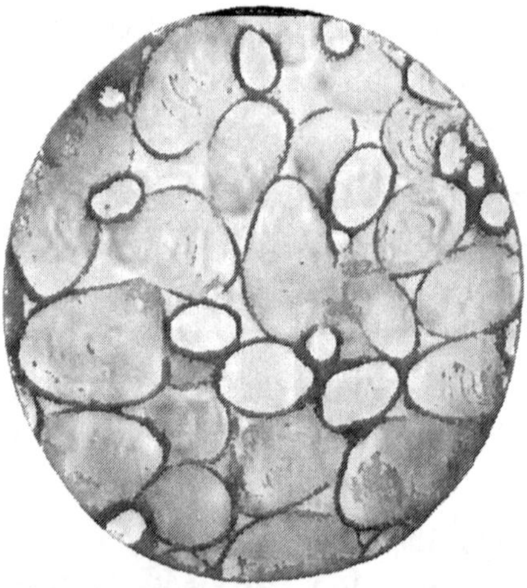

FIG. 59.—Starch grains from a potato tuber. (After Duncan J. Reid.)

other parts of the plant. Some of it is used immediately to nourish these parts, but often this food accumulates faster than needed. This is what always occurs in certain parts of the plant, such, for example, as the tubers (underground stems) of potatoes (Figs. 59 and 60), the roots of turnips, the seeds of beans, peanuts, and other plants, the fruits of all plants, the leaf-base of the onion (forming the scaly bulbs or "onions"), and all buds when they are forming. In these *storage organs* the soluble sugar is removed from solution by being converted by starch-forming leucoplasts (*amyloplasts*) into starch, and thus the storage organs finally become gorged with an excess of food. It is on this account that they are valuable as food for man.

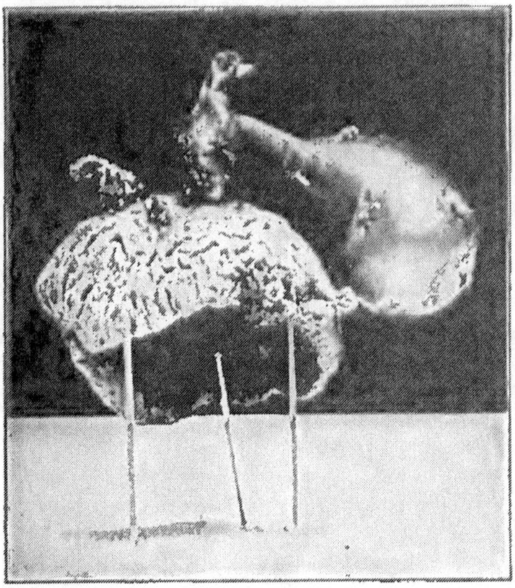

FIG. 60.—Young potato tuber, developed (in light) as a branch of a sprout of an old seed-tuber. Part of the food elaborated and digested in the leaves of the parent plant was translocated down the leaf-stalk and stem, and stored in the older tuber, part of which is shown in the figure. After this piece was cut off, the stored food began to be digested and translocated to the developing "eye" or bud, accompanied by the development of the latter into the young tuber. Ordinarily such changes, in the potato, occur only underground and in the dark.

81. The Need and Source of Nitrogen.—Protein foods differ from carbohydrates and fats by containing nitrogen which the latter lack. Notwithstanding the fact that four-fifths of the atmosphere is nitrogen, green plants are unable to use this free nitrogen until it has been combined with other substances, such, for example, as potassium, calcium, magnesium, ammonium, and others, forming potassium nitrate (KNO_3), calcium nitrate ($Ca(NO_3)_2$), ammonium nitrate $(NH_4)NO_3$, and so forth. Nitrates and ammonia may result from the disintegration of plant and animal bodies, but the supply must continually be renewed by drawing upon the free nitrogen

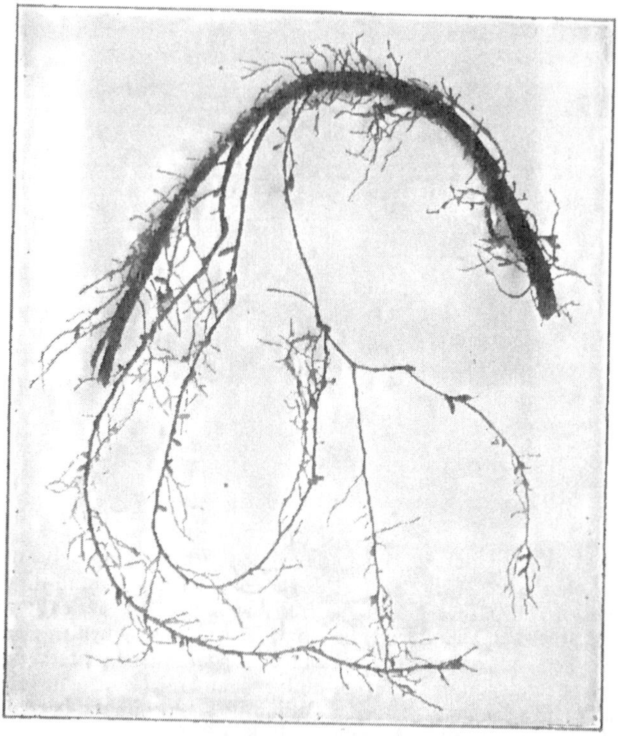

FIG. 61.—Root-tubercles on yellow sweet clover (*Melilotus lutea*), caused by and containing *Pseudomonas radicicola*.

of the air. Ammonia results chiefly from the decomposition of plants and animals, and for the formation of nitrates we are chiefly dependent upon non-green plants, including certain bacteria and fungi. Two important nitrogen-fixing bacteria live in the soil; one (*Nitrosomonas*) has the power to form nitrites from ammonia, and the other (*Nitrobacter*) forms nitrates from nitrites. Only the nitrates are available to plants. A third kind of nitrifying organism, *Pseudomonas radicicola* lives, as its name implies, in roots, and chiefly in those of leguminous plants, such as clover, lupine, locust, peas, beans, alfalfa, and their near relatives. The presence of the bacterium causes little swellings or *nodules* on the roots (Figs. 61 and 228). The ability to "fix" atmospheric nitrogen is possessed by several other species of bacteria, and also by some of the molds.

Root-nodules, caused by nitrogen-fixing organisms, occur also on roots of certain non-leguminous plants, including Elæagnaceæ (Oleaster family), Myricaceæ (Bayberry family), Podocarpineæ, the genus *Alnus*, of the Betulaceæ (Birch family), and Cycadaceæ (Cycas family). The roots of Cycas contain two kinds of nitrogen-fixing organisms, *Pseudomonas radicicola* and *Azotobacter* (Fig. 241).

82. Value of Leguminous Crops.—Because of the presence in their roots of organisms that can use the free nitrogen of the air to form compounds of nitrogen, leguminous crops are of inestimable value to agriculture. In fact, they are absolutely necessary in order to maintain the fertility of the soil. When any leguminous crops are harvested, the roots are left in the soil with their tubercles rich in compounds of nitrogen, and the compounds (nitrates) are available to the next non-leguminous crop, such as oats or corn. This is one of the main reasons why good farmers always practice a rotation of crops, alternating leguminous with non-leguminous plants, for thereby the richness of the soil in *available* nitrogen is maintained. Thus, for example, a certain field in Illinois was planted to corn for 28 years in succession. The yield of corn for the last year was 22 bushels per acre. On a second field, planted for the same length of time with alternate crops of corn and oats, the final yield of corn was 36 bushels; while a third field in which corn, oats, and clover were planted alternately, the final yield of corn was 59 bushels—over twice the yield without rotation with a legume. This increase in yield was due chiefly to the enrichment of the soil in nitrates by the organisms that form tubercles on the roots of the clover. If the entire clover crop (tops and all) is plowed under occasionally, so as to serve as "green manure," the results will be better than when the clover tops are always removed as hay.

83. Manufacture of Proteins.—Proteins are formed *de novo* only in living plant cells, by combining the products of photosynthesis with the nitrogen supplied in the form of nitrates. Their formation may be favored by light, but unlike the process of photosynthesis, protein-formation does not require either light or chlorophyll. The formation of proteins occurs in large measure in foliage-leaves, but may take place in any living cell. The manner of their formation is not as well understood as is that of carbohydrates.

84. Fats.—Fats may occur in plant cells in either liquid or solid form. We are most familiar with the liquid fats, such as the various oils derived from plants. Fat occurs in the solid form in the cocoanut. In the tallow-tree (*Sapium sebiferum*) it is so abundant, as a waxy coating on the seeds, that it is used in eastern Asia for making candles. Fats commonly occur in droplets in the protoplasm, or as an emulsion in the cell-sap, but the place and method of their formation have never been clearly determined.

85. Digestion.—We have learned above (paragraph 42) that substances can enter a plant only in solution. It is also true that substances, even when inside the cell, can-

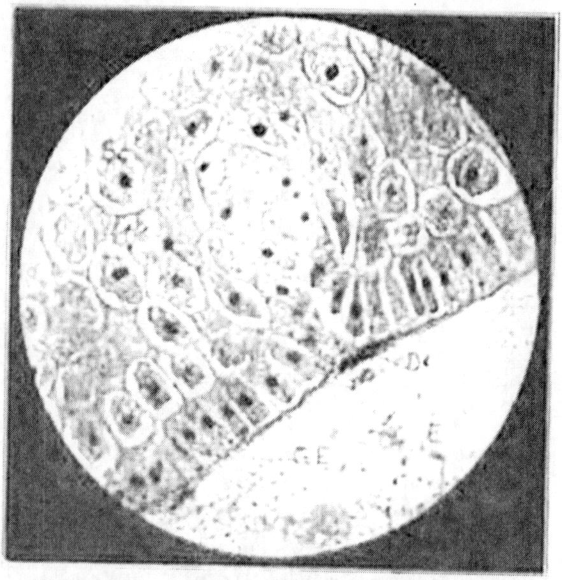

FIG. 62.—Portion of a cross-section of a grain of Indian corn (*Zea Mays*). *G.E*, Glandular epithelium of the scutellum which secretes diastase; *G*, a simple racemose gland in the tissue of the scutellum; *D*, duct of the latter, emptying into the starchy endosperm surrounding the embryo. (Photomicrograph by the author.)

not be utilized as food by the plant unless they are in solution. In order that the protoplasm can be nourished, therefore, all insoluble stored foods must be converted into soluble substances and dissolved. *The process of converting an insoluble food into a soluble substance and dissolving it is digestion.* This change, like the various processes in photosynthesis, is brought about by various *enzymes*, which have the power of converting insoluble starch, proteins, and fats, into soluble substances. Starch is converted by *diastase* (one of the earliest known enzymes), proteins by *proteases*, and fatty substances (lipoids) by *lipase*.

FIG. 63.—Venus's flytrap (*Dionæa muscipula*). Insects are captured by the rapid closing together of the two valves of the leaf-blade. When the valves come together the rigid marginal teeth interlock, making escape impossible. The digestive enzyme is secreted by glands distributed over the surface of the valves. (After John Ellis.)

Digestive enzymes are probably secreted by every active plant-cell. In the corn grain the corn starch (endosperm), surrounding the embryo, is digested during germination by diastase secreted by a glandular epithe-

FIG. 64.—Bladderwort (*Utricularia sp.*). Aquatic insects are held captive in the tiny floating bladders, where they are digested and absorbed.

FIG. 65.—A sundew (*Drosera intermedia*), showing the glandular tipped tentacles on the leaves. When an insect alights on a leaf he is held by the sticky secretion; the tentacles then bend over in contact with his body, holding him more firmly, and pouring out a protein-digesting enzyme secreted by their glands.

lium of the embryo. Often this glandular layer is invaginated, so as to form a true gland (Fig. 62).

A special case of plant nutrition is presented by the insectivorous plants, of which there are many kinds. They are all characterized by the possession of some device for capturing insects that visit them, and by the ability to secrete a proteolytic enzyme capable of digesting the protein tissues of their prey. These plants can also digest any meat fed to them artificially. After being digested the protein food is absorbed by osmosis. The Venus's flytrap (*Dionæa muscipula*), numerous species of bladderwort (*Utricularia*), and several species of sundew (*Drosera*) serve to illustrate the insectivorous plants (Figs. 63–65). Although these plants are able to digest protein, experiments have shown that a protein diet is not necessary either for their life or healthy growth.

86. Assimilation.—After food has been elaborated and digested it still is not a part of the living protoplasm, but only lies within the vacuoles of the protoplast. It is no more a part of the plant than is food in our hands or stomachs a part of our bodies. One step more is necessary; the digested food must be incorporated into, and made part of, the living protoplasm itself. It must be transformed from lifeless matter into living matter. As in the case of enzyme action, the process by which this remarkable change is brought about is not understood. By multitudes of accurate, painstaking experiments, however, one great fundamental truth has been established, namely, that non-living matter can be converted into living matter only by the action of other living matter already existing. Proteins, sugars, and fats have all been manufactured from simpler substances, artificially in the laboratory, without the aid of living organisms; and they may all be digested artificially in a test-tube, also without the aid of living organisms; but, although the attempt has often been made, no one has ever succeeded in artificially producing even the minutest drop of living protoplasm. Only living protoplasm, acting directly on non-living matter, can bring about that marvellous change. This fact is concisely expressed by the Latin phrase, "*Omne vivum e vivo*" (All life from life).

87. Biogenesis.—That living matter is *always* descended from preceding living matter, and that it *never* arises spontaneously from the non-living is the principle of *biogenesis*.[1] Opposed to this principle is the principle of *abiogenesis*,[2] which teaches that living matter may originate from non-living without the intervention of other living matter. This was formerly quite generally believed. Men thought, for example, that putrid meat might become transformed directly into the maggots (young flies) so often found in it; but we now know that maggots in decaying meat always arise from the eggs of flies that have previously visited the meat and deposited their eggs there. Thanks to the painstaking experiments and clear thinking of Redi, Pasteur, Tyndall, and others, belief in the principle of biogenesis is now practically universal among scientists.

That living matter could not, under favorable conditions, originate from non-living matter, or that it did not in the beginning, or never does now, cannot, of course,

[1] Biogenesis, from the Greek words *bios* (βίος), life, and *genesis* (γένεσις) generation.

[2] Abiogenesis. The prefix α (Greek *alpha*) deprives the remainder of the word of its meaning, or reverses the meaning.

be demonstrated; one can never, experimentally or otherwise, prove a universal negative. The principle of biogenesis affirms that, in experiments conducted with the utmost skill, and with every possible precaution to exclude all traces of living matter, no faintest manifestation of life has ever been detected; we therefore logically conclude that, however life may have been *originally* created, it never originates now from non-living matter, but always from living matter only.

88. Dissimilation.—Nothing is more unstable than protoplasm. No sooner is new protoplasm formed by the process of assimilation than it begins to disintegrate, forming various new substances, such as cell-walls, gums, resins, latex, coloring matters (in flowers and other plant parts), the perfumes of flowers, the poisons of poisonous plants, and the substances that give the various flavors and tastes to different kinds of plants. The process by which all such substances are formed by protoplasm is called *secretion*. Thus we see that *protoplasm is in a state of continual formation and disintegration*. The sum total of all these changes, both constructive and destructive, is called *metabolism*. *It is metabolism, above everything else, that distinguishes living from non-living matter.* We also see that death is essential to life; unless protoplasm perishes no new protoplasm can be formed. All life, it is true, comes from life; but only on the condition that that which is already living shall perish.

89. Economic Value of Plant Secretions.—Many of the substances secreted by protoplasm are commercial products. This is notably true of wood, all of which consists of lignified cell-walls; of cork, which consists of suberized cell-walls; of the various gums, such as gum arabic, gum mastic, and gum tragacanth; of the resins; and of turpentine, rubber, vegetable dye-stuffs, perfumes, and various other articles of commerce. Other plant secretions may play an important rôle in practical agriculture, in connection with the rotation of crops, as indicated in paragraph 90(*b*), below.

90. Rotation of Crops.—Closely connected with nutrition and secretion is the question of crop rotation in agriculture. Farmers have known for ages that if one kind of plant is grown in the same soil year after year the yield is greatly diminished. Under such conditions, for example, the yield of wheat will diminish from 25 or 30 bushels to 12 or 15 bushels per acre, and also deteriorate in quality. Various hypotheses and theories have been proposed from time to time to account for this fact, but only three of these theories are here noted, as follows:

(*a*) *Nutrition Theory.*—We have seen above that growing plants withdraw from the soil various so-called mineral "nutrients," in solution in the soil-water. These are essential to the healthy, vigorous growth of the plant. Different kinds of plants absorb these compounds in different proportion, and one theory of crop rotation is based upon this fact. It is argued that, by following one kind of crop with another, different demands are made on the soil, and the compound of which the soil was impoverished or "exhausted" by the first crop is renewed by capillary action from lower or adjacent regions. Its renewal is also hastened by the application of suitable fertilizer. Especially is this true in the case of nitrogen, which is renewed by alternating with non-leguminous plants, leguminous crops, whose root-tubercle organisms renew the nitrates, as explained in paragraph 82. This theory was advocated by the great agricultural chemist, Liebig. Undoubtedly it is correct, as far as it goes, but a more thorough consideration of the question indicates that it is not adequate as a complete explanation.

(*b*) *Theory of Toxic Excreta.*—A second hypothesis is that advanced by certain investigators in the Bureau of Soils of the United States Department of Agriculture.[1] This is based on the fact that the roots of plants are known to excrete substances which are poisonous or toxic to the species producing them. These toxic substances accumulate in the soil during a succession of the same kind of crops, and thus gradually render it toxic to that kind of plants. By following with a succession of different kinds of crops the toxic excreta of the first are either removed by seepage of soil-water, or destroyed, either by being oxidized, or by the addition of other substances which render them harmless. By this theory the function of fertilizers is not so much to renew exhausted mineral "nutrients," as to render harmless the accumulated excreta of the previous crop.

(*c*) *Sanitary Theory.*—This theory has been carefully worked out by Professor Bolley, of the North Dakota Agricultural College. By thorough studies of the wheat crop he has been enabled to make the following positive statements:[2] Constant or rather constant culture of wheat on the same lands brings about *wheat-sickness*, or wheat-sick soil. Wheat does not thrive well in the presence of its own dead bodies, no matter how fertile the soil. Constant wheat cropping does not especially

[1] A similar hypothesis was advanced by A. P. DeCandolle in his *Physiologie Végétale*, Paris, 1832.

[2] The phraseology of Professor Bolley (North Dakota Agric. Coll. Bull. 107), is closely followed.

exhaust or use up the mineral "nutrients" more rapidly than a succession of the different kinds of crops, nor does it introduce into the soil any permanent excrement toxic to wheat. It does, however, tend to introduce with the seed, stubble, roots, *et cetera* a number of kinds (at least five) of parasitic fungi that cause diseases of the wheat plants. These fungi destroy, blight, and rot off the roots of the plants, and live internally in the straw and the seeds. The accumulation of these fungi in fertile soils brings about the condition of wheat-sickness, "wheat-tired" soil. The fungi attack the roots, leaves, stems, young developing grains, and seedlings, and the value of crop-rotation lies in growing a series of different kinds of crops that do not transmit or bear each other's diseases. Crop-rotation is not primarily to conserve the fertility of the soil, but is a sanitary measure, tending to eradicate contagious disease. The reproductive bodies (*spores*) of these fungi are carried from field to field and persist in the field for some time, but lose their vitality during the few seasons when other crops are being cultivated. It is thus seen that one farmer, by careless methods of agriculture, may not only suffer a loss of yield of his own crops, but may also infect his neighbors' fields. In addition to crop-rotation, this trouble may be reduced or avoided by carefully sterilizing all seed, before sowing, by soaking them in a weak solution of formaldehyde, and also by sterilizing the soil in a similar manner. The validity of this theory is based upon extended studies of wheat, oats, barley, and flax: it doubtless holds true also for other crops.

These three theories are all based upon thorough experimental investigation, and it is probable that all three contribute to a rational basis for the rotation of crops.

CHAPTER VIII

FERMENTATION

91. Importance of Fermentation.—In Chapter VII (paragraph 78) reference was made to *enzymes*, which have the power of causing marked chemical changes in other substances without being thereby permanently transformed or used up themselves. The number of different kinds of enzymes now known is very great, and it is probable that further investigation will reveal still others not now recognized. One of the most interesting and illuminating results of their study is the revelation of the fact that *one or more kinds of ferments or enzymes are produced by every living cell* (plant or animal), and that life itself involves, and is in large measure dependent upon, a series of fermentations. This truth, which is becoming more and more firmly established by scientific research, was recognized as early as 1839 by Schwann, one of the founders of the cell-theory.[1] His famous work, "Microscopical Researches," contains the following passage:

"I have been unable to avoid mentioning fermentation, because it is the most fully and exactly known operation of cells, and represents, in the simplest fashion, the process which is repeated by every cell of the living body." In fact, a knowledge of enzymes and fermentation is necessary in order to understand some of the most

[1] Cf. p. 15.

fundamental processes of plant physiology. Fermentation is most commonly associated in our minds with yeast.

92. Yeast.—Practically everyone is acquainted with yeast, which was the earliest recognized agent of fermentation. We are now most familiar with it in the form of small cakes, purchased at the grocer's for use in making bread and other "raised" dough. Our grandparents bought it in liquid form from the local baker; and in breweries and large bakeries it is used in the liquid form in making beer and bread. If a small piece of a "compressed yeast" cake, about the size of a pea seed, is placed with a little sugar and water in a fermentation-tube (Fig. 66), and set in a warm place the mixture will soon begin to "work," and tiny bubbles of gas will be seen rising in increasing numbers to the top of the tube. The process which gives rise to these bubbles is *alcoholic fermentation.*

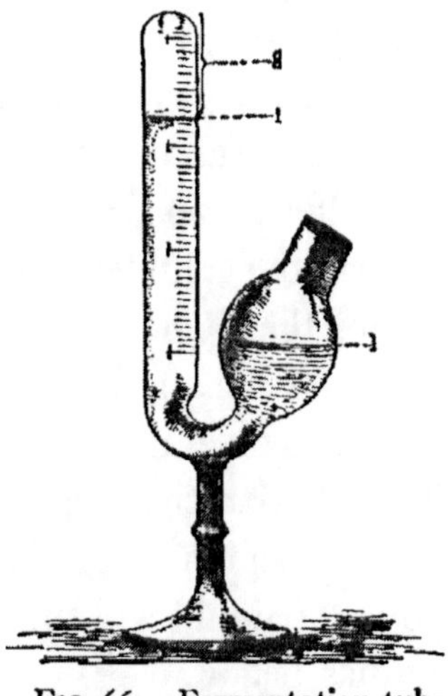

FIG. 66.—Fermentation-tube. *l*, level of fermenting liquid; *g*, space filled with gas (CO_2) given off by fermentation.

93. Conditions Necessary for Alcoholic Fermentation.—If two other tubes are prepared precisely like the first one, except that ice-water is used in one and boiling water in the other, and are set, the first in a cold place (*e.g.*, the refrigerator), and the second in a very warm place, fermentation will occur either very tardily or not at all. If a third fermentation-tube is set up with sugar but no yeast, and a fourth tube with yeast but no sugar, no fermentation will take place. In other words, in order to have fermentation three conditions must be realized: (1) a ferment, (2) something for the ferment to act upon, (3) suitable external conditions.[1]

94. Products of Alcoholic Fermentation.—If we place a large quantity of the fermenting mixture in a deep glass cylinder, and cover over the top so as to hinder the escape of the gas given off, the gas will collect in quantity in the space above the liquid. If, after fermentation has been allowed to proceed vigorously for a few hours, we insert in the cylinder a lighted splinter of wood or a lighted candle, the flame will at once go out, showing that the oxygen of the air, which supports combustion, has largely disappeared and has been replaced by another gas. The test with the flame should, of course, be made also at the very beginning of the experiment, to show that the air above the liquid will support combustion before fermentation has begun.

95. Carbon Dioxide Formed.—In order to ascertain what gas has taken the place of oxygen, we may next insert a fine wire, bent into a small circular loop at the end, and dipped in lime-water. A film of lime-water will extend across the space enclosed by the loop. Lime-water has the characteristic property of turning milky in the presence of carbon dioxide, and in this test the film of lime-water will at once turn white or milky, showing that the gas given off by fermentation is carbon dioxide. It is the formation of bubbles of this gas in bread dough that causes the dough to become "light" and to "rise."

[1] The student may devise an experiment of his own to ascertain whether or not light is necessary to fermentation.

96. Alcohol Formed.—If a large quantity of fermenting liquid—as much as a pint or a quart—is boiled, and the vapor that first comes off is condensed to a liquid, this liquid will have the characteristic odor of alcohol, and will burn with a pale, almost colorless flame. It is, in fact, alcohol, and it is on this account that this kind of fermentation is called *alcoholic fermentation*, to distinguish it from other kinds. Carbon dioxide and alcohol are, therefore, two products of the fermentation of sugar by yeast. If the proportions of yeast, sugar, and water, and the temperature are properly adjusted, and if the fermentation is allowed to continue long enough, it will be found that nearly all the sugar has disappeared, having been converted by the yeast into carbon dioxide and alcohol. Not all of the sugar will be converted for, as Pasteur, the great student of fermentation, demonstrated, small amounts of other substances such as, for example, succinic acid and glycerine, are formed by fermentation, and these finally begin to check the activity of the ferment.

97. Heat Produced.—If a delicate and accurate thermometer is inserted into a fermenting yeast-mixture, and the temperature recorded from time to time, it will be found that the mixture grows gradually warmer, indicating that fermentation produces heat. The experiment will succeed best if the yeast mixture is placed in a Dewar flask, or, what amounts to the same thing, in a "thermos" bottle, which is double-walled, and thus retains more of the heat produced than does an ordinary, single-walled container. It is important to keep in mind the three major results of alcoholic fermentation: (1) the formation of alcohol; (2) the formation of carbon dioxide; (3) the increase of temperature. We shall see, in the next chapter, that the last two are also the results of another important life-process of plants.

98. What is Yeast?—For centuries men employed yeast in baking and brewing without having the remotest idea as to what it really is, or of how it causes fermentation. This was because they did not inquire into the matter. It was not until 1680 that Leeuwenhoek, a Dutch naturalist, discovered that liquid yeast always contains tiny floating globules. It was 150 years after this that a French scientist, Cagniard de la Tour, discovered that yeast is a living organism, and soon thereafter another observer, Turpin, demonstrated that *yeast is really a plant*, closely related to the fungi. Thanks to the painstaking work of many other students, and especially of Pasteur, we now have a detailed knowledge of the structure and activity of the yeast plant. It is related to the sac-fungi (Ascomycetes).

99. Microscopic Appearance.—If a drop of yeast mixture that has been fermenting vigorously is examined under the microscope, the individual yeast plants may be readily observed (Fig. 67). They are seen to be unicellular plants, globular or ellipsoidal in form, of various sizes according to age, and devoid of chlorophyll. The nucleus can be seen only after the cell is stained. Many of the larger cells will be seen to have small outgrowths or buds, also of various sizes according to age. It is by the formation of the buds, that is, by *budding*, that the plant

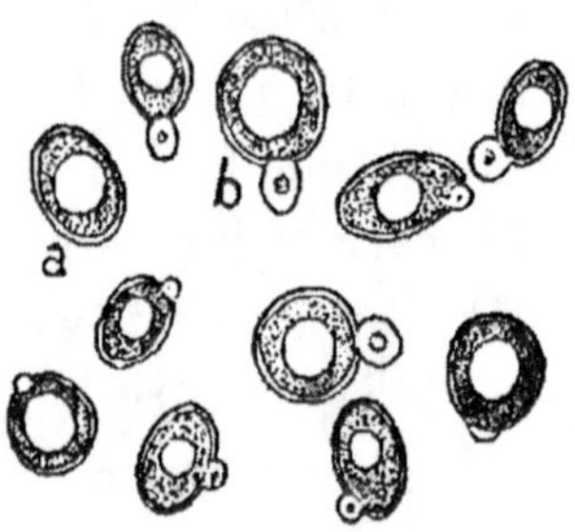

FIG. 67.—Cells of yeast (*Saccharomyces sp.*). Some of the cells are budding. The clear spaces are vacuoles.

reproduces itself. When the buds reach a certain size, they separate from the parent plant, continue to take in nourishment from the surrounding liquid by osmosis, increase in size to maturity, and then give rise to other plants, by repeating the process of budding.[1] Under favorable conditions new plants are formed very rapidly by budding, so that in the course of a few hours the total number of yeast plants will have enormously increased, notwithstanding the fact that some of them in the meantime may have died. This increase in number may be noted with the naked eye, by observing the increase of turbidity or opalescence of the yeast-mixture after it has stood for an hour or more. The yeast cakes of commerce consist largely of starch and millions of tiny yeast plants, skimmed from the surface of a fermenting liquid, and then pressed together.

100. The Active Agent in Fermentation.—After it became recognized that the presence of the yeast plant is necessary, in order to have alcoholic fermentation, it required careful study before it was discovered that if the yeast cells, after being disintegrated by grinding, are all filtered out of the mixture, the filtered liquid still retains the power to cause fermentation. From this it was learned that the active agent, or immediate cause of the process, is not the yeast itself, but some substance or substances produced by the yeast. These substances are the real ferments or enzymes, and are secreted by the living protoplasm of the yeast. At least three different enzymes are known to be produced by yeast. The one

[1] Another process of reproduction of yeast, by the production of *endospores*, need not here be described.

that is active in converting sugar into carbon dioxide and alcohol is a *zymase*, called *alcoholase*.

101. How Enzymes Work.—It has previously been stated that enzymes have the ability to cause changes in other substances without themselves being altered or consumed thereby. The mystery of this fact has never been fully explained, but the simile used by Huxley helps us to form a crude mental picture of the process. "There can be no doubt," says Huxley, "that the constituent elements of fully 98 per cent. of the sugar which has vanished during fermentation have simply undergone rearrangement; like the soldiers of a brigade, who at the word of command divide themselves into the independent regiments to which they belong. The brigade is sugar, the regiments are carbonic acid, succinic acid, alcohol, and glycerine." We may add that the commanding officer is the enzyme, secreted by the yeast.

102. Many Kinds of Enzymes.—Two kinds of enzymes have just been mentioned—that which converts starch to sugar (diastase), and that which causes alcoholic fermentation (alcoholase). In our own bodies we are familiar with the *ptyalin*, or "animal diastase," of the saliva, which can also convert starch to sugar, the pepsin of the gastric juice, which can change the insoluble proteins of meat into soluble proteins, the pancreatic juice, and others. Among plants is found *cytase*, which can liquefy the cellulose of cell-walls. It is by this means that the delicate threads of fungi which grow on trees can penetrate the hard, solid wood. The enzyme, secreted by the fungus, softens and liquefies the wood, and the delicate fungal thread may then penetrate with ease. When leaves fall in the autumn, the final stage in the process is the solution of a portion of the cell-walls of a layer of cells (the *abscission-layer*) at the place where the leaf joins the branch. This greatly weakens the attachment, and the leaf falls, often merely from its own weight. The solution of this tissue is caused by an enzyme secreted by the cells adjacent to the abscission layer. Many of the peculiar effects produced by molds and by bacteria are caused by enzymes secreted by these organisms. The ripening of cheese, the formation of alcohol in beer and wine, the changing of sweet to sour or "hard" cider, the turning brown of cut fruit, such as apples, when exposed to the air, and all processes of decay are caused by fermentations produced by enzymes secreted by bacteria, molds, yeast, or other living cells.

103. The Significance of Alcoholic Fermentation.— From what has just preceded, it is seen that the various processes of fermentation are useful or otherwise important to mankind, but we must seek for the real significance of alcoholic fermentation in its use to the organism that secretes the ferment. In this connection we must recall the fact that all the life-processes of plants and animals require energy. The continued release of this energy within the cells usually makes necessary a supply of free oxygen from the air; but some organisms can secure the necessary oxygen by decomposing compounds that contain it—such as carbohydrates, proteins, and fats. Thus we must regard alcoholic fermentation (in part, at least) as a process by which yeast and other organisms or cells secure the necessary energy for their activities when deprived of the free oxygen of the air. Alcohol and other complex compounds result because the processes of oxidation are not completed, owing to the restricted supply of oxygen that can be obtained in the absence of air. *If the oxidation processes could be completed the end products would be carbon dioxide and water.* Organisms that may continue to live without a supply of free oxygen are called *anaerobes.*[1] Either the entire organism may live anaerobically, or this condition may be confined to one or more of its organs, or even to a single cell or group of cells. It is possible for yeast to live in contact with free oxygen, but when this is not present it can secure sufficient oxygen for its needs by alcoholic fermentation alone.[2]

104. Relation of Fermentation to Our Daily Lives.—Reference has already been made to the fact that such diverse operations as the manufacture of all alcoholic drinks and the making of bread are dependent upon fermentations, and we have seen that the process fundamental to all life—the formation of carbohydrates by photosynthesis—probably involves the action of at least six different ferments. The active principles of all the digestive juices of our own bodies are also enzymes—*diastase* in the saliva, *pepsin* in the stomach, *trypsin* in the intestine, and so on. We shall learn, in the next chapter, that all muscular and mental activity, even life itself, is dependent on the fermentative activity of enzymes.

[1] *a* + *aer* (air) + *bios* (life) = living without air.

[2] From a reading of Chapters VII to IX the student will learn that the transformations wrought in other substances by the catalytic agents, called enzymes, are not all of the same nature; some (as alcoholic fermentation, and digestive processes) are destructive, others (as the polymerizations and other transformations in photosynthesis, mentioned on pages 79 and 80) are constructive. The author believes that it contributes to simplicity, without sacrificing clear and accurate thinking, to consider "enzyme" and "ferment" as synonymous terms, and to call all activities of enzymes *fermentations*, whether they are analytic or synthetic.

CHAPTER IX

RESPIRATION

105. Anaerobes and Aerobes.—In the preceding chapter we learned that all plants require energy for their activities, and that this energy is derived by the oxidation of substances within the cell. In the case of yeast and other organisms, when living in an atmosphere devoid of free oxygen, the necessary oxygen is obtained from compounds which contain it, by the process of fermentation, brought about by enzymes. As is well known, many organisms, such as man and most other animals, and most plants, cannot live in the absence of free oxygen; such organisms, called *aerobes*,[1] continually take in oxygen from the air. The using up of oxygen by the cells creates the need for more, and in the case of man and other mammals, the supply is obtained through the lungs by breathing. Plants, however, have no lungs, nor any organs that correspond to lungs.[2]

When oxygen is consumed by plant tissues, its pressure within the plant becomes less than its pressure outside the plant, and therefore more passes in through the stomata and epidermis by the simple physical process of diffusion.

[1] *aero* (air) + *be* (*bios*, life) living in air.

[2] Leaves have sometimes been called "the lungs of plants." From our study of nutrition, it will be readily recognized that leaves may much more appropriately be called the stomachs of plants.

106. Consumption of Oxygen Demonstrated.—The exchange of gases between the atmosphere and the interior of the plant may readily be demonstrated by a simple experiment, as follows. Into each of seven glass cylinders (Fig. 68) fit a partition of wire gauze, so as to divide the space vertically into equal parts. Into the first jar place nothing, and fill the space, on one side only of the wire gauze, in each of the other six jars respectively, with germinating seeds (pea or lupine), living herbaceous stems, living roots (washed free from soil but moist and fresh), green leaves, freshly opening flower buds, and (in the last jar) fresh mushrooms or other fleshy fungi. Test the air in the empty half of each jar with a lighted taper to make sure that it contains sufficient oxygen to support combustion, and then seal all the jars air-tight with rubber stoppers, and set them side by side in any convenient place except in direct sunlight.[1] At the end of 12 to 24 hours again test the air in each of the jars with the lighted taper. The air in the first jar, containing no plant material, will still support combustion, but the taper will be extinguished at once when lowered into each of the other six jars.[2] This shows that the air in each of these jars has become poorer in oxygen, and that it does not now contain enough to support combustion.[3] This

[1] The heat of direct sunlight is unfavorable to the best results.

[2] If the taper is not extinguished in the jar containing the green leaves, the student should be able, from his knowledge of other plant processes, to suggest a probable reason why, and to devise suitable modifications of the experiment so as to demonstrate the respiration of green leaves. *In this and other tests of the air, the cork stopper should not be removed any longer than is absolutely necessary, and the lighted taper should be lowered and removed quickly.*

[3] Does the experiment show that there is *no* oxygen in the jars in which the flame is extinguished?

FIG. 68.—Experiment to demonstrate the exchange of gases that accompanies plant-respiration. Explanation in the text.

observation justifies the inference that living plants take in oxygen.

107. Carbon Dioxide Given Off.—The air in each of the seven cylinders may next be tested with lime-water, by pouring in not more than one or two tablespoonfuls, and mixing it well with the air by tipping the cylinders, holding the halves with the plant material uppermost, and allowing the lime-water to flow back and forth a few times from one end of the jar to the other. Care should be taken not to dirty the lime-water by allowing it to rinse the plant material. After this treatment the lime-water will be found to have turned milky in all of the jars except the one containing no plant tissue. From these results we may correctly infer that carbon dioxide has been given off by the plants.

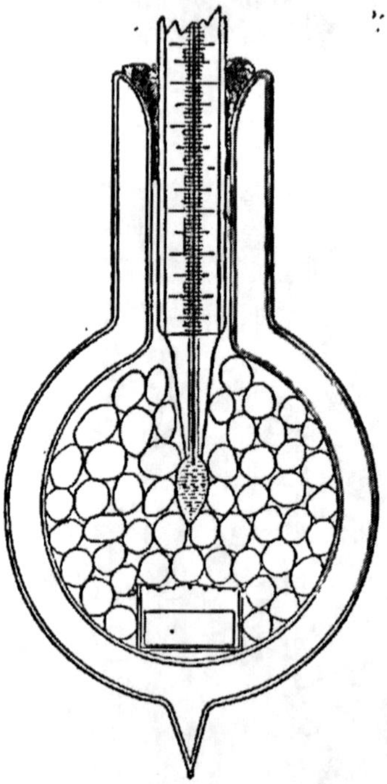

FIG. 69.—A simple calorimeter for studying the temperature transformations in respiration. Respiring seeds are placed in the Dewar bulb (double walled, with a vacuum between the walls). At the bottom of the bulb is a dish containing caustic potash; cotton wool is packed between the thermometer and the neck of the bulb. (After Ganong.)

108. Heat Evolved.—That heat is evolved during the gaseous exchange above demonstrated may be illustrated by placing a delicate thermometer into, say, the germinating seeds. The best results will be obtained by placing the plant material into a double-walled Dewar flask (or a thermos bottle), which will retain most of any heat that may be given off (Fig. 69). If the temperature is recorded at the beginning of the experiment, and again at the end, a rise of temperature will be noted. In one experiment, set up with germinating pea seeds (air dry weight 80 grams) in a Dewar flask as above described, a rise of 19.3° was observed within 96 hours.

109. Respiration Versus Breathing.—In the case of man and other animals, the exchange of gases and evolution of heat, demonstrated by the experiments described above, are an index of respiration. The process of taking in oxygen and giving off of carbon dioxide by animals is called breathing. It is better to restrict the term breathing to the mechanical exchange of gases between the lungs of animals adn the external air, and to confine the term respiration to the oxidation processes of the living protoplasm. It will thus be recognized that *respiration is a function of every living cell*, and that the cells of our fingers, for example, respire just as truly as do those of our lungs and other organs. The lungs, by their mechanical expansion and contraction, merely serve to bring the oxygen of the external air into intimate contact with the blood, which carries it to all respiring tissues of the body. There is no process in plants comparable to this breathing. In the case of some animals without lungs, certain specialized organs (in fishes, the gills) are continually bathed with external oxygen, which passes into the blood *by diffusion.* This more closely resembles the process by which oxygen from the air passes into the plant body. In other animals (*e.g.*, earthworms) there are no special organs for breathing, and the oxygen diffuses through the moist body-walls.

110. Stomata and Gaseous Exchange.—In Chapter IV we described the openings or stomata in the epidermis of leaves, through which water-vapor passed to the outside. We also learned in Chapter VII that the interchange of gases in photosynthesis takes place through the stomata. So, also, does the exchange of gases that

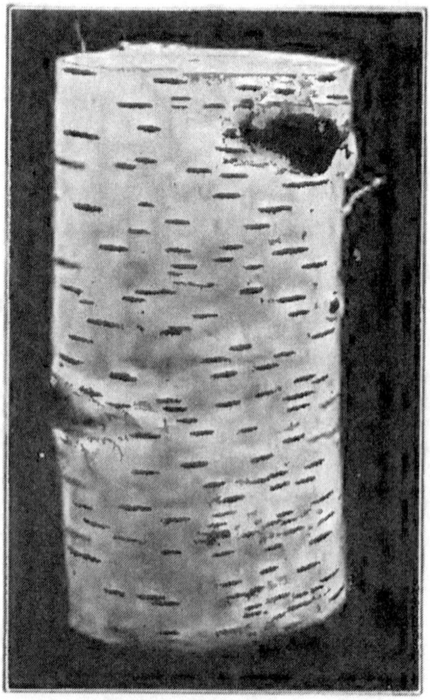

FIG. 70.—White birch (*Betula populifolia*). Portion of a branch showing the prominent lenticels.

accompanies respiration. As the oxygen within the cells is consumed in respiration, more is absorbed from the intercellular spaces. Thus its pressure becomes less within the leaf than without, and consequently oxygen enters by diffusion through the stomata. At the same time the air in the intercellular spaces becomes richer in carbon dioxide than the air outside, and therefore this gas passes out, also by diffusion.

111. Lenticels.—Many living cells and tissues are more deep seated than the mesophyll of leaves, and oxygen obtains access to these cells by different ways in different plants. Only one of these cases may be considered here. If any young woody twig is examined, small "dots" or lines will be discovered on the surface. On closer examination these will be found to be small openings through the bark (Fig. 70). They are known as *lenticels*. The outer portion of the bark, and the older, inner layers of wood are not alive, but the cambium layer, between wood and bark is alive, and therefore needs a continual supply of fresh oxygen. This is supplied through the lenticels in a manner quite analogous to that by which the supply in the leaves is maintained.

112. Respiration and Photosynthesis.—The two processes of respiration and photosynthesis are often confused, but in reality thay have very little in common, except that both result in an exchange of gases with the external air. But it must be kept clearly in mind that the processes themselves are quite distinct from the exchanges of gases that accompany them, or result because of them. Photosynthesis furnishes carbon to the plant in a form available for use; respiration is the physiological process by which the carbon is utilized to supply the energy necessary for all life-processes. The result of the two processes is the continual income and outgo of carbon. The carbon enters and leaves the plant in the same form, namely carbon dioxide. The disintegration of carbohydrates is also accomplished by bacterial decay and other fermentative processes. We thus see that there is a continuous circulation of carbon in nature, known as the *carbon cycle* (Fig. 71). A comparison between the two processes is shown in Table II.

TABLE II.—COMPARISON OF RESPIRATION AND PHOTOSYNTHESIS

1. Photosynthesis Changes inorganic matter into plant-foods (carbohydrates), which are Assimilated and used by the plant	To supply energy for work, To repair waste (Nutrition), In the construction of new parts (Development), including Reproduction.	All of these processes are dependent upon Oxidation within the cells. This process of oxidation is called. . . .	2. Respiration, which involves The taking in of oxygen, The oxidizing of oxidizable matter, The release of all products of these oxidations.

Photosynthesis	Respiration
1. Takes place only in cells containing chlorophyll.	1. Takes place in all active cells.
2. Requires light.	2. Can proceed in darkness.
3. CO_2 absorbed, O set free.	3. O absorbed, CO_2 set free.
4. Carbohydrates formed.	4. Carbohydrates consumed.
5. Plant gains in dry weight.	5. Plant loses in dry weight.
6. Kinetic energy of sunlight becomes potential energy.	6. Potential energy becomes kinetic energy.

113. Plant and Animal Respiration.—There is probably no erroneous notion about plants more tenaciously held, nor more widespread, than the belief that plant respiration is the reverse of animal respiration. This error is due entirely to a confusion of the two processes of respiration and photosynthesis. From what has preceded, however, it should now be clear that plants respire in the same way as animals, using up oxygen in the processes of oxidation within their tissues, renewing the supply from the surrounding air (or, in anaerobic respiration, from the breaking down of chemical compounds rich in oxygen), and releasing the carbon dioxide and other waste products resulting from the oxidations. Heat is developed in both plants and animals. The condensation of water-vapor from the breath shows that water is formed in animal respiration, and careful, delicate experiments have also

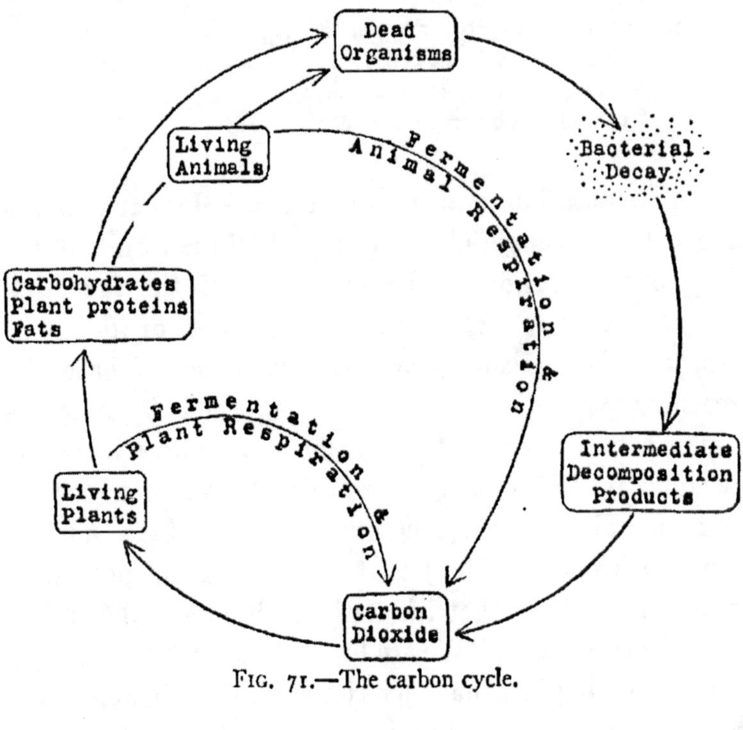

FIG. 71.—The carbon cycle.

shown that water is formed in plant respiration. In both plants and animals respiration converts potential energy (in the form of complex chemical compounds) into kinetic energy—manifest in motion, locomotion, and the overcoming of resistance of various kinds (that is, work). The two processes are compared in the following table:

TABLE III.—COMPARISON OF PLANT AND ANIMAL RESPIRATION

Plant respiration	Animal respiration
1. Oxidations occur within the tissue..........	1. Ditto
2. Oxygen taken in...........................	2. Ditto
3. Carbon dioxide given off..................	3. Ditto
4. Heat evolved..............................	4. Ditto
5. Water-vapor formed........................	5. Ditto
6. Dry weight decreased......................	6. Ditto
7. Potential energy becomes kinetic...........	7. Ditto
8. Occurs in every living cell................	8. Ditto
9. Occurs without ceasing, day and night......	9. Ditto
10. Accomplished by respiratory enzymes.......	10. Ditto

114. Respiration and Fermentation.—Perhaps one of the most surprising and interesting of all the results of the study of respiration is the revelation of the fact that *the real process of respiration* (the oxidation of living tissues, as distinguished from the exchange of gases by breathing, or otherwise) is accomplished by enzymes known as oxidases, and *is therefore, in reality, a form of fermentation.* In fact, the more deeply we study all the fundamental processes of living things, the more it seems to become evident that every chemical process in organisms, in fact, that life itself is absolutely dependent upon fermentations. We are brought face to face with the almost startling fact that such commonplace phenomena as the ripening of fruit, the raising of dough, and the decay of plant tissues, are conditioned by the same class of substances (enzymes), and by the same kind of processes that underlie the digestion of food, the respiration of tissues, and the thinking of human minds. And, moreover, we seem to be led to the odd conclusion that *living organisms do not respire because they take in oxygen, but that they take in oxygen because they have respired.*

CHAPTER X

GROWTH

115. Definition.—*Growth is increase in size* of either the organism as a whole or of any of its parts. By growth the individual protoplast of a cell may become more bulky, the chloroplasts or leucoplasts may become larger, the nucleus bigger, the cell-walls thicker, the cell as a whole may increase in any dimension, and, as a result of this, the tissues and organs, and finally the entire organism, may become larger. Growth does not always involve the whole organism. Cell-walls often grow thicker while the size of the plant as a whole does not alter. Growth often involves a decrease in the size of one or more of the parts; thus, when a potato "sprouts," the tuber itself, giving its substance to nourish the newly formed stems, becomes smaller and lighter in weight, while the stems increase in size and weight. As a whole, however, the potato plant is growing (Fig. 60).

116. Osmotic Pressure and Growth.—Growth does not always involve increase in weight. If, for example, the osmotic pressure increases within a turgid cell, and if the cell-walls are elastic, the cell will grow bigger in one or more dimensions. Not only may this growth involve no increase in weight (as, for example, when the increase in osmotic pressure within a cell is due merely to the changing of starch to sugar), but may even be accompanied by loss of weight on account of waste products being given off by the growing cell. *The immediate cause of all growth is osmotic pressure.*

The great amount of force often exerted by young growing organs, due to the osmotic pressure within their cells, is strikingly illustrated in Fig. 72, showing the rupturing of a concrete pavement by young fern leaves.

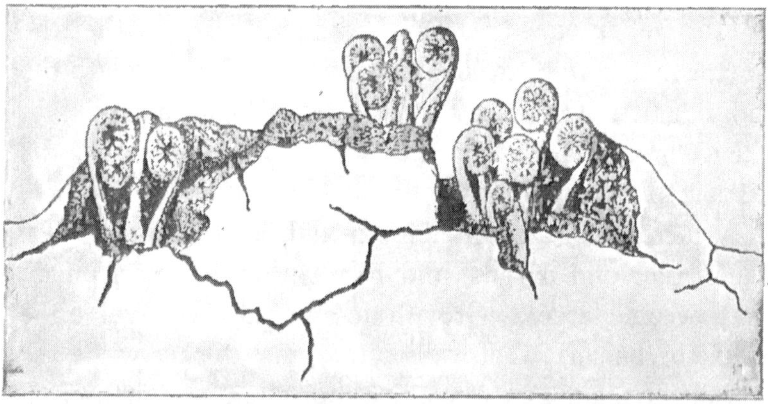

FIG. 72.—The rupturing of concrete by the growth of young leaves of the ostrich fern (*Onoclea Struthiopteris* Hoffm.). (After Stone.)

117. Experiment in Growth.—The relation between osmotic pressure and growth may be demonstrated by a very simple experiment, illustrated in Fig. 73. P is a portion of the herbaceous stem of any convenient plant, fastened securely at one end to an iron clamp (C), lying at the bottom of a glass jar (J). The upper end of the stem is attached by a small thread to the short arm of an index (I), the opposite end of which may move up and down over a graduated scale (S). If the jar is filled with a solution of common salt water, water will pass out of the plant tissue by exosmosis. This will reduce the osmotic pressure (*turgor*) within, and the stem will shorten, on account of the contraction of the elastic cell-walls, causing the long arm of the index to move up over the graduated scale. If the salt-solution is now removed, and the jar filled with tap water, or better, distilled water, the water will enter the cells of the stem by osmosis, increasing the internal osmotic pressure and *turgor* of each cell. As a result the stem as a whole will elongate or grow in length, thereby causing the index to move down over the scale.

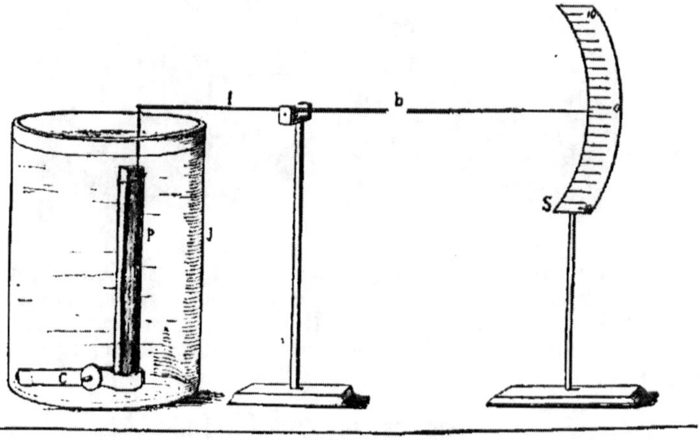

FIG. 73.—Experiment to demonstrate the relation between osmosis and growth in length. *J*, jar containing water, and subsequently salt-solution; *p*, portion of leaf-stalk of Rhubarb; *I*, index-lever (portion omitted at *b*); *S*, scale. Explanation in text.

118. Differential Growth.—Not all the tissues of a stem or other part grow at the same rate.[1] On this account, and since adjacent tissues are closely united, those which elongate or grow more slowly are stretched by those which grow more rapidly. As a result either a state of tension exists, or the organ is distorted, or both. When one epidermis of a leaf grows more rapidly than the other, distortion results, and the leaf becomes "crisped" or crinkled. This is normally the case in some plants, but

[1] The student should endeavor to reason out an explanation for this.

in others the crisping may denote a diseased condition of the leaf.

119. Tissue-Tension.—If a thin surface strip of tissue is cut away for a short distance from a stalk of celery,

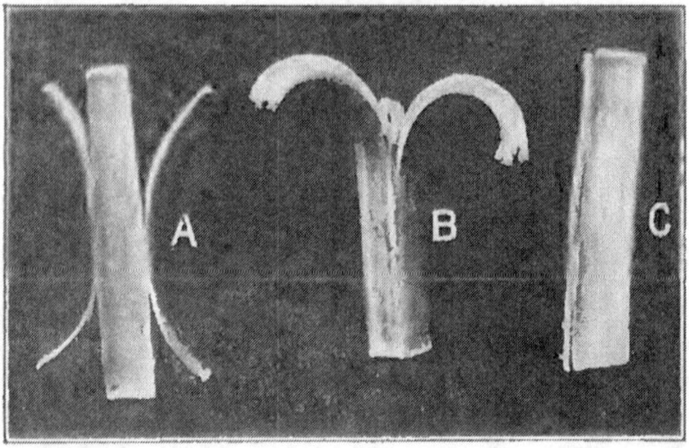

FIG. 74.—Longitudinal tissue-tension in leaf-stalk of rhubarb. In *C* the strip of outer tissues, entirely removed from the main piece, is seen to have shortened, showing that, before being removed, it was in a state of *longitudinal tissue-tension*, owing to the fact that, in growth, the inner tissues elongated more rapidly than the outer, thus stretching the latter lengthwise.

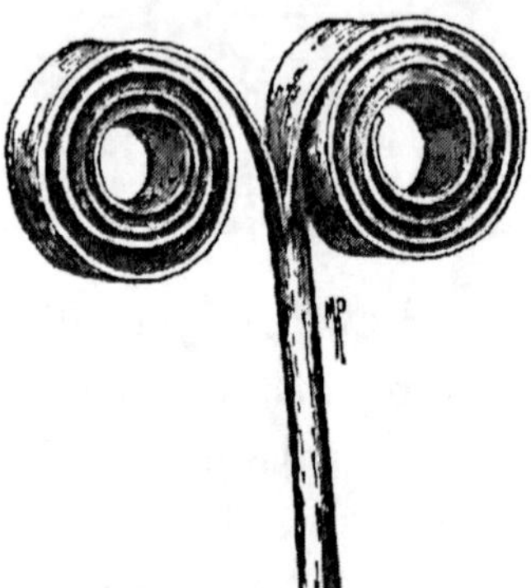

FIG. 75.—Portion of dandelion scape, showing "curls" resulting from longitudinal tissue-tension.

or the thick petiole of a burdock or other leaf, the strip at once curves outward, on account of its *longitudinal tissue-tension.* We are all familiar with this phenomenon (Figs. 74 and 75). When boys make whistles from young willow twigs in spring, a cylinder of bark is removed, and may be easily replaced; but if the cylinder of bark becomes split lengthwise, the edges cannot be made to come together around the wood without considerable stretching. This illustrates *transverse tissue-tension* (Fig. 76). If the preceding statements in this chapter have been understood, the student should now be able to explain these phenomena without further assistance.

FIG. 76.—Portion of stem of a willow, illustrating transverse tissue-tension. By gentle tapping and twisting the cambium layer has been bruised, so that a small cylinder of the bark was easily twisted off.

120. Elongation of Roots.—In order to ascertain the manner of growth of roots, the root of a young seedling of lupine, or other plant, may be carefully marked with dots or lines of India ink, at intervals of 1 millimeter, beginning about 1 millimeter back from the root-tip, and extending for a distance of 15 to 20 millimeters. If the root is again observed, after having been left to grow for about 24 hours, it will be found that the first six or eight marks near the tip have spread apart, those from 3 to 7 millimeters from the tip having separated more than those farther back Those marks most remote from the tip will be found to have separated very little if at all (Fig. 77). By this simple experiment we learn that the growth in length of roots is largely confined to a zone a few millimeters in length directly back of the root-tip. It should also be noted in this connection that the zone of root-hairs begins just back of the zone of growth, no root-hairs being found in the region of elongation.

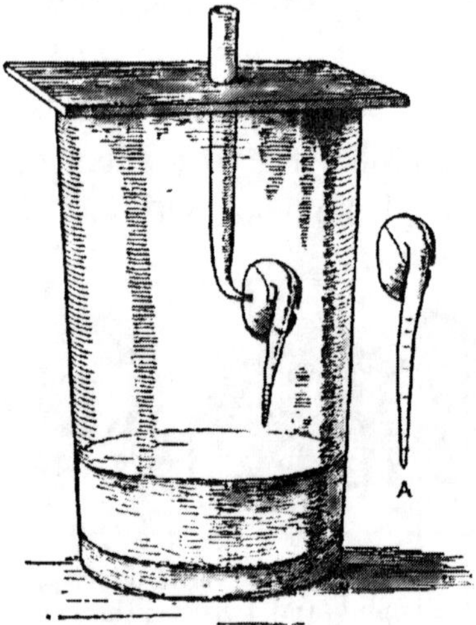

FIG. 77.—Experiment to show the method of growth in length of a root. *A*, 24 hours after the condition shown in the glass.

121. Elongation of Stems.—The manner of elongation of stems may be ascertained by marking the internodes[1] of a young growing stem throughout their entire length. Two or three adjacent internodes near the tip of the stem should be marked. After a period of from 24 to 36 hours the marks will be found to have separated, but, in contrast to the behavior of the root, the marks will be found to have separated through the entire extent of the internode, and several adjacent internodes will be found to have elongated at the same time (Fig. 78). This contributes to the more rapid elongation of the stem, and is

[1] An internode is the space between two successive leaves on the stem.

an advantage to the plant, since the leaves are thereby more rapidly brought into positions of best exposure to air and sunlight. The growth of several internodes at the same time, and their elongation throughout their entire length, carries the tip of the stem forward with much greater force than if growth were confined to a short zone, as in the case of the growing root. But a more rapid and forceful advance of the root-tip through the soil might result in serious or fatal injury, on account of the resistance and obstacles encountered in the soil. Thus the different manner of growth of stems and roots is seen to be of direct advantage to the plant as a whole.

122. Growth of Leaves.—In tropical climates leaves that have once begun to form continue to grow until they reach full size; but in temperate climates, having an alteration of summer and winter, this is not the case. Here the leaves of any given season are all formed during the preceding growing season, and remain over winter

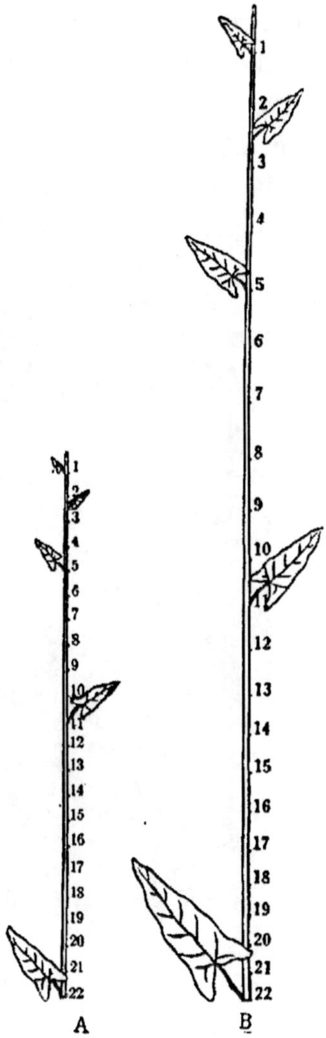

FIG. 78.—Diagram showing mode of growth in length of a portion of a stem of bindweed (*Convolvulus*). *A*, stem with internodes marked off into intervals of 1 cm.; *B*, the same stem 24 hours later, showing the relative elongation of the various internodes. (Cf. Fig. 77.) (Redrawn from Bonnier and Leclerc du Sablon.)

in a resting state in buds. The outer coverings or scales of the bud are modified leaves or parts of leaves. They have almost or entirely lost their character as foliage organs, and while they are forming, their outer (dorsal) surfaces elongate more rapidly than their upper (ventral) surfaces. This causes them to curve together, so as to

FIG. 79.—Opening buds of horse-chestnut (*Æsculus Hippocastanum*). (Cf. Fig. 80.) (Photo by E. M. Kittredge.)

overlap, and form a protection to the embryonic stem, leaves, and other parts within the bud. With the return of warmth and moisture the following spring, the bud-scales resume their growth, but now their inner surfaces elongate more rapidly than their outer, reversing the method of their growth when forming. As a result of this, they begin to open outward. At the same time the embryonic parts within the bud begin to enlarge and this helps to force the bud-scales apart. The young stem-internodes rapidly elongate, the petioles of the leaves increase in length, and gradually the leaf-blades expand

FIG. 80.—Sapling of horse-chestnut (*Æsculus Hippocastanum*), with young leaves not yet wholly expanded. (Cf. Fig. 79.)

as their cells become more and more turgid (Figs. 79 and 80).

123. Permanent and Temporary Growth.—The size finally attained by stems, roots, leaves, and other parts is usually permanent; but some growth is temporary, and certain tissues may manifest various alterations in

FIG. 81.—Sensitive plant (*Mimosa pudica*). *B*, normal position of foliage in light; *A*, position of foliage after the plant was slightly shaken.

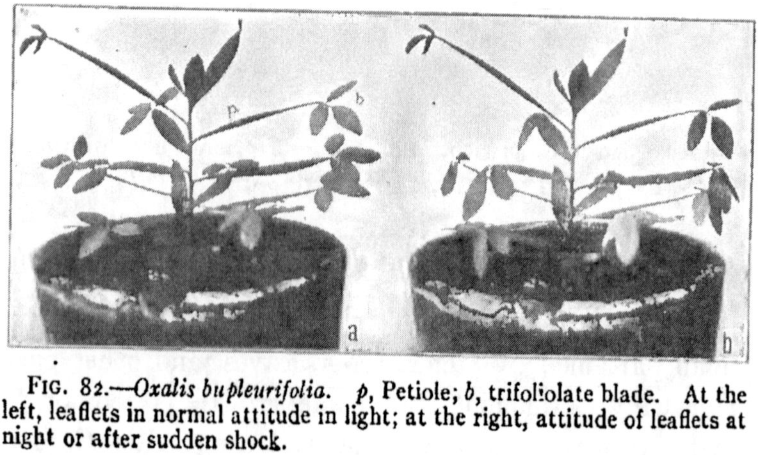

FIG. 82.—*Oxalis bupleurifolia*. *p*, Petiole; *b*, trifoliolate blade. At the left, leaflets in normal attitude in light; at the right, attitude of leaflets at night or after sudden shock.

size according to circumstances. This is illustrated by the petals of flowers (such for example as the tulip), that open and close several times before they drop off. This motion is caused by temporary fluctuations of growth of the upper and lower surfaces of the petals In a similar manner is explained the change of position of the leaflets of certain plants, such as clover, oxalis, bean, and others, at night or in cloudy weather, and the more rapid motion of the leaves of the "sensitive" and other plants (Figs. 81, 82, and 96).

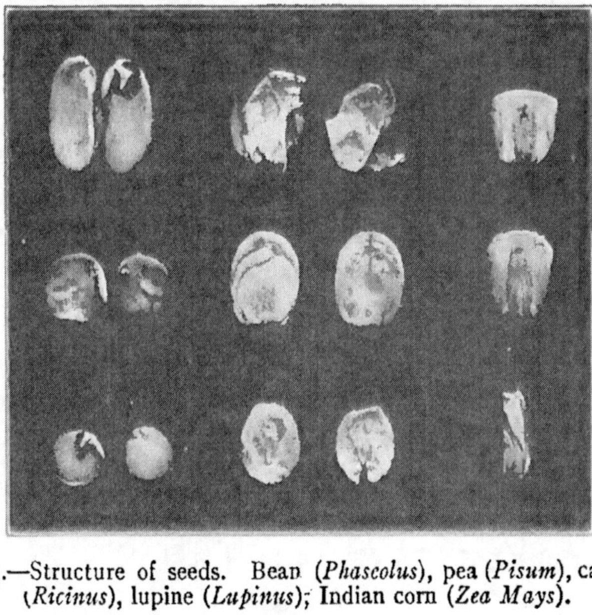

FIG. 83.—Structure of seeds. Bean (*Phascolus*), pea (*Pisum*), castor oil (*Ricinus*), lupine (*Lupinus*); Indian corn (*Zea Mays*).

124. Growth and Nourishment.—When a plant or plant organ is growing, the protoplasm is constantly forming new parts, and therefore must continually be renewed or nourished. The more rapidly new parts are formed, the greater the need for food. This need is provided for in many ways. Young embryo plants in the seed find a rich supply of nourishment, ready made by the parent plant, stored within their tissues (as in the bean or pea), or around them (as in the corn, or castor-oil seed, Fig. 83). They do not have to manufacture their own food at first. Young and rapidly growing plants (seedlings and young saplings) have much larger leaves than mature plants of the same species (Fig. 55). On this account food making, from the raw materials taken in by the plant, may proceed much more rapidly. Plants commonly store food in quantity where it will be needed in the future by rapidly growing new parts, and such storage organs usually become swollen by the abundance of stored food. This is illustrated by "potatoes," which, as is well known, are underground branches (*tubers*) stored with food for the use of young sprouts when they begin to grow in the spring. All bulbs are to be interpreted in the same way. Farmers recognize the need on the part of growing plants for an abundance of food, when they fertilize their fields, thereby placing in the soil a rich supply of the raw materials out of which the growing crops can manufacture food to meet their needs.

CHAPTER XI

ADJUSTMENT TO SURROUNDINGS

125. Environment.—Not only must plants be nourished, and respire in order to live; they must also be in general harmony with their surroundings. The sum total of these surroundings is called the *environment*. Among the *factors of environment* are temperature, water, light, gravity, air, electricity, soil, animals, and other plants. It will not be possible, here, to study the adjustments of the plant to all of these factors, but only to the more important ones, such as gravity, water, and light.

126. Stimulus and Response.—It is the nature of the various parts of a plant to grow in a certain definite relation to their environment. Thus, for example, main stems and roots normally grow parallel to the plumb-line, while their branches grow at an angle to it; foliage-leaves grow naturally in the light, while roots grow naturally in the dark. Any change in the environment requires a readjustment on the part of the plant, if the latter is to remain healthy. If the readjustment cannot be made the given organ, or the entire plant, may become unhealthy, or may die. The change in the environment, considered from the standpoint of its effect on the plant, is called a *stimulus;* the readjustment or attempt at readjustment, a *response*. Thus, if a plant is growing at a certain rate at a certain temperature, any change in the temperature becomes a stimulus to which the plant responds by growing either more or less rapidly, as the case may be.

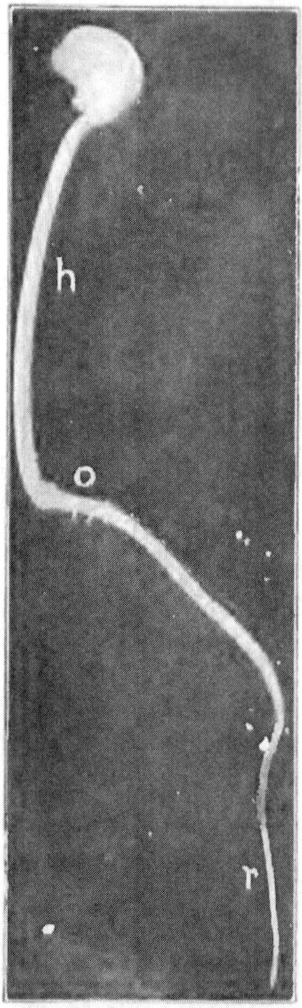

Fig. 84.—Seedling of white lupine (*Lupinus albus*), after having been placed horizontally in the dark for 48 hours. The hypocotyl (*h*) has responded negatively, and the root (*r*) positively to the stimulus of gravity. The portion (*o*) remains in the original horizontal position.

127. Relation of Roots and Stems to Gravity.—It is common knowledge that, in general, roots grow downward, while stems grow upward. If a germinating seed of lupine is so placed that the axis of the emerging embryo-plant is horizontal, the position of the elongating root and shoot after a given interval of time (*e.g.* 48 hours) will be as shown in Fig. 84. The result is the same whether the plant is placed in diffused light or in the dark. The difference in the direction of growth may not, therefore, be attributed to the action of light. If the seedling is so placed that the only external influence is gravity—the attraction of the earth—the result is as shown in the figure. We must, therefore, conclude that the result is due to the earth's gravitational attraction.

The correctness of this conclusion may be assured by subjecting the seedling to another influence than gravity, but, like it, acting on both root and shoot, at right angles to their long axis. Such an influence is the centrifugal tendency produced by motion in a circle. If

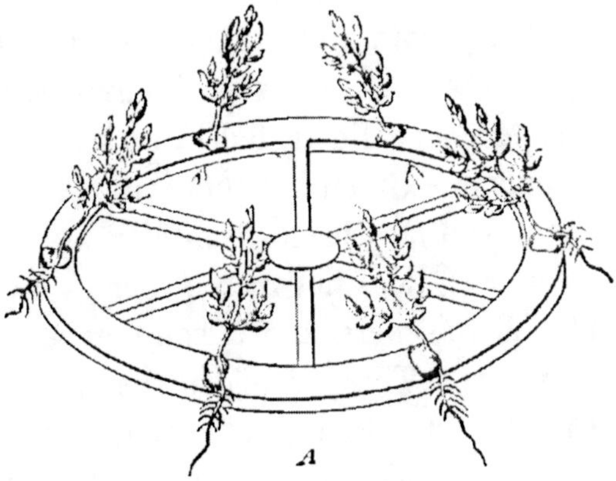

A

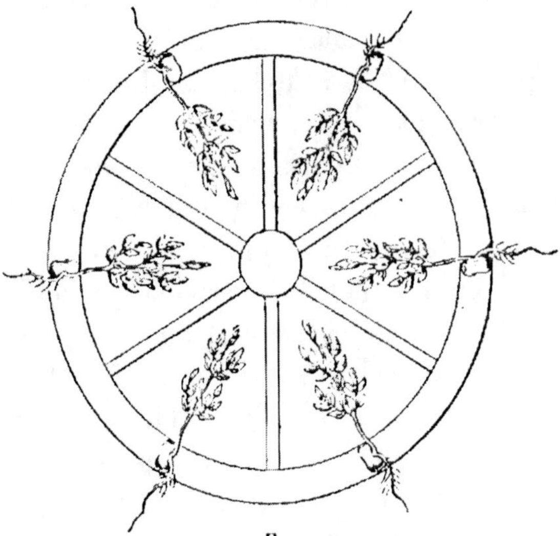

B

FIG. 85.—Knight's experiment, substituting centrifugal "force" for gravity. (After Knight.)

seedlings are fastened to a wheel, with the root and shoot pointing in various directions, and the wheel rapidly rotated, the growing root will bend until it points in the direction of the "pull" (centrifugal tendency), while the shoot will curve in the opposite direction (Fig. 85).

The causal relationship between gravity and the direction of growth of roots and shoots was first established by the English botanist, Thomas Andrew Knight, who devised the experiment illustrated in Fig. 78.

128. Geotropism.—Careful thought about these results will make it clear that the horizontally placed root, in the first experiment, does not merely bend down because of its weight. If this were so, we would expect the shoot to bend down also. The curving is the response of the organs to the stimulus of the pull. The property of an organ by virtue of which it may detect the *direction* of the pull of gravity is *geotropism.* It is thus seen that geotropism is a particular kind of irritability. Organs which respond by a curvature in the direction of the pull are *positively geotropic;* those which respond by a curvature in the opposite direction are *negatively geotropic.*

129. Zone of Curvature.—The following simple experiment shows that the geotropic curvature always takes place in a definite region. A germinating bean or other seed, with the sprout (*hypocotyl*) about 15 to 20 millimeters long, is pinned to a strip of cork, fastened to the bottom of a Petri dish (Fig. 86). The sprout is marked with fine lines of India ink 2 millimeters apart, beginning 2 millimeters back from the tip, as in the study of growth (page 118). Up to this point in the operations care must be exercised to keep the sprout as nearly parallel with the plumb-line as possible. By rotating the cork, or the entire Petri dish, the sprout is now fixed at right angles to the plumb-line, and the Petri dish covered and set in the dark.[1] The air in the dish may be kept moist by a strip of damp filter-paper placed around the circumference of the dish, inside.

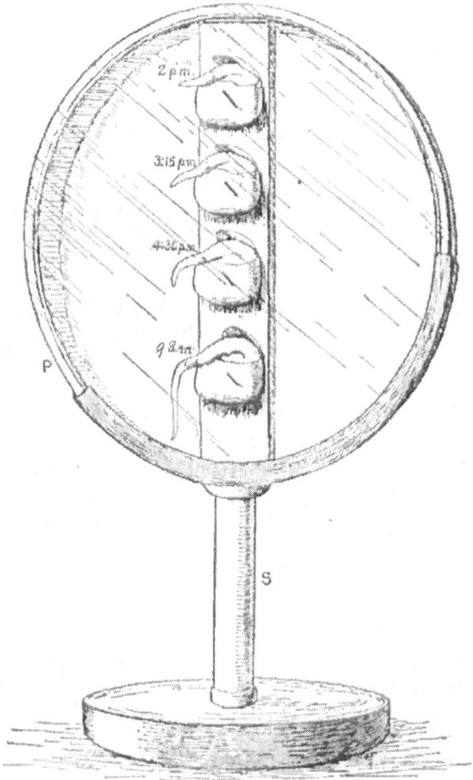

FIG. 86.—Experiment to demonstrate positive geotropism in the root of a seedling of lupine (*Lupinus albus*). *S*, metal stand; *P*, Petri dish, with edges lined with moist filter-paper. The seedling is pinned to a strip of sheet cork. The four views are of the *same* seedling at the successive hours as indicated. (Apparatus after W. T. Bovie.)

At the end of 12 hours, more or less, the sprout, on account of its positive geotropism, will have responded to the pull of gravity by curving downward, until the por-

[1] Why set in the dark?

9

tion between the curvature and the tip is parallel to the plumb-line. Examination of the ink-marks will show that *the zone of curvature is the same as the zone of maximum*

FIG. 87.—Negative geotropism in a barrigona palm (*Colpothrinax Wrightii*). By some accident the palm, when younger, had been bent over.

FIG. 88.—Mullein (*Verbascum thapsus*) showing geotropic recovery of the terminal inflorescence, after having been bent over.

growth in length. The stimulus of gravity has modified the distribution of the rate of growth in such a way that the upper side of the sprout has grown more rapidly than the under side. After the sprout has become oriented in a vertical line, growth takes place by equal amounts, in equal periods of time, throughout the entire diameter, thus resulting in growth directly downward.[1]

Geotropic response in nature is illustrated in Figs.

FIG. 89.—Negative geotropism in a fleshy fungus growing on a treetrunk.

87–89. Its value is evident in insuring good light-exposure and the efficient distribution of seeds and spores.

130. Problems to Solve.—Many interesting questions now arise. How does the root, for example, "detect"

[1] Granting, of course, that all environmental conditions remain uniform on all sides.

the fact that its axis is not parallel to the plumb-line? Have the root and the shoot a nervous system, or a brain? How is the bending accomplished? These questions cannot be discussed here, but they should be given careful thought. They lead us into one of the most fascinating realms of plant study.

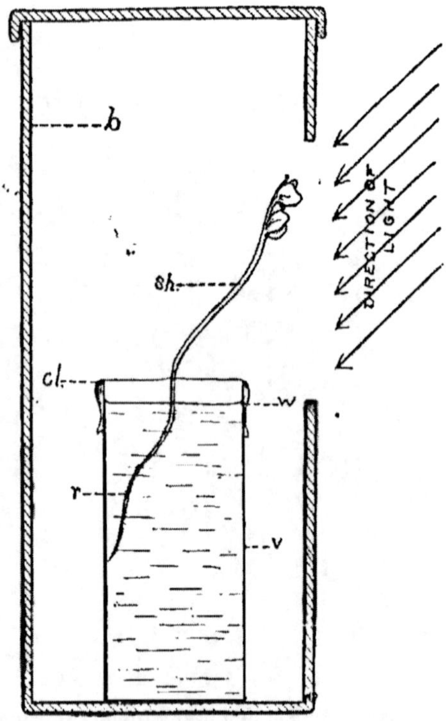

Fig. 90.—Phototropic response of a seedling of white mustard (*Brassica alba*). *b*, box, admitting light only through a narrow slit at the right; *v*, vial; *w*, water-surface; *cl*, cheese-cloth; *sh*, shoot; *r*, root.

131. Effect of Light on Direction of Growth.—The fact that stems ordinarily grow toward, and roots away from the light, as mentioned above, is common knowledge. That this is the normal *response* of roots and stems to the *stimulus* of light may be shown by a very simple experiment. A young seedling of mustard, or any other convenient plant, is allowed to develop in complete darkness in ordinary tap-water, until its root and stem are

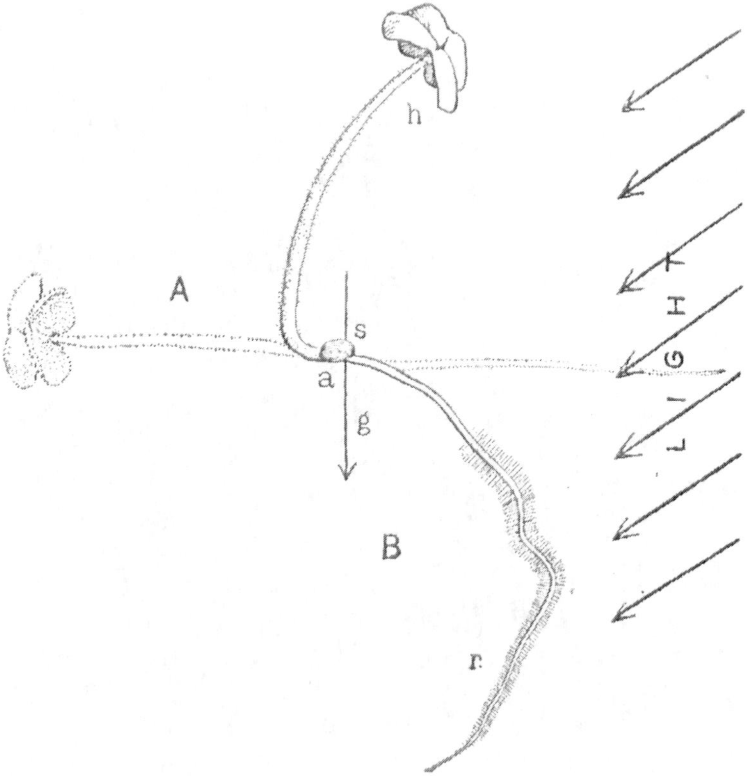

FIG. 91.—Seedling of white mustard (*Brassica alba*) showing the combined effect of light and gravity on the direction of growth of root and shoot. The dotted line figure indicates the position of root and shoot at the beginning of the experiment. The change indicated was accomplished in about 48 hours. (Cf. Fig. 84.)

each about 1 inch long. Being subjected to only the influence of gravity, the root grows vertically downward, the stem vertically upward. If the bottle and plant are then placed inside a covered box, to which the light is admitted only through a narrow slit in one side, the stimulus of the one-sided illumination will be followed by a curvature of the root away from the light, and of the stem toward the light, as shown in Fig. 90.

FIG. 92.—Mountain palm (*Gaussia sp.*), growing on a steep, west-facing cliff. The stems show a phototropic curvature toward the source of most abundant light.

The result of the simultaneous stimulation of root and shoot by light and gravity is illustrated in Fig. 91.

132. Phototropism.—The property of an organ by virtue of which it may detect the *direction of the source* of incident light rays is *phototropism.* Organs which respond by a curvature in the direction of the source of light are *positively phototropic;* those which respond by a curvature in the opposite direction are *negatively phototropic.* Like geotropism, phototropism is a special kind of irritability. Organs growing in the light are, of course, subject to the influence of both light and gravity at the same time.

Fig. 93.—Seedlings of the white lupine (*Lupinus albus*). At the left, grown under normal illumination; at the right, grown in darkness. Both cultures are of the same age.

Phototropic response on a large scale, in nature, is shown in Fig. 92.

133. Effect of Light on Rate of Growth.—Every one is familiar with the fact that stems grown in darkness, or in reduced light, are commonly much elongated, and bleached to a pale yellow color, or even to white. The chlorophyll has failed to develop. This condition is called *etiolation*. Early studies of this phenomenon seemed to indicate that light retarded growth in length, but more thorough and more extended observations clearly showed that such is not always the case. The

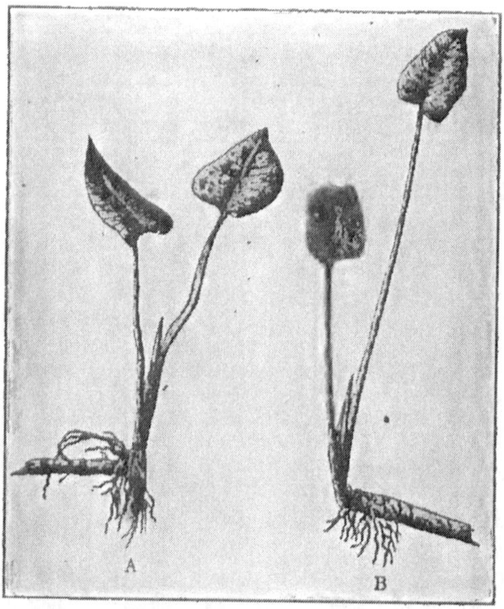

FIG. 94.—*Calla palustris.* –*A*, Normal plant, grown in daylight; *B* etiolated plant of the same age, grown in darkness. (After D. T. MacDougal.)

stems of many kinds of plants (*e.g.*, potato, pea, bean) undoubtedly grow much longer in darkness than in light (Fig. 93), but in other species the difference, if any, is much less (Fig. 94). A disturbance of the normal illumination causes a general disturbance of the functions of the organ or of the entire plant, so that not only growth, but differentiation of tissues (development), nutrition, and metabolism in general are more or less upset, and proceed

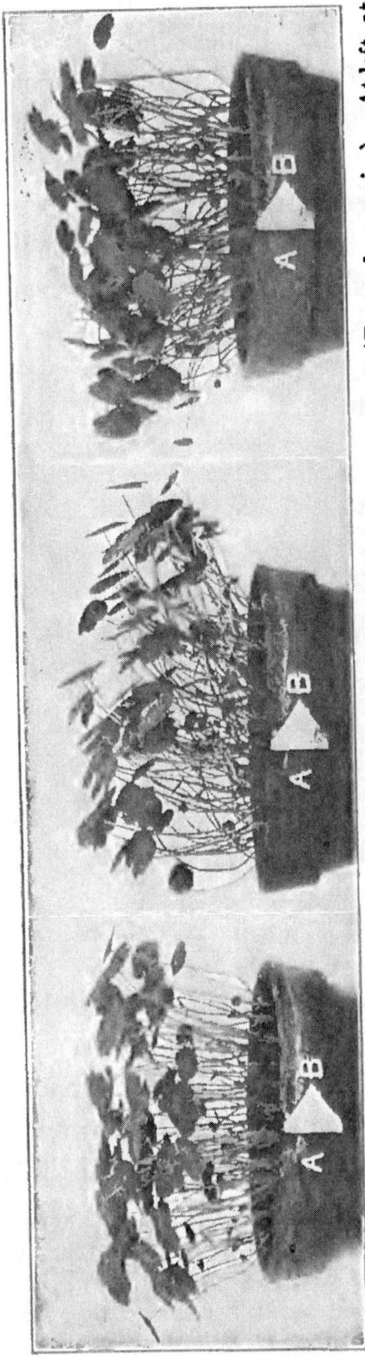

FIG. 95.—Experiment to illustrate adjustable light position. Seedlings of nasturtium (*Tropæolum majus*). At left, at beginning, seedlings grown under equilateral illumination; in middle, after 48 hours of illumination from the right side only; at right, same culture as in the middle, after receiving illumination for 48 hours from the left side only.

in an abnormal manner.[1] Under conditions of normal illumination (granted, of course, that all other conditions are normal), the physiological processes of the plant are *regulated* in a normal manner; but when the illumination is abnormal, healthy regulation ceases, and the organ behaves abnormally. This abnormal behavior includes the failure of chlorophyll to develop, and irregularities of growth. With many plants the stems grow abnormally long and slender, suggesting that absence of light favors more rapid growth in length.

FIG. 96.—Potted plants of an oxalis showing the position of the leaflets during the day (*A*) and the night (*B*)—the so-called "sleep" of plants.

134. Relation of Leaves to Light.—More than all other organs of the plant, the foliage-leaf is developed and adjusted with reference to illumination. Its form, dimensions, and internal structure, and its attitude and position on the stem are chiefly expressions of the surround-

[1] It is often stated in "popular" writings that stems grown in darkness "reach for" or "seek" the light. A careful consideration by the student of all that these terms imply, when predicated of a plant, will lead at once to a recognition of their incorrectness, and even of their absurdity.

ing conditions of light, and clearly indicate that the chief

FIG. 97.—House geranium (*Pelargonium*), showing back and side views of the same plant, grown with the same side always facing a window. (Cf Fig. 98.)

FIG. 98.—House geranium (*Pelargonium*). At the left, front view of the same plant as shown in Fig. 97. At the right, about three days after having been reversed, in front of the window. Note that only the upper, younger leaves are properly adjusted to receive the light rays on their upper surfaces; the lower, older leaves were not able to change the "fixed" light position they previously assumed.

function of leaves is to bring the plant into suitable relation to light. Its flat expanded form makes possible the favorable exposure to light of a large amount of chlorophyll, upon which the plant is absolutely dependent for the manufacture of its food. Leaves that develop in reduced light-intensity (shade), ordinarily dispose of their

FIG. 99.—Geotropic correlation among the branches of a young spruce tree. After the terminal bud of the sapling was destroyed one of the lateral branches (normally transversely geotropic) became negatively geotropic; ultimately it assumed a vertical position and became the "leader" of the tree.

tissue in such a way as to become thinner and of larger area than when developed in more intense light. When the light-intensity is increased, the palisade layer often becomes double (Fig. 27). If a leafy stem is bent, so as to bring the leaf-blade into poor light-exposure, the leaf-stalk, in some plants, will bend and twist so as to restore the blade to a suitable light-relation.

The leaves of some plants (*e.g.*, nasturtium) remain adjustable to the direction of incident light during their active life (Fig. 95); the leaflets of legumes and some other

FIG. 100.—Vertically growing branch of a maple, side view, showing elongation of the petioles of the lower leaves, which serves to prevent their being shaded too much by the leaf-blades above them. (Cf. Fig. 101.)

plants (Fig. 96) fold together each night and on cloudy days, thus manifesting the so-called "sleep" of plants. Whether this response is of value to the plant is not entirely certain. In other plants (*e.g.*, the house geranium) the leaves have a *fixed light-position*, and after reaching maturity are not able to readjust themselves to changed conditions of illumination (Figs. 97 and 98).

135. Correlation within the Plant.—It is of interest to note that the parts of a plant are not only sensitive to the stimulus of their surroundings, but are correlated, or adjusted to each other. This correlation modifies their reaction to external stimulation. Thus, if the "leader,"

FIG. 101.—Adjustment of leaves, by the lengthening of the petioles, to secure the best illumination, in maple. Top view of same branch as in Fig. 100.

or main stem, of a tree is destroyed, one or more of the lateral branches will turn upward, in what *appears* to be an "endeavor" to perform the functions of a leader (Fig. 99). In other words, the destruction of the leader alters the mode of reaction of the lateral branches to the pull of gravity.

136. Correlation among Leaves.—On a vertical and equally illuminated branch, as of maple, the petioles of the lower leaves are longer than those above them, and the stalks of opposite leaves are usually about equal in

FIG. 102.—Garden nasturtium (*Tropæolum majus*), showing leaf-mosaic in seedlings. Top view; compare Fig. 95, showing other views of the same seedlings.

length (Figs. 100 and 101). But on horizontally growing branches, the attitude of the leaves is profoundly altered. The length of the petioles, and their attitude is such as to insure the placing of the blades in positions for the most favorable illumination. This often results in a marked twisting and bending of the leaf-stalks. Blades of opposite leaves often do not appear to be opposite each other, and are often of very unlike size. Such an arrangement of the blades forms a *leaf-mosaic* (Figs. 102 and 103). If a leaf is removed from a group, or even if a leaflet is

FIG. 103.—Leaf-mosaic in the Boston ivy.

removed from the blade of a compound leaf, the remaining leaves or leaflets will alter their positions with reference to each other so as to occupy the space most advantageously and economically (Fig. 104).

137. Advantages of Power of Adjustment.—Very little thought will enable one to understand at once the pro-

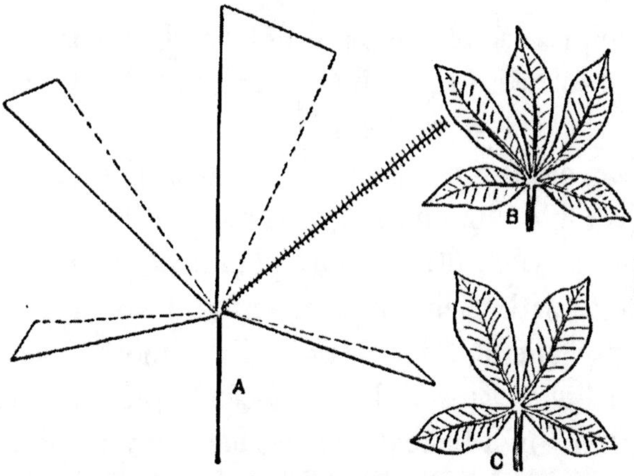

FIG. 104.—Effect of removal of a leaflet from a palmately compound leaf (*e.g.* Woodbine). *B*, normal leaf; *C*, after removal of upper right-hand leaflet. *A*, Unbroken lines represent average normal position of leaflets; dotted lines, average position of leaflets after operation; barred line, position of leaflet removed. (*A*, after Zeleny.)

FIG. 105.—Motherwort (*Leonurus Cardiaca*), showing adjustment of leaves to light. This plant grew at the edge of shrubbery, receiving relatively little light from behind.

found significance to the plant of its ability so to adjust its organs as to bring them into harmony with surrounding influences. If a stem, bent over, could not erect itself, if leaves could not assume positions that secure the most favorable illumination, if stems and leaves were not correlated to each other, most plants would soon be out of harmony with their environment and would sicken and die. Fully one-half the leaves of the motherwort, illustrated in Fig. 105, would have been deprived of suitable illumination by adjacent plants, had they not possessed this power of adjustment.

138. Purpose of Part III.—Chapters I to XI have dealt with all parts of the plant except the flower, and all the activities studied have been primarily for the sake of preserving the life of the individual plant. Flowers function primarily for the race to which the individual plant belongs; but they can be really understood only after a thorough study of the life histories of some of the lower, non-flowering plants. The study of life histories will be taken up in Part III.

PART III

STRUCTURE AND LIFE HISTORIES

CHAPTER XII

LIFE HISTORY OF A FERN

139. Morphology.—In the preceding chapters we considered various physiological processes, the primary result of which was to maintain the life of the individual plant. Most of those processes are carried on by all plants. Every one knows, however, that plants differ widely from each other in both structure and habit of life. In other words, we recognize the fact of *variation*. This means that different plants solve the same problems of life in different ways. For example, some plants expose a large amount of chlorophyll to sunlight by forming thin leaf-blades of relatively large area; while others, such as the cactus, accomplish the same result by developing thick, succulent green stems, and dispensing with leaves entirely. Some leafy plants raise their foliage up to the light on strong woody stems, able to stand alone; while others secure this result by climbing up on other plants. In many cases the organs of plants are disguised, appearing to be what, in reality, they are not; stems may masquerade as leaves, and leaves as stems. That phase of botany which concerns itself with a comparative study of structures, and seeks to interpret the real structural nature of an organ, no matter how it may be disguised, is termed the science of form, or *morphology*.

140. Life History.—Every plant, in the course of its existence, passes through a series of changes in orderly sequence. Like an animal, every plant begins life as a single cell, the *egg*, or the equivalent of an egg. Except in some of the lower forms, the egg develops into an

FIG. 106.—A fern (*Anisosorus hirsutus*), showing portion of the stem above ground.

embryo, and the embryo matures into an *adult*. By a series of more or less complicated processes the adult eventually gives rise to another egg, like the one from which it came, thus completing one life-cycle and initiating another. These various changes constitute the *life history* of the individual. The various stages of life history common to most plants are nowhere more clearly

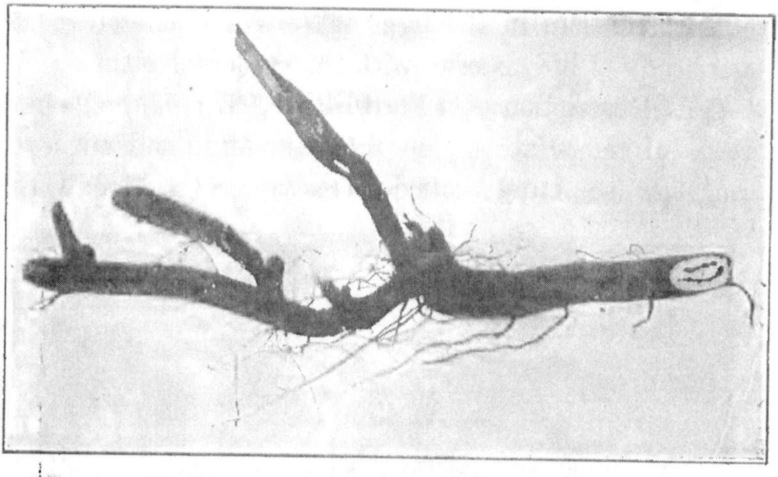

FIG. 107.—Portion of the rhizome of the common brake (*Pteris aquilina*) showing a cross-section view at the right. The two dark areas are sclerenchyma.

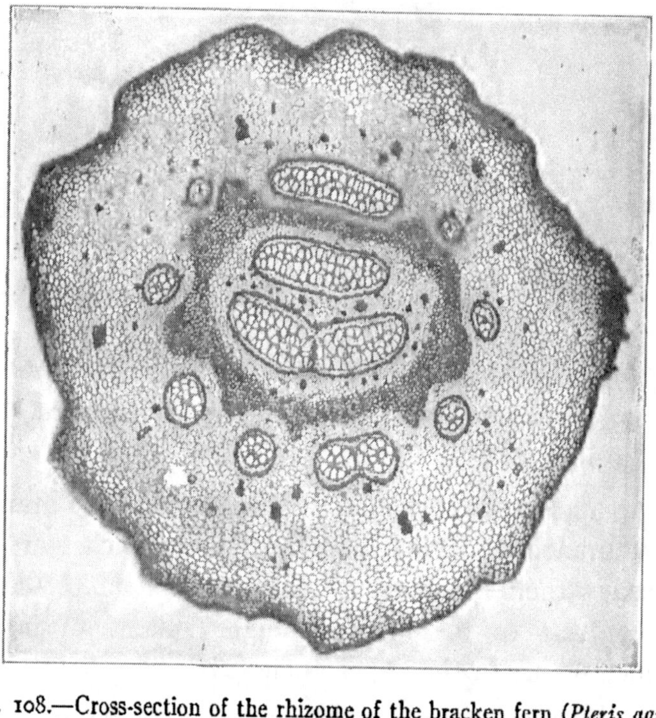

FIG. 108.—Cross-section of the rhizome of the bracken fern (*Pteris aquilina*), showing the tissue systems. Greatly magnified.

illustrated than in the ferns. We shall therefore begin our study of life histories with that group of plants.

141. Description of a Fern Plant.—The more common ferns of temperate regions have underground stems or *rhizomes* (sometimes called *root-stocks*), so that only the

FIG. 109.—Tree ferns on the military road between Cayey and Caguas, Porto Rico. (Photo by M. A. Howe.)

leaves appear above ground.[1] The stem may be branched or unbranched. When branched, the branches are produced without reference to the insertion of the leaves, in contrast to the habit of higher plants of forming branches only in the upper angle (*axil*) between the stem

[1] The leaves of ferns are often called *fronds*.

and leaf-stalk. There is always a terminal bud at the tip of the fern-stem (and of the branches when any occur); and the leaves are usually attached just back of this tip. The stems are commonly (though not always) covered by hairs or scales (Fig. 106), and on their older portions, at some distance back from the tip, may be seen

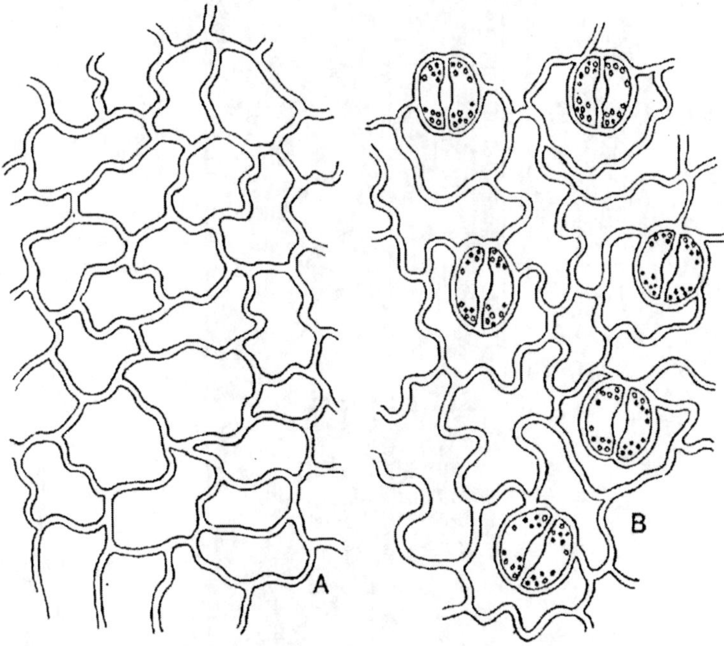

FIG. 110.—*A*, Upper epidermis; *B*, lower epidermis, of the fern, *Drynaria meyeniana*. (Camera lucida drawing.)

the *scars*, or the ends of leaf-stalks, left by old leaves that have died and fallen away. The rhizome bears true roots (Fig. 107), and its tissues are differentiated into epidermal, fundamental, mechanical, and conducting systems (Fig. 108). In tropical countries there are "tree ferns," with upright stems, and this type of fern is common among the fossil plants of earlier geological ages (Fig. 109).

142. Two Kinds of Fern-leaves.—Careful examination of the leaves of some mature ferns will disclose the fact that they are not all alike. Some of them are merely *foliage-leaves*, and do not differ in any essential point from

FIG. 111.—*Osmunda Claytoniana.* Young sporophylls, showing circinate vernation. Note the spore-bearing pinnæ.

the foliage-leaves of higher plants, such as the maple or lily; they possess stomata (Fig. 110), and also resemble the leaves of higher plants in their internal structure. All fern-leaves, however, have a very characteristic arrangement in the embryonic or bud condition, being coiled up from the tip. As the leaves grow they unroll, and in some ferns, at certain stages, they often closely resemble the neck of a violin (Fig. 111). The leaf-blade possesses veins of fibro-vascular bundles that pass down

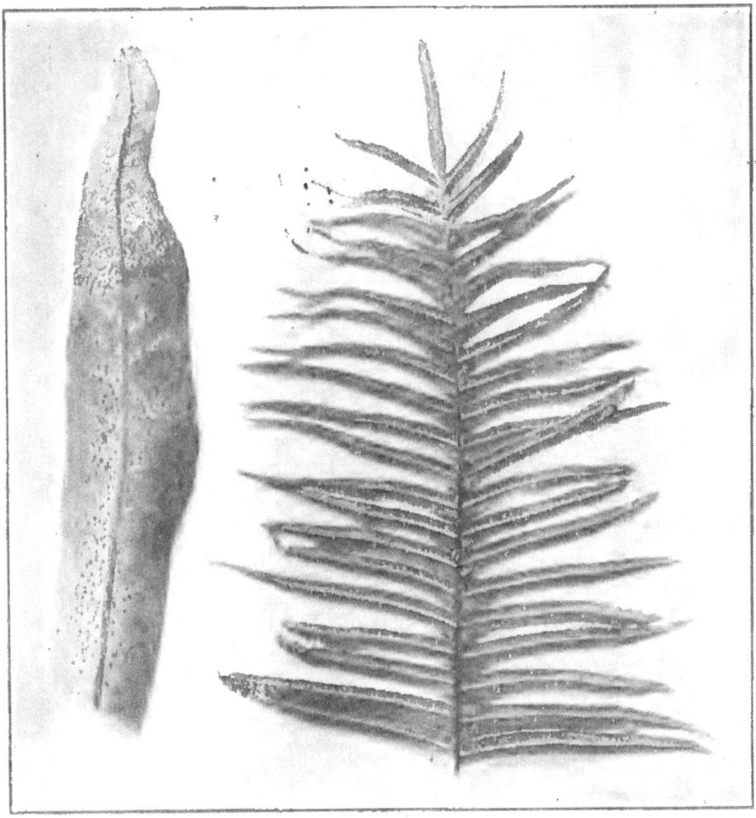

FIG. 112.—Portions of the sporophylls of two ferns to show the sori. On the left *Polypodium punctatum* (L.)Sw.; on the right a variety of *Pteris longifolia*, with sporangia marginal on the pinnules.

the leaf-stalk and through the stem to the roots. Because of the possession of these vascular bundles, ferns (and all other plants of which this is true) are called *vascular plants*. These leaves perform all the functions performed by the foliage-leaves of other plants, the most important of which are photosynthesis and transpiration.

143. Spore-bearing Leaves.—The second type of fern-leaf bears, on its underside, numerous "fruit-dots" or *sori*

FIG. 113.—Sporophylls of two ferns. At the left, a species of *Polypodium* (*Phymatodes*), having no indusium; at the right, *Diplazium zelanicum.*

(singular *sorus*) (Figs. 112 and 113). These structures have to do with reproduction. A single sorus of such a fern as, for example, *Polypodium irioides*, is composed of a cluster of tiny stalked cases. The cases contain minute unicellular reproductive bodies called *spores*, and the en-

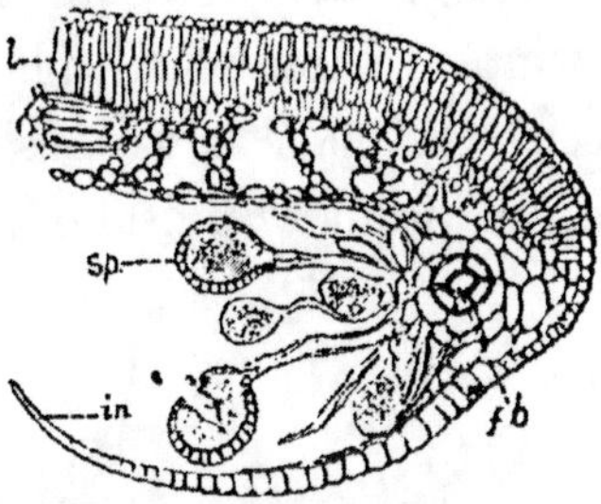

FIG. 114.—Cross-section through the marginal sorus of a sporophyll of the bracken fern (*Pteris aquilina*). *l*, palisade layer; *fb*, vascular bundle; *sp*, sporangium; *in*, indusium. (Greatly magnified.)

tire structure is a *sporangium*. The place where the sporangia are attached to the leaf is the *sporangiophore*[1]

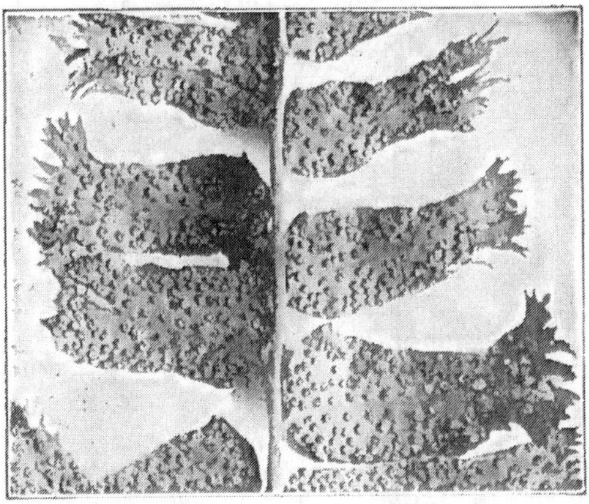

FIG. 115.—*Cyrtomium falcatum*. Under (dorsal) surface of a portion of a sporophyll, showing the numerous sori on the pinnæ.

(Fig. 114), and over all is often found a thin membranous covering, the *indusium* (Figs. 114 and 115). In some ferns the indusium is lacking, and the sorus is naked. Spore-

[1] Also called *receptacle*.

bearing leaves are called *sporophylls*, and plants that bear sporophylls are called *sporophytes*.

144. Types of Foliage-leaf.—In some ferns the foliage-leaf presents a simple, unbranched blade, and petiole; but in other species the blade is variously branched. In such cases the larger, primary divisions are called *pinnæ*,

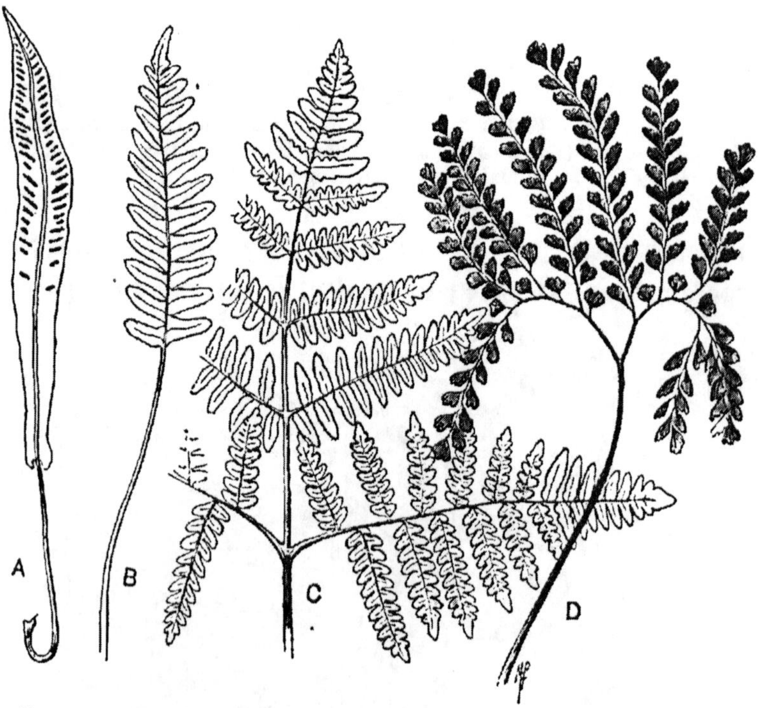

FIG. 116.—Fern leaves, showing various degrees of subdivision or branching of the blade. *A, Phyllitis; B, Polypodium; C, Pteris; D, Adiantum.*

and the secondary subdivisions *pinnules*. Illustrations of these various types are shown in Fig. 116.

145. Sporangia.—As noted above each sporangium consists of a spore-case borne on a stalk (Fig. 117). The structure of the case varies considerably in various groups of ferns, but it usually possesses walls only one cell thick, with a clearly differentiated region, the *annulus*, composed of cells whose radial and inner cell-walls are greatly thickened. Various types of spore-cases are illustrated in

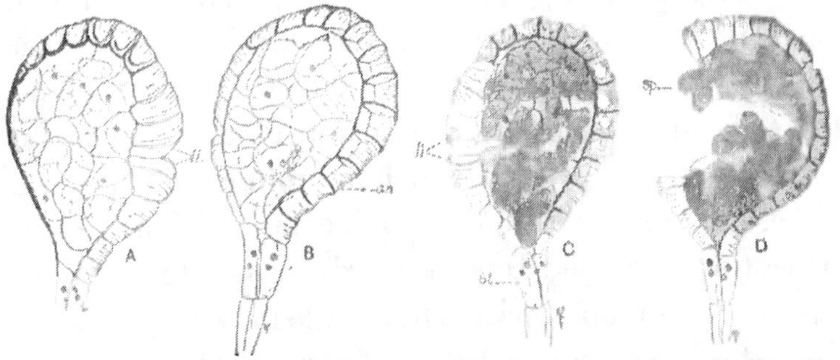

FIG. 117.—Sporangia of an undetermined species of fern; *li*, lip-cells; *an*, annulus; *st*, stalk; *sp*, mature spores. Each of the four nuclei in the upper cells of the stalk is in the terminal cell of one of the four rows of cells that compose the stalk.

Fig. 118. Among the group of ferns which are now most common, and to which the bracken fern (or "brake"), the maiden-hair fern, the common polypody, and others

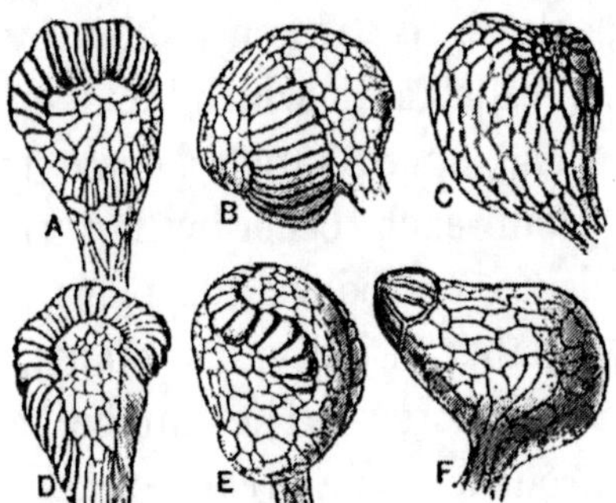

FIG. 118.—Types of fern sporangia. *A*, *Loxsoma Cunninghami; B*, *Gleichenia circinata; C, Todea barbara; D, Thyrsopteris elegans; E, Matonia pectinata; F, Lygodium japonicum.* (Redrawn from various sources.)

belong, the sporangium always originates from a single epidermal cell. Ferns whose sporangia thus originate are called *leptosporangiate* ferns. The walls of their spore-cases are always only one cell thick, and always possess some form of annulus.

146. Spores.—As the sporangia mature the spore-case itself becomes differentiated into two distinct kinds of tissue, namely, *sterile tissue* on the outside, forming the wall, and *fertile tissue* within. In most species of ferns the fertile tissue of each sporangium becomes organized into 16 relatively large cells, rich in protoplasm. As soon as these cells are mature they divide once, and then, without resting, a second time, thus giving rise to four cells each. Each group of four cells is called a *tetrad;* each cell of a tetrad becomes a spore. There is always an even number of spores (usually 64) formed in each spore-case, and the cells from which they are formed by the two successive cell-divisions (*tetrad-divisions*) are *spore-mother-cells*. The spores finally become separated from each other by the dissolving of the middle layer (*middle lamella*) of the cell-wall between adjacent spores. The solution of this middle layer is accomplished by an enzyme secreted by the cells, and which acts upon this particular layer. The spores finally come to lie dry and perfectly free from each other within the spore-case. Their purpose is to reproduce the plant, and especially to multiply the number of individual plants.

147. Number of Spores.—The number of spores produced by a vigorous fern is a great revelation to one who has never given such matters careful thought. Professor Bower, of Glasgow, has called attention to this fact in the following words:

"A rough estimate may be made of the numerical output of spores from a large plant of the Shield fern, as follows: In each sporangium 48[1]

[1] Bower gives this number as the characteristic output for the species *Aspidium Filix-mas*. In other species the number may be 64.

spores may be formed; a sorus will consist of fully 100 sporangia, usually more; 20 is a moderate estimate of the sori on an average pinna; there may be fully 50 fertile pinnæ on one well-developed leaf, and a strong plant would bear 10 fertile leaves. $48 \times 100 \times 20 \times 50 \times 10 = 48{,}000{,}000$. The output of spores on a strong plant in the single season will thus, on a moderate estimate, approach the enormous number of fifty millions."

148. Types of Sporophylls:—In many ferns the leaves serve both vegetative and reproductive functions in about

FIG. 119.—The cinnamon fern (*Osmunda cinnamomea*), showing foliage leaves and sporophylls.

equal degree, as in the case of *Polypodium* mentioned above. In some species, however, there are two kinds of leaves—one devoted entirely to vegetative functions, and another to the reproductive, or spore-producing function (Fig. 119); between these two extremes all grades of transition are found (Fig. 120). But however widely the sporo-

FIG. 120.—Clayton's fern (*Osmunda Claytoniana*), showing sporophylls in the center, surrounded by foliage leaves.

phyll departs from a foliage-leaf in appearance, it must, nevertheless, be regarded as morphologically a leaf. As partial evidence of the true foliar nature of sporophylls, there may be cited the interesting experiment of Atkinson, who, by removing the true foliage-leaves just beginning to unfold

FIG. 121.—A fern (*Tectoria cicularia*) that bears bulbils on both the upper and lower surfaces of its leaves. Plantlets develop from the bulbils while they are still attached.

in the spring, was able to induce developing sporophylls to alter their character, and become transformed into foliage-leaves. Similar results were also obtained by Goebel. These experiments indicate that foliage-leaves and sporophylls are very closely related to each other, and demonstrate clearly that foliage-leaves may be produced by the *sterilization* of spore-bearing leaves.

FIG. 122.—Walking fern (*Camptosorus rhizophyllus*). The smaller, lower plant originated at the tip of a leaf of the larger plant, and one of its leaves has, in turn, struck root.

The interesting question here naturally arises as to whether, in the evolutionary development of the plant kingdom, through long geological ages, foliage-leaves have in general originated by the sterilization of spore-bearing organs.

149. Vegetative Multiplication.—In addition to reproduction by spores, ferns may also be propagated vegetatively in at least four ways. By one of these methods, the rhizome is cut into several pieces, and from every

FIG. 123.—A Boston fern (*Nephrolepis*), reproducing vegetatively by means of runners or stolons. (After R. C. Benedict.)

piece that contains a bud a new plant will develop. By the second method, the plant is propagated by means of *bulbils*, which occur on the foliage-leaves of several species. In the fern *Tectoria cicutaria*, bulbils occur on both the upper and under sides of the leaf (Fig. 121). These bulbils fall to the ground, and under suitable conditions of light, moisture, and temperature give rise to new fern-plants. One of the ferns native to the eastern United States

(*Cystopteris bulbifera*) received its specific name from the fact that it bears bulbils. A third method is illustrated in the very interesting "walking fern" (*Camptosorus rhizophyllus*), where the tips of the long acuminate leaves rest upon the moist ground, take root, and develop an entire new plant at the distance of the leaf's length from the parent fern (Fig. 122). The result of several repetitions of this suggested the common name "walking fern." A fourth method is by means of *stolons* or "runners" (Fig. 123).

150. Dispersal of Spores.—After the spores are mature the essential need is that they become dispersed, so that

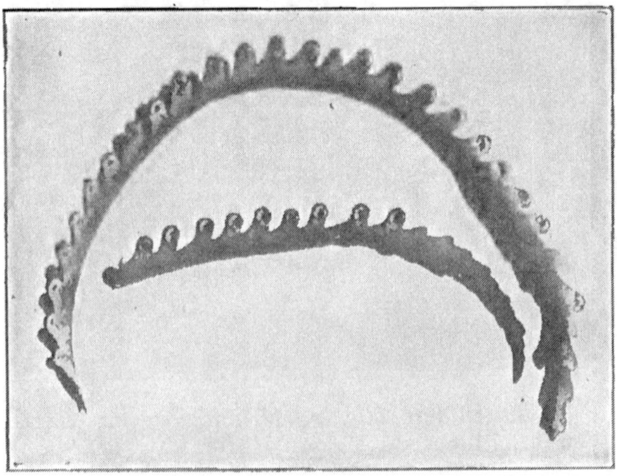

FIG. 124.—Tips of two sporophylls of the fern, *Drynaria meyeniana*, showing the large marginal sori. The black dots adjacent to the leaf-tips are spores projected onto white paper by the snapping of the sporangia. The specimens were covered with a bell-jar.

they may find favorable conditions of moisture, temperature, light, and soil for development; for, with rare exceptions, such conditions do not obtain within the spore-case. Moreover, if the spores remained within the sporangia they would be so greatly crowded that only a very small percentage of them would be able to develop into new plants. When the spores are ripe, the spore-case opens, and by various movements the spores are expelled. That sporangia are able to throw the spores to a considerable distance may be shown in a very simple way by placing a portion of a sporophyll with mature sporangia on a sheet of white paper, with the fruit-dots uppermost, and covering it with a large bell-jar. Within a few hours the scattered spores may be seen against the white background of the paper, and the greatest distance to which they have been thrown may be easily measured (Fig. 124).

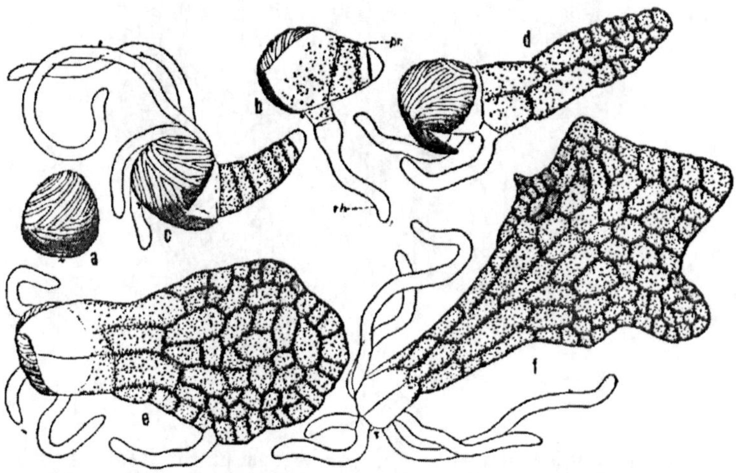

FIG. 125.—Germination of the spores of a fern. *a*, Before germination; *b*, early stage, showing protonema (*pr.*), and first rhizoid (*rh*); *c*, *d*, *e*, *f*, successive stages in the development of the prothallus.

151. Germination of Spores.—After dispersal, and under favoring conditions of temperature, moisture and light, the spore begins to absorb water, and soon commences to grow. As the internal osmotic pressure increases, the walls of the spore are burst apart, and a tiny tube, the *germ-tube*, or *protonema* (first thread), begins to develop. This process is *germination*. Shortly, near the wall of the spore, a smaller, slender tube develops as a branch of the germ-tube (Fig. 125). This is the first of innumerable root-like bodies, or *rhizoids*, which will help to hold the new plant firmly to the soil, and also serve to take in water and dissolved mineral nutrients.

152. The Prothallus.—Before the germ-tube has greatly enlarged, it becomes divided into two cells, and then, by

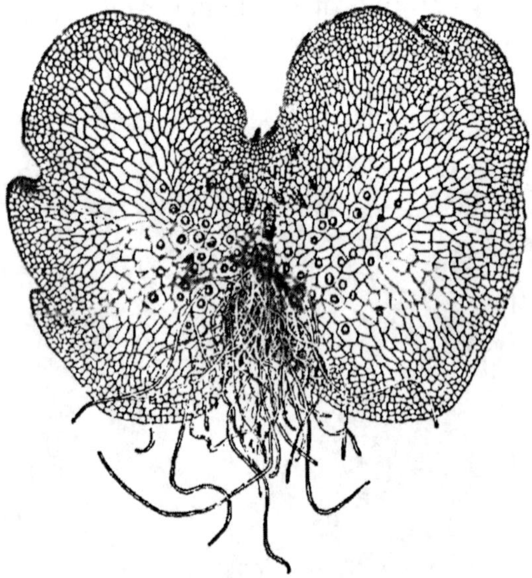

FIG. 126.—Prothallus of a fern. Archegonia on the (central) cushion, near the notch; antheridia among the rhizoids, below. (After Margaret C. Ferguson.)

successive cell-divisions, into an increasing number. Meanwhile chlorophyll bodies begin to appear, but never in the rhizoids. The final product of these cell-divisions and growth is a tiny, flat, green body, often (but not always) heart-shaped, with a central portion, the *cushion*, several cells thick, and a marginal part, the *wings*, of only one cell in thickness. Because of its flatness this little plant (for such it is) is called a *thallus;* and because it precedes, in the order of reproduction, the new sporophyte, it is called the *prothallus* (Fig. 126). It is usually possible to divide the prothallus into right and left halves, similar in shape and in other characters, and hence it is said to possess *bilateral symmetry.*

CHAPTER XIII

LIFE HISTORY OF A FERN (Concluded)

The prothallus, as just described, bears little resemblance, indeed, to the fern plant with which we are commonly familiar. In fact the relation between the two was not understood, nor even suspected, until about 1848, when Count Lesczyc-Suminski, a Polish botanist, first gave a connected description of the life history of the fern. We shall now proceed to follow the steps which lead from the prothallus to the new sporophyte.

153. Dorso-ventral Differentiation.—The appearance of the first root-like body, or rhizoid, was noted above. As the prothallus develops the rhizoids become more and more numerous, forming a mass of fine thread-like bodies on the under side, opposite the notch, of the heart-shaped prothallus. The presence of rhizoids, and of other structures soon to be described, make it easy to distinguish at once the surface that bears them from the opposite surface. Since the surface bearing the rhizoids lies normally next to the substratum it was called the *dentral* surface, while the opposite surface was called *vorsal*. As now used, the terms dorsal and ventral are morphological terms, and have no reference to the manner in which the prothallus lies. Normally the ventral surface is the under one and the dorsal surface the upper, but the application of the terms would not be changed if the differentiated prothallus should happen, by any chance, to lie upside down. The dorsal surface would then be the under surface, and the ventral surface the upper one. Organisms or organs having two such surfaces clearly distinguishable are said to have *dorso-ventral differentiation.* Among many other structures thus differentiated are foliage-leaves, sporophylls, man, fishes, and other animals.

154. Reproductive Organs : Archegonia.—Examination of the ventral surface of a mature prothallus with a lens

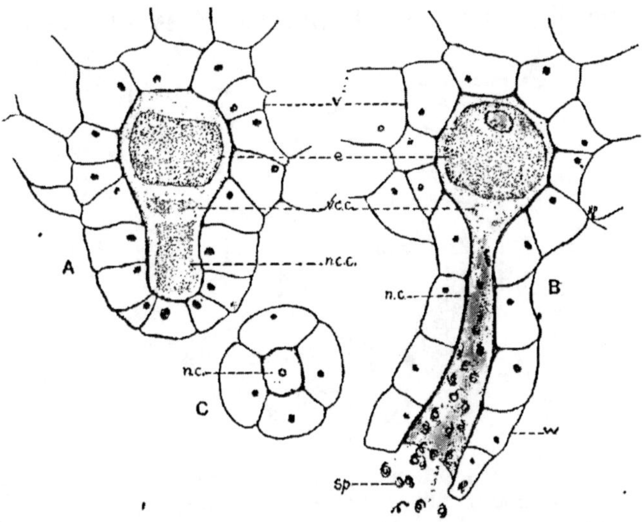

FIG. 127.—Archegonia of a fern (*Adiantum*). *A*, young archegonium; *B*, mature; *C*, top view, showing terminal cells of the four rows of wall cells; *v*, wall of venter; *e*, egg; *v.c.c*, ventral canal-cell; *n.c*, neck-canal; *sp*, sperms entering the neck-canal. *A* and *B* in longitudinal section.

will reveal near the notch and on the cushion, several tiny flask-shaped bodies, the *archegonia.* Each archegonium consists of a wall, one cell thick, and contents (Fig. 127). The *neck* projects away from the surface, and is usually slightly curved, while the remainder, the *venter,* is imbedded in the tissue of the cushion. As the archegonium approaches maturity it is seen to contain three cells; a long *neck-canal cell*, nearly filling the neck, an *egg-cell* or *ovum*, filling the venter, and between these two a *ventral-canal cell.* The egg is the female reproductive cell. As it matures, the other two cells become disintegrated into a mucilaginous mass that fills the neck-canal. Since the archegonia contain the eggs they are the female reproductive organs.

155. Reproductive Organs: Antheridia.—Search among the rhizoids will reveal another class of organs, the

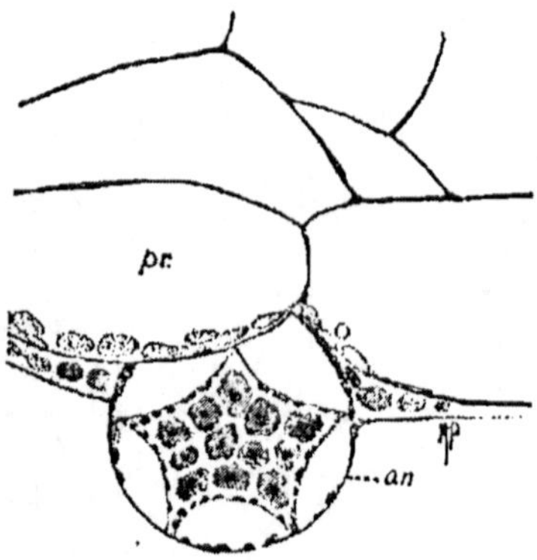

FIG. 128.—Portion of a cross-section of a prothallus of a fern (*Adiantum*), showing an antheridium (*an*), and sporogenous cells within. (Drawn from preparation of E. W. Olive.)

antheridia, globular and also having walls only one cell thick. These are the male reproductive organs. At maturity they contain a large number of tiny motile cells, composed chiefly of a coiled nucleus, and able to swim about in water by the vigorous lashing of numerous little thread-like cilia attached to one end. These are the *sperms*, or male reproductive cells (Figs. 128 and 129).

156. Fertilization.—Neither the eggs nor the sperms are able, independently, to reproduce their kind. In order to accomplish this they must unite, and the fusion of the sperm and egg is fertilization. *One of the most significant facts about fertilization in ferns is that free water is required, in order that the sperms may reach the egg by their own locomotion.* When the antheridia and archegonia are mature, a suitable amount of water (such as would result from a rain or a copious dew), soaking through the

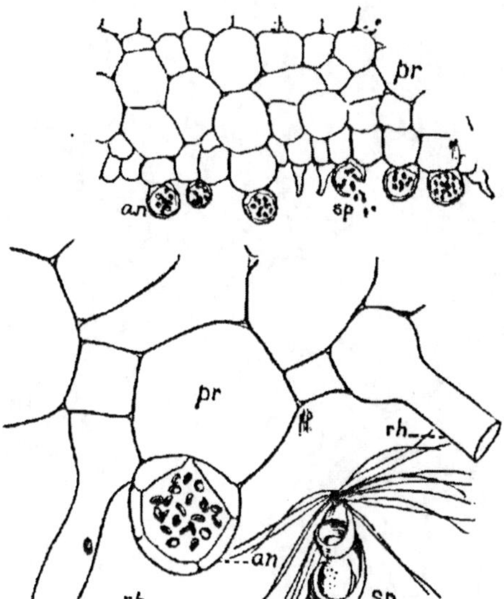

FIG. 129.—Fern prothallus; cross-sections showing antheridia (*an*), sperms (*sp*), and rhizoids (*rh*). Below at the right is a sperm (*sp*) greatly enlarged.

archegonial walls, will cause the mucilaginous matter in the neck-canal to swell. This in turn will rupture the archegonia at their distal ends, and a portion of the contents of the neck-canal will become extruded, while the egg will remain in the venter. The same conditions of moisture will cause the rupture of the antheridia, and the sperms will be set free (Fig. 129). The mucilaginous matter extruded from the archegonia contains a substance (malic acid, in some ferns) which stimulates the sperms to swim toward it. This they are enabled to do by the free external water. On reaching the archegonia, they enter it, and swim down the neck-canal to the egg. The sperm that first reaches the egg penetrates it, and passes through

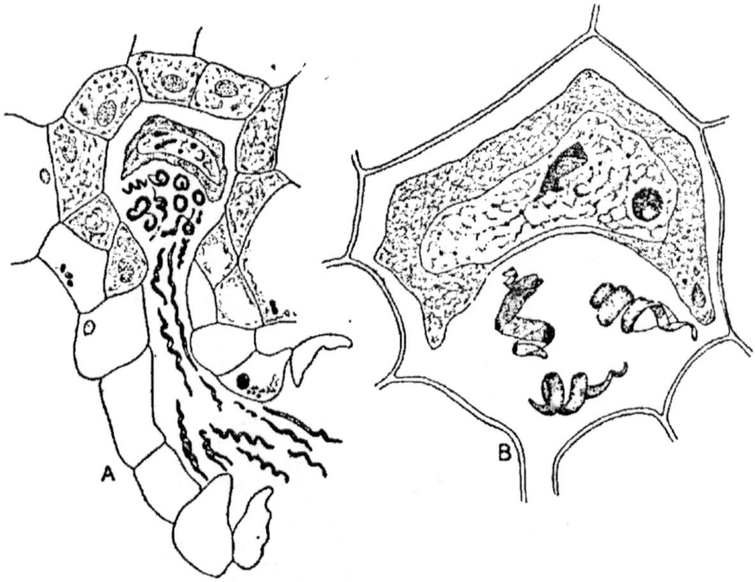

FIG. 130.—Fertilization in the fern, *Onoclea*. *A*, longitudinal section of archegonium, showing the egg in the venter, and numerous sperms passing down the neck-canal. *B*, an egg-cell in the venter. One sperm has entered the nucleus, three sperms have failed to enter the egg. (After W. R. Shaw.)

its cytoplasm until it reaches the egg-nucleus, with which it fuses, thus completing the act of *fertilization* (Fig. 130). As soon as one sperm enters the egg-cell, the latter at once forms a *fertilization-membrane* about itself, through which the remaining sperms cannot enter.

157. Nature of the Fertilized Egg.—It will at once be recognized that the fertilized egg, resulting from a union with the sperm, possesses a double or *diploid* nature.[1] In recognition of its dual nature it is called the *oösperm* (egg and sperm).[2] The oösperm, however, like the unfertilized egg, is still only one cell, though its nucleus comprises substances contributed by both egg and sperm. In some cases the egg and sperm that unite in fertilization may come from different parents; their fusion is then called *cross-fertilization*.

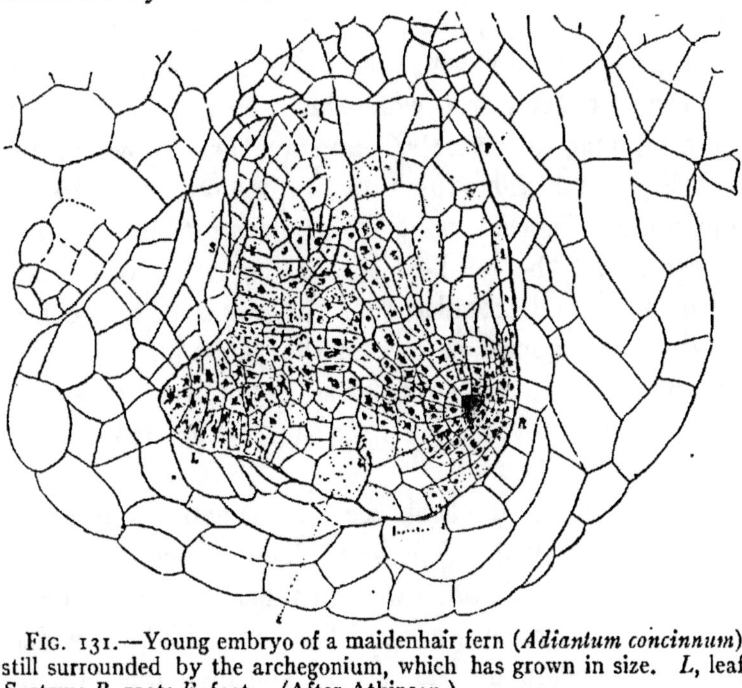

FIG. 131.—Young embryo of a maidenhair fern (*Adiantum concinnum*); still surrounded by the archegonium, which has grown in size. *L*, leaf, *S*, stem; *R*, root; *F*, foot. (After Atkinson.)

158. Development of the Fertilized Egg.—After fertilization the egg begins to develop, undergoing a series of nuclear and cell-divisions, accompanied by increase in

[1] As distinguished from the unfertilized egg, which is of a single, or *haploid* nature.

[2] The term *oöspore* is often used here, but this term lacks the advantage of indicating the real nature of the fertilized egg.

size. The cell-wall of the first division (in all of the family Polypodiaceæ) is parallel to the axis of the archegonial neck. The second wall, at right angles to the first, divides the oösperm into four cells. The beginning of these divisions marks the beginning of the *embryo*. By further cell-divisions each of the first four cells develops a mass of embryonic tissue. The two cells on one side of the first wall formed represent, the one the embryonic *stem*, and the other the embryonic leaf, or *cotyledon*. One of the two cells on the opposite side of the first wall, develops into the embryonic *root*, while the other develops into an organ peculiar to the embryonic stage, and known as the *foot* (Fig. 131). The function of the foot is to absorb nourishment for the young embryo from the prothallus, by osmosis. The need of such an organ becomes apparent when it is recalled that the oösperm, and consequently the embryo, lie free in the venter of the archegonium, without any organic or structural connection with the prothallus. This necessary connection is early established by the foot.

159. Growth of the Embryo.—As the embryo continues to grow, the root develops first. The advantage of this will become evident when we remember that the primary and most fundamental need of the young plant is water, which is taken in by the roots. The next most fundamental need is nourishment, and as plant food is manufactured in chlorophyll-bearing organs, and usually in leaves, we would expect the early development of leaves. Such is the case, the growth of the first leaf being secondary only to that of the root, and in advance of the stem. The development of the stem follows, and finally spore-bearing leaves appear (Fig. 132). We then have an organism similar to that with which we started—a full-grown fern-plant, capable of producing spores, which can develop into prothallia again, with antheridia and archegonia, producing sperms and eggs, and so on. Thus we see that the steps in the life history of a fern constitute a *life-cycle*. At whatever point or with whatever structure we start, if we follow the course of development we are brought back again to the same point, or the same kind of structure with which we began.

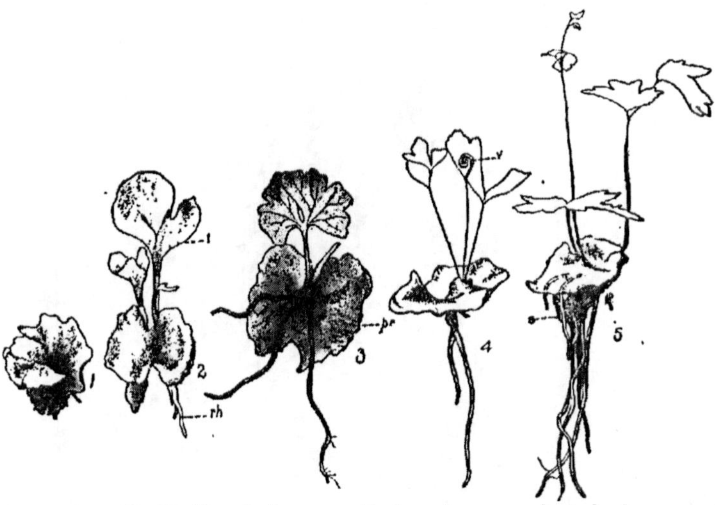

FIG. 132.—Prothallia of a fern. 1, Before the sporophyte had appeared; 2–5, with sporophytes attached; *l*, cotyledon or first leaf of the sporophyte; *v*, circinate vernation of a leaf; *s*, mass of soil adhering to the rhizoids and roots.

160. Simpler Ferns.—In addition to the leptosporangiate ferns, which have served as a basis for the generalized description given above, there is another group, having a more primitive type of organization. Representatives of this group include the "moonworts" (species of *Botrychium*, Fig. 133), and the "adder's tongue" (*Ophioglossum vulgatum*, Fig. 134). The species of

Botrychium usually (though not invariably) possess but one foliage-leaf, and a fertile spike, both of which are

FIG. 133.—Rattlesnake fern (*Botrychium virginianum* (L.) Sw.).

more or less branched. Abnormal forms are not uncommon in which the fertile spike is more or less *steril-*

FIG. 134.—Adder's tongue fern (*Ophioglossum vulgatum* L.). *R*, runner or stolon.

ized, sometimes being entirely so; while in other cases sporangia occur on the foliage-leaf. As in the replacement of sporophylls by sterile leaves in the ostrich fern, *Onoclea struthiopteris* (paragraph 148), these abnormalities indicate the close relationship between leaves and spore-bearing organs, and clearly show that the latter may be completely transformed, by sterilization, into foliage-leaves.

In *Ophioglossum* the foliage-leaf and spore-bearing spike are both unbranched, the latter suggesting an adder's tongue, whence the name, *Ophioglossum*. In both *Ophioglossum* and *Botrychium* the sporangia originate from *a group* of epidermal and sub-epidermal cells, and are consequently imbedded in the surrounding tissue. Their walls are more than one cell in thickness, the annulus is lacking, and they open by a slit. Ferns of this type are called *eusporangiate*. Their prothallia are usually fleshy and subterranean, bear the antheridia and archegonia on the dorsal instead of on the ventral surface, and are perennial, often living on after the sporophyte has died. In general the sporophyte possesses less sterile tissue in proportion to the fertile tissue than is the case with the leptosporangiate forms. These characters mark the group as more primitive than the leptosporangiate ferns, and they are much less numerous, only about 100 species being known from the entire world, while of the leptosporangiate ferns between 3,000 and 4,000 species have been described.

CHAPTER XIV

FUNDAMENTAL PRINCIPLES

161. Two Kinds of Reproduction.—In the two preceding chapters attention has been called to three ways of obtaining new fern-plants, namely, by spores, by vegetative multiplication, and by fertilized eggs. The first two methods may be grouped together as asexual, while the second is sexual, as shown in the following table.

Reproduction	Asexual, involving cell-divisions only.	By the giving off of multi-cellular portions or outgrowths of vegetative tissue.	Artificial (slips, cuttings, etc.).
			Natural (tubers, bulbs, gemmæ).
		By the giving off of special reproductive bodies of one or few cells, called *spores*.	
	Sexual, involving cell-fusions.		

162. Vegetative Multiplication.—Vegetative multiplication may be accomplished either without or with the intervention of man. In the first case the plant produces special reproductive bodies such as tubers, bulbs, offsets and stolons, which become separated from the plant without assistance, and develop into new individuals. In the second case a similar result is accomplished through the removal by the gardener of portions of the parent plant, such as slips, cuttings, leaves (*e.g.*, in the begonia), or by bending branches over until they touch the ground, and there take root, after which the newly rooted portion may be severed from the parent plant. This is called *layering*. The production of new individuals by the artificial methods of the gardener is called propagation; but between these methods and the multiplication by special bodies, given off spontaneously by the plant, no hard and fast line can be drawn. Some plants, for example, become layered without the gardener's assistance; other plants (as the willow), by self-pruning, spontaneously give off branches from which new plants may develop; while, on the other hand, the gardener may cut a tuber, such as the "potato" into a number of pieces, from each of which a new plant will develop. In this practice artificial propagation and vegetative multiplication are combined.

163. Reproduction by Spores.—The essential fact about a spore is that it is an individual cell or small group of cells, produced primarily for reproductive purposes, given off by the plant, and capable *by itself* of producing a new individual. *The essence of all reproduction is the separation of the reproducing cell or body from the parent plant.* If a bud or a bulb remains attached to the plant that formed it, it produces only a branch or other organ, but not a new individual. So, also, a spore must be separated from the parent plant in order to *reproduce* the latter. In many cases spores may germinate before they are set free, but the separation must come sooner or later. No hard and fast line can be drawn between spores and gemmæ.

164. Sexual Reproduction.—In marked contrast to reproduction by spores, is the reproduction by means of sperms and eggs, *involving cell- and nuclear-fusions*, known as fertilization. Eggs and sperms are called *gametes*,[1] the egg being the *female gamete*, the sperm the *male gamete*. The diploid cell, resulting from the union of two gametes, is called a *zygote*, and this term is often extended

[1] From the Greek word, γάμος (*gamos*), meaning marriage.

to apply to the resulting diploid organism through all stages of its development to maturity.

165. Two Kinds of Generations.—A study of the life history of the fern disclosed two distinct phases or generations, one bearing spores, and therefore called the *sporophyte* (spore-bearing plant), the other bearing gametes and for that reason called the *gametophyte* (gamete-bearing plant). The gametophyte of the fern was seen to be entirely independent of the sporophyte, capable of manufacturing its own food by means of its own chlorophyll, not dependent upon any other plant, and in some groups being perennial, living on from year to year, and giving rise to sporophytes that live for only one season. The sporophyte, on the other hand, is *at first*, entirely dependent upon the gametophyte for its nutrition, living as a parasite upon the prothallus, from which it absorbs its nourishment by means of the special organ, the foot. Gradually, however, the sporophyte puts forth roots, capable of taking in water and dissolved mineral substances from the soil, and chlorophyll-bearing organs (the fronds or leaves), capable of manufacturing organic food. As the sporophyte becomes independent, the gametophyte (with few exceptions, as noted above), perishes. A comparison of the two generations shows that the sporophyte is the much more complex of the two, being clearly differentiated into roots, and leafy shoot. The difference in the origin of these two generations results in a very fundamental difference in the nature of all the cells in each. Since the sporophyte is derived from an oösperm (zygote), formed by the fusion of the two gametes, all of its cells are diploid, containing material derived from both its male and female parentage. The gametophyte, on the other hand, being derived from a single reproductive cell (the spore), without nuclear or cell-fusions, is composed of cells of a single or haploid nature.

166. Alternation of Generations.—Our study of the fern also brought out another fact of very fundamental importance. Sporophytes do not produce sporophytes, nor gametophytes, gametophytes; but there is always an *alternation of generations*, sporophytes producing gametophytes, and gametophytes, sporophytes.

The order of sequence in the life-cycle is as follows:

sporophyte→spore→gametophyte→gametes→oösperm→sporophyte.

The order of structures and processes involved in the life-cycle is as follows:

OUTLINE OF LIFE HISTORY OF A FERN

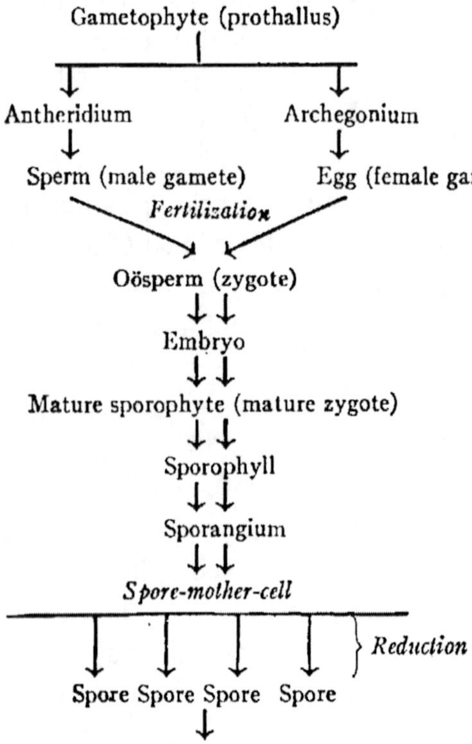

The fact of a cycle in the life history is brought out clearly in the following diagram:

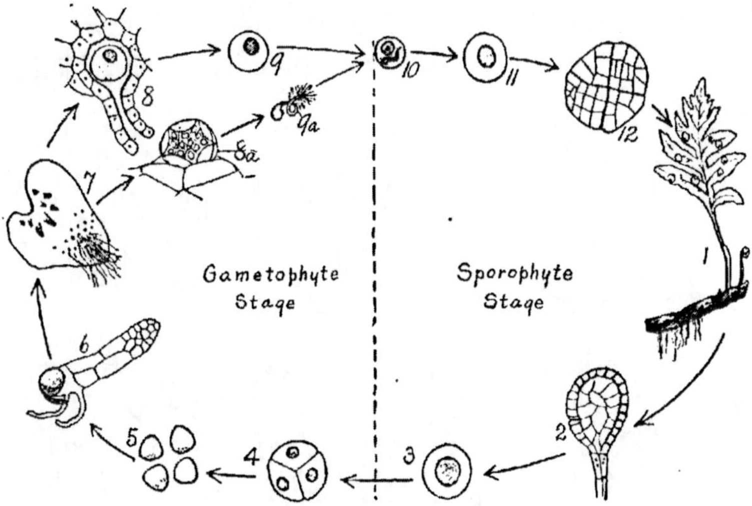

FIG. 135.—Diagram of life-cycle of a fern.

167. Reduction.—Since the sporophyte (descended from the diploid oösperm) has cells of a double nature, resulting from fertilization, and since the spores which give rise to the gametophyte are of a single (or haploid) nature, there must occur, at some stage in the life of the sporophyte, a process of *reduction*, restoring the cells, made diploid by fertilization, to the haploid condition. Painstaking studies of cellular structure and processes has disclosed the fact that this reduction takes place during the two successive divisions (tetrad-divisions) of the spore-mother-cell, resulting in the formation of four spores. The diploid condition persists in all the cells of the sporophyte, and through every cell-division, up to the two divisions preceding spore-formation, just as the single or haploid condition persists in all the cells of the gametophyte, up to the very act of fertilization.

168. Nature and Method of Reduction.—In order thoroughly to understand fertilization and reduction one must have a knowledge of the structure and behavior of the nucleus in cell-division and cell-fusion. This subject

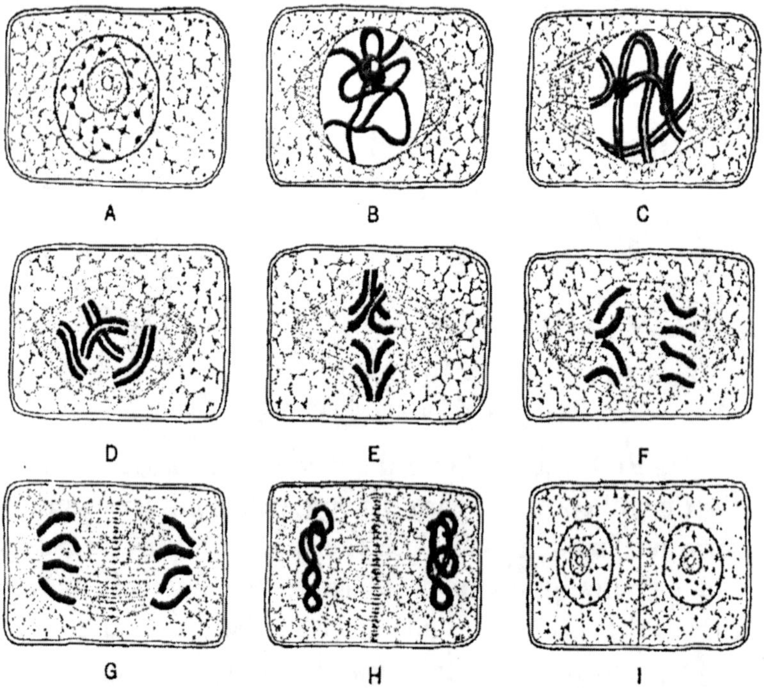

FIG. 136.—Diagram illustrating various stages of indirect nuclear division (mitosis). *A*, resting nucleus of the mother-cell; *B*, formation of nuclear skein or spirem; *C*, longitudinal splitting of the spirem; *D*, the chromosomes (four in number) have been formed by the transverse segmentation of the spirem; *E*, chromosomes arranged on the equator of the nuclear spindle; *F* and *G*, early and late *anaphase*, the chromosomes moving to the pales of the spindle; *H*, formation of daughter spirems; *I*, resting stage of the two daughter-cells.

is too difficult and too extended to be thoroughly treated in an introductory study, but the salient facts are as follows. The nucleus of all cells comprises at least four substances: *nuclear sap*, a threadwork of *linin*, and a

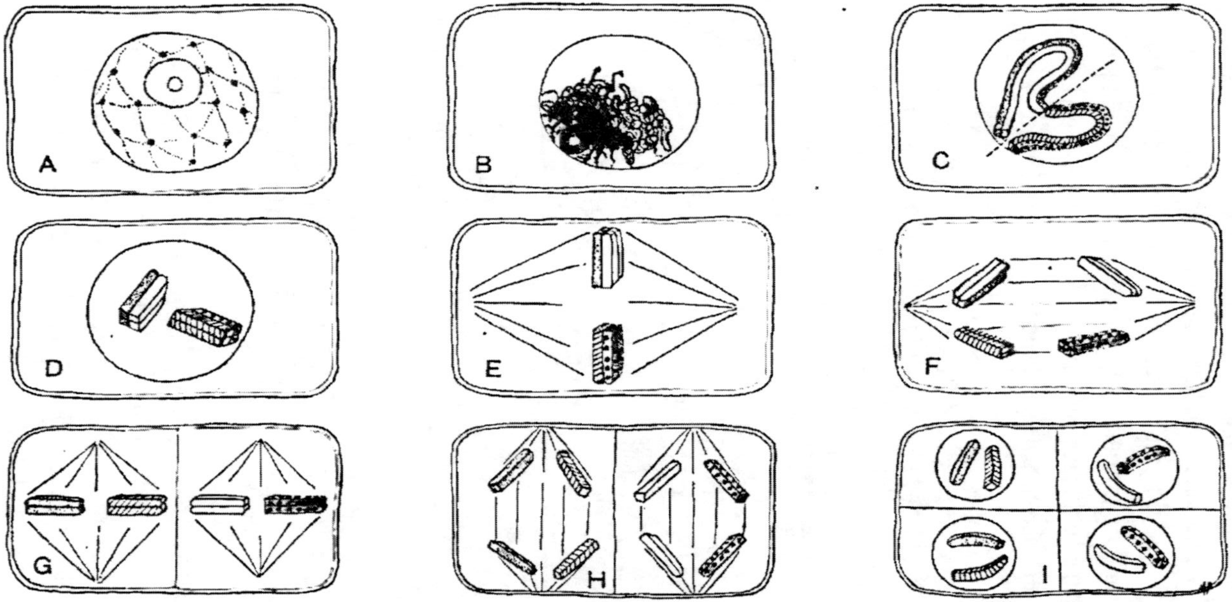

FIG. 137.—Diagram illustrating various stages in the reduction division (maiosis) of a spore-mother-cell of a plant; *A*, resting stage of the mother-cell-nucleus; *B*, the nuclear skein or spirem, in synizesis (during synapsis); *C*, the spirem after synapsis, showing its double (diploid) nature; the dotted line indicates the segmentation of the spirem into two diploid chromosomes, each of which has split longitudinally in *D*; *E*, the diploid chromosomes on the equator of the spindle of the first (heterotypic) division; *F*, late anaphase; *G*, metaphase of the second or homotypic division; *H*, late anaphase of same, two haploid chromosomes approaching the poles of each spindle; *I*, the four daughter-cells (spores) of the tetrad.

substance called *chromatin;*[1] all these are enclosed by a *nuclear membrane.* In the non-dividing nucleus the chromatin is distributed on the linin threads in the form of minute granules (Fig. 136). At one of the stages preliminary to nuclear division the linin network, with the chromatin, becomes transformed into a thickened *skein,*

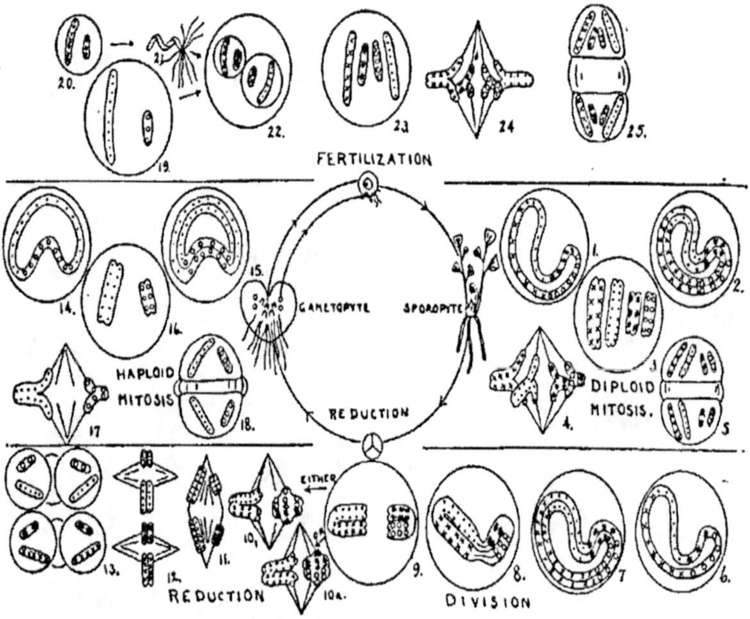

FIG. 138.—Diagram of a cytological life-cycle, based on a hypothetical fern with four chromosomes in the sporophyte. The nuclear phenomena are based on those of the thread-worm (*Ascaris*). Each chromosome is designated by a characteristic mark so that it may be traced throughout the diagram. (After R. F. Griggs.)

which shortly becomes split into two, throughout its entire length. The skein finally becomes divided transversely into a number of double chromatin bodies or *chromosomes.* The number of these chromosomes is characteristic, and always the same for each species of plant. The nuclear

[1] Because it stains readily when treated with aniline dyes.

membrane then disappears, and, by a complicated mechanism, not entirely understood, the two halves of the chromosomes are separated and carried apart to opposite sides of the cell. After this division of the nucleus, a new cell-wall forms, dividing the entire cell into halves; new nuclear membranes develop, and the chromosomes in each *daughter-nucleus* become gradually retransformed into a resting nucleus, like the one with which we started.

In reduction (Fig. 137) a new resting nucleus is not organized after the first nuclear division, but this division is followed at once by a second, or *reducing division*, by which the number of chromosomes in each nucleus is *reduced* by one-half. This is the process of tetrad-division, by which spores are formed from the spore-mother-cells. The reduced number of chromosomes persists throughout the gametophyte-phase, including the formation of both egg and sperm. When the latter unite the nucleus of the zygote will, of course, possess the doubled number of chromosomes, which then persists throughout the body of the sporophyte (mature zygote), until the stage of spore-formation is again reached. These facts are shown diagrammatically in Fig. 138.

169. Inheritance.—It is, of course, common knowledge that men do not gather grapes of thorns, nor figs of thistles. A given species of fern always reproduces the same species, and this is true of all plants. It requires only a brief reflection to realize that this must be so, for the beginning of every living thing is always merely a piece of an antecedent organism, the parent. The offspring would, therefore, naturally partake of the nature of its parent—it is a piece of it—was originally a part of it. Resemblance between ancestor and descendant is commonly regarded as inheritance, but only a little careful thinking will lead us to see that resemblance and inheritance are by no means synonymous. The real nature of inheritance is well illustrated by the inheritance of property by a son from his father. The thing inherited is not an external appearance, but a material substance (land, buildings, a business), which is handed from one to another. So it is in reproduction. *That which one generation of plants inherits from another is the substance of the reproductive cells*—the protoplasm of the spore, oösperm, tuber, or bulb—*plus a certain characteristic organization of this protoplasm, and the effects of its past history.*

170. Inheritance Versus Expression.—That inheritance and expression are not the same thing is plainly shown in the life history of the fern, for the gametophyte clearly derives its living matter by inheritance from the sporophyte, and the sporophyte, in turn, its living matter from the gametophyte, and yet the two generations look so little alike that men for centuries knew them both without recognizing the fact that they were merely two different phases in the life history of the same species of plant. So, often, among human beings, children may bear very little if any resemblance to their parents, but may closely resemble their grandparents. Clearly we do not inherit the color of our eyes or hair, the shapes of our noses, the peculiarities of our voices, or our mental traits from our parents, nor even from our more remote ancestors. What we do inherit is a tiny particle of protoplasm having a certain characteristic composition, structure, and past history. This protoplasm is capable, under certain combinations of circumstances, of developing into a mature organism, resembling the one from which it came, but under other combinations of circumstances the external appearance—the expression—may resemble that of the parent only a very little, or not at all. *Inheritance may therefore be defined as the recurrence in successive generations, of a similar cellular constitution.* Expression of this cellular condition is greatly modified by circumstances, which are never precisely the same for any two individuals.

171. Variation.—The preceding sentence explains, in part, why it is that no two individuals are ever precisely alike—precisely similar circumstances surrounding developing organisms never occur twice; that is, the environment varies. Besides this, internal changes may take place in the reproductive cells. For either one or both of these reasons, constant variation is the rule for living things. This subject will be considered more at length in Chapters XXXII and XXXIII.

172. Adjustment to Environment.—By the term environment is meant all the circumstances that surround a cell, tissue, organ, or organism at any given time, or throughout its existence. The environment of tissues and organs includes surrounding tissues and organs, and the environment of cells includes the neighboring tissues and cells. *The most essential thing in the life of every plant or animal is to keep in harmony with its environment.* Every change of environment necessitates an *adjustment* on the part of the plant in order to maintain this harmony. Adjustments are most easily made when the plant is young and plastic, and especially while it is developing to maturity. If the amount of water in the soil is diminished the young plant will send its roots deeper, if light is entirely cut off no chlorophyll will form. A leaf, or the prothallus of ferns, is bilaterally symmetrical because the environment is uniform on all sides; the same organs have dorso-ventral differentiation largely because the environment is unlike above and below. The motility of sperms is an adjustment to water in the environment. Thus variations in the environment may result in different expressions of inheritance, just as variations in inheritance would be followed by differences in expression, even in an unchanging environment. In order correctly to understand a plant nothing is more necessary than to remember that its characteristics are the result, not of its inheritance alone, nor of its environment only, *but of the interaction between the two.*

173. Struggle for Existence.—In Chapter XII attention was called to the fact that a moderate-sized fern produces each year about 50,000,000 spores. If each one of these spores ultimately produced a mature fern-plant, and if we allowed only 1 square foot of "elbow room" for each plant, the progeny of one parent only, in one season would require at least 50,000,000 square feet, or nearly 1⅔ square miles. If each of these plants in turn, produced 50,000,000 offspring the next season, the descendants of only one fern plant would, in only two years, cover the stupendous area of over 83,000,000 square miles, or an area equal to that of the North American Continent. It has been calculated that a single plant of hedge mustard may produce as many as 730,000 seeds. If each seed developed another full-grown plant, and if the plants were distributed 73 to each square meter, there would be enough mustard plants to cover an area equal to 2,000 times the dry surface of the earth. One may easily imagine the result if all the seeds produced by one of our large forest trees were able to mature. And yet the total number of any given kind of fern, of hedge mustard, or of forest tree does not appreciably change from year to year. The reason, of course, is that not all of the spores and seeds produced are allowed to come to maturity. The direct result of the enormous number of spores and seeds produced is a *struggle for existence*—for sufficient soil, water, light, and food to insure a healthy, mature plant.

174. Elimination of the Unfit.—As a result of variation certain individuals will succeed better than others in the struggle for existence. Those most poorly adapted to their surroundings will perish, and only the more vigorous ones—those best adjusted to their surroundings—will persist. The result of this struggle for existence was called by Herbert Spencer the "*survival of the fittest.*" What really takes place in nature is the elimination, by death, of the unfit. Darwin called this *natural selection*, implying that the result is similar to that when plant breeders select out of a progeny the best individual for further breeding. What really takes place in nature, however, is not so much the selection of the fittest, but a rejection of the unfit. Thus, among the 50,000,000 progeny of a single fern-plant, some are sure to have a weaker constitution than others; to develop a weaker root-system, less chlorophyll in their leaves, a less number of sporophylls or spores, or to be inferior in other ways. The result will be that, in the course of only a few years, the descendants of the most vigorous or otherwise superior plants will alone be left to perpetuate the race.

175. Problems to Solve.—In the preceding paragraphs we have called attention to a number of the problems which arise from the study of so lowly an organism as a fern. Some of these have been partially solved—probably none of them has been completely solved. In fact, we may say that our ignorance of life-processes greatly exceeds our knowledge. Very much more remains to be ascertained than has already been found out; for example, what is protoplasm? Nobody really knows. We have analyzed the substance chemically, we have carefully examined and tried (but without complete success) to describe its structure. We know it is more than merely a chemical compound. It is a historical substance. A watch, as such, is not. The metal and parts of which a watch is made, have, it is true, a past history; but the watch comes from the hands of its maker *de novo*, without any past history *as a watch*. But not so the plant cell. It has an ancestry *as a cell;* its protoplasm has what we may call a physiological memory of the past. It is what it is, not merely because of its present condition, but because its ancestral cells have had certain experiences. We can never understand a plant protoplast merely by studying it; we must know something of its genealogy and its past history.

What is the origin of the sporophyte, and how did there come to be two alternating generations? What is the meaning of fertilization; what the mechanism and laws of inheritance? How did there come to be on the earth such plants as ferns? What was the origin of life? What is life? No one can give complete answers to these questions; but the purpose of the study of botany is to help fit us to seek the answers intelligently. To those who are interested in problems of this sort, nothing can be more fascinating, nor more profitable.

CHAPTER XV

LIFE HISTORY OF A MOSS

176. Variety of Mosses.—There have been described and named over 12,000 different species of *Musci*, or mosses. Obviously, in an introductory study, we can only get a glimpse of so large a group. A comparative study of the species has led to the recognition of three distinct orders as follows:

Musci:
1. Sphagnales (the peat-mosses)
2. Andreæales (the black mosses)
3. Bryales (the true mosses)

Of these the Sphagnales are considered the most primitive, and the Bryales most highly developed. The Sphagnales will be considered first.

177. Habitat of Sphagnum.—Peat-mosses, as the name implies, grow in swamps and lake margins, usually in dense clumps or thick mats, in places forming the familiar peat-bogs of northern regions. They are usually of a very pale green color, often almost white, especially just below the top, and frequently with a tinge of red or yellow.

178. Description of Sphagnum.—The plant consists of an upright central axis or stem, with a central, pith-like portion of thin-walled parenchyma (Fig. 139.) The cell-walls of the outer portion, or *cortex*, are thicker and often tinted with a reddish pigment. The cortex varies in thickness from four cells in the main stem, to one or two cells in the smaller branches. The leaves are only one cell thick, and are densely crowded on the stem, having, at maturity, what is known as the two-fifths arrangement; that is, if one starts with a given leaf and follows upward in a spiral around the stem, he will pass five leaves before he comes to one vertically above that with which he started,

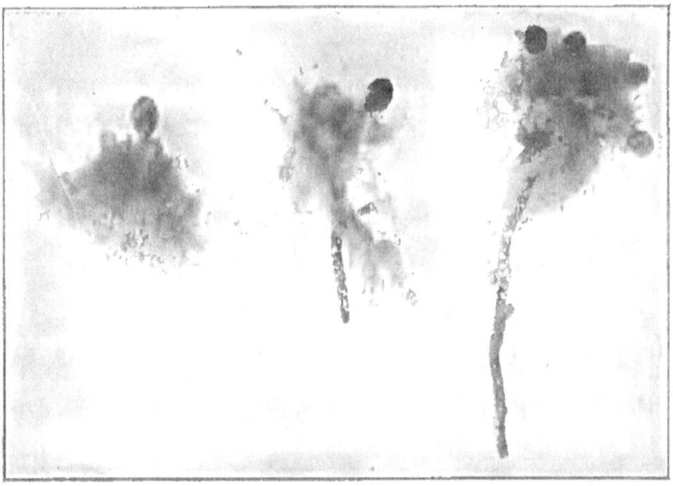

FIG. 139.—*Sphagnum sp.* Upper portions of leafy plants, showing sporogonia.

and in doing this he will have passed twice around the stem. The leaves of sphagnum never have a mid-rib or other veins, and correlated with this is the entire absence of any fibro-vascular bundles in the stem. This is one of the features that marks the plant as of lower organization than the fern. The stem forms numerous branches, usually one for every fourth leaf, and glandular hairs are usually met with at the bases of very young leaves (Figs. 140 and 141).

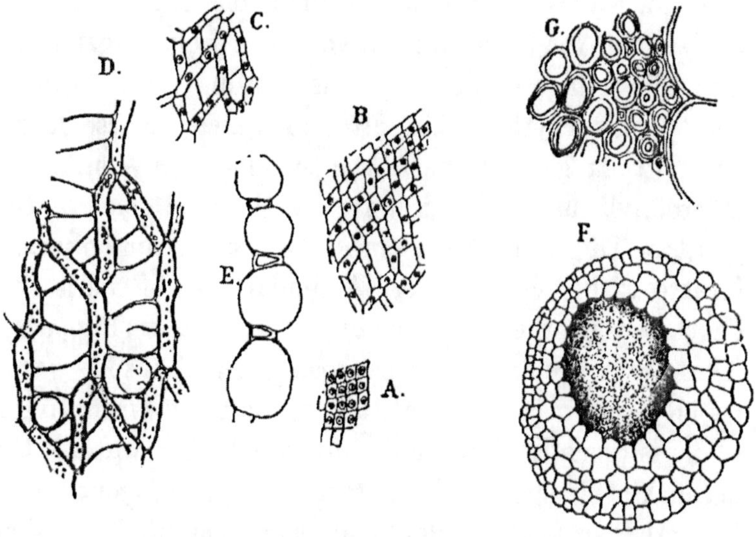

FIG. 140.—*Sphagnum cymbifolium*, Ehrb. *A*, *B*, *C*, cells from a young leaf, × about 300; *D*, cells from a mature leaf; *E*, section of a similar leaf; *F*, cross-section of an old stem, showing the thick, large celled cortex, × about 25; *G*, Sclerenchyma cells from the central portion of the stem, × about 300. (After Campbell.)

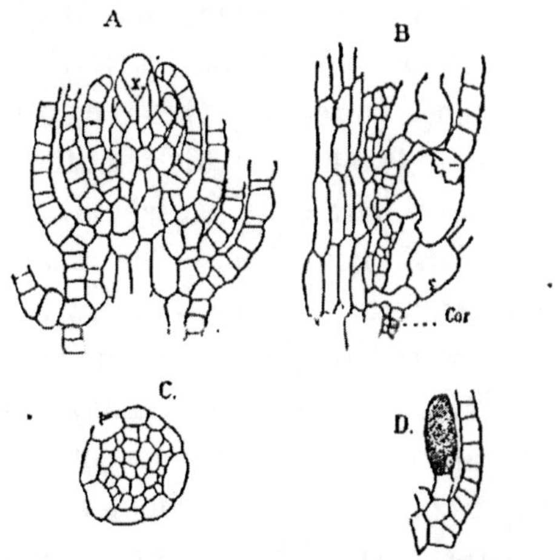

FIG. 141.—*Sphagnum cymbifolium*, Ehrb. *A*, median longitudinal section of a slender branch; *x*, the apical cell; *B*, part of a section of the same farther down, showing the enlarged cells at the bases of the leaves, and the double cortex (*cor*); *C*, cross-section near the apex of a slender branch; *D*, glandular hair at the base of a young leaf; all × 525. (After Campbell.)

As the leaves mature, part of their cells increase greatly in size, and the protoplasm becomes entirely transformed into thickenings of the cell-walls, leaving the cells quite empty of everything but air and water. These large, empty cells greatly mask the smaller ones containing chlorophyll, and this accounts for the pale color of the plants. The walls of the empty cells are commonly perforated with several pores. A similar type of cell is also developed in the outer layers of the stem (Fig. 141). These cells are extremely hygroscopic, and absorb water rapidly and in large quantities, so that the entire living plant is usually thoroughly saturated with water. On account of its sponge-like nature, sphagnum is much used by florists in packing plants for shipment, and in other ways.

179. Sterile and Fertile Branches.—Two kinds of branches occur: sterile and fertile. The organs of reproduction (antheridia and archegonia) occur only on the fertile branches, but antheridia and archegonia never on the same branch. In some species they occur on separate plants (*diœcious*—two households); in other species on the same plant (*monœcious*—one household).

180. Antheridial Branches.—The male branches, or *antheridiophores*, bear leaves that vary in color from green to yellow and red, and the antheridia occur in the axils of these leaves (Fig. 142). They consist of a relatively long stalk, composed of four rows of cells, or less, and bearing, at maturity, the globular capsule containing the sperms (Fig. 143). The sperms are coiled, with about two complete turns, and bear two long thread-like *cilia* at their anterior end. In locomotion the end bearing the cilia precedes. At the opposite or posterior end occurs a small appendage composed of starch, which ultimately drops off. It will be seen at once that the sperms of sphagnum differ from those of ferns in having only two cilia instead of many. When the antheridium is ripe the cells swell, and the capsule is thus forced open.

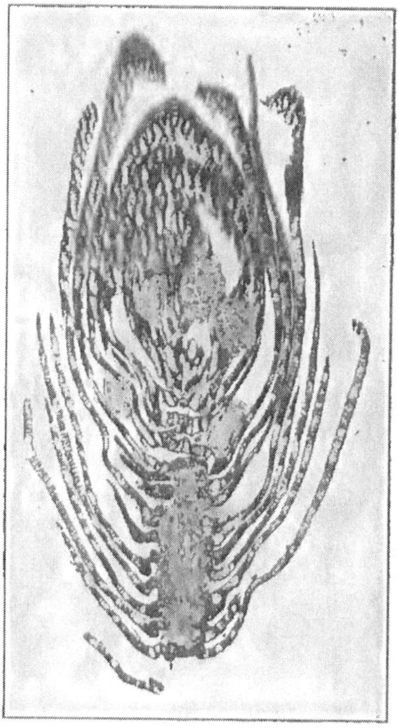

FIG. 142.—*Sphagnum*. Photomicrograph of a longitudinal section of an antheridial branch, showing five antheridia. (Cf. Fig. 143.)

181. Archegonial Branches.—The female branches, or *archegoniophores*, usually occur near the upper end of the plant, and bear the archegonia at their tips. As in the case of the fern, each archegonium consists of a neck (slightly twisted in *Sphagnum*), with neck-canal, a venter, containing the egg, and a basal stalk, or *pedicle*, not found in the ferns. Several archegonia commonly

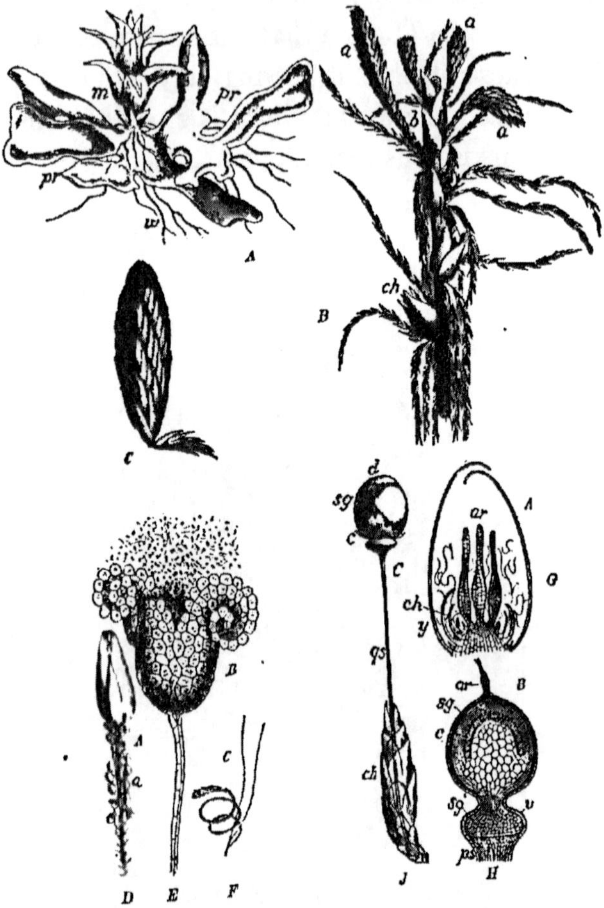

FIG. 143.—*Sphagnum acutifolium*, Ehrb. *A*, prothallus (*pr*), with a young leafy branch just developing from it; *B*, portion of a leafy plant; *a*, male cones; *ch*, female branches; *C*, male branch or cone, enlarged with a portion of the vegetative branch adhering to its base; *D*, the same, with a portion of the leaves removed so as to disclose the antheridia; *E*, antheridium discharging spores; *F*, a single sperm; *G*, longitudinal section of a female branch, showing the archegonia (*ar*); *H*, longitudinal section through a sporogonium; sg^1, the foot; *ps*, pseudopodium; *c*, calyptra; *sg*, sporogonium, with dome of sporogenous tissue; *ar*, old neck of the archegonium; *J*. *Sphagnum squarrosum* Pers.; *d*, operculum; *c*, remains of calyptra; *qs*, mature pseudopodium; *ch*, perichætium. (Cf. Figs. 139 and 142.) (From Schimper.)

occurs together in a group on a single female branch. A number of enlarged leaves surrounding the archegonia constitute a *perichætium*. The antheridial and archegonial branches at first occur close together near the summit of the branch, but the branch often elongates in the region between the two, thus separating them.

182. Asexual Multiplication.—One of the sterile branches, near the apex of the plant, usually develops more strongly than the others, and each year the old stem below dies off, and the young branch becomes established as a new plant. Under favorable conditions young plantlets, called *innovation branches*, may develop on the sterile branches, at the tip and back from the tip, strike root, and become established as independent plants (Fig. 144).

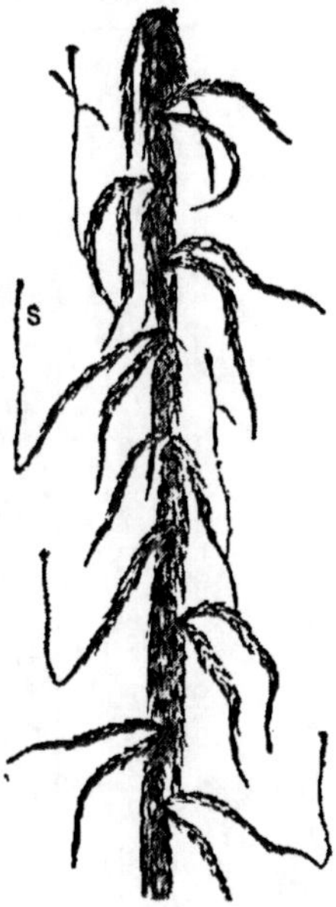

FIG. 144.—*Sphagnum cuspidatum*, showing innovation, or short, branches. (After Schimper.)

183. Sexual Reproduction.—Fertilization is accomplished in a manner similar to that in the fern, a film of water being required in order that the motile sperm may swim to the neck-canal, down which it passes, to the venter and into the egg, where the two nuclei unite. Fertilization probably occurs, as a rule, in winter, for young embryos are usually found in very early spring. The first division-wall of the oösperm is horizontal, or nearly at right angles to the axis of the neck, and thus at right angles to the position of the wall in the first division of the leptosporangiate ferns. As the cell-divisions follow each other in rapid succession, the upper cells of the developing embryo become organized into a large globular spore-case, containing a thick central column (*columella*), surrounded by a dome of spores, and, outside of all, the wall of the sporangium. As the spore-case

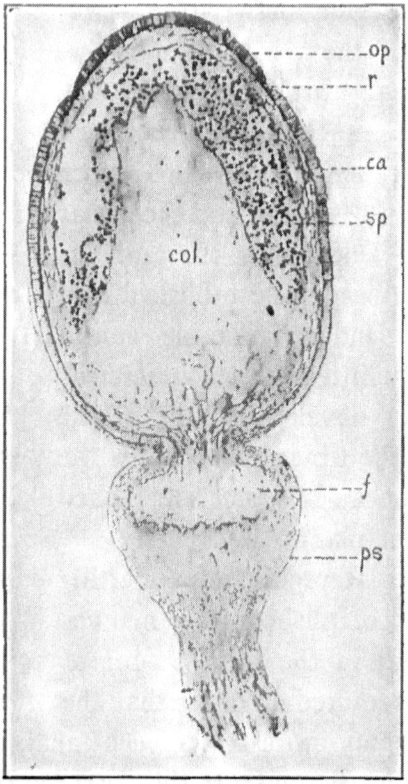

FIG. 145.—*Sphagnum sp.* Photomicrograph of a longitudinal section through a sporogonium and portion of the pseudopodium. *op*, operculum; *r*, annulus; *ca*, wall of capsule; *sp*, spores; *col*, columella; *f*, foot; *ps*, pseudopodium.

enlarges the wall of the archegonium is ruptured and the top portion of it is carried up as a cap on the spore-case, forming the *calyptra*. The lower cells produced by the dividing oösperm become organized into a much swollen *foot*, imbedded in the tissues below, and connected with the spore-case by a very short stalk (Figs. 143 and 145).

184. The Sporophyte.—It will have been recognized already that the simple structure just described, since it bears spores, is the sporophyte stage of *Sphagnum.*[1] While the sporophyte is maturing, the apex of the female branch elongates, forming a leafless stalk, a half inch or more in length. This stalk is called the *pseudopodium* (false foot). The development of the pseudopodium, coincident with that of the sporophyte is very interesting, and the question at once naturally arises, as to how this correlation is brought about. No positive explanation has ever been given, but it seems probable that, as the sporophyte begins to develop, the cells of the foot excrete some substance which stimulates the cells in which it is imbedded to divide and enlarge, resulting finally in the formation of the pseudopodium. The advantage of the pseudopodium in facilitating the distribution of spores by raising the spore-case higher into the air and well above the perichætial and other leaves, is obvious.

The sporophyte of *Sphagnum* possesses no chlorophyll, and consequently does not elaborate any food, obtaining its entire supply from the sphagnum-plant by absorption through the foot. Numerous groups of stomatal guard-cells occur on the wall of the spore-case, but they have no slit between them—no true stomata—and are therefore functionless. There are also, underneath the guard-cells, no intercellular spaces, such as are always associated with true stomata. The presence of these functionless stomata is thought by some botanists to indicate that the

[1] Such simply organized sporophytes are commonly called *sporogonia* (singular *sporogonium*).

sporophytes of the ancestors of *Sphagnum* possessed true stomata and the function of photosynthesis.

185. Formation of Spores.—As the spore-case develops, the inner cells become differentiated into two kinds, one composing the larger part of the tissue, and the other, larger and richer in protoplasm, forming a dome of *sporogenous* or spore-forming tissue near the upper wall (Fig. 145). From this tissue, spore-mother-cells are developed, and from each of these, by reducing divisions, as in the fern, four spores.

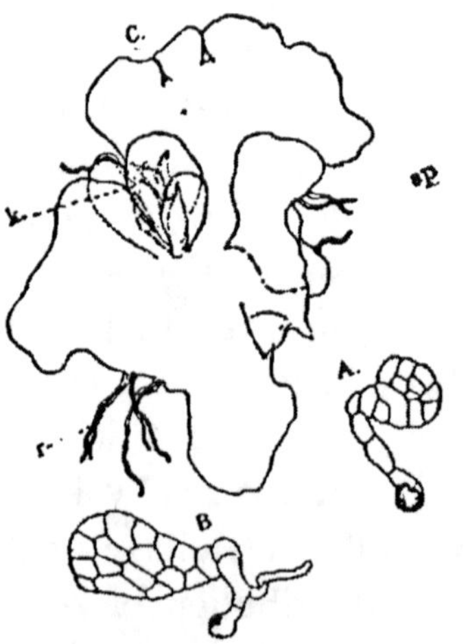

FIG. 146.—*Sphagnum sp. A, B*, young protonemata; *C*, older protonema with leafy bud, *k; r*, marginal rhizoids. (After Campbell.)

186. Asexual Reproduction.—While the spores are maturing, a circular groove (*annulus*) is formed near the apex of the spore-case, and the cells in this zone have thinner walls than those adjacent (Fig. 145). At the maturity of the spore-case these cells become dry, and are easily torn apart, thus forming a lid, or *operculum*, at the summit of the spore-case. The falling away of the operculum affords an opportunity for the scattering of the spores. Under favorable conditions the spores germinate, putting forth a very short, green protonema, as in the case of fern-spores. The tip of the protonema soon broadens out, forming a prothallus, much like that of the fern in shape, but being only one cell thick (Fig. 146). Rhizoids form on the under side, and from the margin other threads develop, having chlorophyll, and resembling the protonema. At the tips of each of these threads a thallus may also form, and in this way vegetative multiplication is brought about. From each thallus arises an upright leafy branch—the sphagnum-plant described above. The reader has already recognized that this complex phase of sphagnum is the gametophyte.

187. Life-cycle of Sphagnum.—The life-cycle of sphagnum may be summarized as follows:

OUTLINE OF LIFE HISTORY OF SPHAGNUM

Sphagnum-plant (*gametophyte*)
↓
Antheridial branch — Archegonial branch
↓ ↓
Antheridia — Archegonia
↓ ↓
Sperm (male gamete) — Egg (female gamete)
Fertilization
↘ ↙
Oösperm (zygote)
↓↓
Embryo
↓↓
Mature Sporophyte (mature zygote)
↓↓
Sporangium
↓↓
Spore-mother-cell
↓ ↓ ↓ ↓ } *Reduction*
Spore Spore Spore Spore
↓
Protonema
↓
Thallus
↓
Sphagnum-plant (*gametophyte*)

188. Diagram of Life-cycle.—The life-cycle of Sphagnum may be diagrammatically represented as follows:

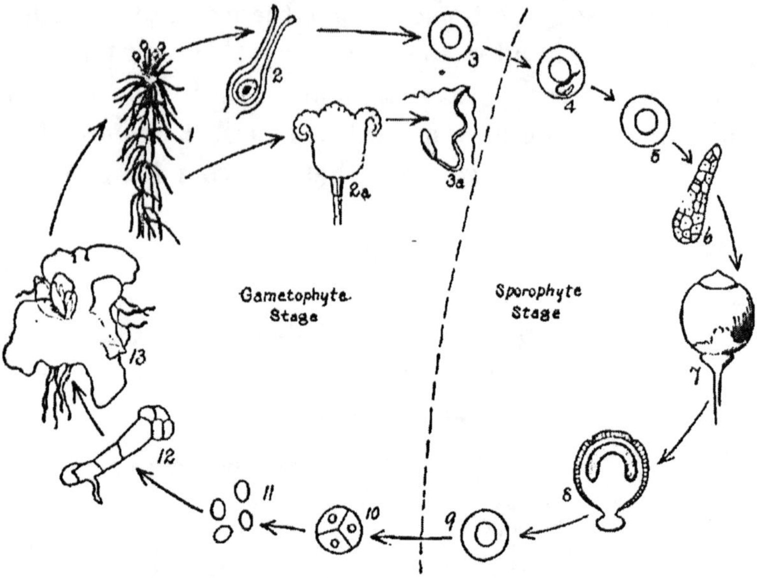

FIG. 147.—Diagram of life-cycle of sphagnum.

189. Other Mosses.—The so-called "true mosses," with which we are perhaps more familar than with sphagnum, cannot be studied here in detail, but it may be said that, in broad outline, their life histories are closely similar to that of sphagnum. The protonema does not produce a thallus, but the leafy branches, or moss-plants, arise directly from the filamentous protonema (Fig. 148). They are both monœcious and diœcious. In the "true mosses" no pseudopodium is formed, but the stalk of the sporophyte (so very short in *Sphagnum*), elongates to form a *seta*, often over 1 inch in length. In the spore-case, or capsule, there is much less sporogenous or fertile tissue, in proportion to sterile tissue, than in *Sphagnum*. Moreover, at the base of the capsules, in the true mosses, occur functional stomata, opening into intercellular spaces, and surrounded by chlorophyll-bearing cells. Thus photosynthesis may be carried on, though of course to a very limited degree. The sporophyte of the true mosses seems to occupy an intermediate position between those of *Sphagnum* and the fern, and, as we ascend from the lower form in *Sphagnum* to the higher form in the fern, *the transition is largely characterized by a decrease in the amount of fertile tissue and an increase in the relative amount of sterile tissue of the sporophytes.*

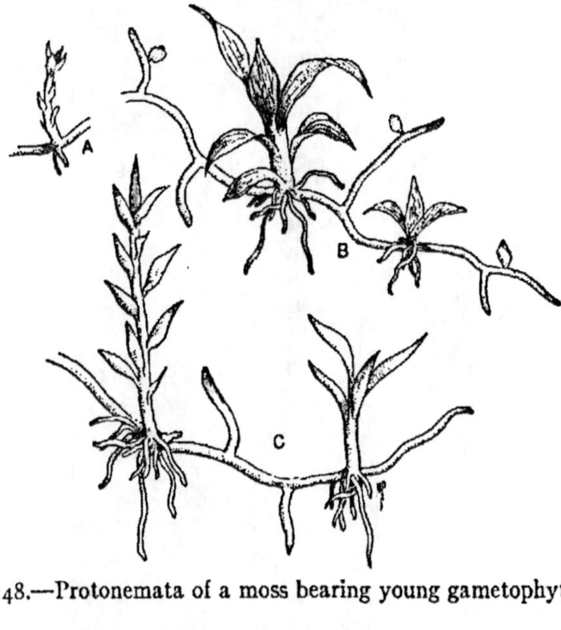

FIG. 148.—Protonemata of a moss bearing young gametophyte buds.

190. Vegetative Multiplication.—Extensive experiments seem to indicate that every living cell of a moss-plant can develop protonemata—or in other words is a potential spore. These protonemata like those produced by the germination of spores, produce buds which may develop into mature plants. The production of entire plants or of parts of plants in this way, by portions of the vegetative body, is called *regeneration.* In some species of mosses the

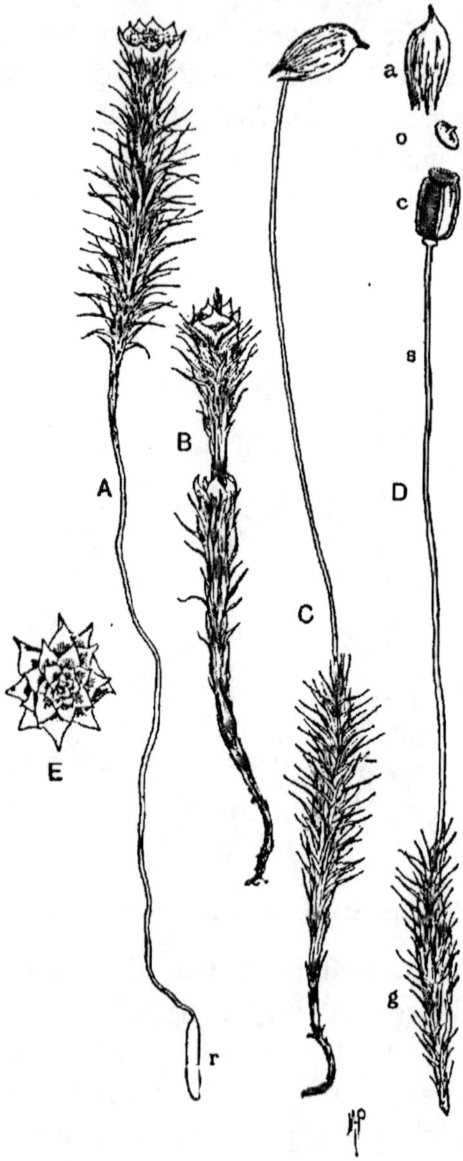

FIG. 149.—Hair-cap moss (*Polytrichum commune*). *A*, male plant; *B*, same, proliferating; *C*, female plant, bearing sporogonium; *D*, same; *g*, gametophyte; *s*, seta; *c*, capsule; *o*, operculum; *a*, calyptra, *E*, top view of male plant.

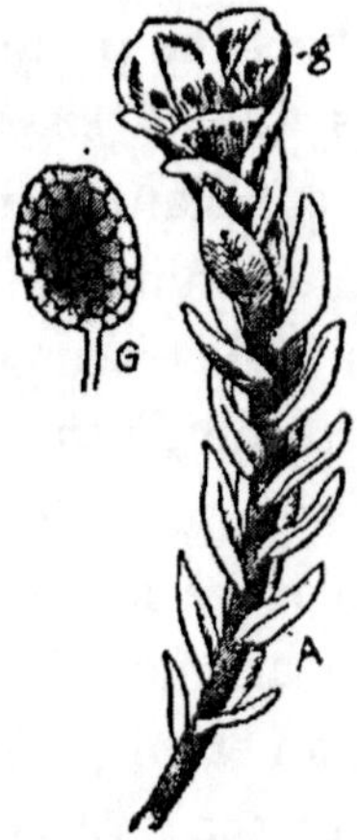

FIG. 150.—A moss (*Tetraphis sp.*), showing gemmæ; *G*, a gemma enlarged. (Cf. Fig. 151.)

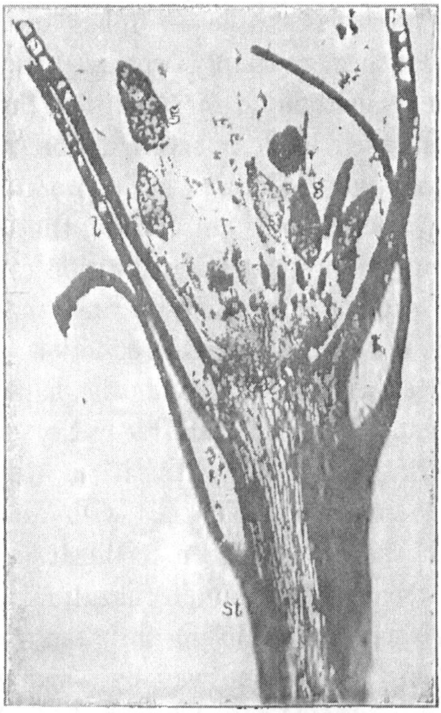

FIG. 151.—Photomicrograph of a longitudinal section of a moss (*Tetraphis*), showing gemmæ (*g*). (Cf. Fig. 150.)

leafy-shoot, and in others the protonemata, may give rise to special small bodies, called *gemmæ*, which may become separated from the parent plant and give rise to new plants (Figs. 150 and 151). Gemmæ will be illustrated more fully in the liverworts to be discussed in the next chapter.

191. Comparison with the Fern.—By comparing *Sphagnum* with a fern several points of interest are brought out. In the first place, we learn that, while the "fern-plant" with which we are familiar is a sporophyte, the sphagnum-plant is a gametophyte. In the second place, while the sporophyte of the fern is at first dependent on the gametophyte for its nutrition, the sporophyte soon becomes entirely independent, and the simply organized gametophyte perishes; while in sphagnum the sporophyte is the much more simply organized, and is dependent upon the gametophyte for nutrition throughout its entire life. In their mode of reproduction, however, the two plants are very similar, each producing haploid gametes of two sexes, male and female, that need to fuse in fertilization; the product of fertilization (zygote) being diploid, and producing a spore-bearing phase; and the spores, haploid again, through reduction, giving rise, without nuclear and cell-fusion to the haploid gametophyte. In each case, in the life-cycle, gametophyte alternates with sporophyte, fertilization with reduction, gametes with spores, haploid cells with diploid. What takes place in the cells between fertilization and reduction, and between reduction and fertilization? This is one of the many fascinating problems in botany still awaiting solution. There is only one way by which the answers to these problems may be ascertained; namely, by accurate, persistent, painstaking observation and experiment.

CHAPTER XVI

LIFE HISTORY OF A LIVERWORT

192. Habitat.—The group of plants ranking next below the mosses in the scale of life is the liverworts (Hepaticæ). They are widely distributed over the earth's surface; being found in a wide climatic range, but usually in moist situations. Some forms (*e.g.*, *Riccia natans*) may grow floating on the surface of water, others (*e.g.*, *Riccia fluitans*)

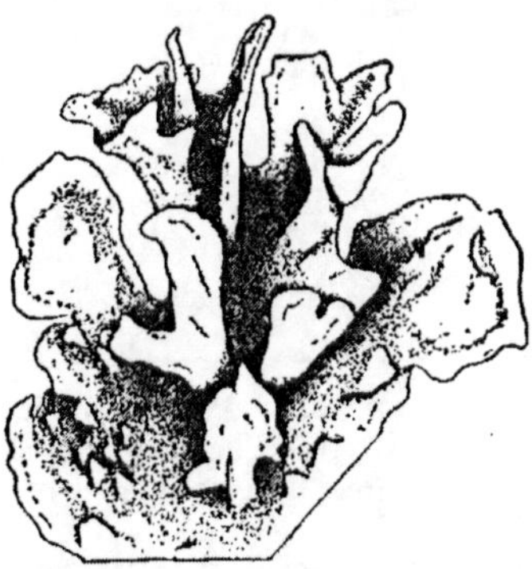

FIG. 152.—*Anthoceros fusiformis.* Portion of lamellate, cristate thallus, which easily retains water. (After M. A. Howe.)

submerged; but, as in mosses, no salt-water forms have been found. A few species grow on other plants (*epiphytic*), or in other situations where the water supply may at times fall very low. Such forms have various contrivances which serve to retain water. Thus, some species of *Anthoceros* (*e.g.*, *A. fusiformis*, *A. fimbriatus*) possess crisped lobes, forming a fringe around the margin which helps the plant to retain water (Figs. 152 and 153). In another species (*A. punctatus*), water is retained in little pits or depressions on the upper surface. The habitat of the liverworts illustrates a step forward in the abandonment by plants of a wholly aquatic life and the establishment of a land vegetation; but the prevailingly moist situations in which most of the species are found,

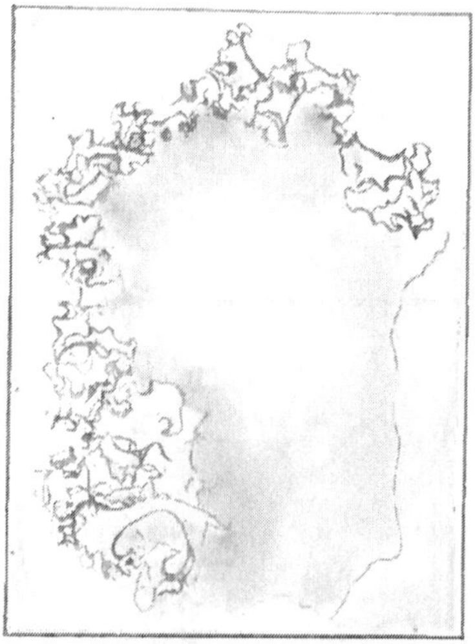

FIG. 153.—*Anthoceros fimbriatus*. Portion of a thallus viewed from below, with the rhizoids omitted. The one-layered crisped lobes at the margin serve to retain moisture. (After Goebel.)

and the need of water for fertilization by swimming sperms (soon to be described), points to an ancestral habitat truly aquatic.

193. Description of the Plant Body.—The plant body of the liverworts shows a marked departure from that of the mosses in the direction of simplicity. There are four main groups or orders of Hepaticæ, as follows:

Hepaticæ
1. Ricciales.
2. Marchantiales.
3. Jungermanniales
4. Anthocerotales.

In the first two and last of these orders the plant body is a thallus, either closely resembling the prothallus of the ferns, or freely branching. In the third order the plant

FIG. 154.—A leafy liverwort (*Porella navicularis*). Male plant, about natural size. (After M. A. Howe.)

body is leafy (*foliose*), and in this respect somewhat resembles certain true mosses, for which it is often mistaken (Figs. 154 and 155). In the first two and last orders the thallus always shows dorso-ventral differentiation.

ANTHOCEROS

194. The Gametophyte.—One of the most important groups is the genus *Anthoceros*, including several different kinds or *species*. The plant body, or thallus (Fig. 156), is roughly circular or semicircular, with numerous rhizoids growing from the ventral surface. It increases in size at numerous *growing points* on the margin of the thallus, and

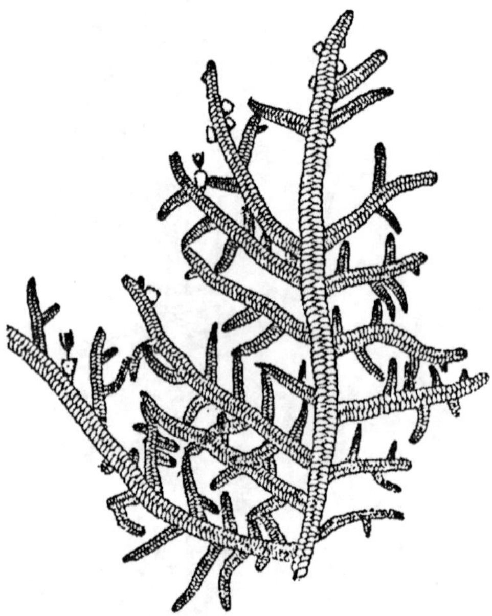

FIG. 155.—A leafy liverwort (*Porella navicularis*). Female plant, about natural size. (After M. A. Howe.)

is green from the presence of chlorophyll in the cells. There is only one chloroplast in a cell, in contrast to the numerous chloroplasts in each cell of the mosses and ferns.

195. Reproductive Organs.—The antheridia are found just back of the *growing points*, near the middle of the lobe. In some species they occur in groups (Figs. 157 and 159), in other species singly (Fig. 158). They develop.

not from epidermal cells as in ferns, but each one from a single cell just underneath the epidermis (subepidermal),

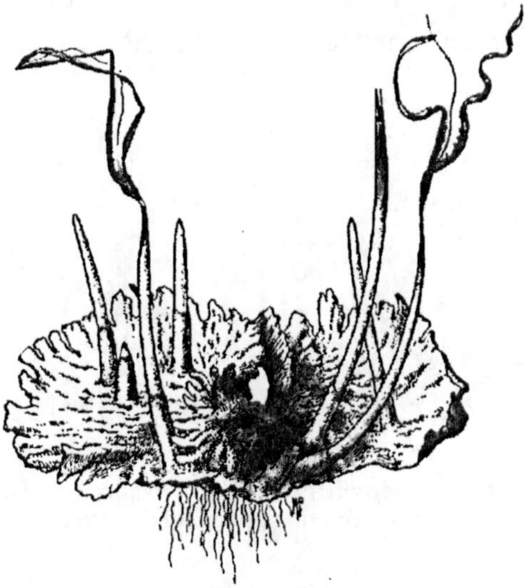

FIG. 156.—*Anthoceros lævis*, showing the lobed thallus of the gametophyte, bearing several upright sporogonia in various stages of development. At the right and left sporogonia dehiscing, and scattering the spores. Note the slender, thread-like columellas, and the lack of differentiation of the sporogonium into seta and capsule. The sheath (calyptra) at the base of the sporogonium is formed chiefly from the vegetative tissues of the gametophyte, and only to a slight extent by the walls of the archegonium.

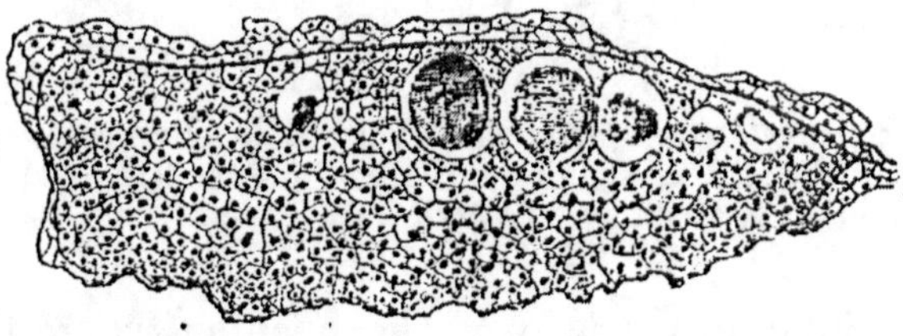

FIG. 157.—*Anthoceros Pearsoni*. Longitudinal section through a well-developed, glandular thickening, in which are embedded a number of antheridia. $\times$ 53. (After M. A. Howe.)

near the dorsal surface. They remain imbedded in the surrounding tissue until mature, closely resembling, in their location and mode of origin, the antheridia of some of the lower, or eusporangiate, ferns, such as *Ophioglosum* and *Botrychium*. The archegonia are also imbedded, with the tip of the neck reaching to the surface (Fig. 159). They are further concealed at maturity by the growth of

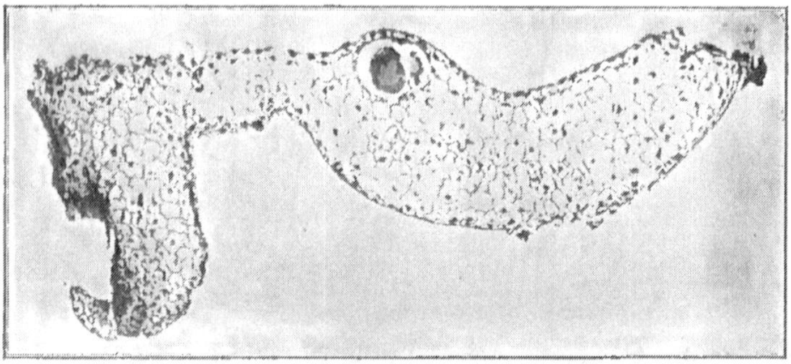

FIG. 158.—Cross-section of the thallus of a hornwort (*Anthoceras sp.*). The oval area is an antheridium, containing sperms, or sperm-mother-cells.

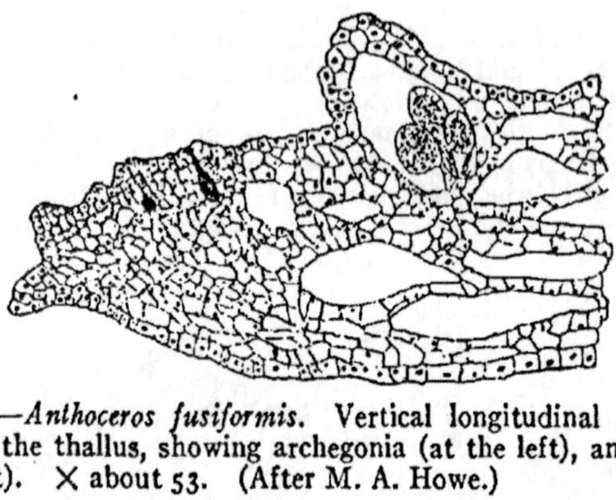

FIG. 159.—*Anthoceros fusiformis*. Vertical longitudinal section near the apex of the thallus, showing archegonia (at the left), and antheridia (at the right). × about 53. (After M. A. Howe.)

a small dome of tissue over the opening where the neck comes to the surface. Both antheridia and archegonia occur on the same plant, sometimes closely intermingled.

196. Symbiosis.—A most interesting case of symbiosis occurs between *Anthoceros* and a much more lowly organized plant—a blue-green alga, of the genus *Nostoc* (Fig. 160). On the ventral surface of the thallus slits occur in the epidermis. These are not stomata, and the intercellular spaces into which they open are fitted with a mucilaginous substance produced by a transformation of the adjacent cell-walls. This mucilage furnishes ideal conditions of food and moisture for the alga, which flourishes there.

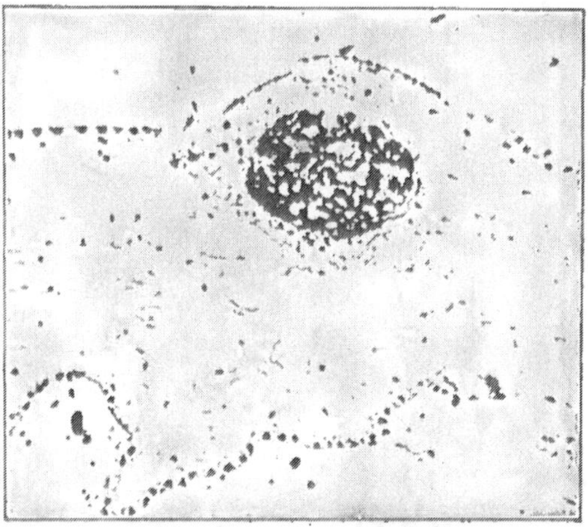

FIG. 160.—Photomicrograph of a cross-section of a liverwort (*Anthoceros fusiformis*). The dark, oval area is a colony of a species of *Nostoc*, an alga that lives symbiotically in the tissues of the liverwort. (Microscopic preparation by M. A. Howe.)

Whether the presence of the alga is of any advantage to the liverwort is not known, but apparently it is of no disadvantage.

197. Vegetative Multiplication.—Liverworts present many interesting devices for vegetative multiplication by the giving off or separation of a portion of the vegetative tissue, and the establishment of this separated piece as an independent plant. No group of plants excels the liverworts in their power to regenerate new individuals from pieces of the plant body. If the thallus is cut into many small pieces with a pair of scissors, each piece can regenerate a new plant. In many species the tips of the lobes of the thallus become separated from the plant naturally, by the dying off of portions back from the tip. In such cases each tip develops an entire new individual. A thorough study of these phenomena has led botanists

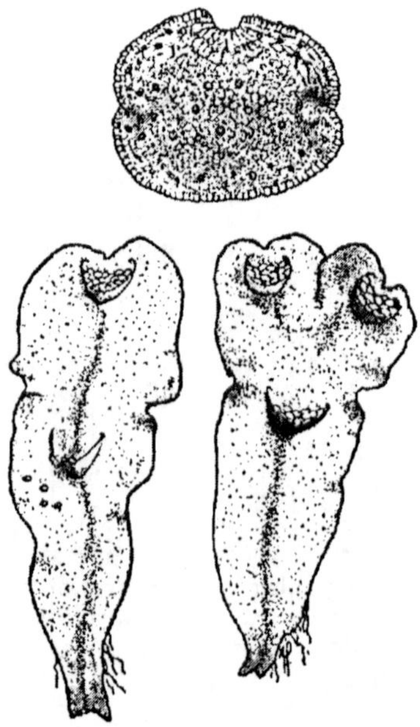

FIG. 161.—A liverwort (*Lunularia*). Below, portions of the thallus, showing the lunar-shaped cupules, with brood-buds, or gemmæ. Above a single gemma, greatly magnified.

to the conclusion that every cell of a liverwort is able to reproduce an entire plant, just as effectually as though it were a spore. Some species produce little multicellular bodies called *gemmæ* (Fig. 161). Other species produce fleshy *tubers*, richly stored with reserve food-materials,[1] and specially valuable in helping the species

[1] Analogous to tuber-formation in the potato.

to tide over periods of drought. Tubers in liverworts were first discovered and recognized in a species of *Anthoceros*. At least two species (*Fossombronia tuberifera* and *Anthoceros tuberosus*) received their specific names from their

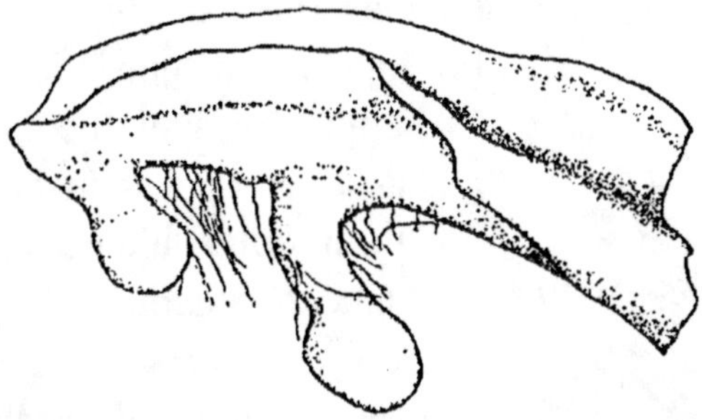

FIG. 162.—*Anthoceros phymatodes*. Portion of thallus showing developing tubers. × about 15. (After M. A. Howe.)

characteristic of forming tubers. In some species the tubers appear as swellings or outgrowths on the underside of the thallus; in others (Figs. 162 and 163) as enlargements of the tips of thallus-lobes. The leafy liverwort, *Bryopteris filicina* (Fig. 164), illustrates vegetative multiplication by stolons.

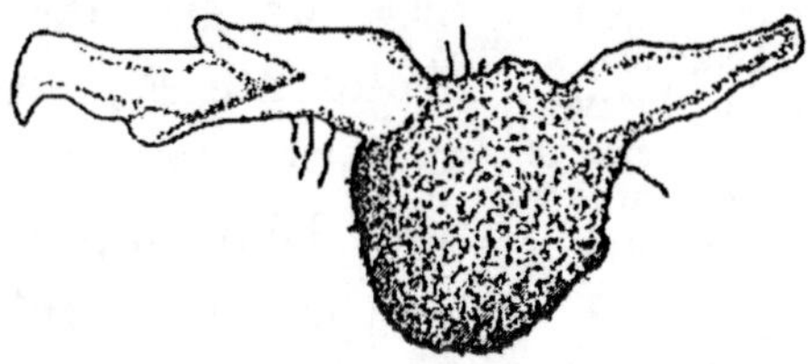

FIG. 163.—*Anthoceros phymatodes*. Mature tuber, sprouting. × about 21. (After M. A. Howe.)

198. The Sporophyte.—After fertilization the oösperm develops a young embryo, and from the lower or basal half the foot develops, with projections reaching down into the tissue of the gametophyte (Fig. 165). After the early stages of development the sporophyte ceases to grow at the apex, and elongates only by the formation and enlargement of new cells just above the foot (*intercalary growth*). Around the base of the sporophyte there develops from the tissue of the gametophyte a *sheath*, but, in contrast with the mosses, no seta is formed. The appearance of the sporophytes, as they appear in clusters, has been aptly likened to tufts of delicaté blades of grass (Fig. 156). Spores are formed from the cylindrical archesporium, between outer and inner layers of sterile tissue. The inner thread-like layer is the columella (Fig. 156). Chlorophyll develops in the sterile cells, and intercellular spaces open to the surface through true stomata (Fig. 166). The sporophyte, therefore, has the function of photosynthesis, and if only a root, or roots, would develop from the basal portion, it could well become established as an independent plant. As it is, it can live only as long as the gametophyte remains active, so as to maintain the supply of water to the sporophyte. The columella serves to conduct water up the sporophyte.

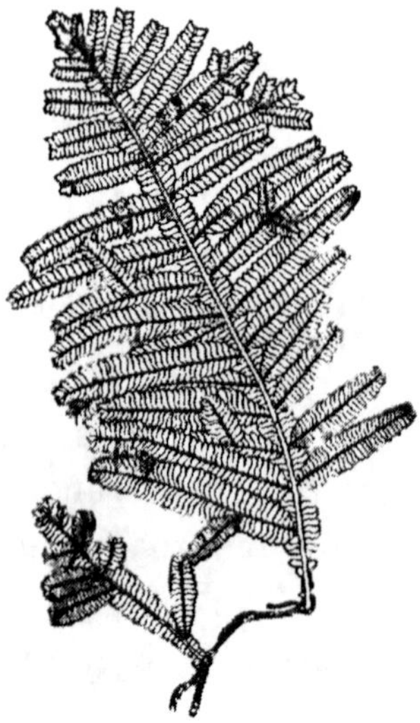

FIG. 164.—*Bryopteris filicina*, showing long shoots and short shoots. The stolons at the base, with reduced leaves, serve not only in vegetative propagation, but also to anchor the plant. (After Goebel.)

199. Formation of Spores.—As in the mosses and ferns, spores arise from spore-mother-cells by reducing divisions (tetrad-formation). In *Anthoceros* they do not all mature at the same time, as in the mosses and ferns, but new spores continue to form in the region of intercalary growth so long as growth continues. As the spores mature the tip of the sporophyte splits open, and the walls spread apart progressively, as spores lower down come to maturity.

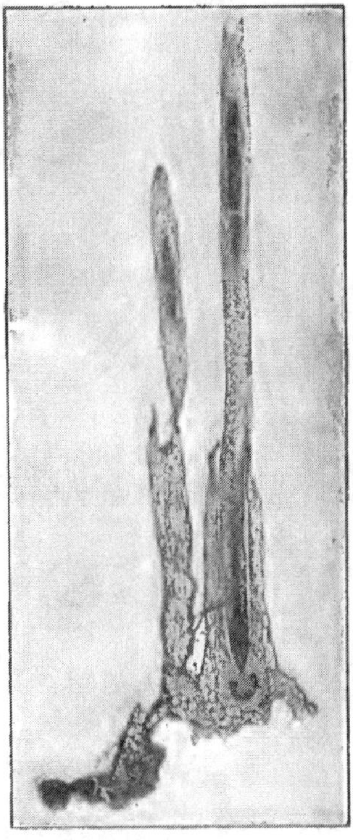

FIG. 165.—*Anthoceros*. Photomicrograph of a longitudinal section of the sporogonium, and portion of the gametophytic thallus. Note the foot of the sporogonium, and the more darkly stained spores at the center, above.

200. Distribution of Spores.—In addition to spores, a portion of the tissue of the archesporium develops sterile cells or cell-rows, called *elaters* (Fig. 166). When these become dry, as the sporogonium splits open from the tip,

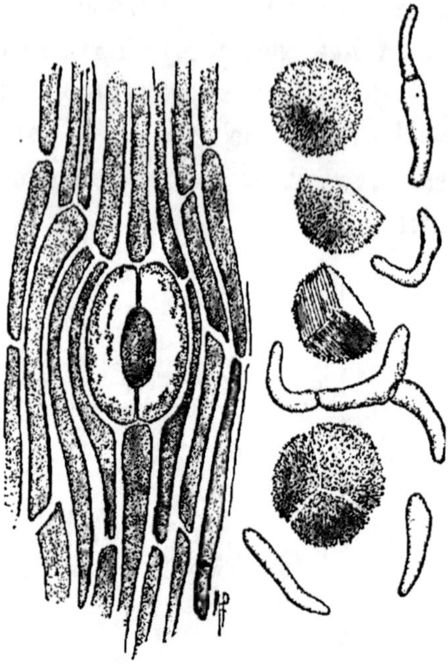

FIG. 166.—*Anthoceros.* At the left, a stoma with guard-cells. At the right, spores and pseudo-elaters.

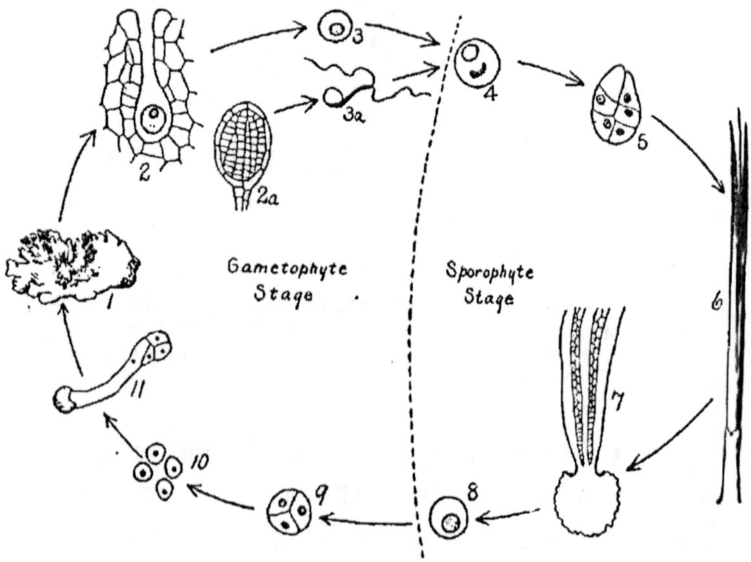

FIG. 167.—Diagram of the life-cycle of *Anthoceros.*

they twist with a jerking motion, which helps to project the spores out to a distance from the parent plant. The advantage of this is self-evident.

201. Germination.—In some, if not all, species of *Anthoceros*, the spores germinate best after a resting period of several weeks or months. Early in germination chlorophyll develops in a plastid contained in the spore, and a germination-tube, or protonema, forms, long in some species, shorter in others, and at the tip of this tube a thallus develops.

202. Summary of Life History.—The life history of *Anthoceros* is, in outline, as follows (it is illustrated diagrammatically in Fig. 167):

OUTLINE OF LIFE HISTORY OF ANTHOCEROS

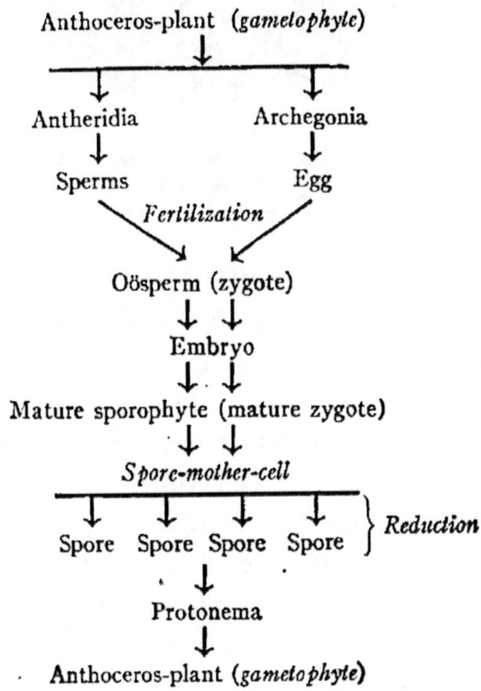

OTHER FORMS

203. Riccia.—About 4,000 species of liverworts have been described, and it is, of course, possible here to refer to only a very few of the forms, chosen because they illustrate some special idea or step in the evolutionary development of plants. In addition to the forms already mentioned, attention should be called to the genus *Riccia*,

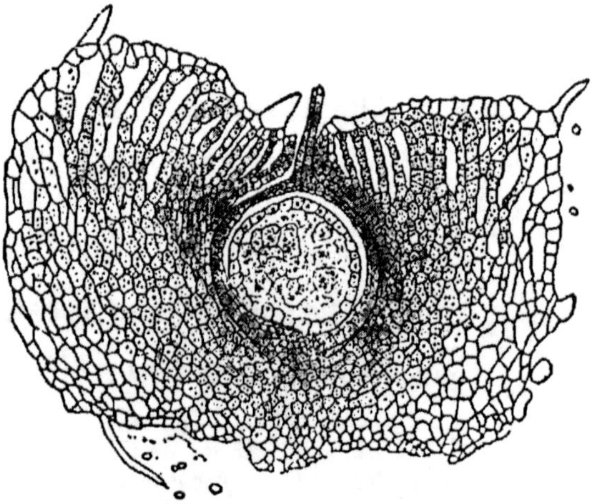

FIG. 168.—A liverwort (*Riccia trichocarpa*), × about 35. Cross-section of the thallus, showing young sporogonium in the enlarged venter of the archegonium. (After M. A. Howe.)

which is of interest because of its aquatic mode of life, and also because of its extremely simple sporophyte—the simplest sporophyte, in fact, of all plants that possess archegonia (*Archegonates*). The fertilized egg of *Riccia* develops a sporophyte which has only fertile cells (spores), except for a wall, one cell thick, enclosing the spores (Fig. 168). In fact, the sporophyte has been reduced to only a very simple spore-case, of short duration; it never projects beyond the venter of the archegonium. Spores are formed in the usual way, as described for the forms previously studied. Except for the sterile wall-cells, all the cells formed by the successive divisions of the oöpserm

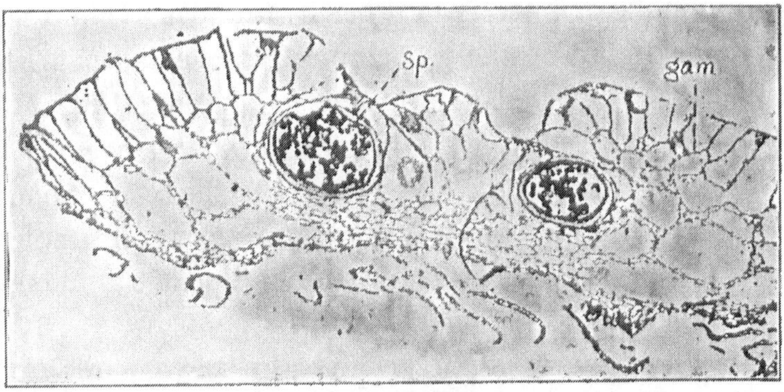

FIG. 169.—*Ricciocarpus.* *sp.*, sporogonium; *gam*, tissue of gametophyte.

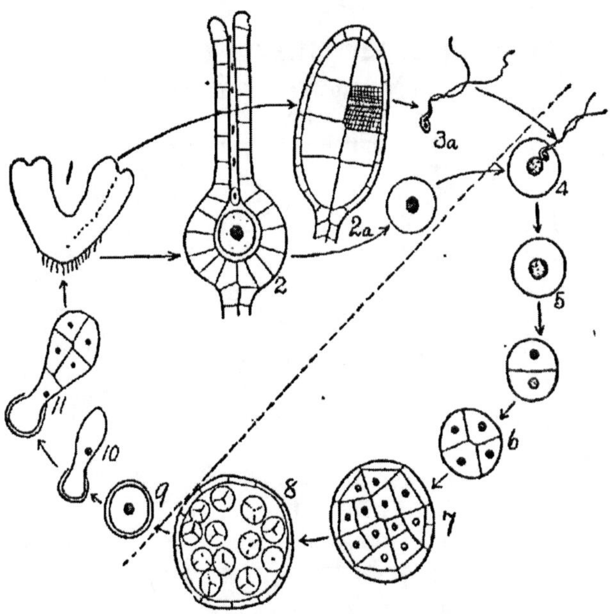

FIG. 170.—Life cycle of *Ricciocarpus.* (After Cardiff.)

become spore-mother-cells, each of which, by the tetrad-division, gives rise to four spores. Meanwhile the wall-cells become disorganized and their substance goes to nourish the spores. By this time the cells of the inner layer of the venter have also become disorganized and their substance, in like manner, is absorbed by the spores (Fig. 169). Thus the tissue of the gametophyte serves as nourishment for the developing, primitive sporophyte. *The phenomenon of an embryo developing into a mature sporophyte is practically eliminated.* As we descend the scale of plant life we find the sporophyte becoming simpler and simpler; and this simplicity consists in the diminution of the amount of sterile tissue.

204. Life History of Riccia.—The life history of *Riccia* is shown in outline as follows, and diagrammatically in Fig. 170. Carefully compare this history with that of *Anthoceros*.

OUTLINE OF LIFE HISTORY OF RICCIA

Riccia-plant (*gametophyte*)
↓
Antheridia — Archegonia
↓ ↓
Sperms — Egg
Fertilization
Oösperm (zygote)
↓↓
Cell-divisions
↓↓
Sporophyte (transient spore-case)
↓↓
Spore-mother-cells
↓ ↓ ↓ ↓ } *Reduction*
Spore Spore Spore Spore
↓
Protonema
↓
Riccia-plant (*gametophyte*)

205. Comparison with Mosses and Ferns.—(*a*) *The Gametophyte.*—The gametophytes of the various kinds of liverworts differ greatly among themselves, but on the whole they are more simply organized than those of the mosses, lacking especially the highly developed, leafy branches or gametophores. The moss-plant represents the highest degree of gametophytic organization known among land-plants, and the leafy branch is practically universal in that group. On the other hand, the vegetative body of the liverworts is, in some forms, simpler than the prothallus of the fern, while in other forms it is much more complicated, becoming a leafy branch in the Jungermanniales, and bearing complex gametophores and other organs in the Marchantiales. But while it may become complex, its organization is always of a lower type than that of the moss-plant. The antheridia are much alike in both mosses and liverworts, and on the whole differ but little from that of the true ferns; but the spermatozoids of the former are always *biciliate*, while those of the true ferns are always *multiciliate*. The archegonia of mosses and liverworts may or may not be stalked, but they are never stalked in the true ferns. With the exception of *Anthoceros* they are never sunk beneath the surface in either mosses or liverworts, but in the ferns the venter is commonly sunk in the tissue of the prothallus.

(*b*) *The Sporophyte.*—The typical sporogonium or sporophyte of liverworts and mosses consists of a stalk or seta, with a foot at one end, imbedded in the tissue of the gametophyte, and a spore-case at the opposite end. There are, however, all degrees of variation of this type of structure. The stalk and foot may be entirely wanting, as in the simple sporophyte of *Riccia;* the stalk may be very greatly reduced, as in *Sphagnum;* or the spore-case may not appear as a clearly defined organ, but may appear to merge very gradually into the stalk, as in *Anthoceros.* In liverworts the spore-case never opens by a lid or operculum, as is universally the case in mosses, but always by valves, formed by longitudinal splittings of the sporangial walls. Elaters may or may not occur in liverworts, but never occur in mosses. The sporogonium of liverworts and mosses never possesses a leafy stem, and never possesses true roots; only one case (that of the moss, *Eriopus remotifolius*) has ever been reported where the sporogonium produces rhizoids from its basal end. To compare the simple sporogonium of liverworts and mosses with the leafy plant of the true ferns, would be quite superfluous. It should, however, be pointed out that the sporophyte of liverworts and mosses lives always, throughout its life, as a parasite on the gametophyte, while the sporophyte of ferns always becomes established, sooner or later, as an independent plant. Except for the very simple columella of *Anthoceros* and the central strand in the seta of mosses, nothing approaching a true vascular bundle occurs in the liverworts and mosses; while, as stated before, the well-developed fibro-vascular system of the ferns has caused them to be known as *vascular* cryptogams.

CHAPTER XVII

LIFE HISTORIES OF ALGÆ

206. The Main Groups of Algæ.—The plants that rank next in the scale of life below the liverworts are the Algæ. On the basis of color they fall naturally into four main groups or *phyla*, as follows:

1. Blue-green algæ (Cyanophyceæ)
2. Green algæ (Chlorophyceæ)
3. Brown algæ (Phæophyceæ)
4. Red algæ (Rhodophyceæ) .

Associated with these differences in color are certain differences of structure, which also lead to a similar grouping. In recent years the above four groups have been further subdivided into seven phyla, on the basis of other characters than color. A study of one of the commoner brown algæ, *Ascophyllum*, will serve to illustrate many fundamental facts about the algæ in general.

ASCOPHYLLUM

207. Habitat of Ascophyllum.—This plant, and the closely related *Fucus*, have become familiar in inland markets, because they are commonly used as a packing in the shipment of crabs and other kinds of "shell fish." *Ascophyllum* and *Fucus*, and their near relatives, constitute the family *Fucaceæ*. For the most part they are inhabitants of the ocean, or of brackish water, or, in rare cases, of fresh water. The two genera mentioned are

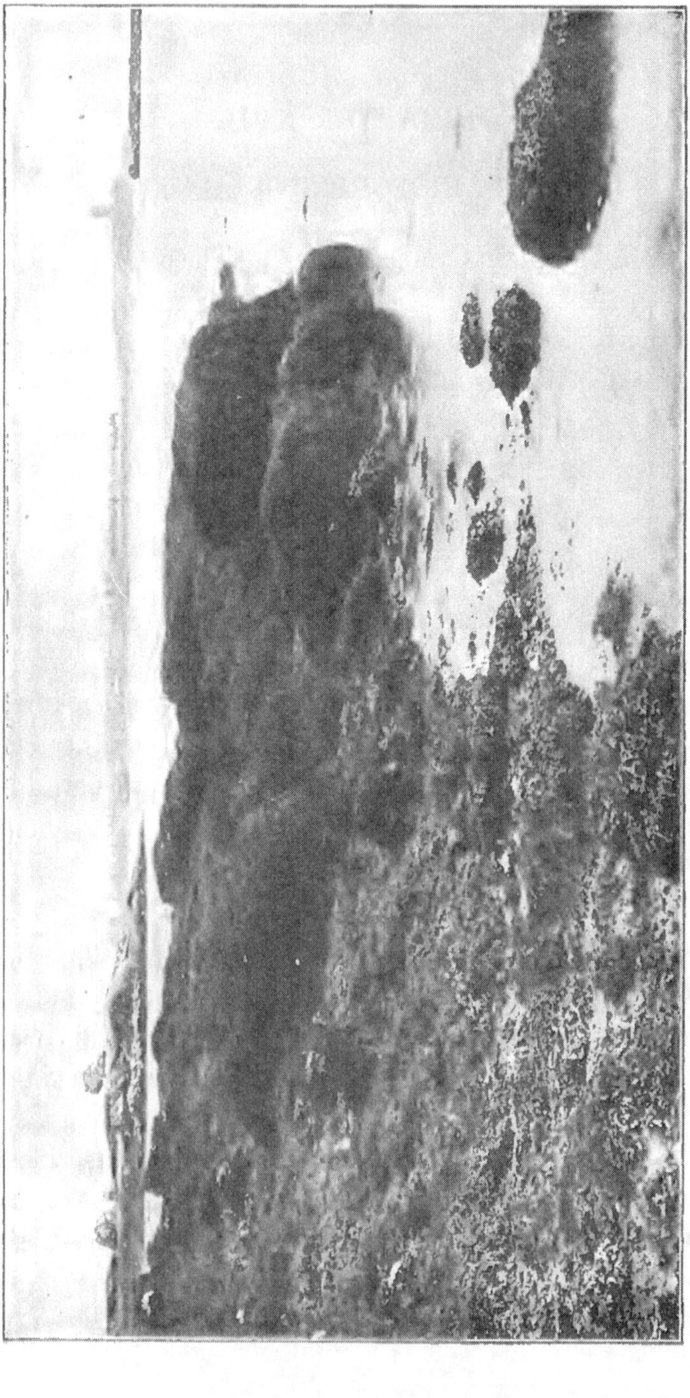

FIG. 171.—*Ascophyllum nodosum* (L.) Le Jolis, and *Fucus*. Hunter's Island, New York City. (Photo by M. A. Howe.)

commonly found attached to rocks between the lines of high and low tide, where they are subjected to alternate submersion and exposure (Fig. 171). The Fucaceæ have an added interest because of their economic uses. They serve as food for the inhabitants of the west coast of South America, and in other countries, and are also widely used as fertilizer, and as a source of iodine. They include

FIG. 172.—Portion of plant of *Ascophyllum nodosum*. × 3/8.

some of the largest plants in the ocean, and one of the genera, *Sargassum*, floating on the surface, helps to form the well-known "Sargasso Sea," of the middle Atlantic ocean.

208. Description of Ascophyllum.—The plant body of *Ascophyllum* is a branched thallus, the branches being relatively narrow (from ¼ to ½ inch), several feet in length, and interrupted at frequent intervals by swellings or nodes, which are air sacs, and add greatly to the buoyancy of the plant in water (Fig. 172). Many of the Fucaceæ possess two kinds of branches, more or less distinct from each other—long branches and short branches, or spurs. This is a phenomenon which occurs in several groups of plants,

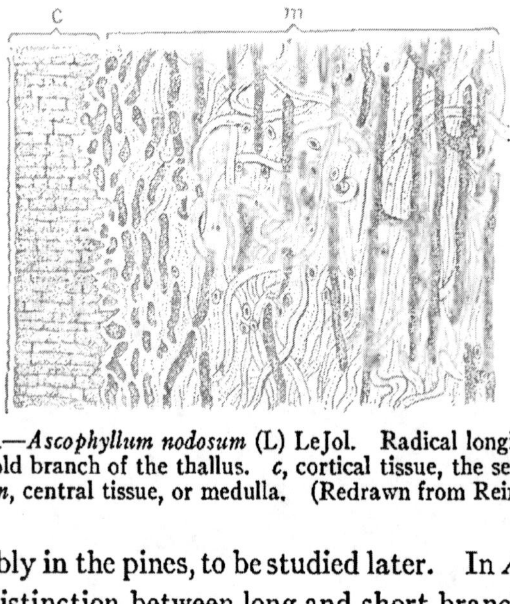

FIG. 173.—*Ascophyllum nodosum* (L) LeJol. Radical longitudinal section of an old branch of the thallus. *c*, cortical tissue, the seat of photosynthesis; *m*, central tissue, or medulla. (Redrawn from Reinke.)

and notably in the pines, to be studied later. In *Ascophyllum* the distinction between long and short branches is not as strongly marked as in some other forms, such, for example, as *Scaberia*. The short branches have enlarged tips, which somewhat resemble the swellings of the main stem. The plant has a "rubbery" appearance, with a smooth, slippery surface, and is usually attached to rocks by a "hold-fast" organ.

209. Anatomy.—A study of the internal structure (Fig. 173) reveals two systems of tissues, more or less clearly distinct:

1. The *cortex*, composed of several external layers of cells, somewhat resembling, in arrangement, the palisade parenchyma of the leaf and, like the latter, having the function of photosynthesis. The outer portion of this layer is further loosely differentiated into an *epidermoidal* tissue, but there is no true epidermis. The outer cell-walls of this layer, forming the external surface of the plant, possess a thick layer of cuticle. The cells of the cortex retain their embryonic character for a long time, and by successive divisions favor the growth of the branch in thickness.

2. The medulla, or central tissue, is composed of cells arranged for the most part in rows, so as to form filaments. This tissue serves chiefly for the conduction of liquids. The walls of its cells are mucilaginous and much swollen, except at certain small pits, the "sieve tubes," closed by a perforated membrane.

210. Photosynthesis.—The cells of the cortex possess several chromoplasts or chromatophores, each containing chlorophyll, by which photosynthesis is possible; but, in addition to chlorophyll, the chromatophores contain also a brown pigment (*phycophæin*), which masks the chlorophyll, and explains the external color that gives the name Phæophyceæ to the family.

211. Vegetative Multiplication.—Vegetative multiplication does not occur in *Ascophyllum*, nor in most of the genera of Phæophyceæ. In the few genera where it has been observed, it is accomplished by a fragmentation of the plant body, or by the death of the older part of the thallus. The pieces thus set free may develop new plants, but these usually remain sterile.

212. Sexual Reproduction.—The reproductive organs of *Ascophyllum* (Fig. 174) are borne in chambers (*conceptacles*) beneath the surface of the enlargements at the tips of the short branches. Since the branches bear

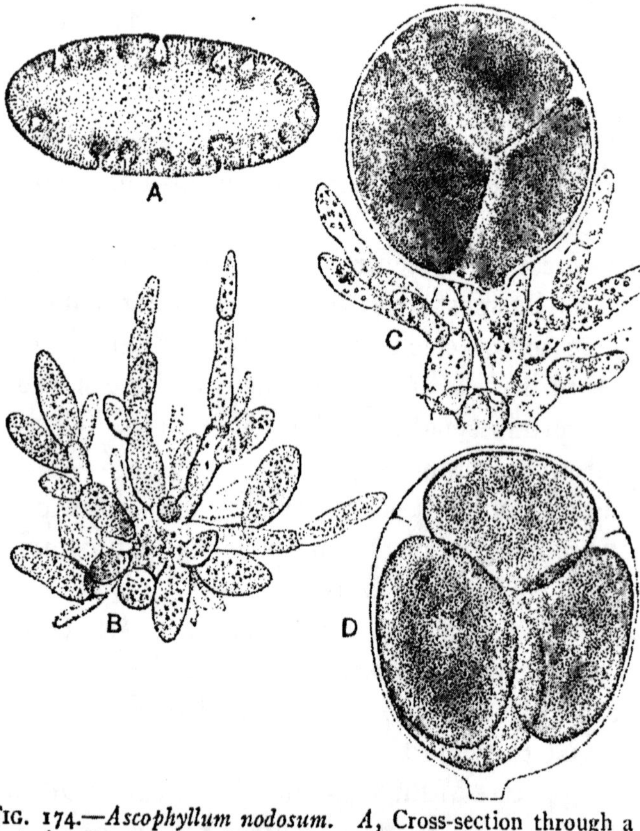

FIG. 174.—*Ascophyllum nodosum*. *A*, Cross-section through a female receptacle; *B*, spermagonia; *C*, ripe oögonium; *D*, eggs, freed from the oögonium, but still enclosed by the separated inner layer of the oögonial wall. (Redrawn from Thuret and Bornet.)

the gametes they are sometimes referred to as gametophores. These chambers open to the exterior by short, narrow canals, the openings of which may be easily seen on the surface of the swollen tips. The inner surface of the conceptacles is covered with more or less branched hairs (*paraphyses*), and associated with these hairs are the organs that bear the sperms and eggs. In some species of Fucaceæ both sperms and eggs are borne in the same conceptacle, and the plant is, accordingly, *monœcious*. This is the case with one of the species of *Fucus* (*F. platycarpus*). In other species, such as those of *Ascophyllum* and *Fucus vesiculosus*, sperms and eggs are borne in separate conceptacles, and even on separate plants, in which latter case the species are *diœcious*.

213. Gametangia.—The organs that bear either kind of gametes (sperms or eggs) are termed *gametangia*. The female gametangium differs in a very fundamental manner from the complex archegonium of the mosses and ferns, for it consists of only one cell, called the *oögonium*. The male gametangium, or *spermagonium*, is likewise unicellular, and the wall is composed of two layers, an inner and an outer layer. The spermagonia are in reality modified branches of the hairs that line the conceptacles. The oögonia are not attached to the hairs, but directly to the inner surface of the conceptacle by a short unicellular stalk.

214. Gametes.—The male gametes, or sperms, are formed by successive divisions of the protoplast of the unicellular spermagonium. Like those of the liverworts and mosses, they bear two long cilia, attached to the side. They also possess a pigment body, usually reddish in color. The oögonia of *Ascophyllum* commonly bear only four eggs, organized out of the protoplast of the oögonium, but in rare cases three or five. In some genera (*e.g.*, *Fucus*) there are eight eggs. The nucleus of the oögonium cell usually divides into eight daughter-nuclei, but in

Ascophyllum all except four (or the exceptional three or five) fail to organize daughter-cells about themselves, and abort. Forms having the full complement of eight eggs, are, therefore, considered more primitive than those with a less number.

215. Fertilization.—The eggs are never fertilized while in the oögonia, nor even while in the conceptacle. The walls of the oögonium burst, and the eggs pass out into the surrounding water. They are covered with a thick layer of mucilaginous substance, and by means of some material, not definitely known, they attract the sperms that happen to have been discharged at the same time and near the same place. No other case is known in plants where the difference in size between egg and sperm is so great as in the Fucaceæ (Fig. 175). The sperms *swarm* about an egg, and finally one of them enters it and its nucleus unites with that of the egg, thus completing fertilization. Soon after fertilization the oösperm or zygote becomes surrounded by a delicate cellulose wall, the *fertilization-membrane.* The setting free of the egg before fertilization marks a lower stage of development than is found in the mosses and ferns.

The process of fertilization in *Fucus* may be easily observed by placing mature eggs and sperms together in sea-water in a watch glass, under the microscope. The sperms, attracted by the chemical stimulus of the substance excreted by the egg, swim toward it, and within about five minutes large numbers of them have become attached to its surface. By the vigorous lashing of their cilia the egg is set in vigorous motion. One of the sperms succeeds in penetrating the cytoplasm of the egg, and reaches its nucleus. The fusion of the two nuclei may occur within 10 minutes after the gametes have been placed together in the water. After the formation of the

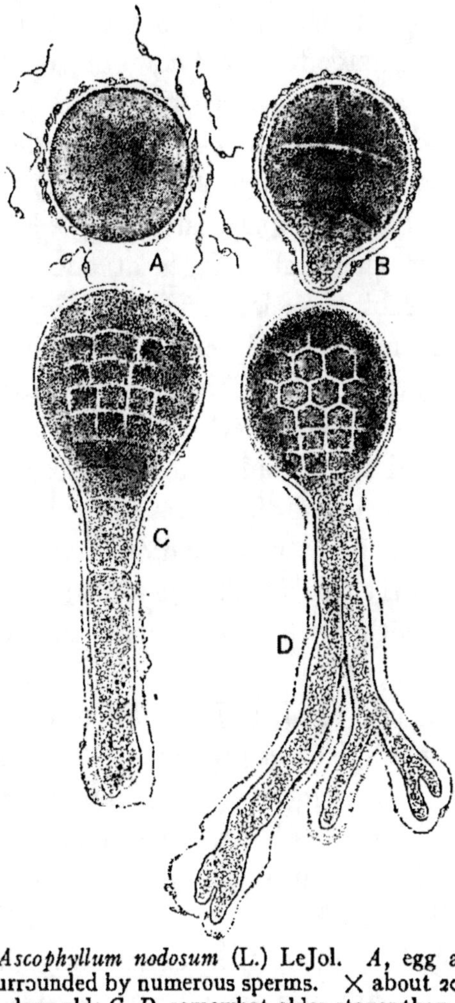

FIG. 175.—*Ascophyllum nodosum* (L.) LeJol. *A*, egg at the time of fertilization, surrounded by numerous sperms. × about 200; *B*, oösperm germinating, 6 days old; *C*, *D*, somewhat older stages than *B*. (Redrawn from Thuret and Bornet.)

fertilization-membrane the sperms seem to avoid the oösperm, quite as though they were repelled by some substance formed at its surface.

216. The Result of Fertilization.—(*a*) The immediate result of fertilization is *physical*—the formation of the fertilization-membrane. Just how this is accomplished is not clearly understood. We know, of course, that the surface of the egg, as in every free mass of protoplasm, acts as a semipermeable membrane or surface, allowing some substances in solution, but not all, to pass through by osmosis. It has been suggested that, when the sperm enters the egg, chemical changes at once occur, which alter the permeability of its surface-membrane, thus permitting, for the first time, the exosmosis of some substance (or substances) which become transformed into the fertilization-membrane on contact with the sea-water. It may be, of course, that the substance composing the membrane is not formed until the sperm enters the egg. However it may be caused, the formation of the membrane is a necessary antecedent to all subsequent changes in the fertilized egg; without its formation the egg dies and disintegrates.

(*b*) The ultimate result of fertilization, as noted in the preceding chapters, is *biological*—the intermingling of the germ-plasms of the egg and sperm, involving the fusion of the two nuclei, the doubling of the chromosome number, and the combination, in one zygote, of the inheritances from two individuals.[1]

217. Artificial Fertilization.—Considering that the formation of the fertilization-membrane is purely physical, biologists began to reason that it ought to be possible to induce it artificially. The experiment was first successfully made by a zoologist, Loeb, with the eggs of sea-urchins

[1] The commingling of the two inheritances was called, by Weismann, *amphimixis*.

and other marine animals. In 1913 it was successfully accomplished by Overton with the eggs of *Fucus*. The eggs were dipped for about a minute, or a minute and a half to two minutes, in a mixture of 50 cc. of sea-water plus 3 cc. of a very weak solution of acetic, butyric, or other fatty acid, and then transferred to normal sea-water. This treatment caused the formation of the fertilization-membrane, quite as in natural fertilization by the sperm. If, after the formation of the membrane, the eggs are placed for 30 minutes in *hypertonic* sea-water (50 cc. of normal sea-water plus 8 to 10 cc. of a weak solution of sodium chloride (common salt), or potassium chloride), and then back into normal sea-water, the eggs begin to divide and continue to develop into young plants. The question as to the chromosome number in the cells of plants formed by artificial fertilization is of very great interest, but has not yet been investigated.

218. Germination of the Oösperm.—After either natural or artificial fertilization the young zygote begins at once to divide, without any period of rest. Of the two cells formed by the first division, one gives rise to the hold-fast organ, by which the new plant is attached to the rocks, while the other develops into the main body of the plant, which resembles the parent plant in all external characters (Fig. 175).

219. Reduction.—As always in normal fertilization, the nucleus of the oösperm is diploid, and the *Ascophyllum* plant that develops from it is also diploid. It is therefore the sporophytic generation. At the end of the first two nuclear divisions of the spermagonia and oögonia, reduction has been accomplished, and the four nuclei that result are haploid. They therefore belong to the haploid or gametophytic generation. In other words they have the same value as spores, and the one-celled stage of the spermagonia and oögonia the same value as spore-mother-cells.

220. Female Gametophyte.—Each of the four cells resulting from the reduction-divisions in the oögonial protoplast divides again, producing a total of eight cells, which constitute a simplified gametophyte. No further divisions occur in the oögonia. In some of the Fucaceæ (*e.g.*, *Fucus vesiculosus*) each of these eight daughter-cells functions as a female gamete or egg; but in *Ascophyllum*, and a few other species, part of the daughter-cells, as stated above, disintegrate or abort, leaving only from one to five. In *Ascophyllum nodosum* one-half of them abort, leaving only four eggs. The female gametophyte is thus seen to be reduced to merely its gametes.

221. Male Gametophyte.—Each of the four cells resulting from the reduction-divisions of the spermagonial protoplast undergoes four divisions in succession, resulting in 64 cells or a total of 256, all of which develop into a male gamete, or sperm. The four daughter-cells, therefore represent a very greatly reduced male gametophyte.

222. Simplification of the Gametophytes.—The important point to note in connection with the life history of *Ascophyllum* is, not only the great simplification of the gametophyte, but the fact that it is reduced to nothing but fertile or reproductive cells. Each of the four spores gives rise only to gametes; no sterile cells, or gametophytic plant bodies are produced.

223. Gametophyte or Sporophyte.—In light of the facts above related, the question as to the real nature of the plant body of *Ascophyllum* becomes of very great interest. Its cells possess the double or sporophytic number of chromosomes, but it bears organs (spermagonia and oögonia) that ultimately contain gametes. Is it, therefore, a gametophyte or a sporophyte? For a long time it was considered a gametophyte, but a clear understanding of the divisions that take place in the gametangia, accompanied by reduction, and the fact that the body-cells are all diploid, lead unmistakably to the conclusion that it is a sporophyte. We have seen that the protoplasts of the young spermagonium and the young oögonium are in reality equivalent or analogous to spore-mother-cells, and that, in each case, their four daughter-cells, with their reduced number of chromosomes, are functionally equivalent or analogous to spores. The spermagonia and oögonia, therefore, which seem at first thought to be sexual organs—simplified antheridia and archegonia—come to be, finally, more truly comparable to sporangia, from which the spores are not set free, as spores, but, while still in the spore-case, develop into either a male or a female gametophyte reduced to nothing but gametes.

The real nature of *Ascophyllum* (and of the other Fucaceæ, for that matter) is just opposite from what a superficial examination would lead us to infer, and we have, in this low form, a condition just the reverse from what is found in the liverworts, mosses, and ferns; in other words, a prominent sporophyte, bearing a greatly simplified gametophyte, that lives upon it as a parasite deriving all of its nourishment from the sporophyte.

224. Alternation of Generations.—Although the gametophytic generation is reduced to its lowest terms, the fundamental fact of alternation is not affected. As soon as the gametes are set free fertilization takes place, producing a fertilized egg, with, of course, the double or diploid number of chromosomes. Every cell of the sporeling, resulting from the germination of the oösperm, and every cell of the mature plant into which it develops, possesses the double number, up to the first two divisions of the

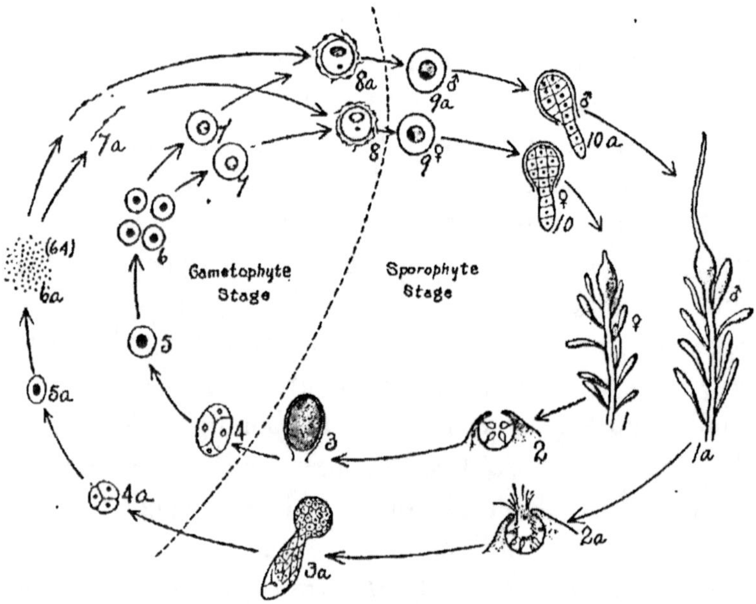

FIG. 176.—Diagram of life-cycle of *Ascophyllum nodosum*.

young gametangia, when reduction gives rise to gametophytic cells. The fusion of these—egg with sperm—in fertilization restores the double or sporophytic number and so on in cycle after cycle (Fig. 176).

225. Diagram of Life History.—The successive steps in the life cycle of *Ascophyllum* may be briefly summarized as follows:

OUTLINE OF LIFE HISTORY OF ASCOPHYLLUM

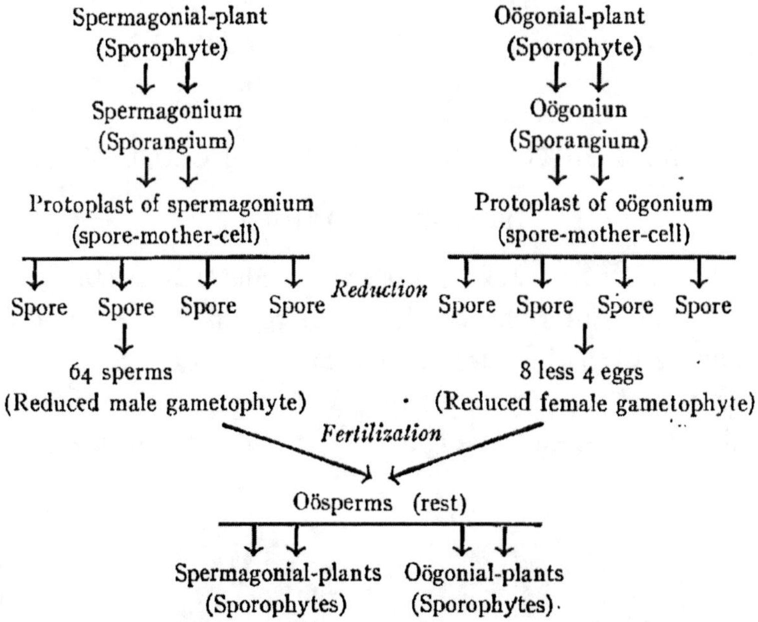

226. The Cause of Sex.—One of the many very interesting things revealed by a study of the life history of *Ascophyllum nodosum* is the fact that part of the fertilized eggs give rise to plants that bear only male gametes, and the remainder to plants that bear only female gametes. Since the fundamentally different individuals develop under identically the same environmental influences, we are forced to the inference that the difference lies in the fertilized eggs themselves. Some of them appear to be male-producing, others female-producing. In what does this fundamental difference consist? Here is a very important problem, but further consideration of it must be postponed until Chapter XXII.

CHAPTER XVIII

LIFE HISTORIES OF ALGÆ (CONCLUDED)

DICTYOTA DICHOTOMA

227. Habitat.—Like *Ascophyllum* and *Fucus*, *Dictyota dichotoma* grows chiefly along the ocean margins in the zone between the lines of high and low tide. It is thus subjected to alternate wetting and drying, and to rhythmically alternating changes of light and temperature. It

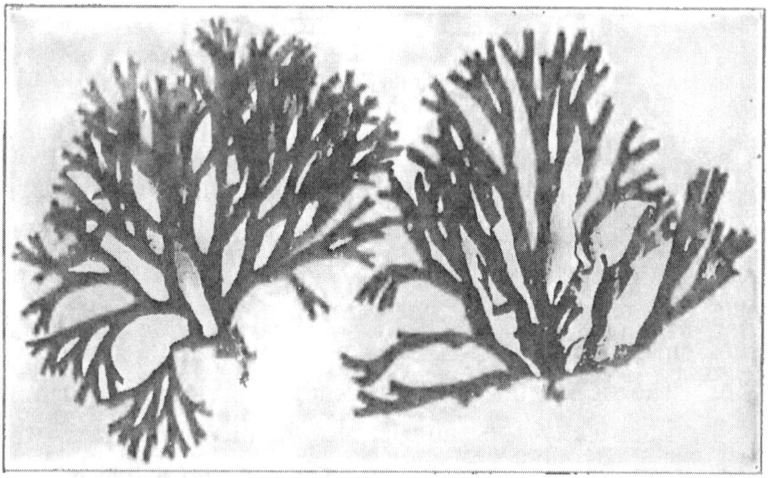

FIG. 177.—*Dictyota dichotoma.* Left, sporogonial plant; right spermagonial (gametophytic) plant. (After W. D. Hoyt.)

is found from as far north as the middle of the Scandinavian peninsula to about 40° south latitude.

228. Description.—The plant body (Fig. 177) is a thallus, flat, and branching profusely by forking at the tips, *i.e.*, *dichotomously* (whence the name *dichotoma*), but showing no differentiation into anything like stem and leaf. One end of the plant is differentiated into a special branching organ, the *hold-fast*, by which it becomes attached to rocks, shells, and other convenient solids. As in *Fucus*, again, the green chlorophyll is masked by a brown pigment, which indicates the relationship of the plant to the Brown seaweeds, or Phæophyceæ. There are two kinds of branches—cylindrical ones which are sterile, and others more strap-shaped, or ribbon-like, which eventually bear the reproductive organs.

Vegetative multiplication may occur by the separation of portions of the thallus, which may become established as independent plants. In some species of *Dictyota*, specially differentiated bodies have been noted, resembling the brood-buds or gemmæ, such as occur in some of the liverworts and mosses.

229. Reproduction.—With reference to reproductive organs, three kinds of plants occur:

1. Plants bearing asexual spores only (asexual).
2. Plants bearing oögonia only (female).
3. Plants bearing antheridia only (male).

But the most interesting feature in this connection is that *the plants of all three groups look very much alike*, except, of course, for their different kinds of reproductive organs, and for unimportant individual variations.

Oögonia and antheridia are both produced *from surface cells*. The surface cell first divides into a smaller stalk-cell, and a larger external one, rich in protoplasm, which forms the gametes. The protoplast of the oögonium does not divide, as in *Ascophyllum* and *Fucus*, but develops into only one very large egg; while the protoplast of the antheridium continues to divide until as many as 1,500 or more sperms are formed in each one. Since the antheridia occur in groups of *sori* (Figs. 178 and 179), the total num-

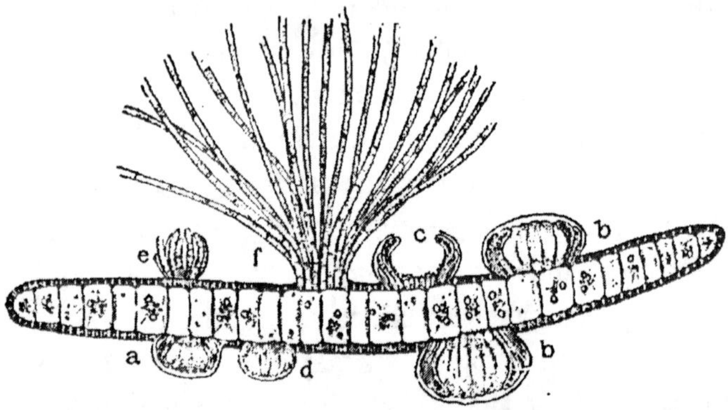

FIG. 178.—*Dictyota dichotoma.* Cross-section of a male thallus, showing the comparative development of the antheridial sori, and the tufts of hairs which are scattered over the frond. *a*, young sorus; *b*, older sorus; *c*, sorus opened. The sperms have been set free. There remain only the cells which form the involucre. *d*, tuft of very young hairs; *e*, tuft of older hairs; *f*, the same fully developed. × about 35. (After Thuret.)

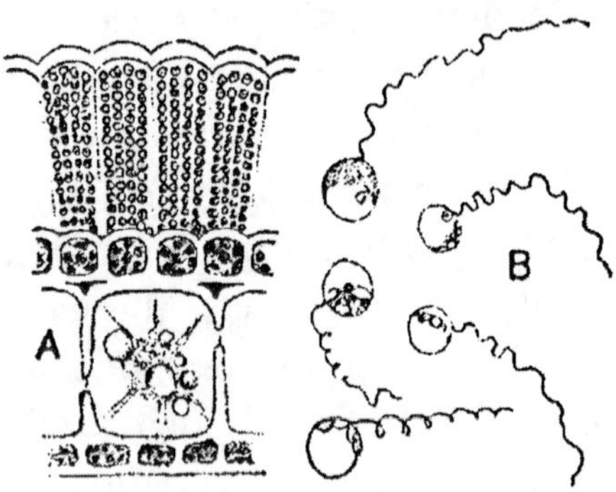

FIG. 179.—*Dictyota dichotoma.* *A*, vertical section through portion of sorus, showing antheridia; *B*, sperms. (Redrawn from J. Lloyd Williams.)

ber of sperms formed on one plant, or even in one sorus, is enormous. The oögonia may occur singly or in groups (Fig. 180).

230. Discharge of Gametes.—As in *Ascophyllum*, both kinds of gametes are set free at the same time, before fertilization. Recent studies have disclosed the very interesting fact that their discharge occurs at rhythmic intervals of about two weeks, synchronizing with the periods of high and low tide. The advantages of this, if any, are not apparent, and the periodicity persists in plants placed in jars of sea-water in the laboratory, and even with branches newly developed in the laboratory, and thus

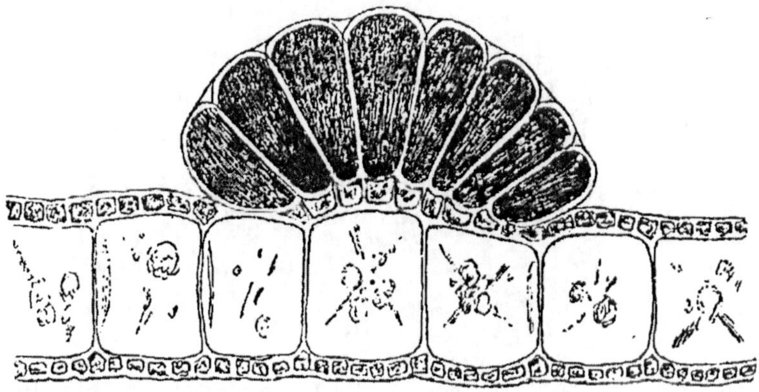

FIG. 180.—*Dictyota dichotoma* (Huds.) Lamx. Longitudinal section of an oögonial sorus. (After Bornet and Thuret.)

never (as branches) subjected to the variations of the tide. So close, however, is the harmony between tidal periods and discharge of gametes, that the exact day of their discharge, at any given station, can be predicted (with an error, at most, of only one day) by consulting the tide-tables for the given station.

231. Fertilization.—From the freshly liberated eggs there diffuses through the water some unknown substance which attracts the sperms. The latter respond to this stimulus by swimming toward the egg. One of them enters it, and makes its way through the cytoplasm to the egg-nucleus (Fig. 181), with which it fuses, thus completing the act of fertilization. The other sperms come to rest outside the egg, and finally disintegrate. If eggs liberated at different periods occur in the water together, the sperms will swim toward those liberated last, in preference to the others. As soon as fertilization has been accomplished, the oösperm begins to divide, and develops into a new plant, which finally comes to resemble externally the ones that bore the antheridia and oögonia.

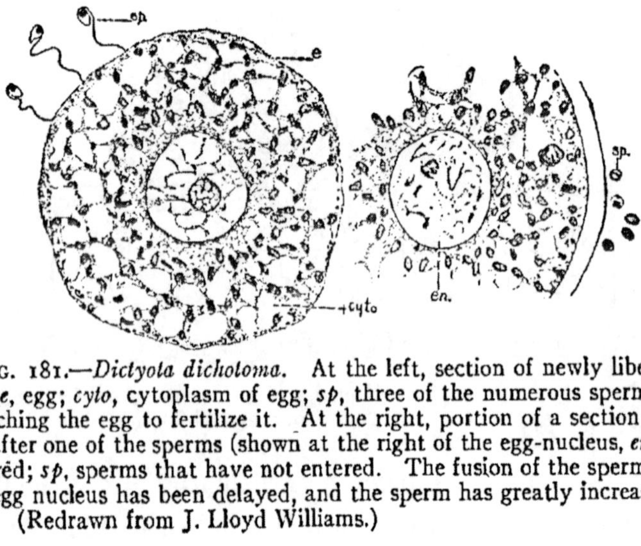

FIG. 181.—*Dictyota dichotoma.* At the left, section of newly liberated egg; *e*, egg; *cyto*, cytoplasm of egg; *sp*, three of the numerous sperms approaching the egg to fertilize it. At the right, portion of a section of an egg after one of the sperms (shown at the right of the egg-nucleus, *en*) has entered; *sp*, sperms that have not entered. The fusion of the sperm with the egg nucleus has been delayed, and the sperm has greatly increased in size. (Redrawn from J. Lloyd Williams.)

232. Asexual Reproduction.—The plants that develop from fertilized eggs never bear antheridia and oögonia, but non-motile, asexual spores only. These are set free at irregular intervals, and never at rhythmic periods like the gametes. They are produced by two successive divisions of a spore-mother-cell, and thus occur in groups of four (tetrads); the plants that bear them are commonly referred to as *tetrasporic plants.* When the tetraspores are set free they soon become attached to some solid object, and, like the fertilized eggs, develop into plants that externally resemble, at maturity, those bearing tetraspores. Thus, *the plants produced by the fertilized eggs and by the tetraspores closely resemble each other in all vegetative characters;* they differ externally only in the kind of reproductive organs they bear.

233. Alternation of Generations.—Although the *Dictyota* plants developed from zygotes and spores look alike,

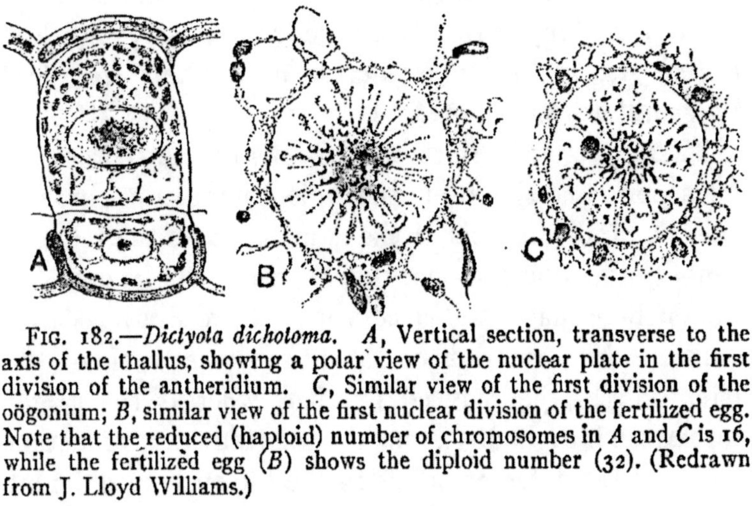

FIG. 182.—*Dictyota dichotoma.* *A*, Vertical section, transverse to the axis of the thallus, showing a polar view of the nuclear plate in the first division of the antheridium. *C*, Similar view of the first division of the oögonium; *B*, similar view of the first nuclear division of the fertilized egg. Note that the reduced (haploid) number of chromosomes in *A* and *C* is 16, while the fertilized egg (*B*) shows the diploid number (32). (Redrawn from J. Lloyd Williams.)

it is obvious that the products of the tetraspore, since they bear gametes, and never spores, are gametophytes; and the products of the fertilized egg, since they bear spores only, and never gametes, are sporophytes. These facts have only recently been established by careful experimental cultures. There is thus a true alternation of generations, although, in marked contrast to the ferns and mosses, the plant bodies of the two generations are vegetatively alike. Obviously we would expect all the cells of the gametophyte to bear the reduced or haploid number of chromosomes, and all the cells of the zygote or sporophyte, the diploid number. Such is the case. Fig. 182,C, shows a section of an oögonium with the nucleus in its first division, and the number of chromosomes (16) may be easily counted. In Fig. 182, A, is shown the dividing nucleus of the antheridium also with 16 chromosomes. In the fertilized egg (Fig. 182, B) the diploid number (32) may readily be counted. Since *Dictyota* is diœcious, we must infer that the tetraspores, though looking alike externally, are fundamentally different internally, since *part of them give rise to antheridial or male plants, and part to oögonial or female plants.*

234. Reduction.—Since all the cells of the sporophyte (tetrasporic plant) contain the diploid number of chromosomes, and all the cells of the gametophytes the reduced number, the question naturally arises, where does reduction take place? It occurs in the two divisions that result in the formation of the tetraspores; each of the latter possess the reduced number, whereas the spore-mother-cell is diploid. From this we learn that reduction may occur at different points in the life-cycle in different forms. In *Ascophyllum* it occurs in the nuclear divisions immediately preceding the formation of the gametes; in *Dictyota*, immediately preceding the formation of the spores, while between reduction and the formation of gametes occur the innumerable cell-divisions that give rise to the body of the gametophyte.

235. Life-cycle of Dictyota.—The life-cycle of *Dictyota* may be diagrammed thus:

OUTLINE OF LIFE HISTORY OF DICTYOTA

Antheridial-plant (Male gametophyte)		Oögonial-plant (Female gametophyte)
↓		↓
Antheridium		Oögonium
↓		↓
Sperm	*Fertilization*	Egg

↘ ↙

Oösperm (zygote)

↓↓

Tetrasporic-plant (Sporophyte)

↓↓

Sporangium

↓↓

Spore-mother-cell

↓	↓	↓	↓	} *Reduction*
Tetra-spore	Tetra-spore	Tetra-spore	Tetra-spore	
↓	↓	↓	↓	
Male gameto-phyte	Male gameto-phyte	Female gameto-phyte	Female gameto phyte	

236. Effect of Environment.—How is the similarity in external appearance of the alternating generations of *Dictyota* to be explained? We cannot say for certain. The two generations start from reproductive cells (zygotes and spores) that are profoundly unlike in their internal organization, but it must be borne in mind that both generations develop under practically identical external conditions—the surrounding ocean-water, with alternate exposure and immersion at low and high tides. This would tend to influence the plant bodies alike, and has been suggested by some botanists as an explanation of the resemblance of the two kinds of generations. In the case of ferns and mosses the environment of the two generations is not alike. The sporophyte, for example, begins life as a parasite on the gametophyte, while the gametophyte leads an independent existence from the start. The reader may also recall other differences. The question we have here raised, however, is a very fundamental one, and will be further discussed in Chapter XXII.

ULOTHRIX

237. Habitat.—The genus *Ulothrix* occurs everywhere, from pole to pole, in fresh water.

238. Description.—The plant body (Fig. 262) is usually a simple thread of cells, though in exceptional cases the cell-divisions result in a *cell-plate* instead of a thread.[1] All the cells are similar in appearance and structure, except the basal one, by which the plant is attached to some solid body. This cell is somewhat larger than the others, possesses less pigment, and is suitably modified to serve as an organ of attachment, or hold-fast. The protoplast of each cell possesses one nucleus, surrounded by the green, cylindrical chloroplast. No other pigment occurs, and therefore *Ulothrix* belongs to the Chlorophyceæ, or green algæ. Photosynthesis, of course, takes place, and a portion of the photosynthate may become transformed into starch, the presence of which is easily demonstrated by the usual test with iodine.

239. Asexual Reproduction.—Every cell of the plant, except the hold-fast, is capable of functioning as a reproductive cell, and two methods of reproduction are common. In one case the entire protoplast of a cell

[1] These two forms of plant bodies are sometimes designated by the terms "linear aggregate" (a filament) and "superficial aggregate" (a plate).

becomes organized into from one to eight motile spores (zoöspores, or swarm-spores), each with *four* cilia and a red "eye-spot." The zoöspore escapes by swimming through a small opening in the cell-wall, attaches itself by its ciliate end, and by a series of cell-divisions produces a new filament like the one from which it came. In this case it is evident that the zoöspore, reproducing without cell-fusion, is an asexual spore, and that the mother-cell from which it came functioned as a sporangium.

240. Sexual Reproduction.—Other cells of the same filament that produced the asexual zoöspores, may, by successive nuclear and cell-divisions, become divided into as many as 16 to 64, or even more, independent motile cells, each with a red "eye-spot," but with only *two* cilia. Like the zoöspores, they escape by swimming through an opening in the wall of the mother-cell. Occasionally one of them comes to rest and begins germination, but the process never continues far enough to produce a new plant. More commonly, two of these cells come together and fuse, showing that they are, in reality, gametes. Since the gametes are similar in size they are termed equal gametes, or *isogametes*. The fusion of two isogametes is called *conjugation*, to distinguish it from the fusion of unequal gametes; it is essentially the same as fertilization. Whether or not reduction occurs, in the nuclear and cell-divisions that result in the formation of the isogametes, is not known.

241. Germination.—After the fusion of the gametes the zygote at once begins to increase in size, but soon its cell-wall becomes thickened, and then the protoplast divides into a number of *swarm-spores*, each of which, when set free, may develop into a new plant.

OUTLINE OF LIFE HISTORY OF ULOTHRIX

Plant Body
(Undifferentiated into gametophyte and sporophyte stages)

↓↓	↓↓
Physiological Sporangium	Physiological Gametangium
↓↓	↓ ↓ } *Reduction*
Zoöspore	Isogamete — Isogamete
↓↓	*Conjugation* ↘ ↙
Plant Body (Undifferentiated into gametophyte and sporophyte stages)	Zygote
	↓↓
	Swarm-spores
	↓↓
	Plant Body

PLEUROCOCCUS

242. Habitat.—Everyone is familiar with the green layer found on the outer surface of the bark of trees, on

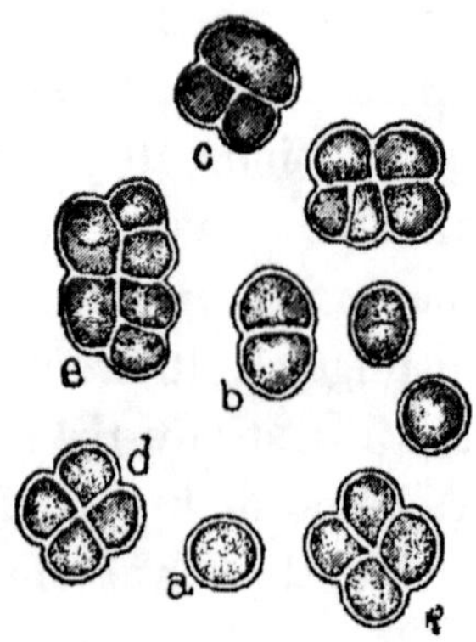

FIG. 183.—Individual plants of green slime (*Pleurococcus vulgaris*), showing the tendency of the cells to remain attached after cell-divisions, thus causing transitions from a one-celled to a multi-cellular plant.

wooden fences, and the moist shaded surfaces of stone steps or rocks. Careful observation will show that this crool is largely due to the presence of countless numbers of a tiny green plant, called *Pleurococcus*, usually of the species *Pleurococcus vulgaris*. The individual plants are so small that they may be seen only with the aid of the microscope (Fig. 183). An examination of the trees in any given locality will disclose the fact that *Pleurococcus* prefers one side of the tree to the other, and that the choice of sides has a direct relation to light, temperature, or moisture—one or all.

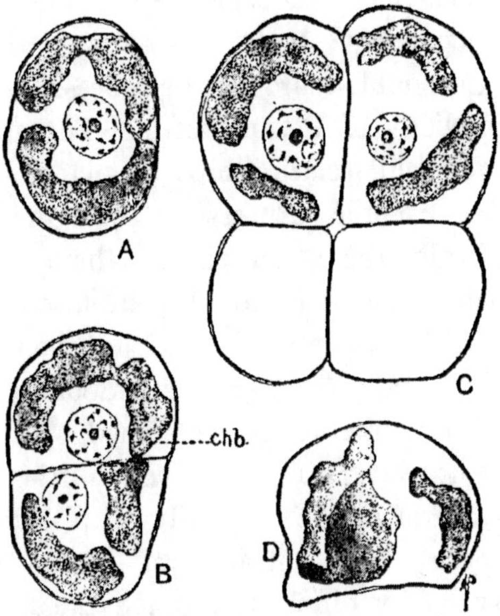

FIG. 184.—*Pleurococcus vulgaris*. Sections of one-, two-, and four-celled plants, showing the nuclei and the large chlorophyll bodies (*chb*) to which the green color of the plants is due. In *D*, the larger chloroplast is shown in perspective. (Camera lucida drawings from a microscopic preparation by E. W. Olive.)

243. Structure.—No plant structure could be much simpler than that of *Pleurococcus*, for the plant body is a single cell, the simplest organic unit capable of independent existence. The protoplast possesses a well-defined nucleus and a chloroplast, and is surrounded by a cellulose cell-wall (Fig. 184). We have here, in fact, a *unicellular organism.*

244. Reproduction.—The reproduction of *Pleurococcus* consists merely of the processes of cell-division, and the final separation of the daughter-cells. The latter may adhere until several divisions have occured, but eventually the middle layer of the cell-wall common to the two adjacent daughter-cells is dissolved, probably by an enzyme. The cells then separate from one another, and become independent plants, increasing in size, and soon repeating the simple reproductive process just described.

245. Simplicity of Pleurococcus.—The structure, life-processes, and life-relationships of plants could hardly find a more simple expression than in *Pleurococcus.* Morphologically the green plant is here reduced to its lowest terms. There is no differentiation into parts—no hold-fast, roots, or rhizoids, no shoot, no special reproductive organs. From the standpoint of physiology, every essential function is performed by the one cell—absorption of water and dissolved nutrient substances by osmosis through the cell-wall and plasma-membrane; photosynthesis, with entrance of carbon dioxide and exit of oxygen by diffusion through the membrane and cell-wall; respiration, with the accompanying exchange of gases in the same way; digestion, assimilation, and growth, resulting finally in reproduction by the division of the entire plant body into new individuals. So far as known, such processes as cell-fusion (in fertilization or conjugation), reduction, and alternation of generations are entirely absent. *Pleurococcus* is a generalized plant, with almost no division of physiological labor. At one time the entire plant body functions vegetatively, that is, for the maintenance of the individual; at another time the entire plant body functions reproductively, that is, for the maintenance of the race to which the individual belongs.

246. Life History of Pleurococcus.—The simple life-history of *Pleurococcus* may be briefly indicated as follows:

OUTLINE OF LIFE HISTORY OF PLEUROCOCCUS

Unicellular plant
↓
Cell-divisions
↓
Temporary cell-aggregates
↓
Separation of daughter-cells

↓	↓	↓	↓
Unicellular plant	Unicellular plant	Unicellular plant	Unicellular plant

CHAPTER XIX

LIFE HISTORIES OF FUNGI

247. The Groups of Fungi.—We are all more or less familiar with fungi, as represented by the common molds, mildews, toadstools, and mushrooms. They are all plants without chlorophyll, and are therefore dependent upon green plants for their nourishment. The Greek word for fungi is *mycetes*, and this word terminates the names of the various groups, as follows:

1. *Phycomycetes*, alga-like fungi; so-called because they closely resemble certain algæ, except for the lack of chlorophyll.
2. *Ascomycetes*, sac-fungi; so-called because their asexual spores are formed in tiny sacs (*asci*)
3. *Basidiomycetes*, with spores borne on little club-shaped hyphæ, or *basidia*. Include the smuts, rusts, and mushrooms.

AN ALGA-LIKE FUNGUS (RHIZOPUS)

248. Habitat.—Everyone is acquainted with "bread mold," a plant without chlorophyll, and having a filamentous plant body. There are many kinds of filamentous fungi, more or less closely related to *Rhizopus*, and growing on various substances or "substrata." They all agree in at least three points: (1) they are always filamentous; (2) they never possess chlorophyll; (3) they always grow on some organic substratum. The substratum is also usually moist. Partly as a result of their presence, the substratum on which they grow is usually disintegrating with decay. From these facts *Rhizopus* is called a *saprophyte*.[1] The most common species is *Rhizopus nigricans*.

249. How Obtained.—*Rhizopus*, or almost any other filamentous fungus, may be readily obtained by sowing its spores on a suitable substratum. But, unlike the higher plants, *Rhizopus* may ordinarily be obtained merely by exposing moist bread, or other nutritive substance, to the air. In the course of time, without one's sowing any spores, colonies of the plant will appear, and this clearly demonstrates the very interesting fact that these spores are always floating in the air in greater or less abundance. When the moist bread is exposed, some of the floating spores come to rest upon it, and there, under favoring conditions of moisture, temperature, and light they germinate, and develop new plants.

250. Description of Plant Body.—The plant body of *Rhizopus* (Fig. 185) consists of a slender, thread-like filament, called the *mycelium*, branching freely, devoid of chlorophyll, and growing over the surface of the substratum. The threads of mycelium are termed *hyphæ*. Careful examination with the microscope discloses the fact that the hyphæ are largely or wholly *aseptate*, that is, not divided by cross-walls or septa. The plant body, therefore, consists of one cell, though there are several to many nuclei distributed through the cytoplasm; such a structure is termed a *coenocyte*.[2]

[1] From the Greek, *sapros* (σαπρός), rotten, + *phyton* (φυτόν), a plant.
[2] Greek, κοινός (*koinos*), common, + κύτος (*kutos*), a hollow (cell).

The protoplasm appears to be *streaming* in a constant current in one direction, and this is thought to be due to the evaporation of water from surfaces more exposed to the air, and the intake of more water from the substratum, by osmosis.

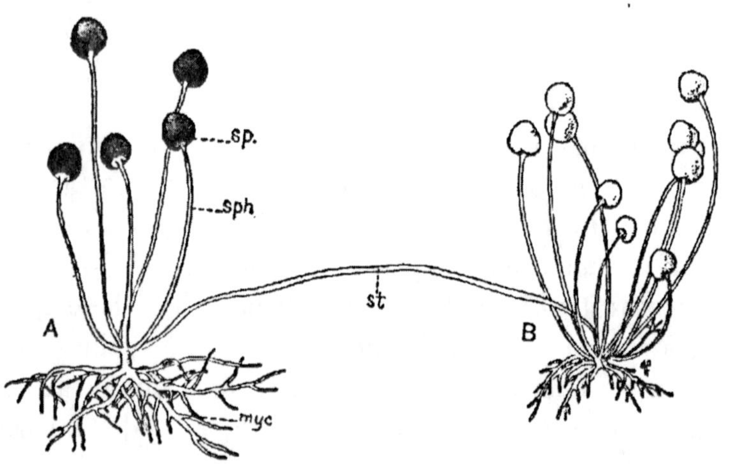

FIG. 185.—Bread mold (*Rhizopus nigricans*). *A*, older plant; *myc*, mycelia; *sph*, sporangiophore; *sp*, sporangium; *st*, stolon produced by *A*, and giving rise at its tip to a new plant, *B*. Greatly enlarged.

251. Secretion of a Powerful Poison.—In the course of some experiments, made in order to determine the cause of sex in the mucors, Blakeslee and Gortner injected into the ear of a healthy rabbit some of the juice, squeezed out of the mycelium of *Rhizopus nigricans*. To their great surprise the animal died almost instantly, before the injection was completed. Further experiments clearly demonstrated that *Rhizopus* contains a powerful poison (or *toxin*), which is soluble in water, but which produces its effect only when introduced into the circulatory system. When this expressed juice was fed to the rabbits, or when they ate the mycelium, no harmful result followed. The discoverers of the toxin suggest that the discovery may possibly throw light on "pellagra" and some of the destructive diseases of cattle, such as "cornstalk-disease," and the "horse-disease," prevalent in some of our western states, and for some time thought to be due to some food-impurity.

252. Vegetative Multiplication.—At various points the mycelium produces one or more upright, aerial hyphæ, 15 to 20 millimeters high, and of larger diameter than the mycelial hyphæ. One or more of these hyphæ eventually bend over and grow for a short time along the surface of the substratum, like the stolons or "runners" of such plants as strawberries. Finally, at their free ends there develop slender hyphæ that penetrate the substratum, like rhizoids, and another group of the larger, aerial hyphæ, one or more of which may repeat the process just described. The formation of these stolons suggested a former name of the plant, *viz.*, *Mucor stolonifer.*

253. Asexual Reproduction.—At the tip of each upright hypha there develops a globular sporangium, and hence the hypha is called a *sporangiophore* (Fig. 186). The protoplasm is constantly streaming up the sporangiophore, getting more and more dense toward the sporangium, and contains large numbers of nuclei. Further down, toward the base of the sporangiophore, the protoplasm becomes thinner and thinner, and the nuclei, fewer in number, finally disintegrate. In the meantime the tip of the sporangiophore increases in size until the globular sporangium is formed, rich in cytoplasm and nuclei. By degrees the protoplasm becomes more dense toward the periphery, and gradually thinner toward the central portion, where large numbers of vacuoles develop. Soon a well-marked cleft separates the denser peripheral protoplasm from the thinner central portion, which now develops into a little column, or *columella* (Fig. 186). In the

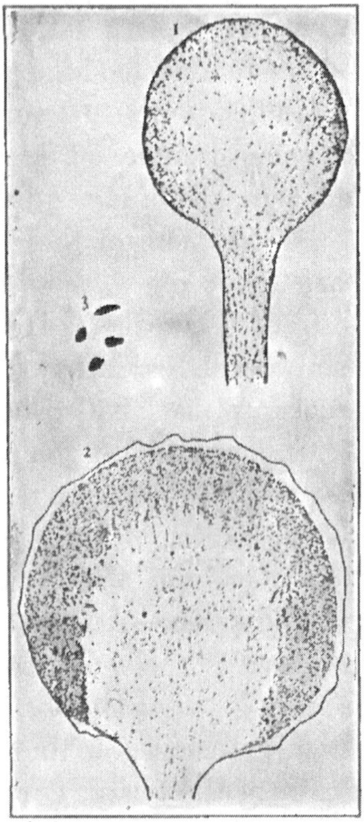

FIG. 186.—*Rhizopus nigricans*: 1, Young sporangium, showing cytoplasm and nuclei streaming up the sporangiophore into the sporangium and out toward the periphery. 2, Sporangium of nearly full size. The differentiation between the dense peripheral and the looser central plasms is clearly shown. Nuclei are still passing from the central to the peripheral regions along the fine strands of cytoplasm. × about 200. (After D. B. Swingle.) (Cf. Figs. 187 and 188.)

meantime innumerable furrows develop in the denser plasm, first at the periphery and then working their way in from the columella cleft. By the time the two sets of furrows meet, the dense protoplasm has been cut up into innumerable, more or less angular masses, each surrounded by a plasma-membrane, and containing from two to six nuclei

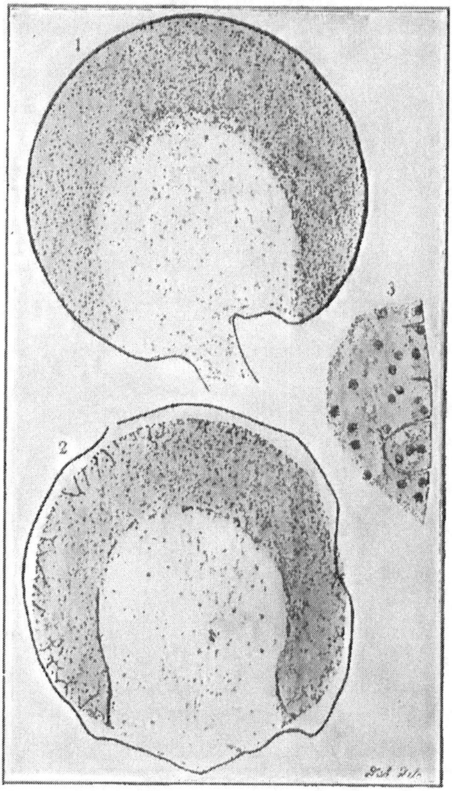

FIG. 187.—*Rhizopus nigricans.* 1, Full-sized sporangium, showing layer of vacuoles nearly formed along the inner surface of the denser plasm, × about 200. 2, Section passing to one side of the sporangiophore, showing columella-cleft being formed by fusion of the vacuoles shown in 1, and by a furrow from the base of the sporangium, × about 200; 3, Detail of another part of same sporangium as shown in 2, showing early cleavage furrows, × about 850. (After D. B. Swingle.) (Cf. Figs. 186 and 188).

each (Fig. 187). These finally become entirely separated from each other, oval in shape, and surrounded by a cellulose wall, having clearly marked ridges (Fig. 188). They are asexual spores, but differ from the spores of ferns, mosses, liverworts, and algæ by usually, if not always, possessing more than one nucleus. They secrete a slimy substance

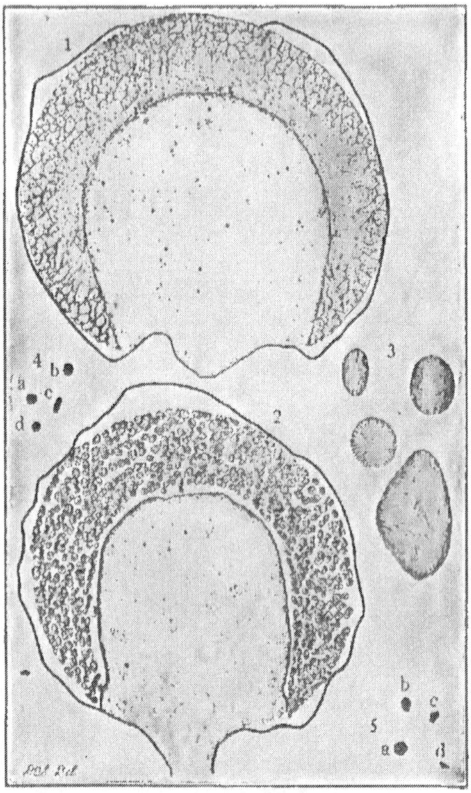

FIG. 188.—*Rhizopus nigricans.* 1, Section of sporangium, showing cleavage of peripheral cytoplasm much further advanced than in Fig. 187. Furrows are here cutting outward from the columella cleft, × about 200; 2, section of sporangium in which the spores are completely formed, rounded up, and surrounded by thin walls. The columella wall is also formed, × about 200; 3, ripe spores in their living condition, showing variations in size, and ridges on their walls, × over 350. (After D. B. Swingle.) (Cf. Figs. 186 and 187.)

in which they are imbedded. When ripe the wall of the sporangium bursts open (Fig. 189), and the spores, thus set free, float away through the air in countless millions. So widely and so thickly are they distributed that a piece of moist bread, or a jar of canned fruit, left exposed for only a brief period, in almost any locality, will, as noted above, soon become "moldy" from the growth of mycelium produced by their germination. On account of the practically universal distribution of "bread

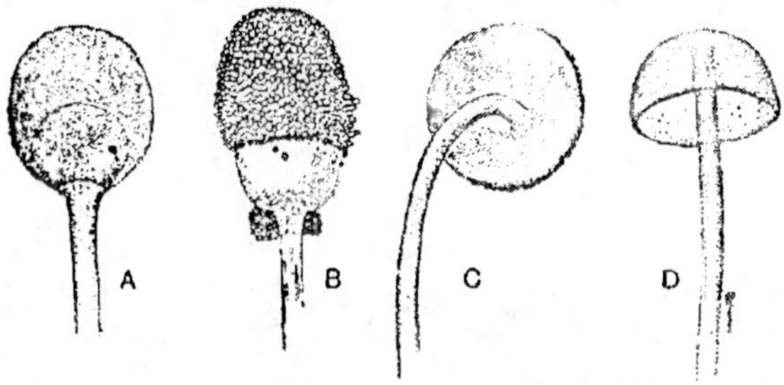

FIG. 189.—*Rhizopus nigricans.* *A*, Young sporangium, showing columella within; *B*, older sporangium, with the wall removed, showing ripe spores covering the columella; *C*, *D*, views of the collapsed columella after dissemination of the spores.

mold" its spores are, of course, commonly present in the air of laboratories, where the mold is a great pest, and has therefore won the appropriate title of "laboratory weed."

254. Sexual Reproduction.—When the hyphæ of mycelia derived from spores of different sex-value are intermingled they frequently develop short lateral branches, which grow out toward each other until their tips come in contact (Fig. 190). The rich protoplasmic contents at the tips are cut off from the remainder of the cœnocytic mycelium, the walls in contact with each other become dissolved,[1] and the two protoplasmic masses fuse. This will be recognized as conjugation; the fusing masses of protoplasm are isogametes, and the cut-off tips of the conjugating branches function as gametangia.

[1] Probably by enzyme action, though this has not been actually demonstrated.

After the zygote is formed, the outer wall thickens and assumes certain external characteristics, easily recognized. It also becomes black as it ripens, and this fact has given rise to the common name, "black mold." In this condition the zygote *rests*, as a *zygospore.*

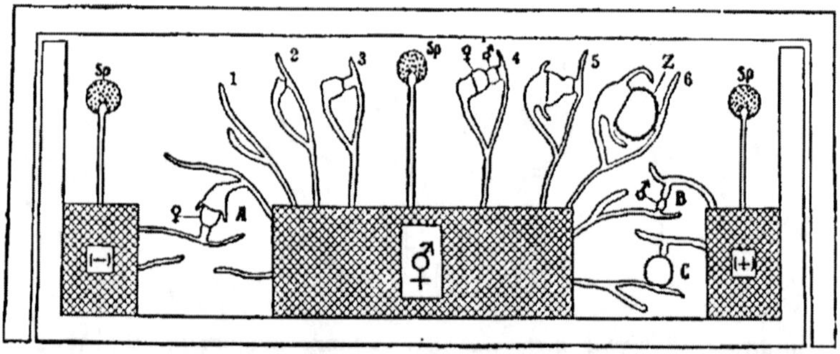

FIG. 190.—Sexual reaction between a hermaphroditic *Mucor* and (+) and (−) races of a diœcious species. Diagrammatic representation of a Petri dish culture showing a heterogamic hermaphroditic mucor (⚥) in the center separated by channels on either side from the (+) and (−) races, respectively, of a diœcious species. *Sp.*, sporangia containing spores by means of which the plant may be reproduced nonsexually. 1–6, stages in development of a hermaphroditic zygospore from unequal male and female gametes. *A*, sexual reaction between a (−) filament and female gamete. *B*, sexual reaction between a (+) filament and male gamete. *C*, a male zygospore formed at stimulus of contact with a (+) filament. (After Blakeslee.)

255. Germination.—At the close of the resting period, and under favorable conditions of temperature and moisture, the zygote germinates, sending out an erect hypha, which at once develops a globular sporangium at its apex. The asexual spores from this sporangium become the starting point of another series of changes like those just described.

256. Sexuality of Rhizopus.—It is well known that, while conjugation often occurs freely between mycelia from different spores, in other cases it fails entirely. The explanation of this was not known until about eight years ago, when it was discovered that there are, in reality, two unlike strains of *Rhizopus*-mycelium, and therefore two kinds of spores. The two kinds of mycelia are designated

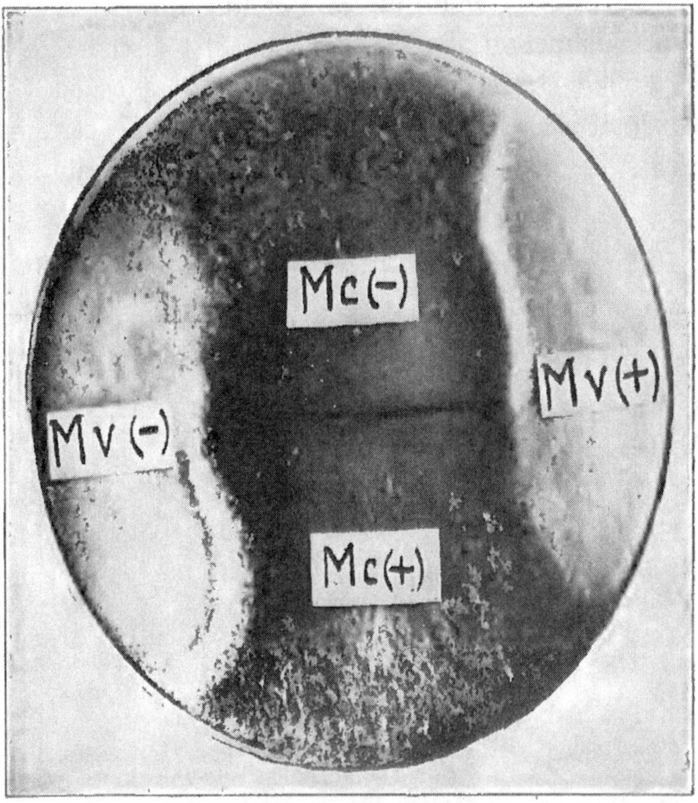

FIG. 191.—Petri-dish culture showing dark line of zygospores between the (+) and (−) strains of a diœcious species of mold, *Choanephora* (*Mc*) and white lines of "imperfect hybridization" between the strains of this species and the opposite strains of Mucor V (*Mv*). Note the total absence of zygospore formation between two (+) or two (−) strains. (After Blakeslee.)

as (+) and (−). When the intermingling hyphæ are of like strains, either all (+) or all (−), conjugation fails completely, but when they are from unlike strains, zygospores form in great abundance. This fact is strikingly shown in Fig. 191, which illustrates the result of growing mycelia from unlike strains side by side. The zone where they come into contact is sharply defined by the line of black zygospores, resulting from conjugation.

257. Distinction of Sexes.—When first discovered, the two unlike strains were designated as (+) and (−), because it was not possible to decide, with certainty, which was male and which female. Externally both

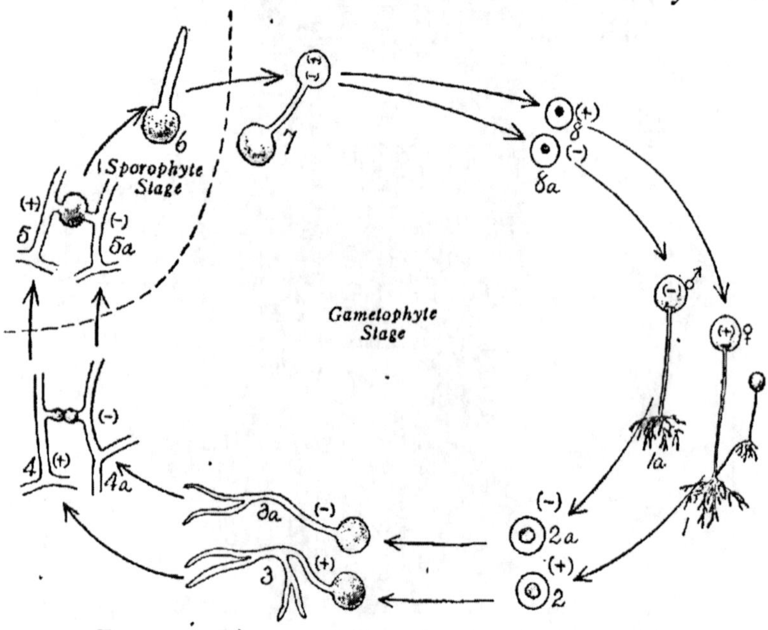

FIG. 192.—Diagram of life-cycle of a diœcious mold.

strains looked very much alike, except that one appeared to be vegetatively more vigorous than the other. Recent experiments seem to indicate that the vegetatively more vigorous (+) strain is female, while the less vigorous (−) strain is male. Not all molds are *diœcious*, like *Rhizopus.* In some species the mycelium from a single spore produces conjugating branches of both (+) and

(−) value, which fuse and form a zygospore. Such mycelia are, of course, monœcious.

The life-cycle of a diœcious mold is illustrated in Fig. 192.

258. Phycomycetes.—*Rhizopus nigricans* represents the group of Phycomycetes, lower fungi, often called "tube-fungi." The group is characterized by the tubular hyphæ without septa. In this cœnocytic character they resemble the filamentous or tubular green algæ (such as *Vaucheria*, or "green felt"), of which they are supposed to be degenerate descendants.

259. Life-cycle of Rhizopus.—The life-cycle of *Rhizopus* may be diagrammed as follows:

OUTLINE OF LIFE HISTORY OF RHIZOPUS

(+) Spore	(−) Spore
↓	↓
Mycelium	Mycelium
↓	↓
Gametangium	Gametangium
↓	↓
(+) Gamete	(−) Gamete

Conjugation

↘ ↙

Zygospore

↓ ↓

Germ-tube

↓ ↓

Sporangium

↓ } *Reduction*

(+) Spores	(−) Spores
↓	↓
(+) Mycelium	(−) Mycelium
↓	↓
Sporangium	Sporangium
↓	↓
(+) Spore	(−) Spore

A SAC-FUNGUS (MICROSPHÆRA)

260. Habitat and Structure.—The fungus, *Microsphæra*, may be found growing on the leaves of the lilac, and is commonly called "powdery mildew." The my-

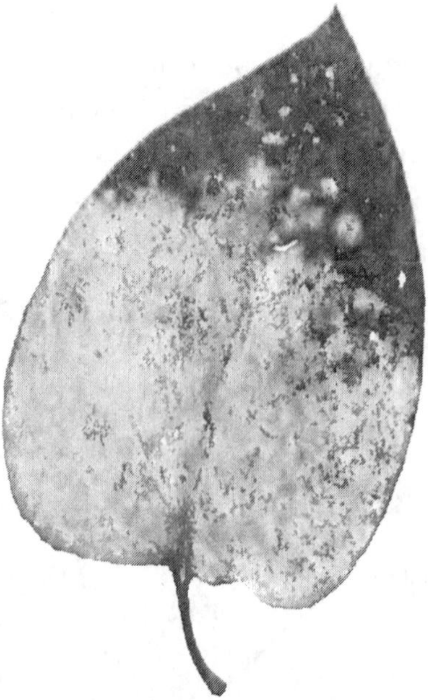

FIG. 193.—Lilac mildew (*Microsphæra Alni*). The white areas are the mycelia of the fungus, growing over the surface of the leaf. The tiny black dots are the perithecia, which contain the asci.

celium is *septate*, and forms a web over the surface of the leaf (Fig. 193), sending down haustoria into the epidermal cells, to secure nourishment, and sending up short branches (*conidiophores*), each bearing a chain of colorless spores (*conidia*).

261. Reproduction by Asci.—In late summer or early fall one may notice, on an infected leaf, among the mycelium, tiny black dots or spheres (Fig. 194), whence the name, *Microsphæra*. Examined with the microscope, these bodies are seen to bear numerous appendages, branched at the end, and with the tips of the branches curved back to form miniature hooks (Fig. 195). When these little spheres are crushed, or when they burst open, they are found to con-

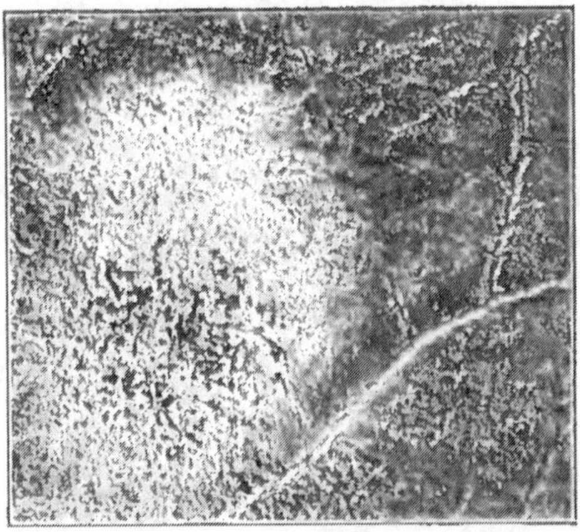

Fig. 194.—Powdery mildew (*Microsphæra Alni*) on lilac leaf. An infected area from the leaf in Fig. 193, greatly magnified.

tain a number of tiny sacs or *asci* (singular *ascus*), whence the name "sac-fungus," or *Ascomycete*. In each ascus are a number of spores or *ascospores*, formed from the contents of the ascus. The young ascus is, therefore, a spore-mother-cell. There are usually eight ascospores in an ascus, but the number may vary.

The spherical case containing the asci is the "spore-fruit" (*ascocarp* or *perithecium*), and results from the fusion of the contents of an antheridium and an oögonium

(Fig. 185). The cells from this point on, to the formation of the ascus, are diploid, and therefore constitute the sporophytic generation.

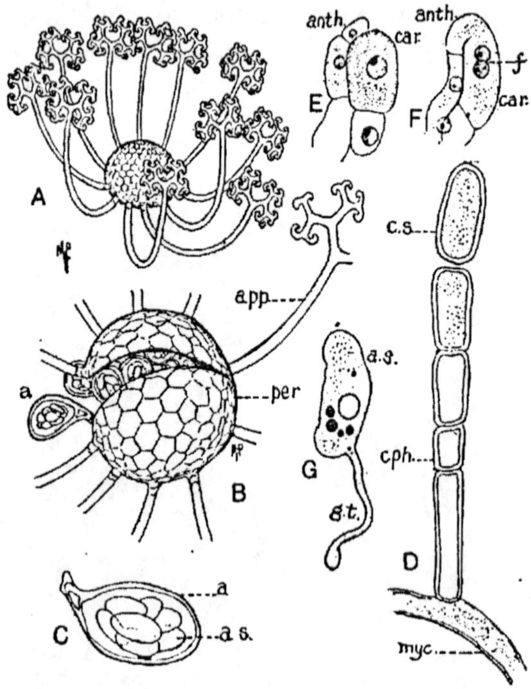

FIG. 195.—Lilac mildew (*Microsphæra Alni*). *A*, perithecium, with appendages; *B*, perithecium, showing asci (*a*); *C*, an ascus, containing ascospores; *D*, conidiophore (*cph*), bearing a chain of conidia (conidiospores, *c.s*); *E*, beginning of fertilization; *anth*, antheridium; *car*, carpogonium; *F*, later stage in fertilization; the contents of the antheridium and carpogonium have fused; *f*, fusion of the two nuclei; *G*, germination of ascospore (*a.s*); *g.t*, germ tube. (*E* and *F* after R. A. Harper.)

226. Germination.—When an ascospore germinates it develops directly into a mycelium.

263. Life-cycle.—The life-cycle of *Microsphæra* may be tabulated as follows:

OUTLINE OF LIFE HISTORY OF MICROSPHÆRA

Spore (conidium) → Mycelium → Antheridium[1]

Spore (conidium) → Mycelium → Oögonium[1]

Antheridium and Oögonium — *Fusion* →

Zygote in ascocarp (Sporophyte)
↓ ↓
Ascogenous hyphæ
↓ ↓
Young asci
↓ } *Reduction*
Ascospores
↓
Mycelium
↓
Conidiophore
↓
Conidium (Conidiospore)

FIG. 196.—A "cup-fungus," *Peziza sylvestris*. (Photo by F. J. Seaver).

[1] In *Microsphæra* there is only a slight morphological differentiation of the gametes.

264. Other Sac-fungi.—Between 25,000 and 30,000 species of sac-fungi have been described. Some of them are filamentous, like the lilac-mildew, while some are fleshy, like the common "cup-fungi" (Fig. 196). The edible morel, *Morchella esculenta*, (Fig. 197) is an Ascomycete, and the common yeast referred to in the chapter on fermentation (Fig. 60) is also classed here because, in one of its methods of reproduction the unicellular plant

FIG. 197.—The morel, *Morchella esculenta.* (Photo by W. A. Murrill.)

body functions as a spore-mother-cell, the protoplast becoming organized into spores (ascospores), and the wall of the mother-cell serving as an ascus.

A "RUST" FUNGUS (WHEAT RUST)

265. Importance.—One of the most important, as well as most difficult, fungi to understand is the wheat rust (*Puccinia graminis*). This fungus is important because it attacks some of the most valuable of all agricultural crops (wheat, oats, rye, barley, etc.), causing, at times, millions of dollars worth of damage.* It is difficult to understand because it is *heterœcious*—that is, lives alternately on two different plants, the barberry and the grain. For many years the form on the grain was supposed to be quite another plant from that on the barberry, which was called *Æcidium berberidis.*

266. Life History.—*a. Red Rust Stage.*—The mycelium of red rust (uredo stage) grows between the cells of the stem and leaves of the wheat, or other grain, and finally during the summer, numerous sporophores, bearing red spores (*urediniospores*), break through the epidermis (Fig. 198), producing reddish or rusty-looking dots and lines, whence the name "rust" for the plant. The one-celled uredinio-spores are easily blown by the wind in great numbers to other wheat plants, where they germinate, and thus spread the rust widely and rapidly.

b. Black Rust Stage.—In late summer the same mycelium develops an entirely different kind of spore, two-celled, and black. These are the final spores of the season, the *teliospores* (or *teleutospores*), and in them the nuclear fusions occur. They rest over winter, and germinate the following spring, each cell usually sending forth a hypha commonly composed of four cells, which constitute the *basidium* (*promycelium*). Each of these cells produces a tiny sporophore, bearing at its tip a single *basidiospore* (*sporidium*). Reduction occurs during germination.

c. Barberry Stage.—The basidiospores are blown by the

* The financial loss from wheat-rust in the United States amounted to $67,000,000 in 1891; in 1904 the loss in North Dakota, South Dakota, and Minnesota alone was estimated at $25,000,000.

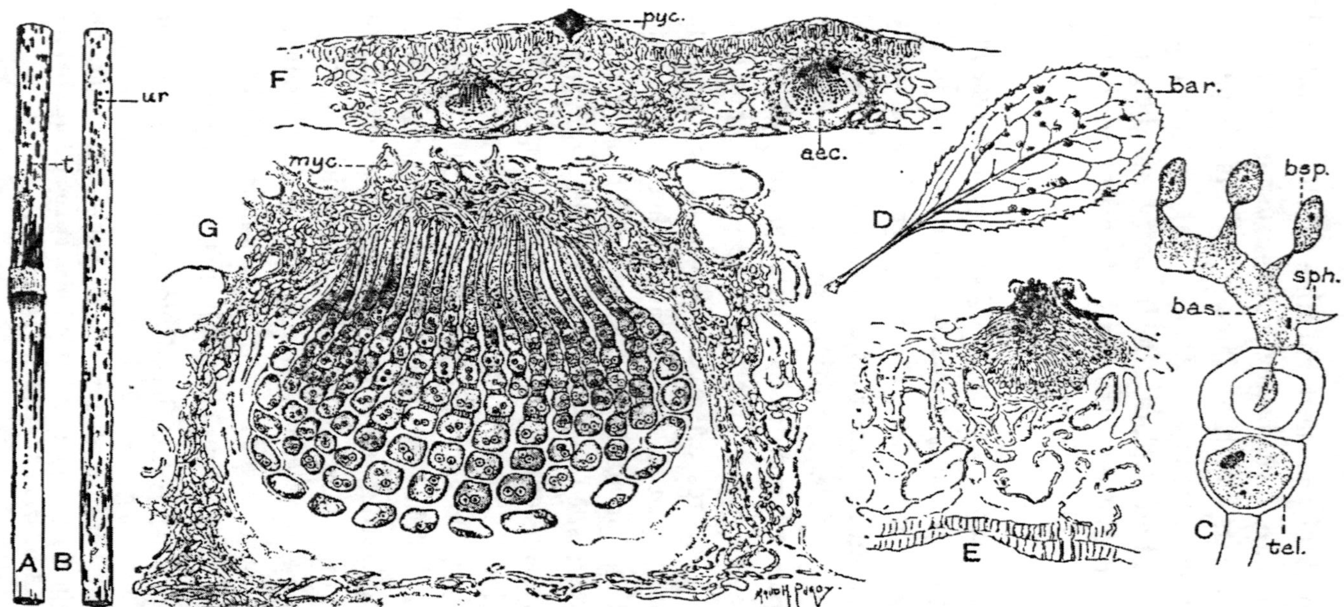

FIG. 198.—Wheat rust (*Puccinia graminis*). *A*, black rust stage on stem of wheat; *t*, sorus of teliospores; *B*, red rust stage; *ur*, sorus of urediniospores; *C*, teliospore germinating; *bas*, basidium; *sph*, sporophore (sterigma); *bsp*, basidiospore (sporidium); *D*, leaf of barberry, showing numerous "cluster-cups" (æcia), bearing æciospores; *E*, longitudinal section through a pycnium (spermagonium), formed at the upper surface of the barberry leaf; *F*, cross-section of a barberry leaf, showing a pycnium (above) and two æcia (*aec*); *G*, longitudinal section of an æcium, greatly enlarged, showing the mycelium of the fungus (*myc*), and the æciospores, each with two nuclei. The walls of the cluster-cup are formed by the mycelium of the fungus. *C*, from *Puccinia Lygodesmiæ*. (*C*, *E*, *F*, and *G*, from preparations of E. W. Olive.)

wind to the leaves of nearby barberry bushes, where they germinate. The resulting mycelium penetrates the epidermis, and ramifies between the cells of the leaf parenchyma, from which it absorbs nourishment. Under certain circumstances, as for example in Australia where barberries do not grow, the barberry stage is eliminated.

Soon this mycelium develops a reproductive structure called the *pycnium* (pycnidium or spermagonium), which breaks through the upper epidermis and produces innumerable *pycniospores* (*spermatia*). The real nature of this structure is not known.

OUTLINE OF LIFE HISTORY OF WHEAT RUST

Rust on Grain

↓↓	↓↓
Urediniospores (early summer)	Teliospores (late summer)
↓↓	↓↓
Germination	Rest (*Nuclear fusion*)
↓↓	↓↓
Mycelium	Germination
↓↓	↓↓
Urediniospores	Basidium
↓↓	↓ } *Reduction*
Germination	Sterigmata
↓↓	↓
Etc.	Basidiospores (sporidia)
	↓
	To barberry
	↓ ↓
	Pycnia — Æcia (*Cell-fusion*)
	↓ — ↓↓
	? — Æciospores
	↓↓
	Rust on grain

Near the lower epidermis are formed the "cluster-cups," or *æcia*[1] (æcidia). They break through to the

[1] Sing. *æcium*.

outer surface, and the countless numbers of *æciospores* are carried by the wind to nearby wheat, where they, in turn, germinate, and the complicated series of events begins again.

267. Diagram of Life History.—The life history of *Puccinia graminis* may be outlined as shown on page 275.

A FLESHY FUNGUS (AGARICUS)

268. Habitat.—Fleshy fungi are found widely distributed, growing in the soil of fields, pastures, and

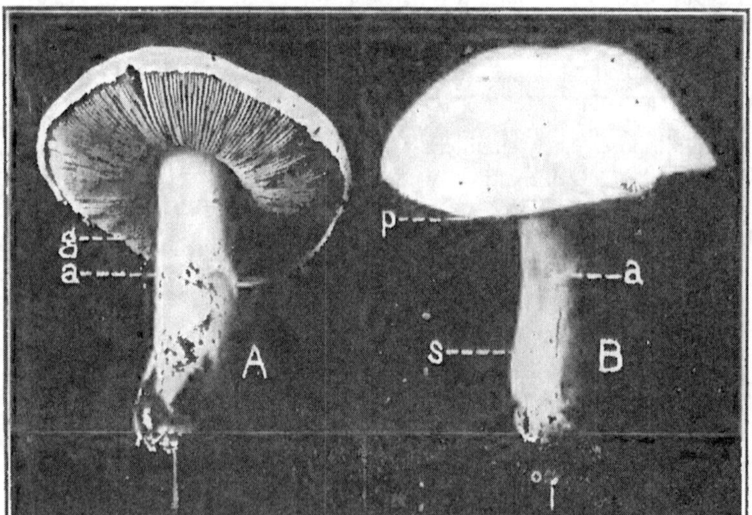

FIG. 199—Meadow mushroom (*Agaricus campestris* L.). *A*, view showing under side of pileus; *g*, gills; *a*, annulus, or remains of the veil attached to the stipe; *B*, side view; *s*, stipe; *a*, annulus; *p*, margin of pileus, showing at intervals the remains of the veil. (After W. A. Murrill.)

woods, or on tree trunks, decaying logs, and elsewhere. The familiar edible mushroom (*Agaricus campestris*), as its name implies, grows commonly in meadows, and is hence often called the "meadow mushroom" (Fig. 199). One of the most poisonous species, *Amanita phalloides*,

(Fig. 200), resembles *Agaricus* superficially and is often mistaken for it. *Amanita* always has, at the base of the stalk, a *cup*, which *Agaricus* lacks.

269. Description.—The body of *Agaricus* consists of a

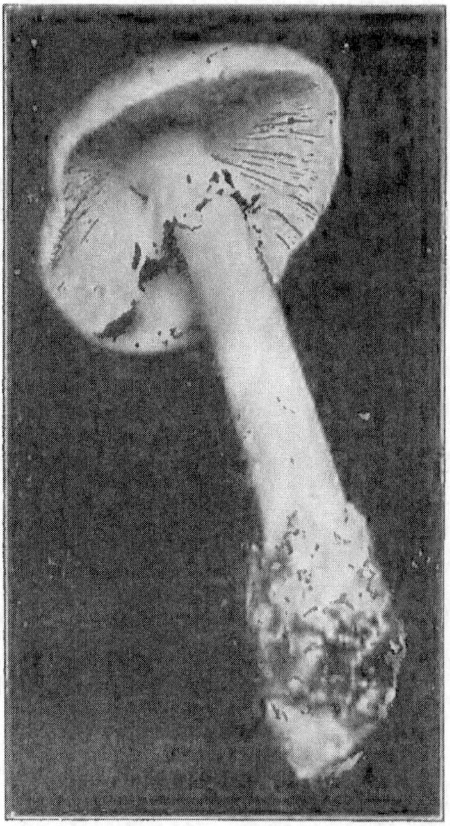

FIG. 200.—The deadly amanita, *Amanita phalloides*. Note the cup at the base of the stipe. (Photo by E. M. Kittredge.)

short fleshy stalk (the *stipe*), having numerous root-like hyphæ (*rhizomorphs*) penetrating the soil from its lower end, and bearing at its upper end an umbrella-shaped expansion, the *pileus*. On the under side of the pileus are numerous thin lamellæ or *gills*. The stalk and pileus are composed of innumerable hyphæ (Fig. 201), closely associated together in a pseudo-tissue, but there is no real

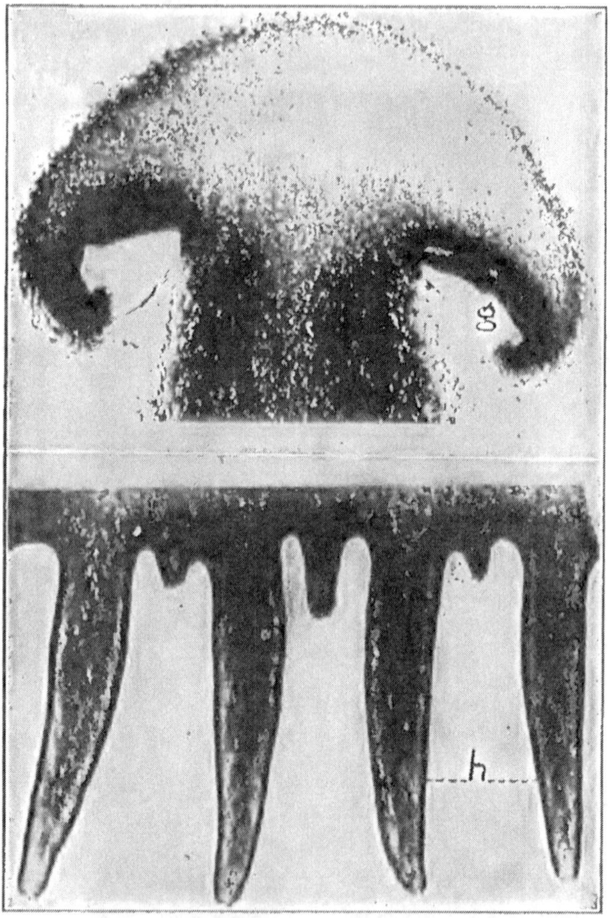

FIG. 201.—*Cortinarius cinnamomeus.* Above, longitudinal section through stipe and pileus, showing gills (*g*); below, longitudinal section through primary and secondary gills; *h*, hymenium or sporogenous surface. (After Gertrude E. Douglas.)

tissue-differentiation, such as occurs in the mosses and ferns and higher plants, though the external layer may usually be peeled off with ease.

270. Reproduction.—If the pileus of *Agaricus* is placed

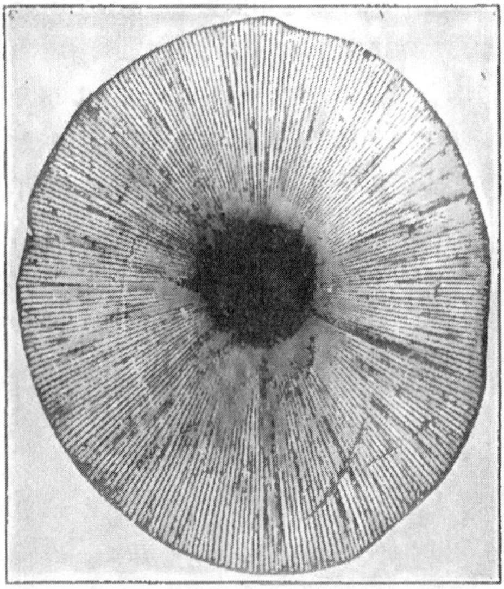

FIG. 202.—Spore-print of the fly agaric (*Amanita muscaria* L.). The spore-print is made by laying the pileus, gills downward, on a sheet of black paper. The white spores fall onto the paper, making the print. (Photo by W. A. Murrill.)

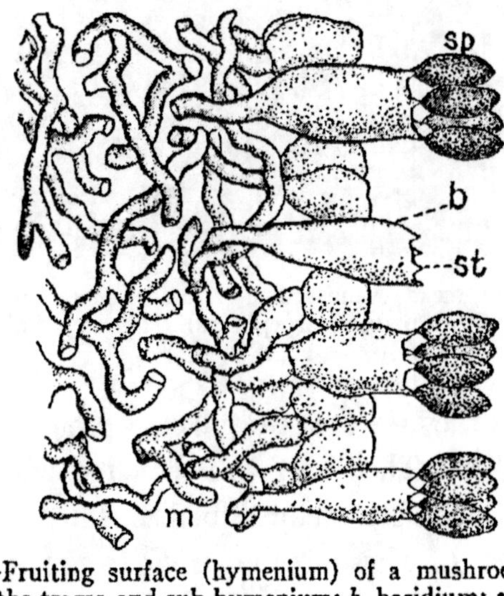

FIG. 203.—Fruiting surface (hymenium) of a mushroom (*Agaricus*). *m*, hyphæ of the trama and sub-hymenium; *b*, basidium; *st*, sterigma; *sp*, spores. (Diagrammatic.)

with the gills down over a piece of white paper, and left for a few hours, a dark purplish deposit will form in lines under each gill. With *Amanita* the color is white. This deposit (the "spore-print") is composed of spores, shed from the surfaces of the gills (Fig. 202). Microscopic examina-

FIG. 204.—The meadow mushroom (*Agaricus campestris*, var. *Columbia.*) Young fruiting bodies (carpophores). The mycelial hyphæ are in the substratum. (Photo by G. F. Atkinson.)

tion discloses the fact that the gills are composed of a network of hyphæ. Their surface is covered with innumerable short, thick, club-shaped bodies, filled with protoplasm (Fig. 203). These are the *basidia* (singular *basidium*). Fungi which bear basidia are grouped together as *Basidiomycetes*. At the tip of each basidium are two tiny projections, the *sterigmata* (singular, *sterigma*)[1], and on the end of each sterigma is a spore (*basidiospore*). In the early stages of development the gills appear white, at maturity they are purplish, and, at about the time the spores are shed, they become dark brown. Although many painstaking experiments have been made in order to secure the germination of the spores, no one has ever been successful. Whether or not the mushroom is produced from spores in nature we can only conjecture. No sexual organs have ever been discovered on any of the fleshy Basidiomycetes.

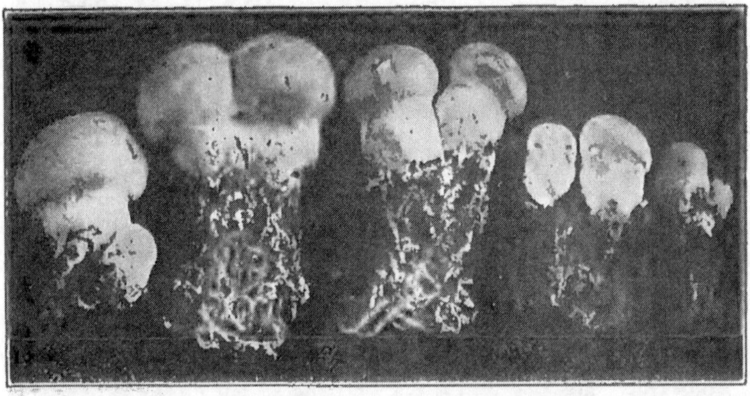

FIG. 205.—The common mushroom (*Agaricus campestris*). Young "buttons." (Photo by G. F. Atkinson.)

271. Vegetative Propagation.—The meadow-mushroom is propagated for food from "bricks" of mycelium, or "spawn" that may be purchased from seedsmen. When portions of these "bricks" are placed in suitably prepared soil, under favorable conditions of moisture and heat, the mycelium resumes its growth, ramifying in all directions through the soil. At numerous points on the mycelium tiny little "buttons" form (Fig. 204). As the

[1] In most of the gill-bearing fungi there are four sterigmata on each basidium, as shown in Fig. 203.

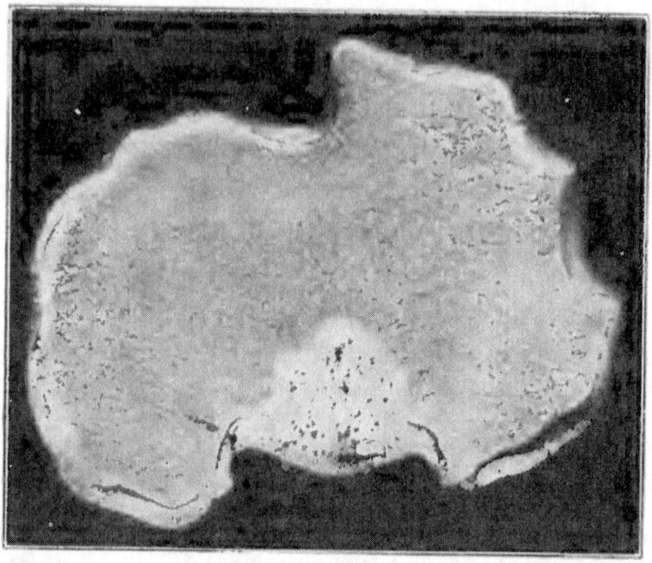

FIG. 206.—A pore-bearing fungus (*Polyporus betulinus*). Under (fruiting) surface, showing the pores.

FIG. 207.—Giant puffballs (*Lycoperdon giganteum* Botsch.). Note the size of the four specimens as compared with the egg and fruit in the center. (After W. A. Murrill.)

buttons enlarge, a little chamber forms near the tip (Fig. 205), and into this chamber some of the hyphæ grow, forming the "gills," with their "fruiting" surface. While the gills are forming other hyphæ form a *veil*, extending from the stipe to the edge of the pileus, and protecting the gills until the spores are ripe. By continued growth of the pileus the veil becomes ruptured, thus allowing the spores to escape. It has been found that the spores do not merely fall from the sterigmata from their own weight, but that they are forcibly expelled.

Entire new mushrooms may also be obtained by growing pieces of a young plant on suitable nutrient media. From such pieces mycelium is produced which ultimately bears the "buttons."

OUTLINE OF LIFE HISTORY OF MEADOW-MUSHROOM

Spore (Basidiospore)
↓
Mycelium
↓
Binucleate cells
↓↓
Young sporophore ("Buttons")
↓↓
Mature sporophore (the "Mushroom") } Stipe, Pileus
↓↓
Gills
↓↓
Hymenium
↓↓
Basidium (*Nuclear fusion*)
↓ } *Reduction*
Sterigma
↓
Spore (Basidiospore)

272. Other Classes of Fleshy Fungi.—In addition to the gill-bearing fungi (Agaricaceæ), there are many other families of Basidiomycetes, one bearing the fruiting surface in tubes (Polyporaceæ, Fig. 206), another on the surface of teeth or spines, on the under surface of the pileus (Hydnaceæ). The common "puff-balls" are Basidiomycetes, with the fruiting surface entirely enclosed in the more or less globular fruiting body, almost the entire contents of which break down into the powder or dust of the ripe puff-ball (Fig. 207). Over 14,000 species of Basidiomycetes have been described.

273. Life-cycle.—The life-cycle of the meadow-mushroom (*Agaricus campestris*) may be indicated as shown on page 283.

OTHER NON-GREEN PLANTS

In addition to the true fungi, there are two other groups of non-green thallophytes which ought to be mentioned here, one (the Myxomycetes) because of their scientific interest; the other (bacteria) because of their economic importance.

274. Myxomycetes.—The myxomycetes are on the border-line between the kingdom of plants and that of animals. In some of their characters they so closely resemble lower animals like the *Amœba*, that they have been claimed by the zoologists, under the name *Mycetozoa* (fungus-like animals). In their method of reproduction they are more like plants than like animals.

The body of the organism is a large naked mass of protoplasm, called a *plasmodium*, commonly found on old decaying logs, in tan-bark, and similar places, where moisture and organic food are abundant. The protoplast flows over the surface on which it grows, like the *Amœba*, taking in nourishment, at times flowing around and thus injecting particles of food, assimilating, and growing in size. The protoplasm may be spread out in sheets or in a delicate network of strands, or both (Fig. 208). When viewed under the microscope the

FIG. 208.—Plasmodium of a slime-mold (myxomycete), *Fuligo septica*, growing on the inner surface of a glass jar. The natural color was bright orange.

protoplasm is seen to be in almost constant motion, flowing for about a minute in one direction; gradually slowing

FIG. 209.—Fruiting bodies of a myxomycete (*Comatricha suksdorfii* E. and E.), greatly enlarged. (Photo from type specimen.)

up, it comes to rest, and then resumes its flowing, but in the opposite direction, also for about a minute. Different species possess different colors, but they never possess chlorophyll.

275. Reproduction.—At a certain stage of development, the plasmodium will begin to form tiny upright stalks, at the top of which will develop a spore-case, containing spores and *capillitium* (Fig. 209). The capillitium consists of hygroscopic threads which aid in the dissemination of the spores. When the spores are ripe they are scattered

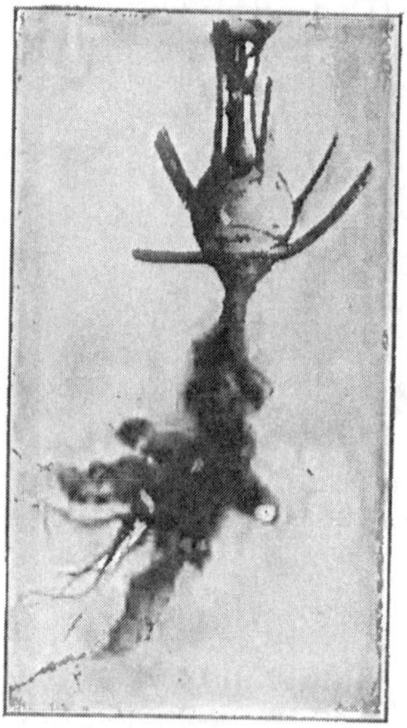

FIG. 210.—Kohlrabi, showing club-root, caused by a myxomycete, *Plasmodiophora brassicæ*. (Cf. Fig. 2.)

by the wind, and each, on germination, produces a swarm-spore. A new plasmodium results from the fusion of these swarm-spores.

276. Economic Importance.—The Myxomycetes have very little economic importance, but the disease of cabbages, kohlrabi, and turnips, known as *club-root*, is caused by a slime-mold growing on the roots (Fig. 210).

277. Bacteria.—The bacteria are among the very

simplest plant structures known. They are one-celled, but of many shapes, and with or without motile cilia. They include the smallest living things known. There are even reasons for believing that some forms are *ultra-microscopic*, that is, too small to be seen with the most powerful microscopes that can be made. Some forms are less than one fifty-thousandth of an inch in diameter. Of some kinds of bacteria, as many as 300 could be placed side by side on the period at the end of this sentence. In fact the word "microbe" means "tiny living thing,"[1] though not all microbes are bacteria. The germ of malaria, for example, is a microscopic animal (*protozoon*), resembling an *Amœba*.

Several genera of bacteria are distinguished according to shape as, for example, *Bacterium* (non-motile rods), *Bacillus* (motile rods), *Micrococcus* (spherical), *Spirillum* (spiral threads) (Fig. 211).

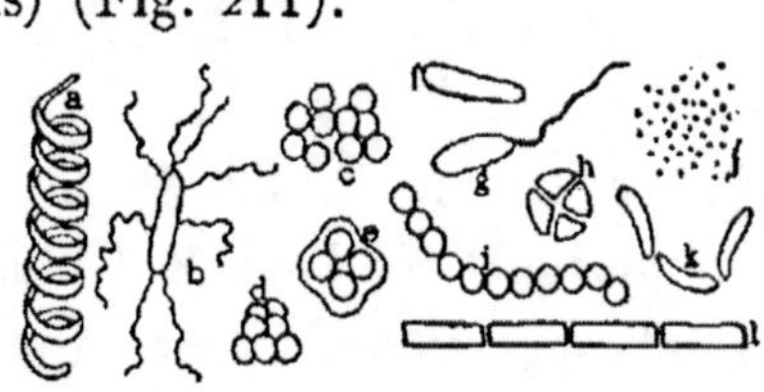

FIG. 211.—Various forms of bacteria. *a, Spirillum; b, Bacillus typhosus; c, Staphylococcus; d, e, j, h, Micrococcus; f, k, l, Bacillus; g, Pseudomonas pycocyanea; i, Streptococcus.*

They are found everywhere and multiply rapidly by cell-division, whence they are called "fission-fungi," or *Schizomycetes*. Not possessing chlorophyll, they are all, of course, either parasitic or saprophytic, some being highly beneficial—in fact indispensable—to man; others highly harmful, causing some of the worst known diseases of both plants and animals.

[1] From the Greek μικρός (*mikros*), small, + βίος (*bios*), life.

CHAPTER XX

ECONOMIC IMPORTANCE OF FUNGI

In the preceding chapter we have frequently referred to ways in which our own lives are related to the life of plants. It would be difficult to say what particular group of plants affects us most, but certainly none more than the fungi. They are among the direct causes of human sorrow and happiness, of health and disease, of poverty and wealth, life and death. They are at once the foundation and the arch enemy of agriculture, the objects and obstacles of commerce, the source and hindrance of human industry.

EDIBLE FUNGI.

278. Mushrooms and Toadstools.—Everyone is familiar with edible "mushrooms;" they are now on sale at every grocery. Nearly everyone thinks there is a difference between mushrooms and "toad-stools," Such, however, is not the case. These two terms are applied indiscriminately by the botanist to any "fleshy" fungus. The word "mushroom" is used by most people to designate the meadow-agaric (*Agaricus campestris*), which is *the* mushroom of commerce, *par excellence*. There are over 1,000 fleshy fungi that are good to eat, and many more that are not poisonous, but non-edible because they are tough, or fibrous, or ill-tasting. Many of those good to eat resemble the meadow-mushroom in having a stalk and gills, and are closely related to it (Fig. 212); while others, like the "puff-balls," belong to an entirely different group. All puff-balls are good to eat when young. Many esteem the *morel* (*Morchella esculenta*) as a great delicacy.

FIG. 212.—Shaggy-mane mushroom (*Coprinus comatus*). Edible before the spores turn black.

279. Criterion of Edibility.—Here, as elsewhere, there is no royal road, no short cut to knowledge. There are absolutely no external characteristics which distinguish edible from poisonous fungi. The only way to tell whether a given species is poisonous or not is to try it. Since this is so, it is best for the amateur not to make the endeavor, but to depend only upon the knowledge of an experienced mycologist. One should first seek to attain skill in determining the *exact species* of his specimen, and then follow the assurance, and especially the warnings, of some reliable book. In general, one should avoid all bright-colored species (although some of them are not poisonous), and all species that have a "cup" at the base of the stalk, or stipe. To insure no mistake in this latter point, one should always be sure that he has the base of the stipe, and has not broken it off above the base. Beginners should also avoid all specimens in the "button" stage of development, as it is more difficult to determine the exact species at that stage.

280. Mushroom Culture.—The growing of mushrooms for the market is a very important industry, especially in some localities. Cultures are usually started from "spawn," obtained from the seedsman in the form of "bricks." These bricks consist largely of mycelium, tightly pressed together. When the bricks are broken up and distributed through a "bed" of soil and manure, properly prepared, the mycelium resumes its growth, and soon begins to produce the "buttons" (Fig. 204), which finally develop into mature mushrooms.

The industry is commonly carried on in cellars and caves. This is not necessary, for the meadow-mushroom, as its name clearly implies, grows in nature in open meadows and pastures. But, since the fungi have no chlorophyll, they do not need the light, and so space can be used for their culture that would not well serve any other useful purpose.

FUNGI THAT CAUSE PLANT DISEASES

281. Government Regulation.—Fungi that grow as parasites on green plants cause serious disturbances of the normal life-processes and structure of their hosts, interfering with healthy growth, and causing plant diseases. Since the fungi are reproduced by spores, these diseases may rapidly spread by contagion. On this account state legislatures and the national Congress have been obliged to pass stringent laws governing international and interstate traffic in plants liable to disease, providing for their careful inspection and quarantine. The United States Government maintains an expert pathologist continuously at the port of New York to inspect plants imported from foreign countries. Sometimes whole cargoes of potatoes or other vegetables are refused entrance at the port, and must then be taken to sea and dumped into the ocean, or else taken to the port of some other country where the regulations are less stringent or less rigidly inforced.

282. Diseases Caused by Phycomycetes.—Among the plant diseases caused by the alga-like fungi may be mentioned:

FIG. 213.—"Little potatoes." A disease caused by the parasitic fungus, *Rhizoctonia* (*Corticium vagum* var. *solani* Burt).

1. The "damping-off fungus" (*Pythium de Baryanum* Hesse), which attacks young seedlings of beans and other plants near the surface of the ground, causing the tissues there to disintegrate, and the entire plant finally to wilt and die.

2. Brown rot of lemons, commonly seen in fruit that has been kept too long or in too damp a place.

3. "Blister-blight" or white "rust" of radishes and their relatives, such as shepherd's purse and mustard.

This fungus is known as *Albugo candida*, or more recently as *Cystopus candidus*.

4. Downy mildew of grapes and cucumbers.

FIG. 214.—Witches' brooms on the hackberry (*Celtis occidentalis*), caused by a gall-mite (*Phytoptus sp.*), or possibly by the mite in conjunction with a powdery mildew (*Sphærotheca phytoptophyla*), which is usually found on the "brooms."

5. Potato rot and "late blight," *Phytophthora infestans* (Mont.) DeBary. This disease was the cause of the failure of the potato crop and the consequent famine in

Ireland, in 1846–47. (The disease known as "little potatoes" (*Rhizoctonia*) and by various other names (Fig. 213), is caused by one of the *Basidiomycetes*.)

283. Ascomycetes.—Among diseases caused by various species of sac-fungi are the following:

FIG. 215.—Ergot (*Claviceps purpurea*). Sclerotia on wild rye (*Elymus virginicus*), at left; marsh grass (*Spartina sp.*), middle; cultivated rye (*Secale cereale*), at right.

1. Peach leaf-curl, plum pockets, and "witches brooms" (Fig. 214).

2. Brown rot of peach and plum. The damage caused by this disease in the state of Georgia alone, in 1900, amounted to nearly $700,000.

FIG. 216.—Two chestnut trees (*Castanea dentata*), killed by the destructive chestnut blight. (After W. A. Murrill.)

3. Alfalfa leaf-spot, the sooty mold of the orange, the powdery mildew of grapes and apples, the wilt disease of cotton and watermelon, the ergot of rye and other cereals (Fig. 215), the black knot of plums and cherries, and the disastrous chestnut disease of the eastern United States.

284. Chestnut Disease.—The chestnut disease (Fig. 216) first appeared in the vicinity of New York City about

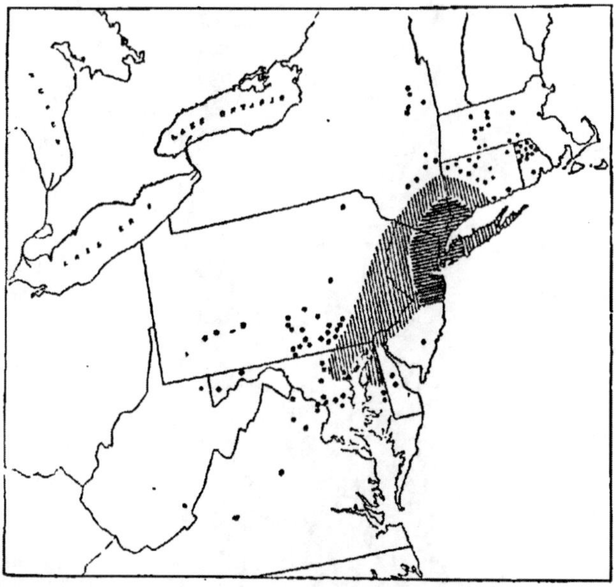

FIG. 217.—Map of the northeastern United States, showing the approximate distribution of the chestnut bark disease in 1911. The disease has spread further since the map was made. Horizontal lines, area where majority of trees are dead; vertical lines, approximate area where infection is complete; dots, location of advance infections. (After Metcalf. U. S. Dept. Agr., Farmers Bull. 467.)

1904, and from there as a center it has rapidly spread until it has destroyed most of the chestnut trees within a radius of 150 to 200 miles of the city (Fig. 217). As many as 17,000 trees have been destroyed in the city of Brooklyn alone, entailing a total loss of several million dollars. The mycelium of the fungus that causes it (*Endothia parasitica*) grows underneath the bark, and for this reason it is practically impossible to check it

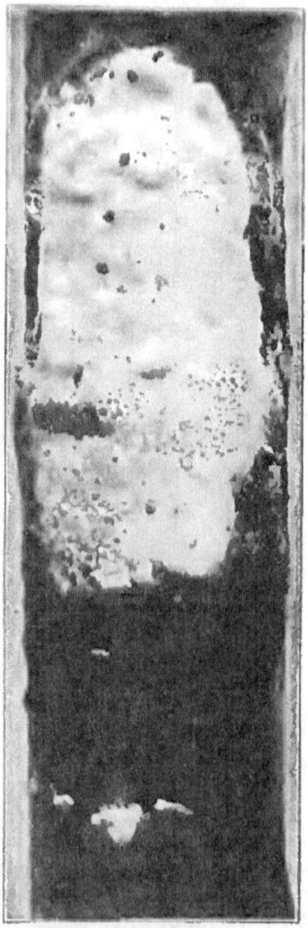

FIG. 218.—Chestnut blight. Portion of a branch of an American chestnut (*Castanea dentata*), which had been artificially inoculated with the spores of the chestnut-blight fungus, *Endothia parasitica* (Murr.) Anders. The white areas are infected spots. (After W. A. Murrill.)

by spraying, as the bark protects the mycelium from all known spraying solutions. The fruiting pustules of the fungus form on the surface (Figs. 218 and 219). The only method of checking the spread of the disease is to cut down and burn all affected trees. Millions of dollars worth of damage has been caused by this disease within the past seven or eight years. The financial loss in New York City and vicinity, alone, has been estimated at much more than $5,000,000, while the loss for the entire United States, up to 1911, was estimated by the Federal

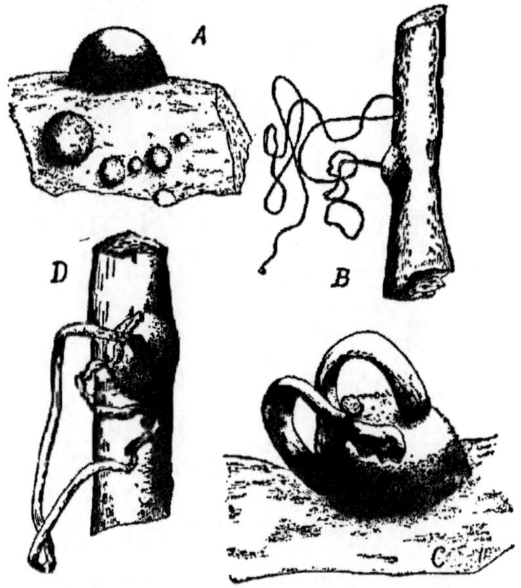

FIG. 219.—Chestnut-blight fungus (*Endothia parasitica*). Fruiting pustules and spore-masses from cultures. × about 8. *A*, stages in the development of the pustules; *B*, *C*, *D*, various forms of spore discharge in a moist atmosphere. (After Murrill.)

Government at not less than $25,000,000. In 1910, the state of Pennsylvania appointed a special commission of experts for the investigation and control of the disease, and appropriated over $275,000 to meet the necessary expense of the work.

285. Grain Smut.—The smuts of wheat, oats, barley, and corn are among the commoner pests of the farmer.

These diseases are caused by fungi of the genus *Ustilago*.[1] The species are often named from the plant affected; for example *Ustilago Avenæ* on oats (*Avena*, Fig. 220),

FIG. 220.—Panicles of oats (*Avena sativa*), with the grains almost completely destroyed and replaced by the oat smut (*Ustilago Avenæ*).

Ustilago Tritici on barley (*Triticum*), *Ustilago Zeæ* on corn (*Zea*, Fig. 221). The mycelium extends through the

[1] A Hemibasidiomycete.

stem, fruiting in the tissues, and commonly destroying the kernel of grain. The innumerable black spores form a sooty powder—whence the common name of "smut."

FIG. 221.—Corn-smut (*Ustilago maydis*) on stalk, tassel, ear, and leaf of *Zea Mays.*

286. Rusts.—The life history of the wheat rust (*Puccinia graminis*) was outlined in Chapter XIX. This fungus has not only caused millions of dollars worth of damage to the wheat crop of the world but has been the cause of legislative enactments. As early as 1760 there was passed in Massachusetts "An Act to prevent Damage to English Grain arising from Barberry Bushes." This act read, in part, as follows:

"Whereas it has been found by experience, that the Blasting of Wheat and other English Grain is often occasioned by Barberry Bushes, to the great loss and damage of the inhabitants of this province:

"Be it therefore enacted by the Governour, Council, and House of Representatives, that whoever, whether community or private person, hath any Barberry Bushes standing or growing in his or their Land, within any of the Towns in this Province, he or they shall cause the same to be extirpated or destroyed on or before the thirteenth Day of June, Anno Domini One Thousand Seven Hundred and Sixty.

"Be it further enacted that if there shall be any Barberry Bushes standing or growing in any land within this Province, after the said 10th day of June, it shall be lawful, by Virtue of this Act, for any Person whosoever to enter the Lands wherein such Barberry Bushes are, first giving one month's notice of his intention to do so to the Owner or Occupant thereof, and to cut them down, or pull them up by the root, and then to present a fair account of his labour and charge therein to the owner or occupant of the said land; and if such owner or occupant shall neglect or refuse by the space of two months next after the presenting said account, to make to such person reasonable payment as aforesaid, then the person who cut down or pulled up such bushes, may bring the action against such owner or occupant, owners or occupants, before any Justice of the Peace, if under forty shillings, or otherwise before the Inferior Court of Common Pleas in the County where such Bushes grew, who upon proof of the cutting down or pulling up of such bushes by the person who brings the action, or such as were employed by him, shall and is hereby respectively empowered to enter up judgment for him to recover double the value of the reasonable expense and labour in such service and award execution accordingly.

"Be it further enacted, that the Surveyors of the Highways, whether public or private, be and hereby are empowered and required *ex officio* to destroy and extirpate all such Barberry Bushes as are or shall be in the Highways in their respective Wards or Districts, and if any such shall remain after the aforesaid tenth Day of June, Anno Domini One Thousand Seven Hundred and Sixty, that then the Town or District in which such bushes are shall pay a Fine of two shillings for every bush standing or growing in such Highway, to be recovered by Bill Plaint, Information, or on the Presentment of a Grand Jury, and to be paid one Half to the Informer and the other Half to the Treasury of the County in which such bushes grew for the use of the County."

In addition to the rust of wheat, there are also rusts of the carnation and the clover caused by species of *Uromyces.* The carnation rust, which first appeared about

1892, is common in the plant houses of commercial florists.

287. Pine Tree Blister-rust.—Among the more important plant diseases recently appearing in the United States is the pine tree blister-rust, introduced from Europe about 1909. One species is *Cronartium pyriforme*, which is the telial stage of *Peridermium pyriforme.* The æcial stage (*Peridermium*) appears on the pine, while the alternating host is the "false toad-flax" (*Comandra umbellata* and *C. pallida*).[1] This fungus attacks species of pine that have less than five leaves to the fascicle, such as *Pinus contorta*, *P. ponderosa*, and *P. rigida.*

Another species (*Cronartium ribicola*) passes its æcial stage on five-leaved pines, where it is commonly known as *Peridermium Strobi*;[2] the telial stage, as its name indicates, is passed on species of *Ribes* (gooseberries and currants) (Fig. 222).

The importance of such a disease as this may be inferred when we consider that the value of the white pine growing in the New England states is estimated at $75,000,000. that of the Lake states at $96,000,000, of the Western states at $60,000,000, and of other National forests at $30,000,000, a total of $261,000,000. The western sugar pine (*Pinus Lambertiana*) has a total value estimated at $150,000,000. Thus, timber to the value of $411,000,000 is threatened with destruction by this one parasitic disease. In order to reduce the danger of infection from the blister-rust, and also from the pine-shoot moth (*Evetria*

[1] The *Comandra* is itself a parasite on the roots of various species of blueberry (*Vaccinium*), and other woody plants.

[2] From *Strobus*, the specific name of the common white pine (*Pinus Strobus*).

buoliana), the United States Department of Agriculture has issued quarantine regulations forbidding the impor-

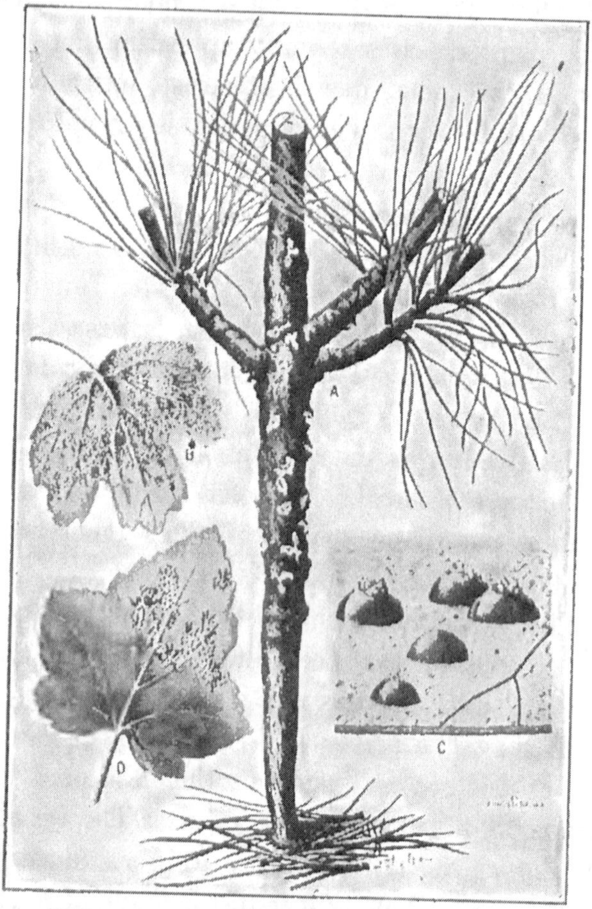

FIG. 222.—White pine blister-rust. *A*, portion of diseased tree, showing pycnidial blisters broken open; from these blisters the disease spreads to neighboring currant or gooseberry bushes; *B*, early summer stage on under surface of a currant leaf; these spores repeat during the summer, at intervals of two weeks; *C*, early summer stage, much magnified; *D*, late summer and fall stage, on the under surface of a currant leaf; from this stage the disease spreads again to pine trees. (After Perley Spaulding, by courtesy of the U. S. Dept. of Agriculture.)

tation of all five-leaved pines and all species and varieties of *Ribes*, except for experimental or scientific purposes by the Department of Agriculture. Since July 1, 1915, the importation of every species of the genus *Pinus* has been forbidden from all European countries and localities. In March, 1916, the Federal Horticultural Board requested all nurserymen in the eastern United States not to ship white pine, gooseberry or currant stock into the Rocky Mountain and Western white pine forest areas.

FIG. 223.—A shelf-fungus (*Fomes applanatus*) on sugar maple.

288. Timber-destroying Fungi.—Everyone recalls the "shelf-fungi," so often seen growing on the trunks of trees (Fig. 223). These forms are the fruiting bodies of the fungus, while the mycelium ramifies through the wood, often in such quantities as to form the "punk," formerly much used in setting off fireworks. The soft fungal threads are enabled to make their way through the hard woody tissue by means of an enzyme which they secrete. The enzyme softens and dissolves the cell-walls of the wood, thus making it possible for the mycelium to penetrate with ease. This process disintegrates the wood, weakens the tree so that it eventually dies or is easily blown over by the wind, and of course renders the wood of little or no value for timber. The fungus gains admission to the tree by means of the spores falling on some surface freshly exposed by trimming the tree, by the accidental breaking of branches, by the "barking" caused by lawnmowers, and in other ways; on account of the disastrous results, all such surfaces should be protected by being painted over as soon as a branch is cut or broken off, or a portion of bark removed. There are many species of wood-destroying fungi, and the financial loss they cause to the lumber industry, not to mention the losses of beautiful shade trees in lawns, parks, and streets, is very considerable.

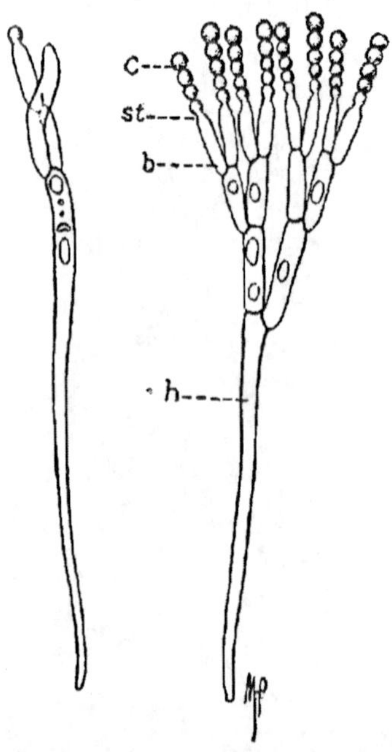

FIG. 224.—*Penicillium glaucum.* *h*, hypha; *b*, basal cell; *st*, sterigma; *c*, spore (*conidium*).

MOLDS

The filamentous fungi, commonly known as molds, belong to various species. The black mold (*Mucor mucedo*) is common on bread, and the blue mold (*Penicillium*) (Fig. 224) on decaying fruit and on fruit canned at home. The appearance of the mold indicates that the fruit was not sufficiently sterilized before the cover was screwed down on the fruit jar. In fact, the entire process of canning is a series of operations intended primarily to kill all germs of bacteria and fungi. The sterilized fruit is then sealed from the air and from access of other germs while it is still hot. The "keeping" of canned goods depends upon the successful exclusion of *every* living spore or other germ. If goods preserved in tin cans have been imperfectly sterilized the gases produced by fermentation will exert a pressure upon the can from the inside, often strong enough to cause a bulging of the ends.

COLD STORAGE

Just as canning has for its object the preservation of vegetable or animal tissues by killing the germs with heat, so cold storage accomplishes the same end by means of extreme cold. Most germs remain inactive below a certain temperature, which may be readily ascertained by experiment. The spoiling of eggs is caused by the presence within the egg of a germ-"flora," which lives upon the yolk and white, producing by its life processes the noxious gases of stale eggs. At certain low temperatures most of the life-processes of the germs are either stopped entirely, or greatly retarded. In the colonial days of America, and later, it was common for dwellers on farms and in villages to preserve meat by burying a quantity of it in the snow during the winter season—a primitive cold storage. During cold storage, however, certain chemical changes take place in the preserved tissue, due to enzyme action. As a result there is a limit to the period that food can be kept in cold storage without deteriorating. All cold-storage plants and refrigerator cars are evidence of the fact that our own lives are profoundly affected by the existence and activity of microscopic forms of plant life.

YEASTS

We are all familiar with "yeast," but many persons do not realize that yeast is a plant, and that there are various species. The baker's yeast is different from the brewer's, and there are more than one kind of the latter—one for example causing "top fermentation," another "bottom fermentation." There are also various "wild" yeasts, present in the air. The nature of fermentation has been discussed in Chapter VIII. It is interesting to reflect that this group of microscopic plants, in its relation to bread making (from one kind of grain) adds to the wealth and happiness of the world, and ministers to one of the most fundamental needs of our physical being, while in its relation to brewing (the formation of alcohol from another kind of grain) it contributes to one of the greatest sources of poverty, misery, and crime.

The use of yeast in bread making dates from prehistoric ages. It is mentioned in old testament history as early as the patriarchal age. It is of interest also to reflect that in the various great migrations of the human race, this little plant must have been preserved and transported with as much care as domestic animals. In such a movement as the colonization of a new continent, as, for example, North and South America, and Australia, provision must have been made for maintaining the supply of yeast for the making of bread.

BACTERIA

289. Extent of Their Influence.—The study of bacteria, the smallest of all known plants, has become so extensive as to form a separate science, bacteriology; and it will not be possible here to more than suggest in outline the numerous important ways in which these tiny plants affect our daily lives. In fact their discovery has practically revolutionized our method of living in many ways.

FIG. 225.—Louis Pasteur, founder of the science of bacteriology.

Modern methods of sanitation and hygiene, public and private, modern house furnishing, as, for example, the substitution of bare floors with rugs in place of carpets, modern views of disease and methods of treating it, and the technique of innumerable industries, both agricultural and manufacturing, have all been profoundly modified

FIG. 226.—Tumors on a black walnut (*Juglans nigra*); probably crown galls caused by bacteria.

or determined altogether by the discovery of bacteria, and the extension of our knowledge concerning them.

290. Bacteria and Plant Diseases.—In addition to the plant diseases caused by fungi, as mentioned above, a number are known to be caused by bacteria. The "wilt" of sweet corn, a disease first discovered on Long Island, is caused by bacteria, as is also the crown gall, a tumorous or cancerous-like disease common in the rose family (peaches, apples, roses, raspberries), and the walnut, grape, and willow (Fig. 226). The "bean blight" and pear blight, the soft rot of the calla-lily, and the "wilt" of cucumbers and melons, are also caused each by its own peculiar kind of bacteria. On account of their nature these diseases may all be transmitted from one plant to another of the same kind.

291. Contagious and Infectious Diseases.—The ease with which such tiny organisms as bacteria can be transferred from one place to another makes the diseases they cause easily transmissible or "catching." We actually do "catch cold"; that is, our all too common "colds" are due to the presence of "cold"-producing germs. Arctic explorers testify to the fact that, notwithstanding the great exposures to which they are subjected, they never "catch cold." This is explained by the absence of the "cold" germs that cause colds in other climates or regions.

When the members of the Peary arctic expedition of 1908–09 were in the field away from the heat and infective dust of the ship, they were practically immune from colds and respiratory troubles. "The fact that colds are due to bacteria was clearly demonstrated in the Arctic. We might be precipitated into icy water with the air many degrees below zero; our clothing saturated with moisture on the march; yet we could sleep in our damp garments without fear of taking cold."[1]

292. Immunity.—This is not the place to discuss the various theories of immunity, but the fact should be noted in passing. It is a common belief that one who has had the measles or the mumps cannot have the same disease again. While this is extremely doubtful, it is known that once having a disease does render one less liable to contract it a second time. When the germs multiply in the body with the first attack, the toxin they produce stimulates the various cells to secrete an *antitoxin*, which counteracts the toxin, or poison. Some persons appear to be naturally immune from certain diseases (*e.g.*, hay fever), while others are specially susceptible.

293. Disease Carriers.—Persons who are immune may, however, unknowingly transmit the disease-germ from one person to another. They are called "carriers." Typhoid fever, caused by *Bacillus typhosus*, is often transmitted by "typhoid carriers," a recent case being that of "Typhoid Mary," a domestic servant near New York City, who for several years endangered the lives of others in homes and hospitals where she was employed. The menace of such persons to public health justifies their permanent isolation.

294. Combating Disease.—There are two ways of combating disease in either plants or animals: (1) to guard against it in advance (*prophylaxis*), thereby endeavoring to prevent its appearance; (2) to treat it after it has appeared. Obviously the former is the more im-

[1] From a letter to the author from John W. Goodsell, M. D., Surgeon of the Peary arctic expedition of 1908–09.

portant and effective. The most effective prophylactic measures are the following:

1. *Personal hygiene*, involving bodily cleanliness, temperate habits, and careful diet. With plant diseases hygienic measures include such practices as sterilizing seeds before planting, by rinsing them in solutions of some germ-killing substance, like formaldehyde; spraying diseased trees with fungicides (fungus-killing solutions); washing the branches and foliage with various solutions, such as whale-oil soap (good for scale insects); and painting the cut surfaces of trees, after trimming, to prevent the mycelium of germinating fungus spores from entering the woody tissue.

2. *Public hygiene, or sanitation*, which means maintaining healthful surroundings. In the case of animal diseases this includes preserving a pure public water supply, proper sewage systems, clean streets, a pure milk supply (especially a healthful condition of the cows and their surroundings), and a careful inspection of meat and all other foods shipped and sold in public.

In the case of plants, sanitation includes preserving a proper drainage and aeration of the soil; maintaining a pure atmosphere, and especially one free from smoke and the poisonous gases that accompany it; fumigating in plant houses with potassium cyanide fumes, or with tobacco smoke to kill scale insects, and other insects, the burning up of trees or other plants infected with a transmissible disease, such for example, as the chestnut bark disease, or barberry bushes carrying wheat rust, and eradication of injurious fungi from the soil of cultivated fields by crop-rotation, as indicated in Chapter VII.

3. *Quarantine.* This is a method of sanitation by which

diseased individuals are prevented by isolation from coming into contact with those who are well. When one member of the family is sick with a contagious disease he

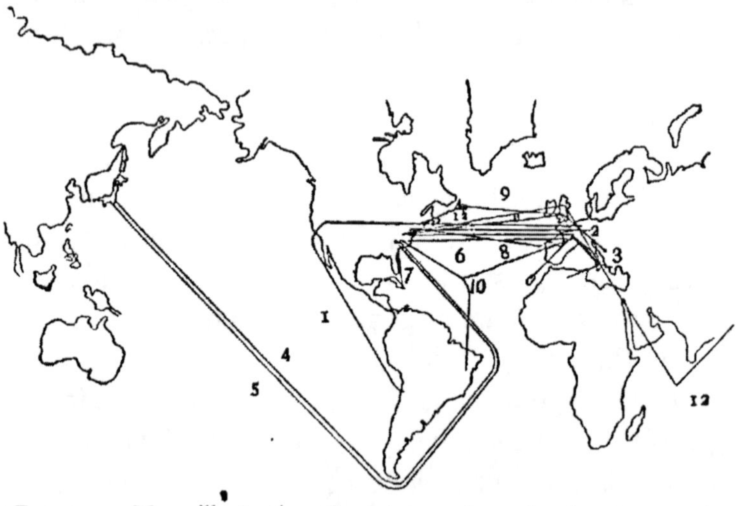

FIG. 227.—Map, illustrating the inter-continental migration of plant diseases. No. 1, potato blight: Chili-Colorado-Europe. No. 2, asparagus rust: Europe, 1805; New Jersey, 1896; South Carolina, 1897; Michigan, 1898; Illinois, 1899; Dakota, Nebraska and Texas, 1900; California, 1901. No. 3, potato cercosporose: Europe, 1854; United States, 1903. No. 4, rice smut: Japan-South Carolina, 1898. No. 5, sorghum smut: Japan-United States, 1884. No. 6, grape anthracnose: Europe-America, 1880, or earlier, now widespread. No. 7, cucumber downy mildew: Cuba, 1868; United States, 1889. No. 8, grape black rot: North America, early; France, 1885; Italy and the Caucasus, 1898. No. 9, potato wart: Hungary, 1896; England, 1900; Newfoundland, 1909; Boston and New York, 1910. No. 10, grape downy mildew: America early; France, 1873; the Rhineland, Savoy and Italy, 1879; The Tyrol and Algiers, 1880; Portugal and Greece, 1881; Alsace, 1882; the Caucasus, 1887; Brazil, 1890. Now known in all countries except Australia. No. 11, grape powdery mildew: United States, early; England, 1845; Belgium and France, 1848; all Europe 1849; Madeira, 1852. Known everywhere now. No. 12, chrysanthemum rust: Japan-England, 1895; America, 1896. (After F. L. Stevens.)

should be confined to one part of the house, apart from the others, and not allowed to mingle with them until well. Hospitals have "isolation wards" where persons with communicable diseases are kept apart from other patients.

Immigrants coming to America from foreign countries are carefully examined, and if they have a contagious disease they are isolated (placed in quarantine) until well.

The United States Government maintains a stringent quarantine against the shipment of diseased plants from one state to another, or from foreign countries into the United States. Some, if not all, of our worst plant diseases have been imported. The map (Fig. 227) shows how the rice smut travelled from Japan to South Carolina in 1898, the chrysanthemum rust from Japan through England (1895) to America (1896), and the potato blight from Chili to Colorado and across North America to Europe (1845). The downy mildew of the grape is an example of a disease probably originating in North America, where it has been known from the earliest times, and travelling thence to France (1873) and other parts of Europe, reaching as far as Greece by 1881, and to Brazil by 1890.

These brief references indicate the importance of maintaining a strict quarantine on plants at all our ports of entry.

4. *Breeding of resistant varieties.* This is one of the most important of all prophylactic measures. Just as some persons are immune to certain contagious diseases, so certain plants in a crop are less susceptible than others, or even entirely immune, to a given disease. By choosing seed each year only from the immune or most resistant individuals, a crop may sometimes be obtained which not only withstands the disease itself, but interferes with or finally stops entirely its spread. No phase of plant breeding is more important than this.

5. *Vaccination.* When bacteria produce poisons (*toxins*) in the system, the cells affected are stimulated to secrete

an *antitoxin* which counteracts the influence of the toxin (Cf. p. 310). The production of these antitoxins may finally completely nullify the effect of the toxin, and then the patient "gets well." The presence of the antitoxin, thus produced, explains why one who has recently recovered from a contagious disease, like measles, or mumps, or whooping cough, is more or less immune for a longer or shorter period. In 1796 the physician Jenner observed that persons who had cowpox, a mild form of smallpox, were commonly immune to the latter. Reasoning from this he developed the method of *vaccination.* By this method the cowpox is first given to a calf or a heifer, or sometimes to an adult cow. At the end of five to seven days pustules occur on the infected surface of the animal. A sticky substance that exudes from these pustules is then collected by sterile instruments and carefully tested to make sure that it does not contain any germs of tuberculosis or other disease. This substance is the *vaccine,* and in vaccination a small portion of it is applied to a scratched or slightly lacerated area on a person's arm. A mild form of the disease results, causing the formation of an antitoxin in the person's blood, and thus rendering him actively immune. The word vaccination is derived from the Latin word *vacca* (a cow), in allusion to the method of obtaining the serum or vaccine. It has been calculated that, in large armies, fully as many lives have been saved from disease by vaccination against typhoid, cholera, and other diseases as are lost in battle.

6. *Serum-therapy.* The treatment of germ diseases by serum-therapy consists in injecting into the blood of the patient an antitoxin, specific for the disease to be treated. The antitoxin is contained in the blood-serum

of some animal that has had the given disease. As in the case of the preparation of vaccine, the animal is first placed in quarantine, under the most perfect sanitary surroundings; if found free from all contagious diseases, and otherwise satisfactory, he is given increasingly large doses of the toxin or the virus that causes the given malady. This treatment may require as long as six weeks, and results in the formation of quantities of the antitoxin in the blood. A quantity of blood is then drawn from the animal, and the blood-serum isolated, filtered, carefully tested for purity, content of antitoxin, and freedom from disease-germs, and finally put up in glass syringe containers ready for use. When a person is exposed to the given disease (*e.g.*, diphtheria), or has actually contracted it, the serum is injected into his circulatory system, where the antitoxin counteracts the toxin of the disease. The patient is thus rendered *passively*[1] *immune.* Serum-therapy is now successfully employed in the treatment of diphtheria, tetanus (lockjaw), hog cholera, and, with more or less success, of infantile paralysis and certain other diseases.

Nothing corresponding to vaccination and serumtherapy is known for a certainty in the treatment of plant diseases.

7. *Antiseptic surgery.* The greatest obstacle to successful surgery has always been the presence of the rich and varied microscopic flora, or plant life, in the air. When a wound was opened or a cut made the germs composing this flora found on the cut surface the most favorable conditions for their growth and multiplication, and the poisons they secreted interfered with the healing of

[1] Passively, because the antitoxin is not produced by the activity of his own cells, as it is in the case of vaccination.

the wound and caused gangrene, or inflammations, more fatal than the disease for which the operation was undertaken. When the discovery of bacteria, and of their universal presence, enabled men to understand these facts it was only a step to the practice of making the operating rooms, the surgical instruments, and the surface to be cut, *absolutely* aseptic or sterile, thus making possible the almost unbelievable achievements of *antiseptic surgery*. Only a step! But what a wonderful and all-important step for the human mind to take. The honor and credit for taking it belong chiefly to the famous English surgeon, Lord Lister.

HELPFUL BACTERIA

295. Bacteria and the Dairy.—Not all bacteria, by any means, are harmful to man. Many of the practices of the dairy, for example, are dependent upon the action of bacteria. This, in part, is thought to explain the peculiarly delicious flavor of June butter. The souring of milk is caused by the action of substances produced by the bacteria present in all unsterilized milk. In fact the familiar flavor of milk is due in large measure to the presence in it of certain bacteria and the substances they produce. When milk is obtained under strictly sanitary conditions ("certified" milk) it loses much, if not all, of its characteristic and familiar flavor. The ripening, flavoring, and other peculiarities of the various varieties of cheese are due in part to the fact that they ripen under the influence of different kinds of bacteria or molds. The "ripening" is caused, in part, by the action on the substance of the cheese of the enzymes peculiar to the various fungi or bacteria growing in it.

and in part by the action of an enzyme (*galactase*) inherent in the milk from which the cheese is made.

296. Vinegar.—Cider vinegar is in every respect a plant product. It is formed from the juice of apples, and ripens or "ages" under the influence of bacteria. These bacteria produce an enzyme which causes "acetic acid

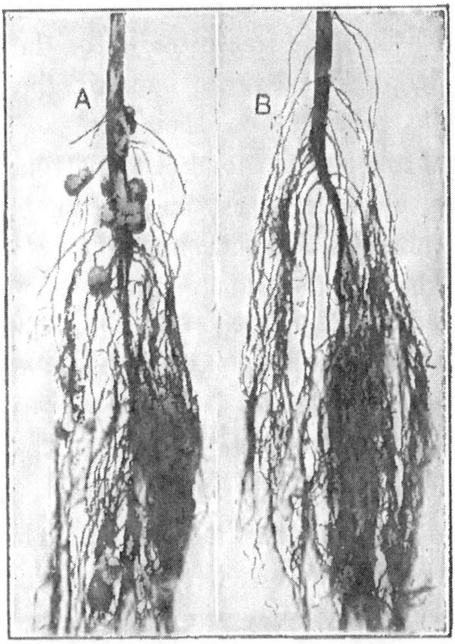

FIG. 228.—Roots of soy bean plants. *A*, from seeds that were soaked in soy bean bacterial culture over night; *B*, roots of check plant (not inoculated). (After Garman and Didlake. Courtesy of Kentucky Agr. Exp. Station.)

fermentation." This is the acid to which vinegar owes its sourness. There is not room here to explain the process of vinegar making in detail.

297. The Secret of Clover.—Farmers have known for many years that a given piece of land produces a larger yield if the same crop is not grown continuously, season after season, but if there is an alternation or *rotation of crops* of different kinds. It was also recognized that the best results are obtained when one of the crops in rotation is a *legume* (a member of the family Leguminosæ) such as clover, peas, beans, vetch, lentils, and others.[1] A clear explanation of the value of rotation was not possible until, in 1889, Hellriegel discovered that legumes are able to utilize the free nitrogen of the air, and that this is made possible by the bacteria that produce the characteristic tubercles on their roots. The researches of Hellriegel and others, at about this time, proved that the fixation of nitrogen is due to the bacterium that causes the tubercles, *Pseudomonas radicicola* (Fig. 61). If clover or other legumes are grown in a sterile soil, free from the presence of all bacteria, the tubercles do not form (Fig. 228), and the fixation of free nitrogen ceases. Thus it is seen that bacteria are essential to one of the oldest and most fundamental practices of agriculture.

289. Nitrifying Bacteria in the Soil.—In addition to the *symbionts* causing leguminous tubercles, there exist, in all soil, at least two other forms of nitrifying bacteria, which grow independently of other plants. The first, by the addition of oxygen, transforms the ammonia in the soil into *nitrites*, while the second, by the addition of more oxygen, transform nitrites into *nitrates*.[2] It is only in the latter form that nitrogen, so indispensible to nutrition, can be utilized at all by plants.

299. The Nitrogen Cycle.—From the above facts it is seen that there is, in nature, a *nitrogen cycle* quite as

[1] The subject of rotation of crops is more fully discussed in paragraph 90 (pp. 91–93).

[2] Cf. Chapter VII, pp. 82–83.

remarkable as the carbon cycle. By respiration and burning, complex compounds of carbon (carbohydrates and hydrocarbons) are broken down and the carbon released, either as pure carbon (C) or as the simple compound, carbon dioxide (CO_2), which is taken in by green plants and recombined into the complex carbohydrates by the process of photosynthesis (page 77).

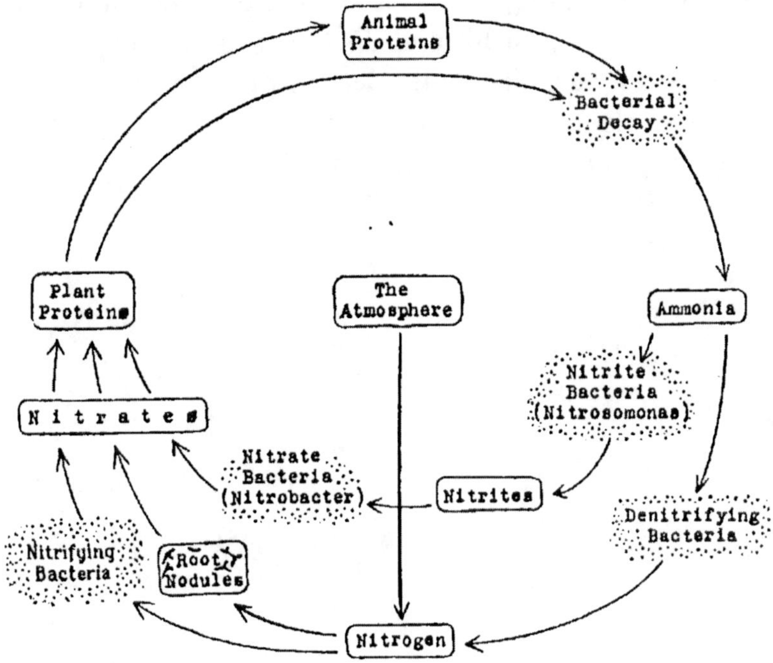

FIG. 229.—The nitrogen cycle.

So also, by the action of *proteolytic* (protein dissolving) enzymes produced by bacteria, certain complex compounds of nitrogen, the proteins, are broken down, by *putrefaction* and similar processes, into simpler compounds, such as ammonia (NH_3), or still further disintegrated until free nitrogen results. Were it not for the nitrogen-fixing bacteria this process would continue until all complex nitrogenous compounds were reduced to ammonia or free nitrogen. All life would then cease, because green plants, upon which animal life is dependent, are unable to live without nitrogen, and they cannot utilize it in the form of ammonia nor of free nitrogen. Without chlorophyll *and the nitrogen-fixing bacteria*, therefore, all life would cease. Thus it is that life and death, health and disease, wealth and poverty, misery and happiness, are dependent upon the activity of tiny plants, too small to be seen, except under the highest powers of the microscope.

CHAPTER XXI

SAPROPHYTISM AND SYMBIOSIS

300. All Food Organic.—In more ways than one it is true that life is dependent upon antecedent life. An illustration of this principle is seen in the case of nutrition, for no living thing, neither plant nor animal, can utilize directly as food the unaltered inorganic elements and compounds derived from the air and soil. This was clearly shown in Chapter VII. While plants are commonly said to obtain their food from the air and soil, strictly speaking this is not true. Carbon, oxygen, hydrogen, phosphates, nitrates, sulphates, *et cetera* are no more plant food than are flour, water, sugar, and salt bread. Just as the elements composing bread would, if eaten separately, make a very unsavory and poor diet, so the inorganic elements and compounds, as such, would not be able at all to nourish plants. They must first be broken down (if compounds), and then recombined into the organic compounds of carbohydrates, proteins, and fats.

301.—Necessity for Chlorophyll.—As we have seen in Chapter VII, this recombination of inorganic chemical elements into organic compounds is the function of chlorophyll. Thus it is that green plants are absolutely essential to all life, and as we learned in Chapter XIX, this explains why all non-green plants are found only in intimate association, either with living green plants or with the organic remains or products of other living things—plants or animals. Not being able to manufacture their own food, they must find it ready made.

SAPROPHYTISM

302. Decay.—Perhaps the simplest case of the nutrition of non-green plants is the absorption of food from the organic remains of other plants or of animals. When the spores or other reproductive bodies of such plants begin to grow upon such a substratum, they secrete various enzymes which begin to disintegrate it, reducing it to simpler, soluble substances. This is the process commonly known as "decay," and the plants which cause it are called *saprophytes*.[1] The word "decay" is derived from a Latin word, *decidere*, which means to fall apart, in allusion to the fact that the decaying substance is being disintegrated or broken down into simpler substances, which are recombined by assimilation, in the cells of the saprophyte, into protoplasm like its own. Such a state of existence is called *saprophytism*.

303. Fungus-saprophytes.—Among the more familiar saprophytic plants may be mentioned the common bread-mold, the fungi that are instrumental in ripening cheese, the so-called "mildews," which often grow on old moist pieces of leather, and numerous other filamentous fungi; the bacteria which cause the decay of meat and other substances, bacteria which cause the retting of flax stems, thus freeing the bast fibers from which linen is made by causing the decay or rotting away of the remainder of the tissue, the bacteria which convert cabbage leaves

[1] From the Greek words *sapros*, rotten + *phyton*, plant.

into sauerkraut, the numerous slime-molds (Myxomycetes), and various other forms, which are more or less intimately connected with human industries, or with public or private hygiene.

Humus, one of the most important compounds of soil, is composed almost entirely of the remains ot plant and animal bodies in various stages of disintegration,

FIG. 230.—Indian-pipe (*Monotropa uniflora*). (Photo by Elsie M. Kittredge.)

and the disintegration is caused, almost entirely, by the action of enzymes secreted by bacterial and fungal saprophytes. Thus we come to realize that these saprophytic plants are absolutely essential to the most fundamental of all human occupations, namely agriculture.

304. Saprophytic Flowering Plants.—Not all saprophytes are fungi. The Indian-pipe (*Monotropa uniflora*,

Fig. 230), and its close relative, the false beech-drops (*Monotropa Hypopitys*, Fig. 231), are examples of flowering plants, wholly devoid of chlorophyll, and therefore unable to manufacture their food, which is absorbed entirely from the humus in which they grow. Other examples are *Lathræa*, and the coral-root (*Corallorhiza*).

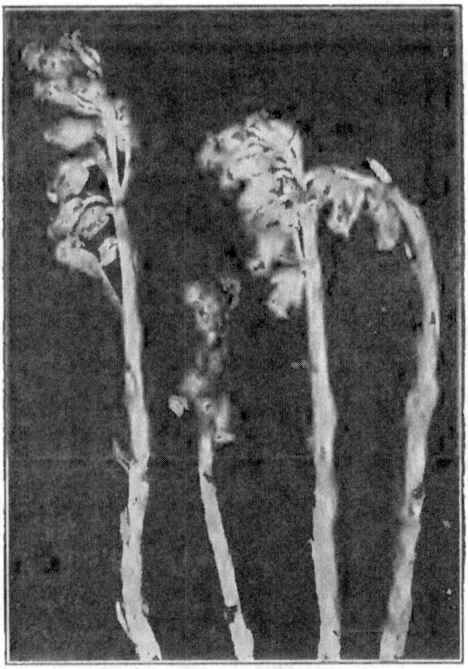

FIG. 231.—False beech drops (*Monotropa Hypopitys*). (Photo by Elsie M. Kittredge.)

SYMBIOSIS

305. Different Kinds of Symbiosis.—The absorption of nourishment from one plant by another involves, of course, the intimate association of the two organisms. Such a vital association is called *symbiosis* (living together), and we find organisms living together in all degrees of intimacy and independence, or of interdependence. One plant may merely live upon another, without deriving any nourishment from it (*epiphytism*); or two plants may be mutually helpful, each contributing something of advantage to the other (*mutualism*); one plant may live at the expense of the other, deriving nourishment from it, but contributing little or nothing in return (*parasitism*); or the two organisms may maintain a loose or disjunctive symbiosis, which may be either (1) *nutritive*, as in those cases where ants cultivate filamentous fungi, maintaining fungus-farms; or (2) *non-nutritive*, as in the cases where certain plants like clover or orchids, are dependent upon insects for the transfer of pollen from one flower to another. These phases of symbiosis are indicated in the following table:

Symbiosis
1. Disjunctive or "social."
   (*a*) Nutritive (*e.g.*, ants and fungus-farms).
   (*b*) Non-nutritive (insects and pollination).
2. Epiphytism.
3. Mutualism.
4. Parasitism.

306. Social Symbiosis.—As an illustration of social symbiosis of a nutritive character may be mentioned the interesting relation established between certain leaf-cutting ants and a filamentous fungus. The ants remove the foliage-leaves from certain trees and use them as "fungus-farms," or a suitable substratum on which to cultivate a certain fungus, portions of which serve as food for the ants (Fig. 232). The spores are sown by the ants and the "crop" harvested in a very systematic manner. The loss of leaves, however, is very deleterious to the life of the tree, and certain species (*e.g.*, *Cecropia* and

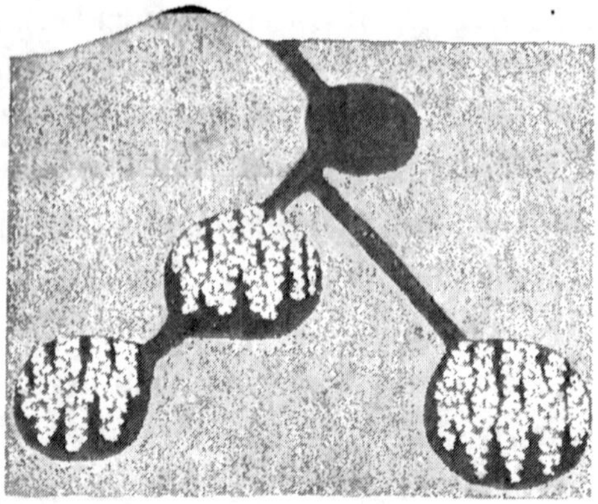

FIG. 232.—Diagram of a nest of a fungus-growing ant (*Trachymyrmex obscurior*), showing four chambers. The pendant white masses in three of the chambers are the mycelium of the fungus—the so-called "fungus-gardens." The species of the fungus has not been definitely determined, but they are thought to belong to the Ascomycetes. (After W. M. Wheeler.)

FIG. 233.—Epiphytes or "air" plants (*Tillandsia sp.*), growing on telephone wires at Ponce, P. R.

Acacia), secrete a substance which is greatly liked by another kind of ants, a smaller, war-like species. These ants, attracted by the much-prized food, make their home on the tree or in special cavities in it, and repel all attempts of the leaf-cutting species to reach the foliage.

FIG. 234.—Epiphytic group of bromeliads and orchids on a tree, in Cuba. (Photo by M. T. Cook.)

Such trees are called ant-loving (*myrmecophylous*), or myrmecophytes.

307. Epiphytism.—Any plant (whether parasite or not) that lives on another, or upon any other convenient support (Fig. 233), is an epiphyte, but the term is commonly restricted to those cases where there is no physiological or nutritional relationship between the two. A vine climbing up a tree is an epiphyte, as are also the *Pleurococcus* and mosses growing on the tree trunks. Epiphytism is specially common in the tropics where orchids,

FIG. 235.—An epiphytic *Clusia*. (From photo by G. V. Nash, taken in Haiti.)

ferns, hohenbergias, and great lianas (vines) are found growing in profusion on other plants (Figs. 234, 235, and 236).

308. Mutualism.—The associating together of two plants in intimate physiological relationship, to their

FIG. 236.—An orchid (*Cattleya sp.*) growing as an epiphyte on a portion of a branch of white birch. Note the aerial roots.

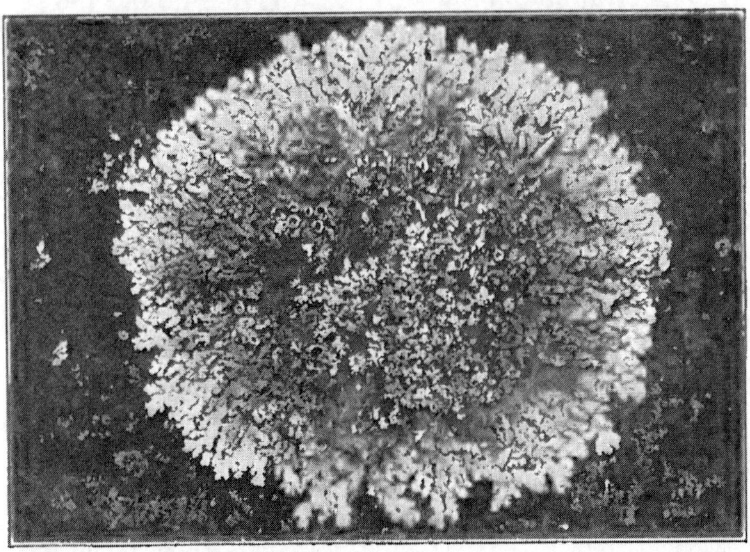

FIG. 237.—A thallose lichen, *Physcia stellaris* (L.) Nyb., growing on a rock. The cup-shaped structures are the fruiting bodies (apothecia). At the left are seen two very young plants.

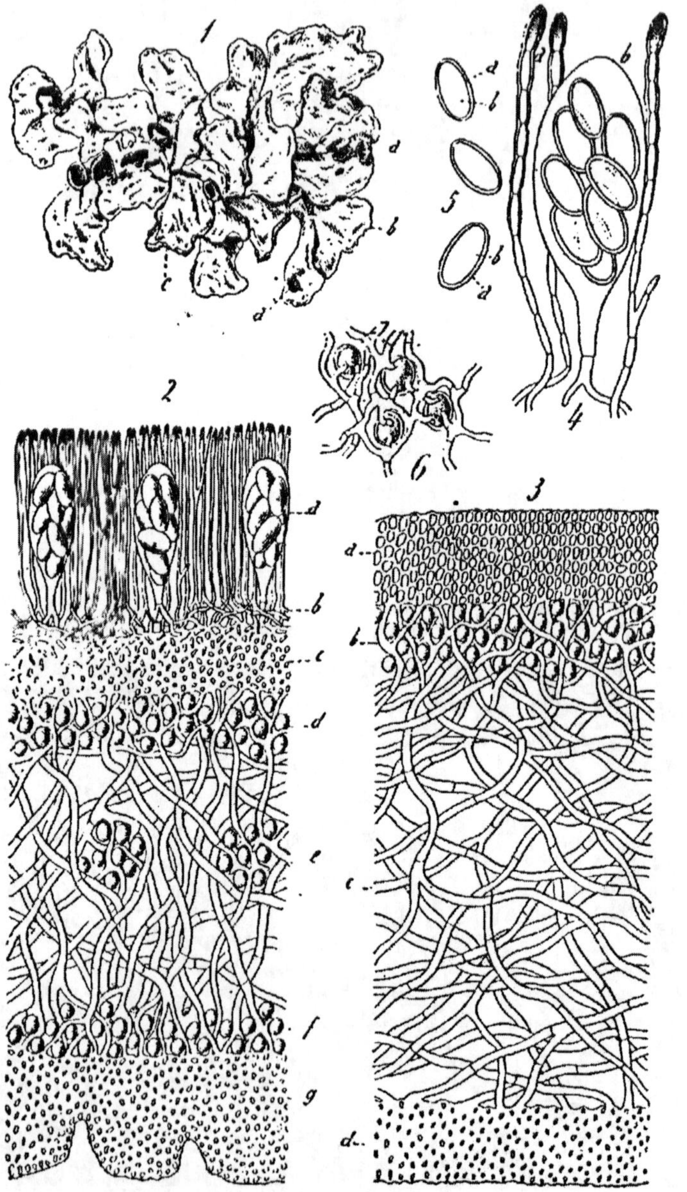

FIG. 238.—A lichen, *Parmelia perlata* (L.) Ach. 1. Plant, slightly reduced in size; *a*, apothecia; *b*, lobe of thallus; *c*, soredial patches. The soredia are vegetative reproductive bodies composed of both algal and fungal elements, and therefore able to reproduce the lichen; the ascospores,

mutual advantage, is admirably illustrated by *lichens*. These plants grow commonly on the trunks and stems of trees, on old boards and fences, and on rocks (Fig. 237). The plant body is a thallus, and, when its inner structure is examined, it is seen to be a composite plant, formed by a species of green alga, resembling *Pleurococcus*, and surrounded by the mycelium of a filamentous fungus (Fig. 238). If supplied with suitable moisture, the alga can live alone, because it has chlorophyll, but the fungus, not having chlorophyll, cannot live alone. By uniting into a common body, each plant supplies what the other needs.

The fungal portion of lichens reproduces by means of spores borne in asci, and is therefore an ascomycete. The *apothecium* ("fruiting" portion of the lichen) is in reality a modified ascocarp (Fig. 238). In some species the apothecia occur at the summit of specialized, upright branches or *podetia* (Fig. 239). Only a few years ago the interesting discovery was made that lichens may be experimentally produced by the artificial union of certain algæ and fungi (Fig. 240). Some of the lichens thus produced resembled those found in nature, while other combinations were entirely new.

An interesting case of the symbiotic association of four genera, if not to their mutual benefit, at least without apparent detriment to either, is found in the roots of some of the Cycadaceæ. All the genera of this family produce

---

alone, cannot do this. 2, Longitudinal section of apothecium; *a*, thecium; *b* and *c*, the two layers of the hypothecium; *d*, upper algal layer; *e*, colonies of algæ distributed through the medullary layer; *f*, lower algal layer; *g*, lower cortical layer. 3, Cross-section of vegetative portion of thallus. 4, Paraphyses (sterile fungal filaments), and spore-sac (ascus), containing ascospores. 5, Ascospores. 6, Algal cells, surrounded by fungal hyphæ with haustoria (absorbing branches). (After Schneider.)

branched, coralloid nodules on their roots (Fig. 241). These roots are caused primarily by infection with the

FIG. 239.—Thallus and erect portions (*podetia*) of two species of lichen of the genus *Cladonia*. The larger podetium is *proliferating*, and bears a number of *apothecia* on the margin of the podetium of the first rank. Apothecia are also shown on the margin of the larger podetia at the right. (Drawn from nature.)

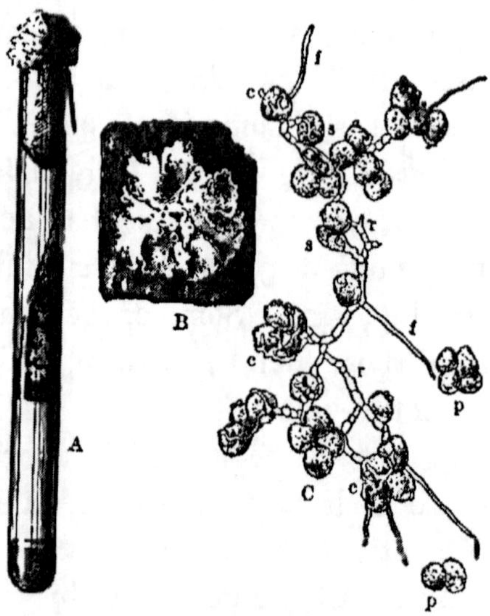

FIG. 240.—A lichen produced synthetically by cultivating the spores of a fungus in association with a green alga. The culture was carried on in a test-tube on sterilized culture media, thus preventing contamination by bacteria and foreign spores. (After Bonnier.)

nitrogen-fixing organism, *Pseudomonas radicicola*. By the development of lenticels at the base of each nodule the epidermis is ruptured, thus affording entrance to another nitrogen-fixer, *Azotobacter*, and also under favorable conditions, to a blue-green alga (*Nostoc*). This is the only known case in which four organisms are associated

FIG. 241.—Root-nodules of *Cycas revoluta*. *n*, one of several cross-sectional views, showing the zone of the symbiont alga, *Nostoc*.

together symbiotically. The alga has never been found in the nodules of *Bowenia*, *Ceratozamia*, *Macrozamia*, nor *Zamia* (all genera of cycads).

309. Grafting.—One of the oldest practices of horticulture is that of grafting a twig or a bud of one species

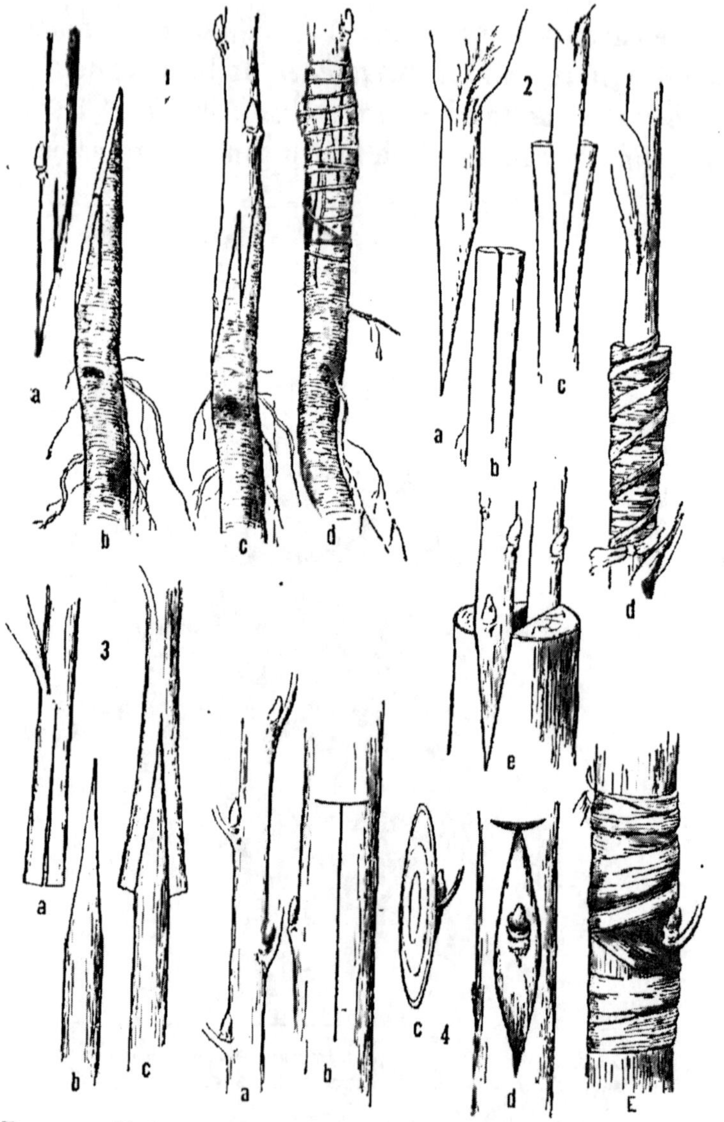

FIG. 242.—Various methods of grafting. (1) Root grafting in its different stages. *a*, Scion cut for insertion; *b*, stock prepared to receive the scion; *c*, stock and scion united; *d*, the same tied up with waxed cord. (2) Cleft grafting (Herbaceous). *a*, Scion ready for insertion; *b*, stock; *c*, stock and scion united; *d*, the same tied up with raffia; *e*, cleft grafting (woody). Stock with two scions. (3) Saddle grafting. *a*, Scion; *b*, stock; *c*, scion and stock joined. (4) Budding. *a*, Budstick; *b*, T-shaped cut in bark of stock; *c*, bud ready for insertion; *d*, stock with bud inserted; *e*, the same tied up with raffia. (From Brooklyn Botanic Garden *Leaflets*.)

onto the main stem or branch of another species. This is accomplished by placing the freshly cut surface of the *scion* against the freshly cut surface of the *stock*,

FIG. 243.—A tomato (*Lycopersicum*), grafted on a potato (*Solanum*). Note the potato tuber on the surface of the soil. *Cf.* Fig. 404.

in such a way that the cambium layers of each come in contact, and then binding the two together (Fig. 242). In time the two tissues become firmly united, growing as one continuous stem. In all grafting the scion maintains essentially its true nature, seldom, if ever, being affected by the characteristics of the stock, which only serves as a channel for the passage of water and food elements to the scion, and receiving in return from the scion the elaborated carbohydrate and other food (Figs. 243 and 404). Scion and stock therefore represent a case of symbiosis artificially brought about. In some cases branches of the same tree rub against each other until the bark is worn through, bringing the cambial layers in contact, and resulting in a "natural" graft.

310. Mycorrhizas.—The roots of many plants (especially of woody plants) enter into intimate association with the mycelia of various fungi growing in the soil.

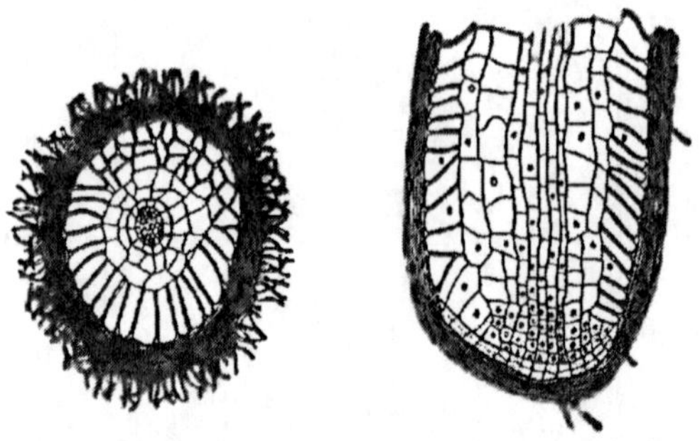

Fig. 244.—Ectotrophic micorhizas. At left, micorhizal mantle on root of hickory (*Carya ovala*), in cross-section; at right, root-tip of an oak (*Quercus*), covered by fungus mantle. (After W. B. McDougall.)

The mycelia either form a mantle or jacket at or near the surface of the young roots (*ectotrophic*, Fig. 244), or they penetrate through the cell-walls into the cell-cavities (*endotrophic*, Fig. 245). Recent careful studies seem to demonstrate that the ectotrophic mycorrhizas, common on the roots of many kinds of trees (hickory, oaks, birch, sugar-maple, larch, beech, hornbeam), are, in reality, evidence of the parasitism of some fungus on the tree. Several species of fleshy fungi are, in this way, parasitic or partly parasitic. In ectotrophic infection the hyphæ penetrate through the epidermis and then grow and branch underneath it, some of the branches growing between the individual epidermal cells by dissolving the middle lamella with enzymes which they secrete. In this manner there is formed a pseudo-tissue, closely analogous to a lichen, which replaces the true epidermis. The fungus doubtless derives some nourishment from the dissolved (digested)

FIG. 245.—Tangential section of root of the red maple (*Acer rubrum*), showing endotrophic micorhiza in the cells. (After W. B. McDougall.)

substance of the middle lamella, as well as from nutrient substances that diffuse out from adjacent cells; but there is no evidence that the tree is in any way benefited by the presence of the fungus.

In some cases the development of the mycorrhiza-mantle inhibits the growth of the root, and stimulates a profuse branching, which is repeated as the branches are infected. This gives rise to a malformation known as "coral root," which is so well developed in one herbaceous species as to give the plant its scientific as well as its common name —*Corallorhiza*, or coral-root.

In endotrophic mycorrhizas the hyphæ penetrate through the cell-walls into the cell-cavities, and in such cases all stages are found from true parasitism of the fungus on the root, through a mutually beneficial relationship, to a parasitism of the root-cells on the fungus. Among common trees having endotrophic mycorrhizas, may be

FIG. 246.—Cancer-root (*Conopholis americana*), of the Broom-rape family (*Orobanchaceæ*). The ovaries are developing into capsules. The plant derives its name from the scaly cone. (Photo by Elsie M. Kittredge.)

mentioned the black maple, horse-chestnut, and black walnut, and most of the heath family (Ericaceæ), such as trailing arbutus, huckleberry, wintergreen, heather, laurel, and rhododendron. This is probably the chief reason why it is so difficult to transplant many of the heaths; the delicate adjustment between the plant and the mycorrhizal fungus is disturbed in transplanting, and the soil conditions in the new habitat are not favorable to its reëstablishment before the plant dies.

The Indian-pipe and the false "beech-drops" (Figs. 230 and 231), both belonging to the heath family, also possess endotrophic mycorrhizas.

FIG. 247.—Dodder (*Cuscuta sp.*), parasitic on geranium (*Pelargonium*). A few seedlings at the left are still rooted in the soil, and are not yet attached to the host-plant. They eventually sever all relation with the soil.

311. Parasitism.—In some cases of symbiosis, as stated above, only one plant derives any benefit from the union, which may or may not be of positive injury to the other. Such is the case with the endotrophic mycorrhizas, already mentioned. There are many instances of the parasitism of one flowering plant on another (Fig. 246). In some of these cases as, for example, the dodder (*Cuscuta*), the parasite may have completely lost the power of elaborating chlorophyll, and thus lack the function of photosynthesis;

FIG. 248.—Dodder (*Cuscuta sp.*), in flower. Parasitic on a golden rod (*Solidago ulmifolia*). (Photo by Elsie M. Kittredge.)

the parasitism is then complete (Figs. 247, 248 and 249). In other cases the parasite may retain its chlorophyll-apparatus, and hence be only partly dependent upon the host, as in the case of the mistletoe (Fig. 250). Such plants are *semi-parasites*. Another example of semi-parasitism is that of the blue-green alga, *Nostoc*, species of which grow in little pockets or cavities in the tissues of the water-fern *Salvinia*, of *Gunnera manicata*,

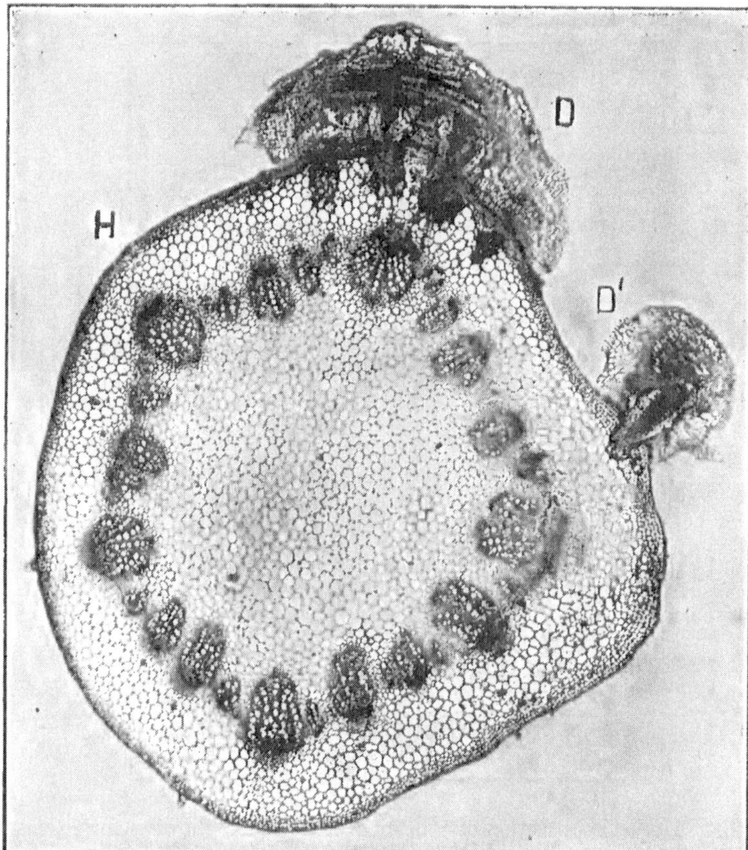

FIG. 249.—Photomicrograph of a cross-section of the stem of a dicotyledonous host-plant infested with the parasite, dodder (*Cuscuta sp.*). Note the haustoria extending from the dodder (D, D′) into the cortex of the host (H). Greatly enlarged.

of *Anthoceros*, and of other plants, without apparent injury to the host (Fig. 160).

312. Artificial Parasites.—By recent experiments certain plants have been induced, by experimental treatment, to grow as parasites on other plants (Fig. 250*a*). The condition to success in such experiments is that the osmotic strength of the cell-sap of the host must be less than, or at least not greater than that of the parasite.

FIG. 250.—Cross-section of a branch of live oak, showing five stems of mistletoe, parasitic on the oak; the upper stem with foliage and fruit. Note the prominent "sinkers" of the parasite, some of them growing laterally for a short distance, close under the surface of the bark, and then radially, deep into the tissue of the wood.

313. Fungal Parasites.—Mention has already been made in Chapter XIV of the parasitism of the entire group of fungi, including the smuts, rusts, and other disease-producing fungi, on flowering plants. The "shelf-fungi," commonly found on forest trees, are economically important because of the enormous financial losses occasioned by the timber-decay which they induce.

314. Parasitism Means Degeneration.—*Most parasites among the flowering plants have suffered the loss of some organ or organs*, and of one or more functions as a result of the parasitic habit. In fact, parasitism must be regarded as an acquired habit, and the parasite among plants, as in human society or elsewhere, as a degenerate form of life. Some plants can live only as parasites (*obligate parasitism*), while others may live either as parasites or as saprophytes (*facultative parasitism*).

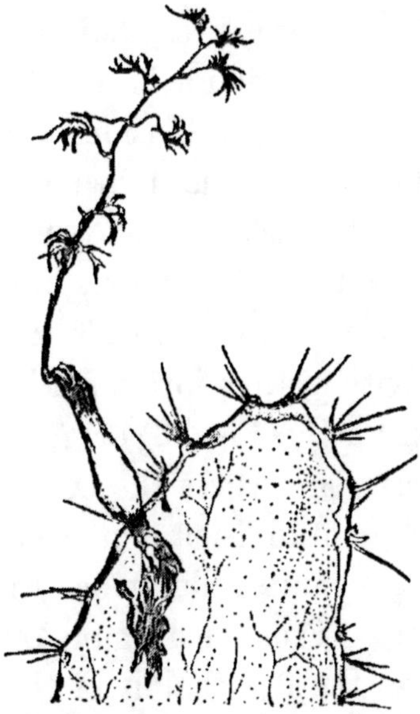

FIG. 250, *a*.—*Cissus laciniata*, parasitic on the cactus (*Opuntia Blakeana*). The parasitism was artificially induced (xeno-parasitism). The host plant has been sectioned to expose the roots of the xeno-parasite. (Redrawn from D. T. MacDougal.)

315. Flowers and Insects.—The dependence of certain plants upon insects to secure the transfer of pollen from one flower or plant to another, will be mentioned more in detail in Chapters XXVII–XXIX.

CHAPTER XXII

THE PROBLEM OF SEX IN PLANTS

316. Cell-division and Reproduction.—As stated in Chapter XIV, the essence of reproduction is the separation, from the body of the parent, of a cell or larger portion, which becomes the starting point of a new individual. In some of the lowest plants, such as certain species of bacteria, cell-division always results in reproduction; that is, the two halves of the divided, one-celled body always separate at the close of cell-division, thus giving rise to two new individuals. A little higher in the scale of life we find such plants as *Pleurococcus*, where cell-division *may* result at once in reproduction, but where there is also a marked tendency for the cells to adhere together at the close of division, thus forming a loosely organized, multi-cellular plant body (Fig. 183). A further advance is illustrated by *Spirogyra*, where the cells normally do not separate at the close of division, but remain together, end to end, producing a multi-cellular body in the form of a filament (Fig. 251). From this simple condition we have seen transitions to the flat thallus of the liverworts; the simple, leafy axis of the mosses, the leafless axis of the moss-sporophyte, and the leafy sporophyte of the ferns. Not that these forms are derived from each other; but they illustrate various degrees of complexity from the simplest unicellular plant body to a complex, multi-cellular body. By a comparison of these forms, we see that while, in some of the lowest forms, cell-division always results in reproduction, in the higher forms it only paves the way

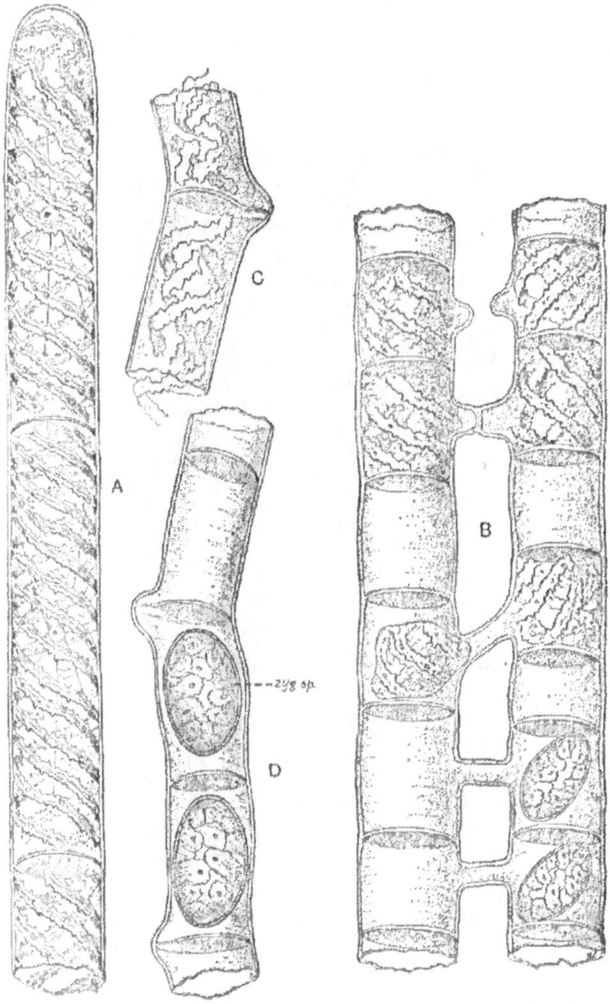

FIG. 251.- *Spirogyra sp.* *A*, terminal portion of vegetative filament; *B*, stages of scalariform conjugation; *C*, preparation for lateral conjugation; *D*, zygospores formed by lateral conjugation.

to increasing the size of the given individual, that is, to growth. In other words, between cell-division and reproduction there is interposed the enlargement or growth of the parent.

317. Vegetative Multiplication.—Attention has also been called to the various methods by which the number of individual plants is increased by the separation of multi-

FIG. 252.—Branch of a willow (*Salix sp.*), showing the formation of fibrous roots. The lower portion of the stem was placed in water for a few days.

cellular portions of the body of the parent. The most familiar of these processes being the artificial propagation of plants by means of cuttings. A portion of stem (Figs. 3 and 252), or sometimes of leaf (Fig. 253), stuck into moist sand will form new roots and ultimately develop an entire new plant. A leaf of begonia laid on moist sand will give rise to several new plants wherever it is cut (Fig. 254). Leaves of the sundew (*Drosera*) frequently strike

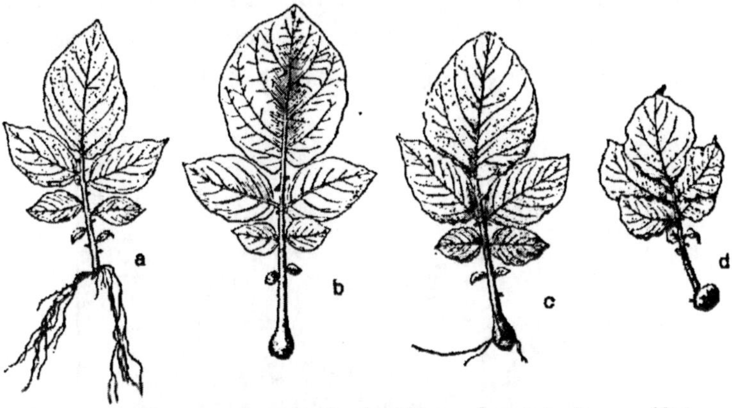

FIG. 253.—Regeneration at the leaf-base of potato leaves (*Solanum tuberosum*). *a*, roots formed; *b*, tuber-like enlargement; *c*, same as *b*, with roots; *d*, formation of true tuber. (After Miss Elsie Kupfer.)

FIG. 254.—Young plantlets developing from the edges of lacerations made in a large leaf of Rex begonia.

root at the tip and develop new plants (Fig. 255), while the leaves of *Bryophyllum* normally produce marginal buds from which new plants develop (Fig. 256). As noted in Chapter XVI, the thallus of a liverwort may be chopped fine and every isolated, intact cell will give rise to a new plant.

Growing plants of the liverwort, *Marchantia*, isolated by the dying of older tissue develop new individuals; the tips of the leaves of the walking fern may strike root

FIG. 255.—*Drosera rotundifolia.* Production of a young plant from the leaf of an older plant.

and originate new plants (Fig. 122), the tips of stolons or runners (as in ferns, eel-grass, strawberries, etc.) may do the same (Figs. 257–259, and 123), isolated sterile branches and "innovation-branches" of *Sphagnum* moss become new individuals (Fig. 144), as may also the familiar tubers and bulbs (such as those of the potato and onion),

FIG. 256.—*Bryophyllum crenatum.* A leaf which has given rise to three plantlets along the margin of the blade.

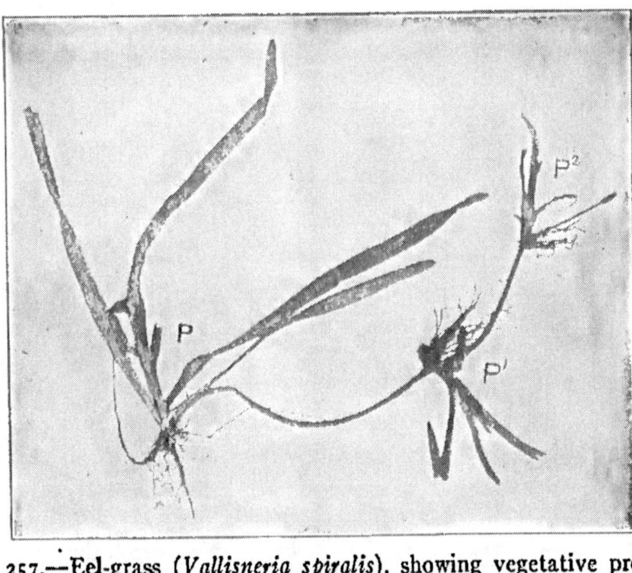

FIG. 257.—Eel-grass (*Vallisneria spiralis*), showing vegetative propagation by stolons. Young plants at P^1 and P^2.

FIG. 258.—*Sempervivum tectorum*, with stolons.

FIG. 259.—*Chlorophytum elatum* R. Br., showing vegetative propagation by runners. P^1, P^2, P^3, new plants; P, parent plant. From P^2 one root, and from P^1 two roots hang down.

and the *gemmæ* of various species of liverworts, mosses, and ferns (Fig. 260).

An interesting form of vegetative multiplication is illustrated by the fern *Woodwardia orientalis*, where new plantlets arise at numerous points on the upper surface of the leaves (Fig. 261). The number of individuals is thereby increased or multiplied, hence the term *vegetative multiplication.*

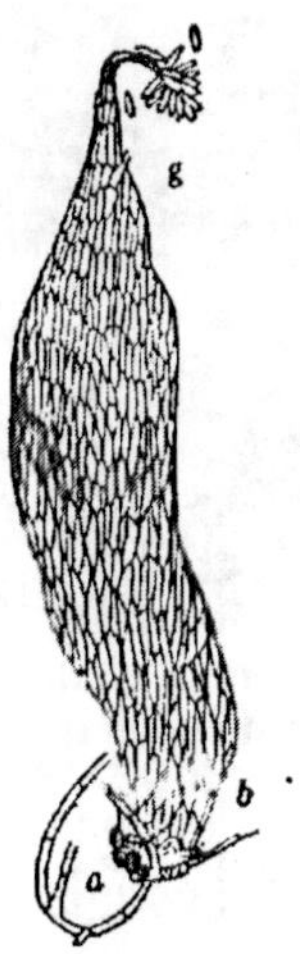

FIG. 260.—*Hymenophyllum sp.* Prothallus. *a*, antheridia; *b*, archegonia; *g*, gemmæ. (After Winifred J. Robinson.)

318. Reproduction by Spores.—In many plants such, for example, as the fern, the parent plant, while retaining its own vegetative organs intact, gives off individual cells (the spores), which become the starting points of new individuals. *The most distinctive thing about a spore is that it escapes, or becomes separated from the parent*, while all the other cells remain organically united.

In some one-celled plants (*e.g.*, yeast, Fig. 67), the entire plant body (except the cell-wall) may become organized into spores, which escape from the cell-wall of the mother-cell. In a number of many-celled plants (*e.g.*, *Ulothrix*) practically every protoplast has the capacity of becoming organized into one or more spores which escape from the old cell-cavity. The next higher step is the restriction of spore formation to certain cells in special organs (sporangia), while the other cells function only vegetatively.

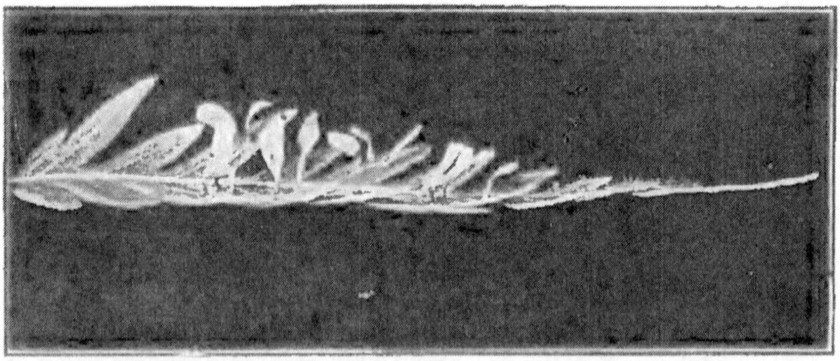

FIG. 261.—*Woodwardia orientalis.* Portion of a leaf bearing numerous young plantlets on its upper surface.

319. Cell-fusions.—Through all the variations of reproduction by spores there is, as a rule, only the separation of protoplasts from the parent body, never a cell-fusion or nuclear-fusion. Some plants, however, such as *Ulothrix* (Fig. 262), have been found to produce two sizes of spores, and the small spores must always unite before they can develop into full-sized, mature individuals.[1] Attention has already been called (Chapter XVIII) to the condition of similar sized gametes (*isogamy*), as in *Spirogyra*, in contrast to that of unequal gametes (*heterogamy*), as in *Ascophyllum* and *Fucus*.

[1] In certain cases (*e.g.*, *Ulothrix*) the microspores may develop small, imperfect individuals without fusion.

320. Maleness and Femaleness.—*Spirogyra.* In nearly all cases of cell-fusion it is possible to recognize some difference, either of structure or of behavior, between the gametes. In *Spirogyra,* for example, it has long been noticed that if one of the cells of a filament passes over to the other filament through the conjugation-tube, *all* the cells of that filament will ordinarily do the same. Thus after conjugation is over *all* the cells in one filament will be found empty, while all the cells of the adjacent, conjugating filament will contain zygotes. This behavior, however, varies under certain conditions and with different species.

Recent studies by York have revealed the fact that the supplying gamete of *Spirogyra* always possesses less starch and a less number of starch-formers (*pyrenoids*) than does the receiving gamete (Fig. 263). It has also been noted that the supplying filaments (male ?) are less vigorous, vegetatively, than the receiving filaments (female ?).

321. Sexuality in Molds.—One of the most interesting of recent discoveries in connection with sex in plants, is that of the existence of two strains of different sexual value in the molds. It was known for a long time that conjugation and the formation of zygotes in these plants could not always be secured when desired; that is, conjugation would not occur between every two individuals. At first it was thought that the explanation lay in the fact that the external conditions (temperature, light, moisture), might not be just right, or that the two adjacent plants were not in the right condition as to age, or nutrition, or otherwise. Finally, as stated in Chapter XIX, Blakeslee, by careful experimental studies, found that there are two unlike strains of many of the molds, and that whenever a

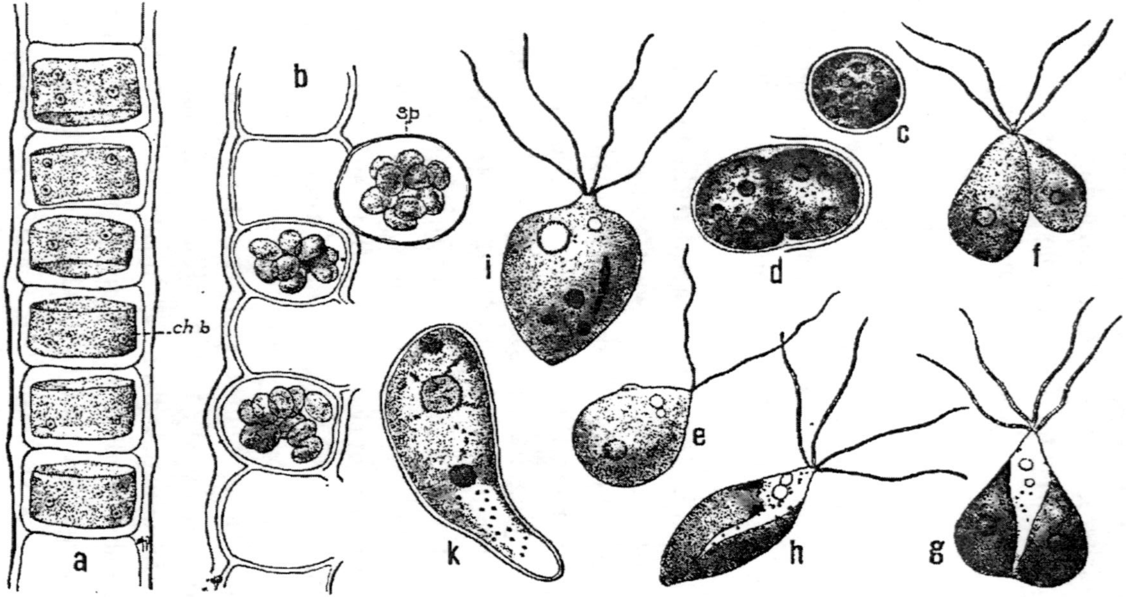

FIG. 262.—*Ulothrix zonata; a*, portion of the filamentous plant-body, showing the chlorophyll band (*ch.b*) in each cell; *b*, the various cells functioning as sporangia; from the upper cell the mass of small zoöspores, or gametes, (*sp*) are escaping; *c*, zygote; when the zygote germinates it produces several zoöspores, each of which develops into a new plant; *d*, beginning of germination of zygote; *e*, isogamous gamete; *f–h*, stages in the conjugation of isogamous gametes; *i*, large zoöspore; *k*, large zoöspore germinating. (*c–k*, after Oltmanns.)

plant of one strain grows next to a plant of another strain, conjugation will always take place between them. These strains he designated, provisionally as (+) and (−) (Fig. 190). The (+) strain is vegetatively more vigorous

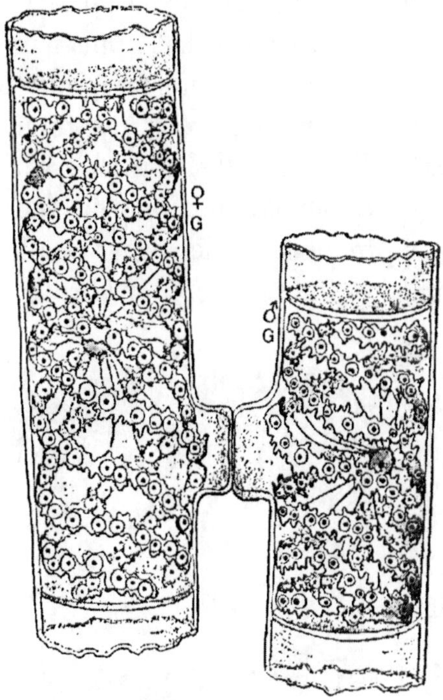

FIG. 263.—*Spirogyra sp.*, illustrating sexual differentiation. Receiving (female) gamete at the left; supplying (male) gamete at the right. (Redrawn from camera lucida drawing by H. H. York.)

than the (−) strain, and the conclusion seems warranted that the (+) race is female and the (−) race male.

322. Sexual Differentiation of Spores.—1. *Physiological.* Even an elementary study of reproduction reveals the fact that spores from the same plant, and even from the same sporangium (as in some of the molds just mentioned), and to all external appearances entirely alike, may produce individuals of different sex-value, some being male and some female.[1] Such was also seen to be the case with the marine alga *Dictyota*,[2] the externally similar male and female gametophytes being produced by spores that are alike in size and other external features.

As a further advance spores that appear to be morphologically alike may produce plants morphologically as well as physiologically different (*Anthoceros*, some molds).

2. *Structural.* In the little club-mosses (*Selaginella*) we found the spores unlike, not only in function but in structure, those producing males being smaller than those producing females—the condition of *heterospory*.

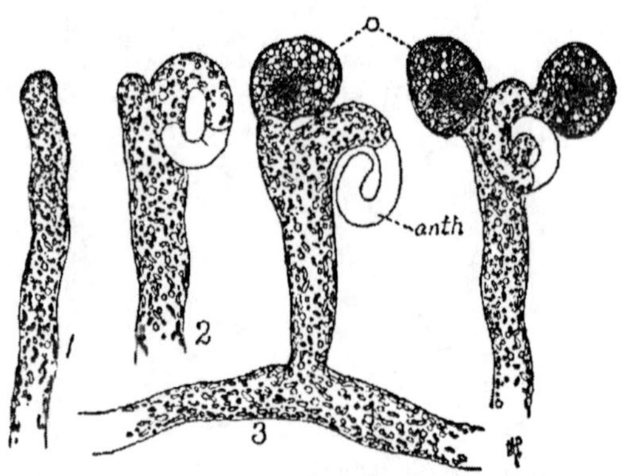

FIG. 264.—*Vaucheria terrestris.* *anth*, antheridium (empty); *o*, oögonia.

323. Differentiation of Sex-organs.—In many lower plants there is no recognizable structural difference between the organs that produce the heterogametes, but a step in advance in this direction is found in such a plant as *Vaucheria* (Fig. 264), where the antheridia are struc-

[1] See, also, pp. 246 and 248.

[2] See Chapter XVIII.

turally very unlike the oögonia. This differentiation is carried a step further with the appearance of the multicellular archegonium in liverworts and mosses.

324. Structural Differentiation of the Sexes.—1. *Partial.*—In some species (though not in all) of the fresh-water alga, *Œdogonium*, the spores are unlike. Large zoöspores produce normal-sized plants that bear eggs and smaller *androspores*. The androspores, intermediate in size between sperms and zoöspores, produce smaller, *male individuals* only, of simple structure, which fasten themselves to the egg-bearing plants, and give rise to sperms, which fertilize the egg.[1]

2. *Complete.*—In the liverworts and mosses commonly, and in the higher plants always, the gametophytes are clearly differentiated into male and female, with unlike vegetative characters which clearly distinguish them. These unlike structural features are called the *secondary sexual characters*. In these groups the sporophytes are not differentiated in structure, but the spores they produce, though structurally alike, are physiologically unlike, some producing male gametophytes, others female.

The most complete expression of maleness and femaleness is found in the seed-bearing plants, where the sporophytes are differentiated into microsporophytes (staminate plants), bearing only microspores which produce male gametophytes (pollen-grains), and megasporophytes (pistillate plants), bearing only megaspores which produce female gametophytes (embryo-sacs). Usually the two kinds of sporophytes are essentially alike, except for the sporophyll-bearing branches (the flowers), but the

[1] It has been suggested that these androspores might be regarded as sperms developing without fertilization, *i.e.*, by *parthenogenesis*.

male and female gametophytes are as unlike as could well be imagined. Illustrations of this condition will be found when we study the Gymnosperms (zamia, cycas, ginkgo), and the Angiosperms (willow, poplar, hop, etc.).

325. Determination of Sex.—1. *Effect of Nutrition.*—Nobody knows the real cause of sex—of maleness and femaleness. We may arrange plants (and animals) in a series so as to show the gradual transition from the simple non-sexual condition to complete differentiation of males and females, but in doing this we should clearly recognize the fact that we have really explained nothing. We have only described events and structures in the order in which it seems probable that they have occurred, in the gradual development of the earth's vegetation.

But while we have never yet been able to determine in advance the sex of a plant or animal, we have been able to determine which sex shall gain expression. For example, we have seen above that male plants are frequently less vigorous and more poorly nourished than female plants. We would, therefore, expect that poor nutrition would cause a suppression of femaleness, and this is precisely what has been found in certain experiments that have been made. When the prothallia of certain ferns that normally bear both antheridia and archegonia are grown under conditions that result in their being poorly nourished, the antheridia develop, but not always the archegonia. In such cases we know that we have not changed the sexual nature of the prothallus, but have only modified its expression.[1] This is further illustrated

[1] In exceptional cases perfect flowers may appear on staminate or pistillate plants, as in papaw (*Carica Papaya*) and willow, suggesting that diœcious plants may, in reality, be of double sex-value, but that only one of the sexes comes normally to expression.

in the gametophytes of the Horsetails (Chapter XXIV), which are usually differentiated into larger ones (female) and smaller ones (male); but under certain conditions (apparently involving differences of nutrition), the female gametophytes may bear antheridia, and the male gametophytes archegonia.

2. *Effect of Constitution of Germ-cells.*—If sex is not determined by external conditions—by environment—then

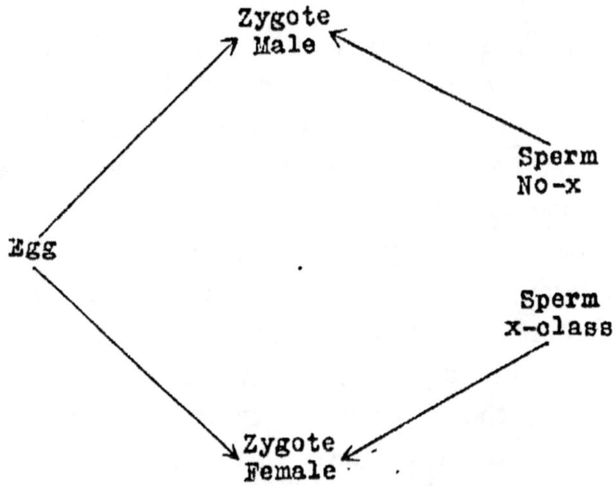

FIG. 265.—Diagram to illustrate determination of sex by the *x*-chromosome.

its explanation must lie in the internal constitution of the germ-cells—in their chemical, physical, or morphological differences. Remarkably careful and accurate observation has, in fact, revealed a constant and fundamental morphological difference in the germ-cells of animals. It has been found, for example in some insects, that the nucleus of every egg possesses a certain clearly distinguished chromosome, called the *x*-chromosome,[1] while in the

[1] The *x*, as in algebra, indicating an unknown, or not understood, factor.

sperms one-half possess it and one-half do not. This x-chromosome is always associated with femaleness. If an egg is fertilized by a sperm possessing the x-chromosome a female zygote is determined, otherwise the zygote will be male, thus:

Egg x + sperm no$-x$ = zygote x (male):
Egg x + sperm x = zygote xx (female).

This condition is illustrated diagrammatically in Fig. 265.

In sea-urchins, and some other animals, this condition may be reversed the sperms being all alike, and the eggs unlike. Careful investigations have, so far, failed to reveal anything corresponding to the x-chromosome in plants, but undoubtedly there are fundamental differences between the eggs and sperms of plants. Possibly these differences are chemical only, and not accompanied by differences of cellular structure.

326. The Meaning of Sex.—Just what is accomplished for plants by the occurrence of two sexes is not entirely understood. Among the lower plants the primitive expressions of sex seem in some cases, to have met a need for better nutrition, or to have resulted in rejuvenating the protoplasts of the gametes; but these explanations are not satisfactory, especially for the higher plants. We do know that fertilization always results in increasing variation. When plants are propagated vegetatively, as by cuttings or by grafting, the characters remain constant in the new plants,[1] but when reproduction is by seeds (resulting from fertilization) we always observe great variation. This is of course, an advantage, for it is only by variation that new characters may appear, and without the appearance

[1] Except in the special case of bud-sporting (p. 532, and Fig. 400).

of new characters there would be no opportunity for the improvement of plants—either by nature or by man.

The results of all studies and discussions of the question of sex lead us to recognize the fact that it is still largely an unsolved mystery. We must make further and more accurate observations, and be careful and logical in our reasoning, before we can hope to solve this difficult problem.

CHAPTER XXIII

FROM ALGA TO FERN

327. Progressive Development.—The largest fact that stands out in a hasty review of the plants we have studied is the increasing simplicity of form and organization from fern to alga, or in reverse order, the increasing complexity from alga to fern. The *Pleurococcus* is a simple globule of living matter. Its organs are all reduced to their lowest terms—cell-wall, cytoplasm, limiting surface (or membrane), nucleus, nuclear membrane, chromatophore—the parts of a cell. The one protoplast performs all the functions of life—takes in raw materials, elaborates food out of these raw materials, digests the food thus made, assimilates it, respires, and reproduces itself. It is difficult to imagine the fundamental life-functions performed under simpler circumstances of structure.

But as soon as plant cells begin to remain united after cell-divison they begin to be differentiated. The single *Pleurococcus* cell is globular, but when two or more remain attached they are flattened at the surfaces in contact (Fig. 183). This is a simple illustration of morphological differentiation. When a cell-mass is formed the outer cell-walls, in contact with the air, become covered with a layer of cuticle, which retards the loss of water. Cell-walls in contact with each other do not possess the cuticle. Thus, by gradual steps the plant body becomes increasingly complex, so that we may arrange a series from algæ to ferns, and from ferns to the higher seed-bearing plants, showing increasing complexity of structure.

328. Division of Physiological Labor.—The differentiation of the plant body into organs—root, stem, leaf, reproductive organs—may be considered as an expression of the *division of physiological labor.* For example, when a sufficiently thick cell-mass is formed the inner cells may be deprived of light; no chlorophyll can then develop, photosynthesis becomes impossible, and the outer-cells must elaborate all the food, not only for themselves, but for the inner, non-green cells as well. Roots that serve to hold the plant in the soil, and to take in water and minerals to be used in the leaves, must be nourished by food elaborated in the green cells. The leaves and branches must be supplied with water taken in by the roots, and a vascular system becomes necessary. So, in these and countless other ways, the vegetative functions become divided among organs specially fitted by their structure to perform them well. Then the reproductive function becomes confined to certain cells, which are nourished by the others. Reproduction itself becomes complicated by the development of two kinds of gametes, and the introduction of cell-fusion as well as cell-division.

Among plants, organization—the development of definite organs for definite work—has the same kind of advantage as the division of labor among men. The "jack-at-all-trades" is not as efficient at any one of them as the specialist. The existence of carpenters, plumbers, masons, tailors, architects, superintendents, teachers, lawyers, stenographers, doctors, means greater efficiency, than could be secured if everyone tried to be all of these.

So the differentiation of the plant body into root, stem, leaves, and organs of reproduction means greater efficiency in the performance of all the functions of life.

329. From Water to Land.—A careful consideration of all available evidence leads to the conviction that plant life originated in the water. For example, the more primitive types of plants have no well-defined *polarity*; that is, they do not present an axis with the opposite ends clearly differentiated for the performance of different functions under unlike surroundings, such as roots adjusted to a life in the soil and darkness, and leaves adjusted to a life in the air and light. Plants submerged in water, such as *Spirogyra*, commonly possess a uniformity of structure, in harmony with their uniform environment. Of course, there are exceptions to this, *Ascophyllum*, *Dictyota*, *Vaucheria*, and other submerged aquatics possess, on one end, hold-fasts which anchor them to the substratum; but these plants probably represent early steps toward a rooted existence on land.

One of the most marked evidences of aquatic life for primitive organisms is their method of reproduction by motile spores and motile gametes; while, at the same time, one of the most distinctive characteristics of the more highly developed land-plants is reproduction by non-motile spores, suited to distribution by wind. The enormous number of spores produced insures a rapid multiplication of individuals, and their dryness insures protection during periods of more or less prolonged drought.

330. Development of the Sporophyte.—For the successful production of large numbers of spores there is needed some provision for richly nourishing the spore-producing tissues. There must be a large amount of chlorophyll-bearing tissue, ample provision for taking in abundant water and minerals, and efficient channels for conducting the raw materials and elaborated food from one part of the plant to another. Moreover, the spore-bearing parts need to be lifted into the air to insure the most efficient distribution of the spores. These needs are admirably met by the sporophyte with roots on one end, green leaves on the other, and sporangia borne at or very near the tips of the branches.

A review, at this time, of the sporophytic phases of the liverworts, mosses, and ferns will show how these sporophytes gradually increase in complexity and importance, from the simple condition in *Riccia*, with almost no sterile tissue, through the sporogonium of the higher liverworts and mosses, to the leafy sporophyte of the ferns. The final step in the development of the sporophyte was the differentiation of megasporophytes, bearing only megaspores, and microsporophytes, bearing only microspores.

331. Decline of the Gametophyte.—As the sporophyte became more highly developed and the dry-land flora more firmly established, the gametophytic phase became less essential and less in evidence, until, in the ferns, the sporophyte became the commonly recognized "plant," and the very existence of the gametophytic phase was, for a long time, not known. Reproduction by spores and by other non-sexual means became entirely sufficient to perpetuate the race.

332. Classification.—By a careful comparison of all kinds of plants, it has been recognized that certain ones are very much alike in fundamental characteristics of structure; they fall naturally into a group. Moreover it is recognized that there are numerous groups, and that the members of any one group differ from those in every other group in some fundamental point. By such comparisons botanists have been able to *classify* all known plants into more or less clearly defined groups and subgroups. The larger the number of characters considered, the smaller the group, and *vice versa*.

The *divisions* of the plant kingdom already studied, and their distinguishing characters are as follows:[1]

Divisions of the Plant Kingdom

1. *Thallophytes.*—Plant body a thallus; no archegonia.
2. *Bryophytes.*—Archegonia; no vascular system.
3. *Pteridophytes.*—Vascular system; no seeds.

These four divisions are, of course, distinguished by other characters than the ones just indicated, but these stand out prominently as positive and negative characteristics of the respective groups.

These three divisions are further subdivided, as shown on the following page.

[1] Adapted from Coulter (J. M.).

TABLE IV.—SUBDIVISIONS OF THE PLANT KINGDOM

1. Thallophyta
   (*a*) Algæ
      (1) Cyanophyceæ
      (2) Chlorophyceæ
      (3) Phæophyceæ
      (4) Rhodophyceæ
   (*b*) Fungi
      (1) Myxomycetes
      (2) Schizomycetes (bacteria)
      (3) Phycomycetes
      (4) Ascomycetes
      (5) Basidiomycetes
      (6) Fungi imperfecti (life histories imperfectly known).
   (*c*) Lichens
2. Bryophyta
   (*a*) Hepaticæ
   (*b*) Musci
3. Pteridophyta (true ferns)[1]
   (*a*) Eusporangiatæ
   (*b*) Leptosporangiatæ
4. Calamophyta (calamites)
   (*a*) Equisetineæ
5. Lepidophyta (lycopods)
   (*a*) Lycopodineæ (club-mosses)
   (*b*) Lepidodendrineæ (little club-mosses)

---

[1] An older classification combined the last three groups or phyla into one, as follows:

3. Pteridophyta (ferns and fern allies)
   (*a*) Filicineæ
   (*b*) Equisetineæ
   (*c*) Lycopodineæ

CHAPTER XXIV

CALAMITES AND LYCOPODS

I. THE HORSETAILS (EQUISETALES)

EQUISETUM

333. Habitat and Distribution.—As the names of some of the various species indicate, representatives of the genus *Equisetum* occur in a rather large variety of habitats. Thus we have the swamp-equisetum (*E. palustre*), meadow-equisetum (*E. pratense*), the field-equisetum (*E. arvense*), and so on. They are frequently found along railroad embankments in exposed situations, while other species occur only in shaded or very moist locations (Fig. 266). They are distributed throughout the northern hemisphere, but only one species has been reported from South America. Twenty species have been described from the temperate and tropical North America, but none has ever been found in Australia. Fossils of near relatives of the genus have been found in the rocks of previous geological ages, and some of the fossils in the coal-bearing rocks of the Carboniferous age are thought to belong to *Equisetum* itself. In temperate America the horsetails vary in height from only a few inches to several feet. One species (*E. debile*), found near Lahore, in India, attains a height of from 10 to 15 feet, needing the support of neighboring trees in order to stand erect, while *E. giganteum*, found from the West Indies to Chili, reaches a maximum height of about 40 feet. In the island of Jamaica it is found in thickets 10 to 15 feet high.

334. Description of the Sporophyte.—The plant body (Fig. 267) consists of a horizontal, much-branched, underground stem, or *rhizome*, from which spring two kinds of sub-aerial branches—sterile and fertile. The cells that

FIG. 266.—*Equisetum fluviatile.* Pure stand in shallow water, at Tully Lake, N. Y. (Photo by W. L. Bray.)

compose the sub-aerial branches are, in many of the species (*e.g.*, *E. arvense*), nearly or quite all formed by the close of the growing season, in the fall, so that in the following spring all that is necessary is the expansion of these cells, causing an elongation of the internodes and the appearance of the branch above ground in early spring.

The sterile branches produce smaller side branches at the nodes. Chlorophyll is formed in the cells of the cortex, and stomata in the epidermis permit the exchange of

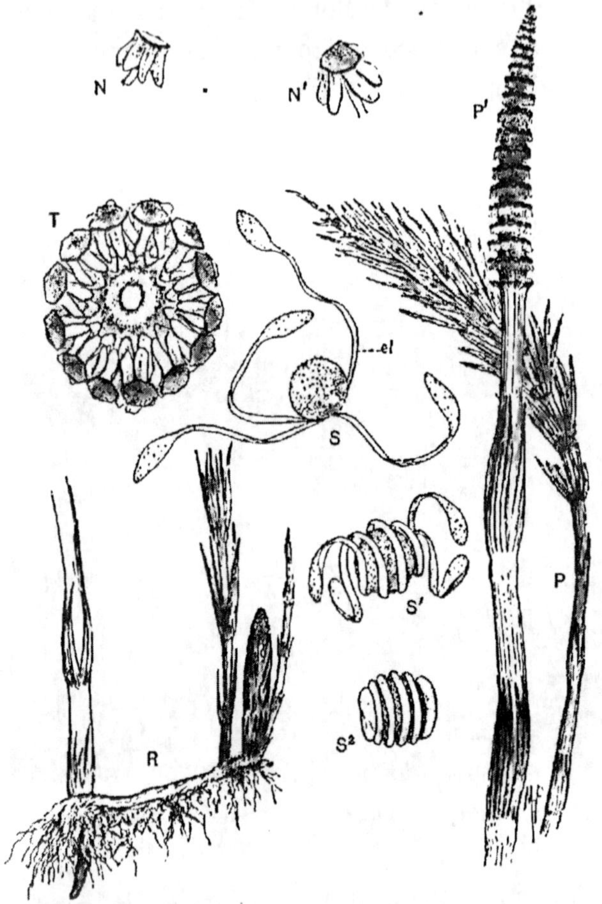

FIG. 267.—*Equisetum arvense.* *P*, sterile branch; *P*[1], fertile branch with strobilus, or cone; *R*, rhizome (underground); *T*, cross-section of cone, showing insertion of sporophylls in a whorl; *N*, *N*[1], sporophylls with pendant sporangia; *S*, *S*[1], *S*[2], spores with coiled elaters (*el*).

gases necessary in photosynthesis and respiration. The sterile branches elaborate practically all of the food necessary to nourish the underground stem and the developing sterile and fertile branches that will appear the following spring. We thus have an excellent illustration of the division of physiological labor—one branch to anchor the plant in the soil, and serve as a storehouse of food and a center of distribution; roots to take in water and dissolved minerals; sterile aerial branches to perform the functions of food-manufacture, and the fertile branches to perform the function of reproduction—bearing the spores, and lifting them high in the air, thus facilitating their distribution by wind.

The fertile branch commonly appears first in the spring, usually bearing no side branches nor foliage-leaves, but only whorls of scale-like leaves at each node. These scales possess little or no power of photosynthesis, and are chiefly protective (Fig. 267). In some instances the fertile branches bear green lateral branches. At the apex of the fertile branch is borne the *strobilus*, or cone, consisting of a central axis (the prolongation of the axis of the branch), bearing a variable number of *sporangiophores*. In the development of the fertile branch the cone is formed first, and is raised above ground by the subsequent formation and elongation of the sterile tissue below it. In some species (*E. arvense*) the fertile branch dies after the shedding of the spores, while in other species (*e.g.*, *E. pratense*), after the spores are shed the entire cone falls away and the fertile branch then takes on the characters of the sterile branches which occur with it.

Each sporangiophore[1] consists of a stalk with a *peltate* shield at the end The axis of the cone soon ceases to

[1] The sporangiophores of *Equisetum* have been interpreted as homologous with leaves, *i.e.*, as sporophylls, but evidence derived in part from a study of the fossil relatives of the modern horsetails indicates that this conclusion may not be correct (Cf. Fig. 268). The term sporangiophore is non-commital as to homology.

elongate between the whorls of sporangiophores, so that the shields occur in close contact. It is this cessation of growth, in fact, that produces the cone; otherwise the sporangiophores would occur in whorls distributed at wider intervals along the axis.

The sporangia arise from a single epidermal cell (*eusporangiate*) on the underside of the shield; there are from five to ten on each shield.

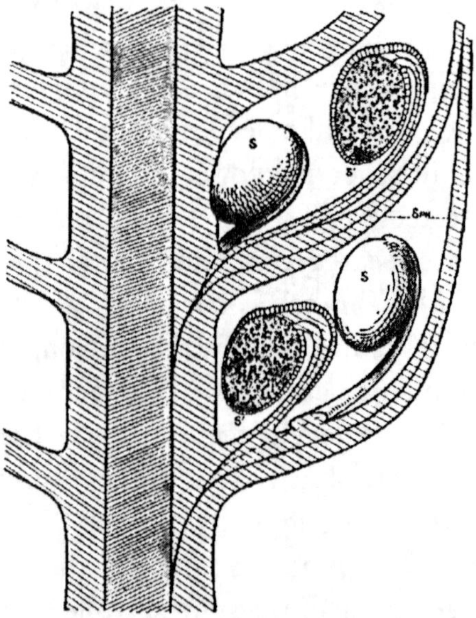

FIG. 268.—*Sphenophyllum cuneifolium*, a fossil species related to the modern horsetails. Diagram of a longitudinal sectional view of an axis bearing sporophylls (*Sph*); *s,s*, sporangia; s^1, s^1, sporangia in longitudinal section, showing spores. A vascular bundle enters the stalk of each sporangium. Enlarged. (Redrawn from Zeiller.) Cf. Fig. 280.

The spores (which are green when ripe) are alike in size (*homosporous*), but they produce two kinds of gametophytes, male and female (diœcious). Therefore they must be unlike physiologically. Under certain circumstances, as already mentioned, (page 359), the female gametophytes may ultimately produce antheridia, and the male ones, archegonia. It is of interest to note that some of the fossil relatives of the modern horsetails were heterosporus.

The structure of the spores is unusual in that they bear four ribbon-like appendages (*elaters*), formed from the outer wall, and closely coiled around the spores (Fig. 267).

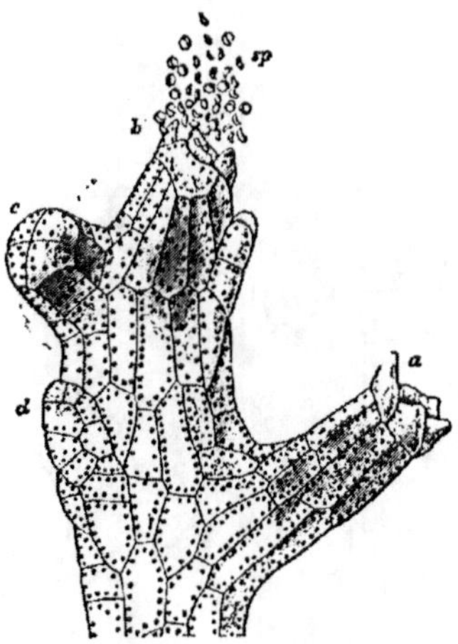

FIG. 269.—*Equisetum palustre.* Portion of a male prothallus, bearing antherida; *a*, *b*, *c*, three antheridia in successive stages of development; *a*, empty; *sp*, escaping sperms and sperm-mother-cells; *c*, antheridium not yet opened; *d*, initial stage in the development of an antheridium. × about 70. (After Sadebeck.)

These appendages uncoil in dry air and recoil with moisture, with a sharp, snapping motion, thus rolling the spores about.

The distribution of the spores is accomplished when they are ripe, by the opening of the dry walls of the sporangia. The shrinking of the walls gradually forces out the spores, and by the uncoiling and snapping of the elaters the spores become entangled and held fast to each other in little flocculent masses. Thus the complete isolation of single spores is prevented, and the advantage of this is recognized at once when we recall that the prothallia are diœcious.

335. The Gametophytes.—Under suitable conditions of moisture and temperature the spores begin to germinate, and by successive cell-divisions produce the lobed prothallia. The male prothallia are one cell in thickness, and bear the antheridia at the tips of the lobes or on the margins (Fig. 269).

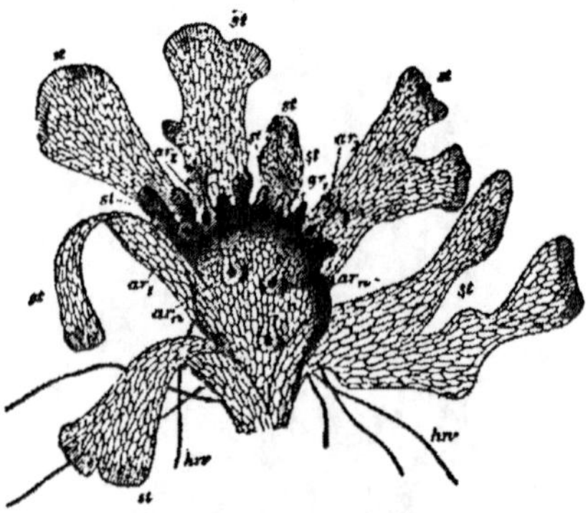

FIG. 270.—Female prothallus of *Equisetum arvense* L. ar_1, young archegonium; ar_2, archegoium before fertilization; *st*, sterile lobe of prothallus; *hw*, rhizoids. Several lobes were removed in order to show the cushion and the archegonia. Enlarged about 20 times. (After Sadebeck.)

The female prothallia form a cushion of relatively thick, spongy tissue (the *meristem*), and on this cushion (as in all Pteridophytes) are borne the archegonia. In contrast to the true ferns, the archegonia are borne on the upper surface of the prothallus, and point upward, in consequence of being negatively geotropic (Fig. 270). From the edges of the cushion numerous thin flaps of green tissue form; these fold over the cushion, enclosing the archegonia, and thus retaining the moisture of dew or rain. This forms a favorable environment for the multiciliate sperms, which are set free from the antheridia of neighboring male prothallia; and swim to the archegonia, and down their neck-canals to the eggs which they fertilize.

336. The New Sporophyte.—As always, the fertilized egg develops into an embryo, and the embryo, *without any*

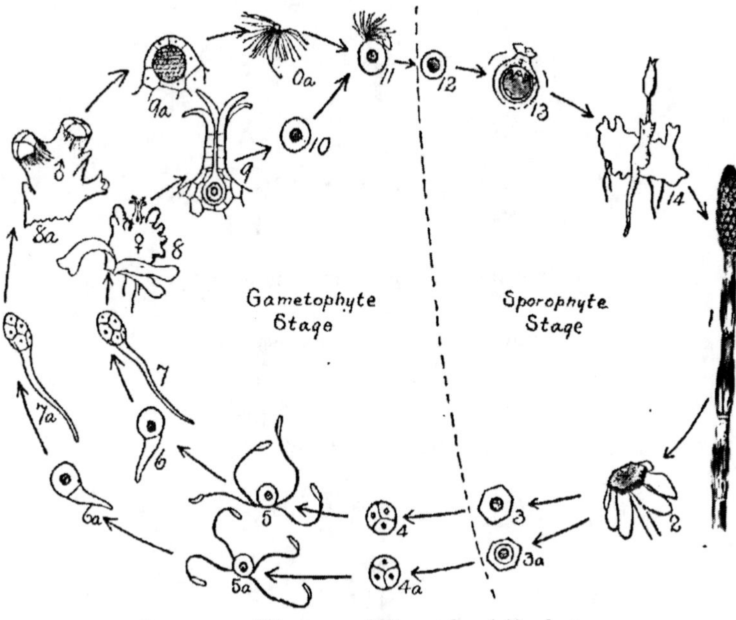

FIG. 271.—Diagram of life-cycle of *Equisetum*.

period of rest, continues to grow until the new sporophyte is formed, with underground rhizome, and finally with the sub-aerial sterile and fertile branches, thus completing the life-cycle[1] (Fig. 271).

[1] In a few species of *Equisetum* modified underground branches, resembling a string of tubers are formed, and these give rise to new plants by vegetative multiplication.

The life history of *Equisetum* may be tabulated as follows:

OUTLINE OF LIFE HISTORY OF EQUISETUM

Rhizome } Sporophyte
↓ ↓
Sterile branch — Fertile branch
↓↓
Strobilus
↓↓
Sporangiophores
↓↓
Sporangia
↙ *Reduction* ↘
Isospore — Isospore
↓ ↓
Male gametophyte — Female gametophyte
↓ ↓
Antheridium — Archegonium
↓ ↓
Sperm — Egg
↘ *Fertilization* ↙
Oösperm
↓↓
Embryo
↓↓
Mature sporophyte

II. THE CLUB-MOSSES (LYCOPODIALES)

LYCOPODIUM

337. Habitat and Distribution.—Nearly all the species of *Lycopodium* prefer moist situations, and one or two of them are aquatic. They are widely distributed over the earth, in both hemispheres, from the torrid to the frigid zones, and commonly grow in shady places. *Lycopodium Selago*, and a few other species are epiphytic. They all prefer a substratum rich in humus or other organic matter. Most of the species are restricted to one hemisphere, but a few occur in both.

338. The Sporophyte.—There are several hundred species of *Lycopodium*. Among those most common in temperate America are *L. clavatum* (Fig. 272), *L. obscurum*

FIG. 272.—*Lycopodium clavatum.*

dendroideum, and *L. lucidulum*. These species commonly grow trailing over the surface of the ground, and from this, and the appearance of their foliage, they are commonly called "ground pine," though of course they have nothing to do with true pines. As is well shown in the figure, the plant-body of the sporophyte of *Lycopodium clavatum* consists of a sterile lower region, bearing foliage-leaves, but no sporophylls, while the fertile region occurs as a clearly recognized cone, formed by the crowding of the sporophylls at the apex of the leafy axis (Fig. 273). The foliage-leaves are all simple and small (*microphyllous*).

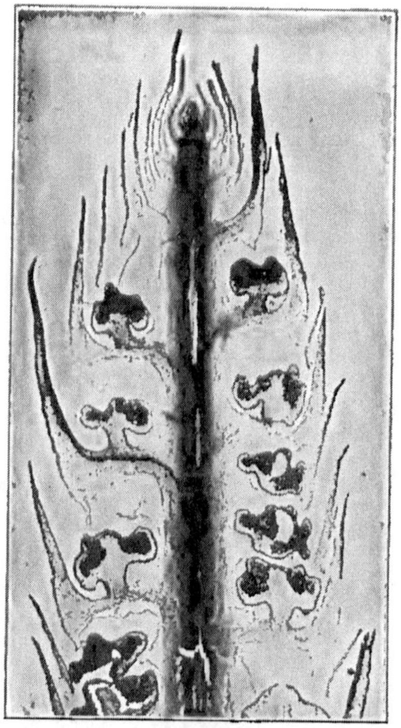

FIG. 273.—*Lycopodium sp.* Photomicrograph of longitudinal section of a cone, showing the sporangia on the upper surface of the sporophylls, near their insertion on the main axis.

A more primitive type is found in *Lycopodium Selago* (Fig. 274). Here the lower region is sterile, but is not as well developed as in other types, for the sporophylls begin to appear lower down on the stem. Moreover the sporophylls are not aggregated into a cone, but are distributed at intervals from near the base to near the apex, with sterile regions intervening. The leaves usually occur in whorls of five, but often they are arranged in spirals.

At the zone of transition from sterile to fertile regions, imperfectly developed (*aborted*) sporangia are often formed, and this (with other evidence) has suggested that, *in the*

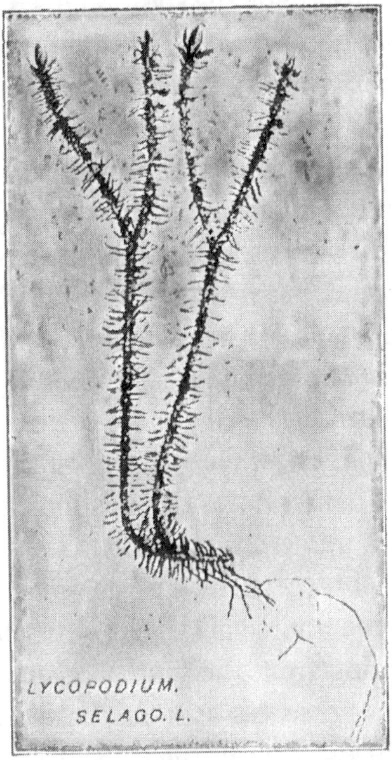

FIG. 274.—*Lycopodium Selago.* (After Bower.)

evolution of the sporophyte, the purely vegetative regions have resulted from a sterilization of fertile tissue. The correctness of this interpretation of the origin of the sterile regions is rendered more probable by the fact that the condition found in *L. Selago* is characteristic of the fossil Lycopods of the coal measures. The possession of a well-developed sterile region with foliage-leaves, and the restriction of the sporophylls to the apices of the branches is of very considerable advantage, making possible an abundant supply of food to a vast number of spores. The branching of *L. Selago* is dichotomous, and the sporangia are borne on the *upper surfaces* of the sporophylls, near their bases.

339. The Gametophyte.—The spores of Lycopods are alike in size (*isospores*), and on germination produce fleshy prothallia, bearing both antheridia and archegonia (monœcious), and partially saprophytic in habit. They commonly have a filamentous fungus growing parasitically within their tissues. The reproductive organs occur at the upper end, surrounded with sterile hairs (*paraphyses*). The whole of the antheridia, and the venters of the archegonia are imbedded in the vegetative tissue. The gametophyte may grow more or less completely imbedded in the soil, but when growing on the surface chlorophyll is formed, and photosynthesis may take place. Its lower end bears numerous rhizoids.

340. The Embryo.—After an egg is fertilized it begins at once to divide and soon develops an embryo. Of the two cells resulting from the first division of the fertilized egg, the lower one serves as a *suspensor*, while the other becomes the ancestor of all the cells of the embryo. The suspensor serves to push the embryo down into the nourishing tissue of the prothallus. The young embryo (Fig. 275) soon becomes differentiated into two distinct regions—the foot (not shown in the figure), and the shoot. As in the mosses and true ferns, the foot serves to absorb nourishment from the gametophyte. But the embryo is dependent upon the gametophyte for only a relatively brief period—shorter than in the mosses and true ferns.

The elongation of the embryo-stem (*hypocotyl*) carries the first leaves (*cotyledons*) up above the surface of the soil, while at the same time the first root (*radicle*) is develop-

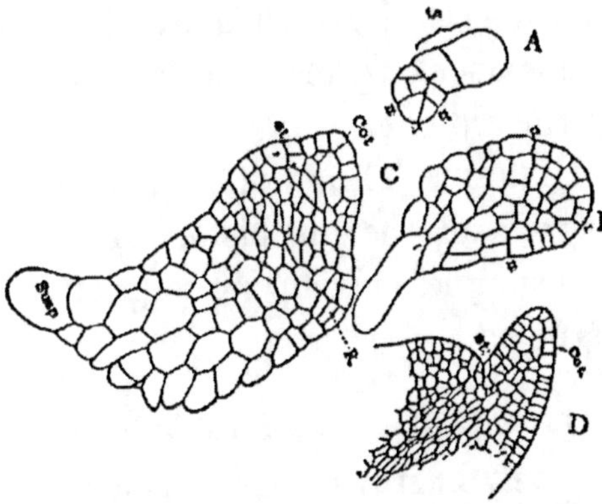

FIG. 275.—*Lycopodium phlegmaria.* Development of embryo. *st*, stem; *cot*, cotyledon; *sus*, suspensor; *R*, root. (After D. H. Campbell.)

FIG. 276.—Young sporophyte of *Lycopodium cernuum* L., with the gametophyte, having irregular lobes of chlorophyll-bearing tissue attached on one side. (After Treub.)

ing at its base (Fig. 276). If the prothallus is deeply buried the hypocotyl becomes more elongated before the cotyledons are formed.

341. Vegetative Multiplication.—Several species of *Lycopodium* bear gemmæ. They are conspicuous on

Lycopodium lucidulum (which is common in the northern United States), and are borne near, but not in, the axils of the leaves. A young rootlet commonly appears on the gemma while it is still attached to the plant. After it falls off, the axis elongates, and a new sporophyte is formed, like the old one.

342. Life History.—The student should be able to make his own diagram of the life history of *Lycopodium*, following the examples given in connection with forms previously studied.

III. LITTLE CLUB-MOSSES (SELAGINELLALES)

SELAGINELLA (LITTLE CLUB-MOSS)

343. Habitat and Distribution.—The little club-mosses (species of *Selaginella*) are found in every continent and on most of the larger islands. They usually grow only in moist situations, and are very common in conservatories, under the plant benches, and in pots and hanging baskets.

344. The Sporophyte.—The plant body (sporophyte) consists of a much-branched stem (Fig. 277), bearing scale-like, but green foliage-leaves, sessile and more or less closely appressed to the stem. At the tips of the branches the foliage-leaves are replaced by sporophylls, so arranged as to form a clearly distinguished cone (Figs. 278 and 281). Near the base of the leaves, on the surface next the stem, is formed a thin, membraneous flap, the *ligule* (Figs. 279 and 280). The possession of a ligule is one of the fundamental distinguishing characteristics of *Selaginella*.

345. Two Kinds of Spores. Heterospory.—If we examine a longitudinal section of a cone, we shall normally find a sporangium in the axil of each sporophyll. In exceptional cases the lower or basal leaves of the cone are

FIG. 277.—*Selaginella Wildenovii.*

FIG. 278.—*Selaginella amœna.* Branch bearing numerous terminal cones.

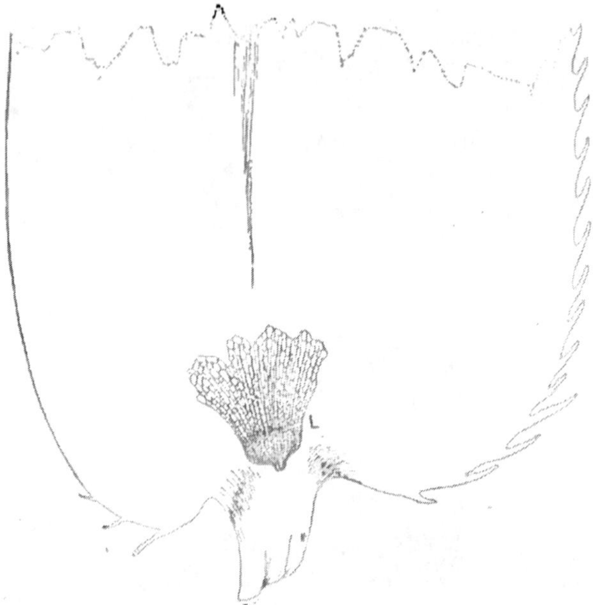

FIG. 279.—*Selaginella Watsoniana.* Base of foliage leaf, showing ligule, *L.* Enlarged about 36 times.

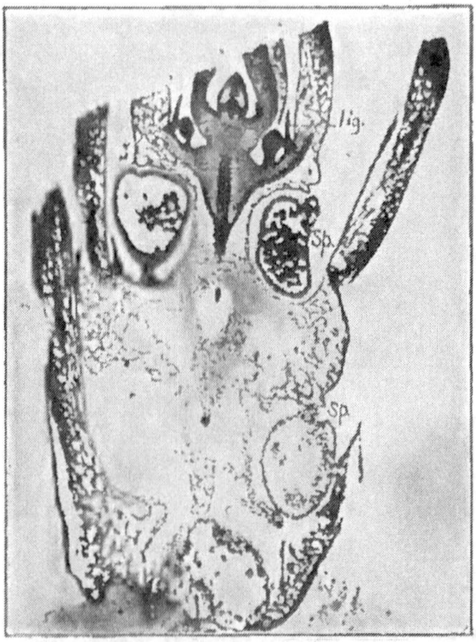

FIG. 280.—*Selaginella sp.* Photomicrograph of a longitudinal section through the tip of a cone, showing sporangia (*sp*), and ligules (*lig.*). (Cf. Fig. 268.)

sterile. The lower sporangia are larger than the upper ones, and bear four large spores (*megaspores*). They are *megasporangia*, and the leaves are *megasporophylls*. The

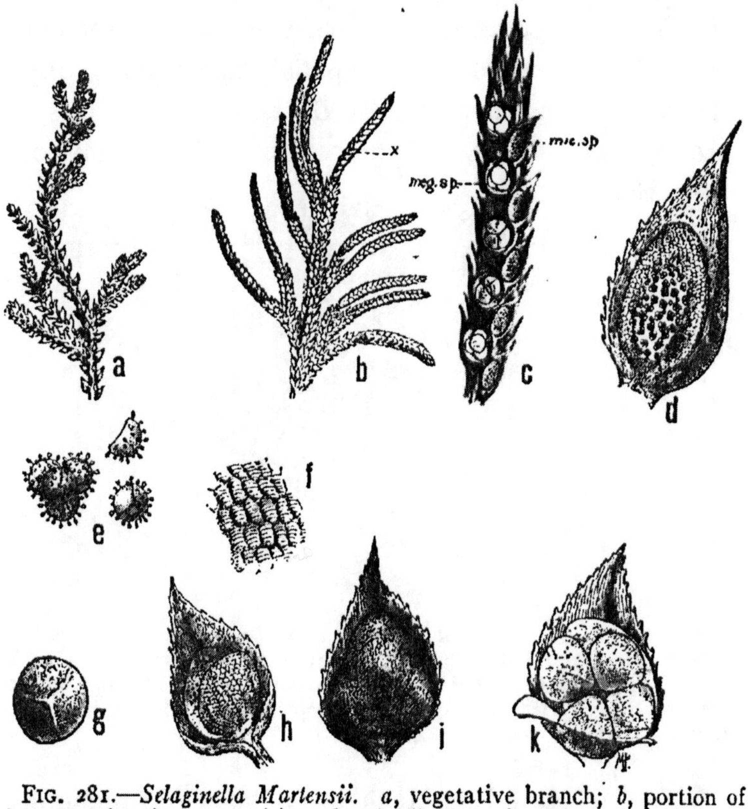

FIG. 281.—*Selaginella Martensii.* *a*, vegetative branch; *b*, portion of the stem, bearing cones (*x*); *c*, longitudinal section of a cone, showing microsporangia (*mic. sp.*) in the axils of microsporophylls, and megasporangia in the axils of megasporophylls; *d*, microsporangium with microsporophyll; *e*, microspores; *f*, portion of wall of sporangium, greatly magnified; *g*, megaspore; *h*, microsporangium opened, and most of the microspores scattered; *i*, megasporangium, with megasporophyll; *k*, same, opened, showing the four megaspores.

smaller sporangia (*microsporangia*) are subtended by *microsporophylls*, and bear numerous small spores (*microspores*). In some species the two kinds of sporophylls alternate along the axis of the cone (Fig. 281). The larger number of microspores results from the fact that every spore-mother-cell, by tetrad-division, develops spores, while in the megasporangia only one spore-mother-cell develops spores, the other cells serving to nourish that one. The microspores develop only male gametophytes, the megaspores, female. In dissemination, the spores are ejected to some distance from the parent plant (Fig. 282).

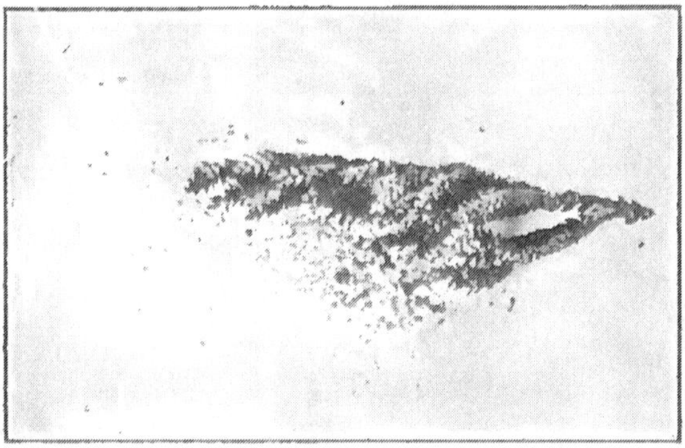

FIG. 282.—*Selaginella Martensii.* Dissemination of spores. The branch was covered with a glass bell-jar to avoid currents of air. The "dust" is composed of both microspores and megaspores, and indicates the distance to which the spores are projected from the dehiscing sporangia. × 23.

346. The Male Gametophyte.—The male gametophyte is developed entirely within the wall of the microspore. The first division gives rise to a vegetative (or sterile) and a fertile cell. The vegetative tissue never develops beyond the one-celled stage. By several divisions the fertile cell develops a simple antheridium containing four sperms. Each sperm bears two long, slender cilia (Fig. 284).

347. The Female Gametophyte.—*The megaspores begin to germinate while still in the sporangium.* This will be recognized at once as a new feature in life history. By successive divisions the protoplasm of the spore becomes a multicellular body, *the prothallus*, with richer cells near the apex. Here a number of archegonia form (Fig. 283), and the enlargement of the prothallus, or gametophyte, causes a splitting apart of the old, thick walls of the megaspore, so that the female gametophyte protrudes (Fig. 284, 9).

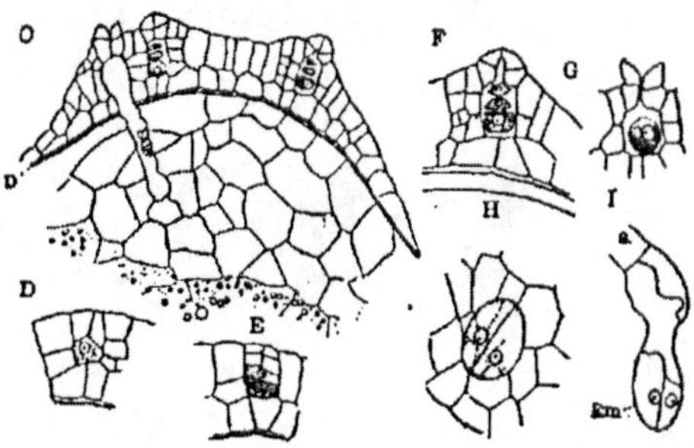

FIG. 283.—*Selaginella Kraussiana*. *C*, section of mature female gametophyte, showing three archegonia, two containing eggs, and one (at the left) an embryo with suspensor (*sus.*). *D–G*, Stages in the development the archegonium; *H*, very young embryo (two-celled stage), after first division of the fertilized egg; *I*, older embryo (*Em*), with suspensor (*s*). (After Campbell.)

It bears no chlorophyll, living entirely as a parasite on the parental sporophyte, from whence it derives all the food with which it nourishes the embryo.

348. Fertilization.—As throughout the ferns, calamites, and lycopods, fertilization is accomplished by the swimming of the sperm to the mouth of the archegonium, and down the neck-canal to the ripe egg in the venter. Thus while *Selaginella* is, in other respects, a land-plant, it retains the aquatic method of fertilization. External water is absolutely necessary in order that the sperm may reach the egg.

349. The Embryo.—After fertilization the oösperm begins to divide. The cell nearest the neck of the archegonium, after the first division of the egg, is a suspensor, but becomes much longer than in *Lycopodium*, and thrusts the developing embryo deep down among the nourishing cells of the gametophyte. *By the possession of a suspensor the Lycopodiales and Selaginellales are distinguished from the Pteridophytes and Calamites.*

The embryo does not cease growth, and pass through a resting period, but continues to develop, until its root and shoot, with two cotyledons, emerge from the prothallus,

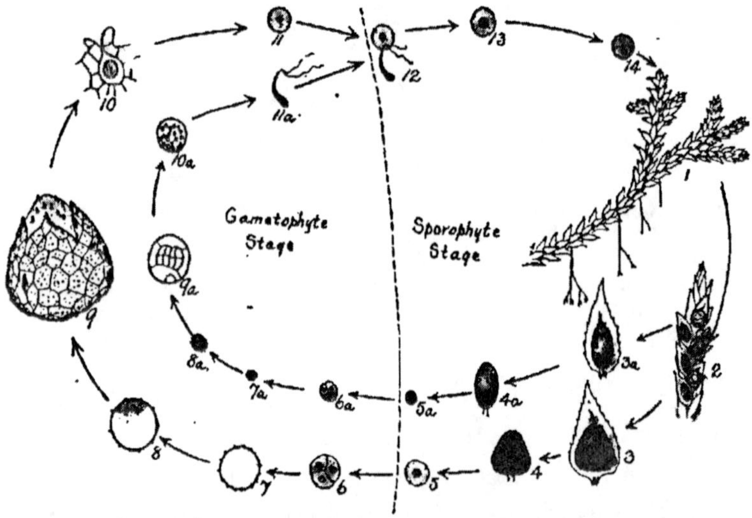

FIG. 284.—Diagram of life-cycle of *Selaginella*. (Modified from J. H. Schaffner.)

and the young sporophyte gradually becomes established as an independent, green plant (Fig. 284). It is only after the development of a vigorous leafy shoot, with chlorophyll apparatus, capable of elaborating an abundance of food, that the strobilus is organized with its axis and green sporophylls.

OUTLINE OF LIFE HISTORY OF SELAGINELLA

Sporophyte

↓↓		↓↓
Microsporophyll		Megasporophyll
↓↓		↓↓
Microsporangium		Megasporangium
↓	← *Reduction* →	↓
Microspore		Megaspore
↓		↓
Male gametophyte		Female gametophyte
↓		↓
Antheridium		Archegonium
↓		↓
Sperm	*Fertilization*	Egg
↘		↙

Oösperm
↓↓
Embryo
↓↓
Mature sporophyte

350. Marks of Progress.—With the introduction of heterospory we recognize a distinctly new feature of the sporophyte generation. Structural differentiations associated with difference in sex have hitherto been confined to the gametophytic generation, but now such distinctions appear for the first time in the sporophyte. This is a long step forward, and marks *Selaginella* as a more highly organized form than the lycopods, horsetails, and ferns. Other marks of progress are:

1. The reduction of the vegetative tissue of the gametophytes (to only one cell in the case of the male gametophyte).

2. The entire dependence of the gametophytes upon the sporophytes for nutrition.

3. The retention of the female gametophyte, throughout its entire existence, almost entirely within the wall of the megaspore.

CHAPTER XXV

SEED-BEARING PLANTS

THE CYCADS

351. Description.—The cycads, while native only in the tropics, are familiar to all persons who have visited conservatories. One of the commoner species in cultivation (*Cycas revoluta*) is often labelled, "Sago palm." In

FIG. 285.—*Cycas revoluta*, showing terminal bud of foliage-leaves just opening. (Compare Fig. 286.)

fact, in some respects it bears a superficial resemblance to a palm, while in other characters it suggests the ferns. There is a short, thick, cylindrical, unbranched stem or *trunk*, bearing a crown of beautiful, leathery, green leaves, having prominent midribs and pinnately divided (Fig. 285). The leaves endure for a year or more (varying with the species), and are then replaced by a fresh crown. The duration of each crop of leaves is said to vary according as the plant grows wild, or in botanic gardens and

FIG. 286.—*Cycas revoluta*. Terminal bud of foliage leaves just opening. Nearer view of Fig. 285. Note the circinate vernation of the leaf-pinnules, but not of the entire leaf.

conservatories. Thus, when temperature and rainfall are excessive, *Cycas circinalis* may produce two crowns of leaves a year, instead of the one crown commonly produced in green houses.

The young leaves are curled up at the tips, unrolling as they grow. In the genus *Cycas* only the leaflets are

FIG. 287.—*Macrozamia Moorei.* Two staminate cones; the older one above.

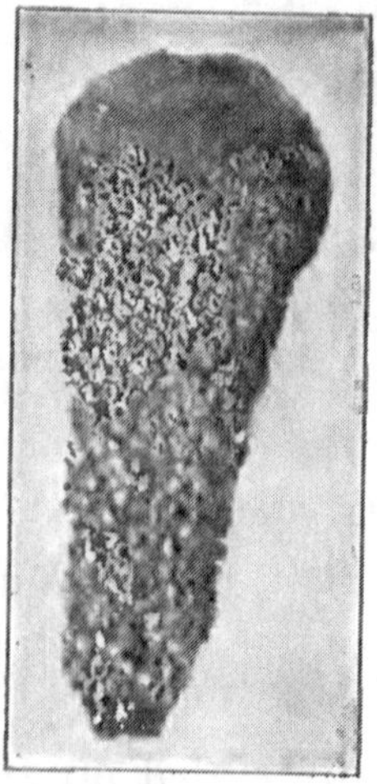

FIG. 288.—*Macrozamia Moorei.* Microsporophyll (lower surface), showing microsporangia (pollen-sacs), after the shedding of the pollen.

curled (Fig. 286), while in the related American genus, *Zamia*, the entire leaf is curled as well. The plants are diœcious, but the two sexes so closely resemble each other that they cannot be distinguished except by their sporophylls when in fruit.

FIG. 289.—*Macrozamia Moorei*, showing two lateral carpellate cones.

352. Microsporophylls.—The microsporophylls are grouped into a cone (Fig. 287). This means that they are *not on the main stem*, for the cone is really a branch, bearing only sporophylls. The microsporangia, bearing microspores, occur *in groups* (sori), on the under surface of the sporophylls (Fig. 288).

FIG. 290.—*Cycas revoluta.* Greenhouse specimen (at left) in flower. (Photo from the New York Botanical Garden.)

353. Megasporophylls.—The megasporophylls, or *carpels*, occur either in axillary cones (Fig. 289), or in groups

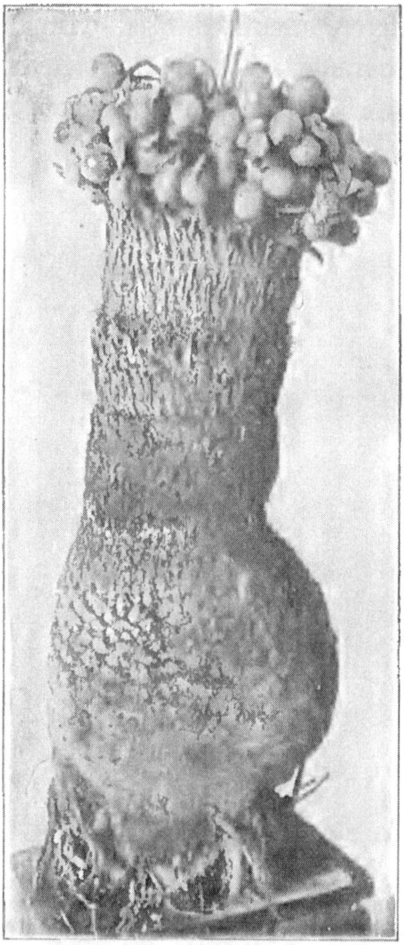

FIG. 291.—*Cycas media.* Trunk, with foliage leaves removed, showing crown of megasporophylls (carpels). (Specimen in Brooklyn Botanic Garden.) (Cf. Fig. 289.)

at the summit of the *main stem*, surrounding the growing point of the stem, and surrounded by the foliage-leaves (Figs. 290 and 291). In the latter case they possess a pinnately divided blade, with mid-rib and petiole (Fig. 292). The genera that bear the megasporophylls on the main stem resemble the ferns, and in this respect are the simplest, or most primitively organized, of all living seed-plants.

354. Megasporangia.—Unlike the microsporangia, the megasporangia of *Cycas* occur, not in groups, but solitary

FIG. 292.—Young megasporophyll (carpel) of *Cycas revoluta*, bearing six young ovules, destined, after fertilization, to mature into seeds. Note the relatively large amount of leaf-blade above the ovules, as compared with *Cycas media* (Fig. 293). (Specimen from C. C. Chamberlain.)

on the lower part of the sporophyll, at the margin, occupying the position of the pinnate divisions (Figs. 292–294). In genera bearing *carpellate cones* the megasporangia occur in pairs on the under surface of each scale (megasporophyll; Fig. 295). In the Cycads and higher plants the megasporangia are called *ovules*.

355. Ovules.—The young megasporangia or ovules of Cycads consist of two distinct regions of sterile tissue—an inner *nucellus*, and an outer covering, or *integument*,

FIG. 293.—Megasporophyll (carpel) of *Cycas media*, bearing one ripe naked (gymnospermous) seed, and three ovules which failed to become seeds, doubtless through not being fertilized. (Compare Fig. 292.)

which is an outgrowth of the ovule just below the nucellus. The integument serves to protect the more delicate tissues within, and later becomes transformed into the *seed-coat* (Figs. 296–298). Only one of the four megaspores develops within the nucellus.

356. Female Gametophyte.—As in *Selaginella*, the megaspores begin to germinate while still in the sporangium, but now a new feature is introduced into life history;

FIG. 294.—*Cycas media.* Carpel (megasporophyll) with six ripened ovules or seeds.

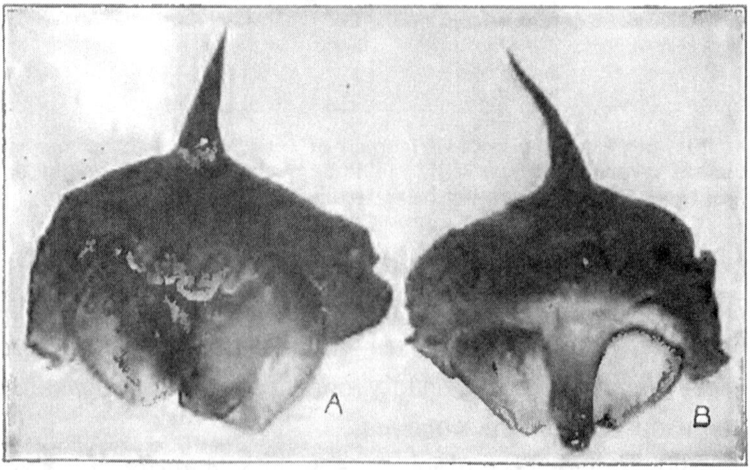

FIG. 295.—*Macrozamia Moorei.* A scale (megasporophyll) from a carpellate cone, bearing two ovules, maturing into seeds. *A*, top view; *B*, bottom view. About half size.

the megaspores of Cycads never leave the sporangium. The developing female gametophyte is nourished entirely as

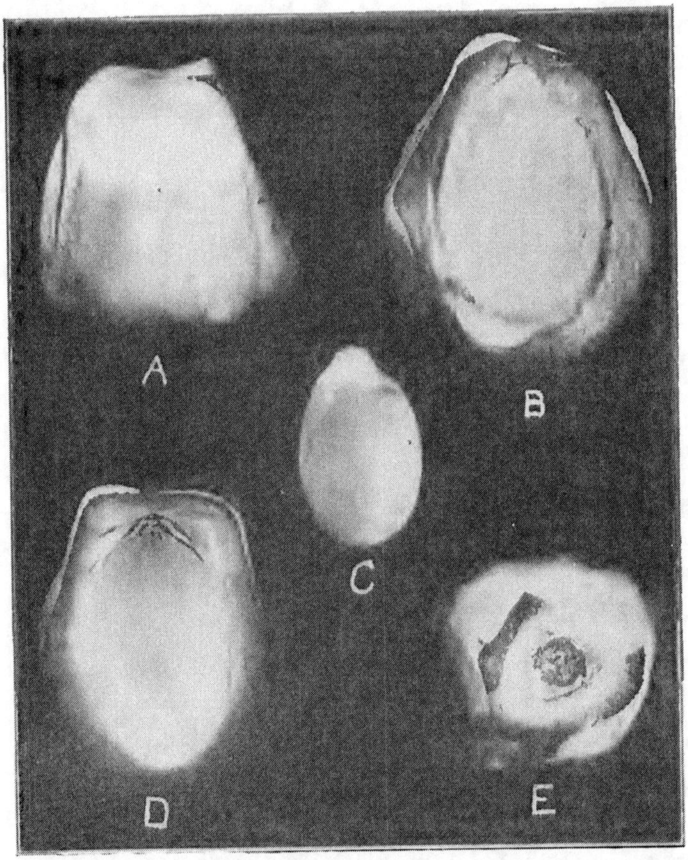

FIG. 296.—Ovule of *Macrozamia Moorei.* *A*, external view; *B*, portion of integument removed, showing egg-shaped gametophyte. The dark strip on the upper left-hand portion of the latter is where a piece of the now membranous nucellus was peeled off; *C*, gametophyte, entire, with nucellar cap at the upper end; *D*, longitudinal section; *E*, end view, with part of the integument removed, disclosing the tiny crater-like pollen-chambers, at the bottom of which the necks of the archegonia open. (Cf. Fig. 297.) About natural size.

a parasite, by the tissue of the nucellus. The latter becomes almost entirely consumed, so that when a longitudinal section is made of a mature ovule (Fig. 297), the remainder of the nucellus appears only as a thin membrane adhering to the outer surface of the prothallus, or *endosperm*, as it is here called. When the egg fails to become fertilized the gametophyte may protrude, develop chlorophyll, and lead a brief, semi-independent existence.

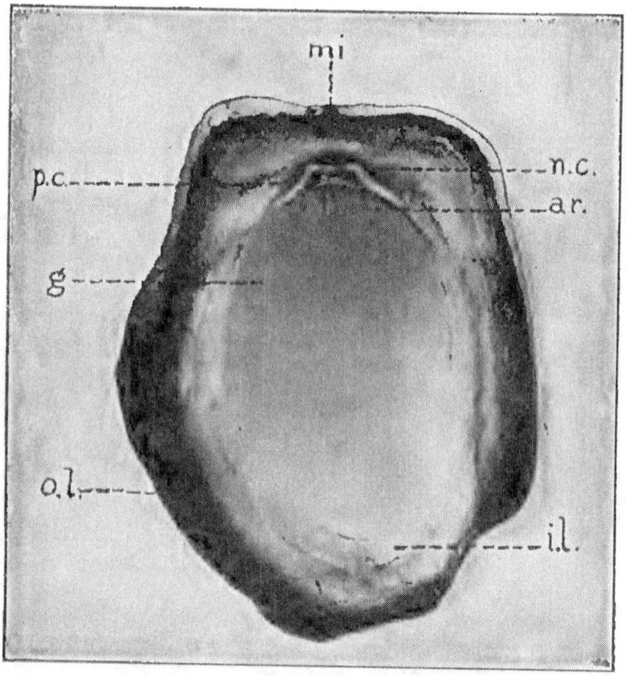

FIG. 297.—Photograph of a longitudinal section of an ovule of *Macrozamia Moorei*. *mi*, micropyle; *n.c*, nucellar cap; *a.r*, archegonia (the venters only showing); *il*, inner, hard layer, *o.l*, outer, fleshy layer of the integument; *g*, gametophyte; *p.c*, pollen chamber. Enlarged from *D*, Fig. 296.

Several archegonia develop in the apical end, imbedded in the tissue of the prothallus, and with their neck-canals opening at the surface into a *pollen-chamber* (Fig. 297). They resemble somewhat the archegonia of the lower orders studied, but possess only two neck cells, and no neck-canal cells. The large egg-cell in the venter is the largest known in the plant kingdom.

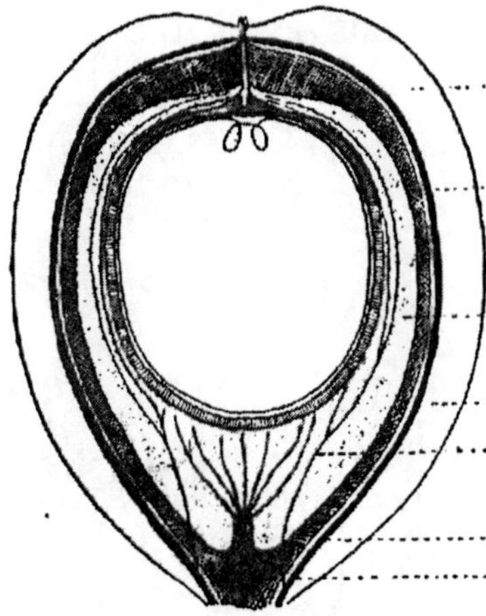

FIG. 298.—*Cycas circinalis.* Diagram of longitudinal section of a nearly mature seed; *o*, outer fleshy layer, with a bundle (o^1) of the outer vascular system; *s*, stony layer of integument; *i*, inner fleshy layer, with a bundle (i^1) of the inner vascular system; *c*, central vascular bundle. (After Marie C. Stopes.)

357. Male Gametophyte.—The germination of the microspore and the development of the male gametophyte involve only cell-divisions, but not the growth of new tissue. *The mature gametophyte is called a pollen-grain.* It consists of three cells: a prothallial cell, a tube-cell, and a generative cell (Fig. 299). There is no structure that can be positively identified as an antheridium, unless the prothallial cell is considered (as by some), as representing the antheridium. The pollen-grain has two coats—an outer and an inner.

358. Pollination.—When the pollen is mature it is scattered by the wind, and some of the grains lodge, by chance, in the pollen-chamber of the ovules on neighboring female plants. The transfer of pollen to the female plant is *pollination.*

359. Germination of the Pollen-grain.—In the pollen-chamber the conditions favor the germination of the

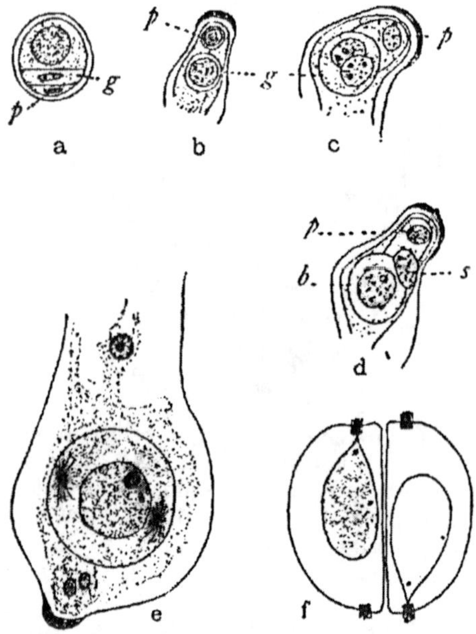

FIG. 299.—*Cycas revoluta.* *a*, Pollen grains at shedding stage; × 500; *b*, later stage, showing prothallial cell (*p*) and generative cell (*g*), the tube-nucleus not shown; × 200; *c*, generative cell divided, giving rise to stalk- and body-cells; × 500; *d*, the stalk-cell-nucleus (*s*) being crowded out, and blepharoplasts appearing in the body cell (*b*); × 500; *e*, the body-cell shortly before division, showing two well-developed blepharoplasts; × 750; *f*, the two male cells resulting from the division of the body-cell; the beaks of the nuclei are attached to the cilia-bearing bands; × 200. Reduced about two-thirds in reproduction. (After Ikeno.)

pollen. This is also a new feature in life history. In germination the pollen-grain develops absorbing organs (*haustoria*), which penetrate the tissue of the nucellar-cap (Fig. 300), and also larger tubes which carry the generative cell further down into the pollen-chamber. As the tube elongates the generative cell passes down it, becoming divided into two sperm-cells. These sperm-cells are remarkably interesting little bodies, bearing a large num-

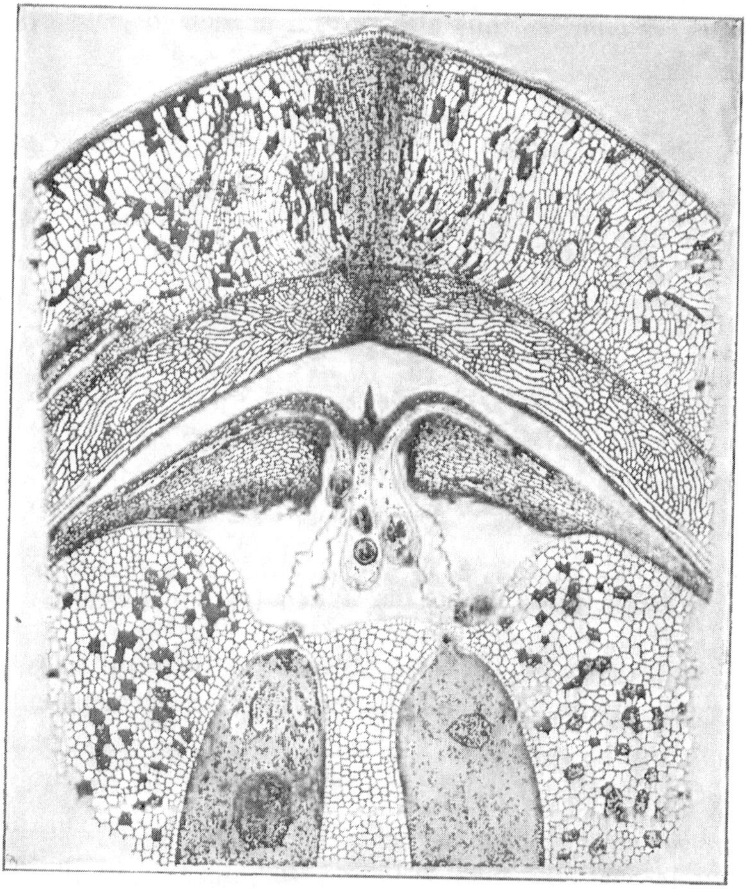

FIG. 300.—*Dioon edule:* upper part of an ovule at the time of fertilization, showing integument, nucellus, male gametophytes (germinating pollen-grains), and female gametophytes (embryo-sacs). Reconstructed from sections of several ovules. (After Chamberlain.)

ber of cilia, by the motion of which they are carried, in the completion of their journey to the egg, through the watery solution emptied from the pollen-tube, to and through the neck-canal of the archegonium, into the archegonial chamber. Fertilization, here as always, is completed by the fusion of the sperm and the egg-nuclei (Fig. 301). The behavior of these little sperms in an allied genus, *Zamia*, is thus described by their discoverer,[1] Webber:

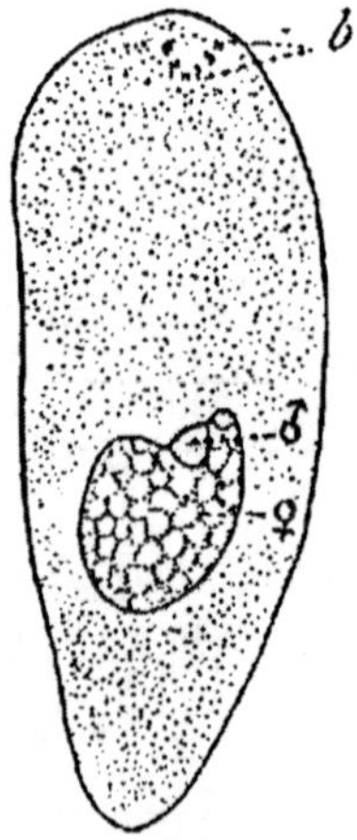

FIG. 301.—Fertilization in *Zamia floridana*. The male and female nuclei are fusing; *b*, remains of the cilia of the sperm. (After Webber.)

"In removing the nearly mature pollen-tubes the spermatozoids are found to be in various stages of development, as would be expected. In many cases tubes have been observed, before cutting them off, in which the two spermatozoids had pulled apart and were swimming free in the protoplasm. In some instances their movement in the pollen-tube, before it is injured, can be observed with the aid of a hand lens.

"It is an interesting sight to see the two giant spermatozoids moving around vigorously in the pollen-tube,

[1] Sperms were discovered in *Cycas* by two Japanese botanists, Hirasé and Ikeno.

bumping against each other and the wall of the tube in their reckless haste. They seldom escape from the upper cut end of the pollen-tube, although they as frequently swim toward this end of the tube as the other end, so far as could be observed. In many cases the pollen-tubes were cut so that the spermatozoids escaped into the solution, and in numerous other cases mature turgid tubes burst in the process of cutting, discharging the uninjured spermatozoids in the sugar solution. The writer was thus able in many cases to study the spermatozoids swimming free and observe their unobstructed motion.

"The motion of the spermatozoids when swimming free in sugar solution is in no way different from their motion when in the pollen-tube. The general motion is a continuous rotation of the body, always in the same direction, around an axis passing through the apex of the helicoid spiral. Viewed from the head end or apex of the spiral the rotation is in the direction of the hands of a clock, and contrary to the turns of the spiral band. They roll around, first here, then there, resembling in this respect the motion of *Pandorina*. After moving about rapidly for from five to fifteen minutes they usually cease all progressive motion, but continue to rotate for a considerably longer period. The rotary motion also soon ceases, but the cilia continue to vibrate for a considreably longer time. The spermatozoids of *Zamia* also have an amœboid motion, which is particularly noticeable while they are inclosed in the pollen-tube. The apex of the spiral as a whole frequently rotates in a most remarkable way, turning in a circle, pushing out first this way and then that way with the greatest freedom of motion, as if selecting a point of exit or ingress. In other cases the base or the side of the spermatozoid body may be considerably extended as a blunt point in pushing between two obstacles. The whole body seems flexible and changeable in the highest degree and is eminently fitted for its difficult task of finding and swimming through the narrow passage between the neck-cells of the archegonia."

A point to be specially noted here, is that while a pollen-tube is introduced in the process of fertilization, the final act is accomplished as in lower aquatic forms, by the swimming of the sperms through liquid. The pollen-tube alone, as in higher plants, should suffice in Cycads to bring the sperm to the egg, and the retention of locomotion of the sperm, after the appearance of the pollen-tube, can be interpreted only as the persistence, by inheritance, of a character that was a fundamental necessity in lower forms.[1]

360. The Seed.—During the processes of germination of the pollen-grains and fertilization, the ovule is increasing in size, and developing different tissues and juices. The outer wall of the nucellus hardens, while the integument becomes succulent and pulp-like, so that externally the structure resembles a plum. It cannot, however, be compared to a plum in morphology (*i.e.*, cannot be homologized with a plum), for a plum is a ripened ovary, while the so-called "fruit" of the Cycads is a ripened ovule or seed.

361. The Embryo.—After fertilization the oösperm develops into an embryo-sporophyte (Fig. 302). This is often delayed until after the seed is planted, so that *after the embryo has once begun to form it continues to grow,*

[1] The accomplishment of fertilization by the mediation of a pollen-tube (siphon) is called *siphonogamy*.

without undergoing any resting period, until the new sporophyte has emerged from the seed and become established

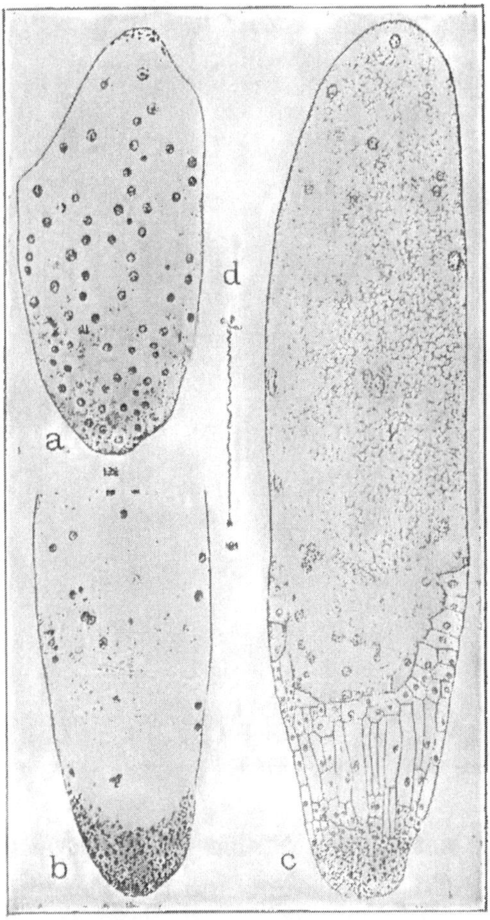

FIG. 302.—*Zamia floridana*. *a*, free nuclei of proembryo; × 16; *b*, tissue at base of proembryo; × 24; *c*, differentiation into suspensor and embryo; × 29; *d*, young embryo showing long suspensor, natural size. (After Coulter and Chamberlain.)

in the soil as an independent plant (Fig. 303). In its early stages the embryo derives its nourishment as a parasite from the female gametophyte (prothallus, or endosperm).

362. Gymnospermy.—The fact that the seed is not enclosed within the carpels, or walls of the ovary, but continues wholly exposed throughout its existence, until

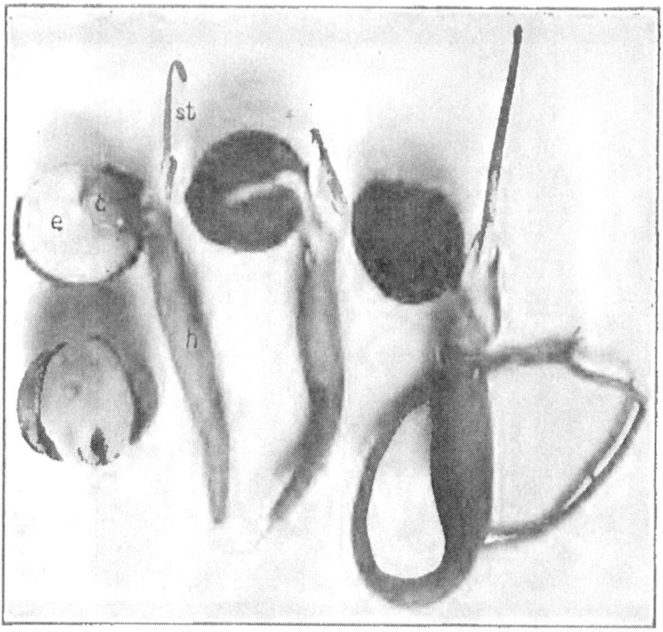

FIG. 303.—*Cycas media.* Germinating seeds. *e*, endosperm (gametophyte); *c*, cotyledons; *st*, leaf-stalk; *h*, hypocotyl, showing early enlargement to form the thick trunk shown in Fig. 291.

shed, is one of the most significant of all the features of the cycads. On this feature, and its opposite, the great division of seed-bearing plants (*Spermatophytes*) is separated into two classes as follows:

Spermatophytes { Gymnosperms
Angiosperms

The word gymnosperm means "naked seed,"[1] while

[1] From the Greek, *gymnos* (γυμνός), naked + *sperma* (σπέρμα), seed.

angiosperm means "enclosed seed."[1] The fundamental distinction between gymnospermy and angiospermy was first made clear by one of the greatest of English botanists, Robert Brown, in 1827 (Fig. 10).

363. Comparison with Ferns.—The cycads resemble the true ferns in several points—in the vernation of their leaves (coiled in the bud), in the venation of the leaves (forked veins), in the possession of sori (for microsporangia), in having multiciliate sperms, in having sporophylls (megasporophylls) that closely resemble foliage leaves, and in having the embryo dependent at first upon the prothallus for nourishment, but later becoming established as an independent plant.

They differ from ferns in having the non-green gametophyte dependent for nourishment throughout its life upon the tissues of the sporophyte. In the heterosporous habit they differ from the true ferns, but resemble the higher fern relatives, like *Selaginella*. *Their greatest step forward is the development of a seed.* They are the first true seed-bearing plants to be met with among living species, as we ascend from the Algæ. How closely *Selaginella* approaches the formation of a true seed may be seen by referring to the condition in the megasporangium following fertilization (Fig. 284). *If* the female gametophyte of *Selaginella* should remain within the walls of the megaspore; *if* the embryo should undergo a period of rest after the formation of the young stem and first leaves, and *if* this entire structure should remain within the megasporangium, we should have a true seed in *Selaginella*.

The cycad seed is primitive (or imperfect as a seed),

[1] From the Greek, *angeion* (ἀγγεῖον), a vessel + *sperma* (σπέρμα), seed.

in frequently not having the embryo develop until after the seed is planted, and in not having the embryo undergo a period of rest between its formation and its final development into a mature sporophyte; the absence of an embryo characterizes some of the fossil relatives of *Cycas*.

The genus *Cycas* is the only living genus of plants which produces seeds without developing either a cone or a flower, but *produces the seeds on sporophylls borne on the main stem.* It is the simplest of all living seed-plants, to this extent, being in this respect as lowly organized as the ferns.

OUTLINE OF LIFE HISTORY OF A CYCAD

The Cycad plant
(Sporophyte)

↓↓		↓↓
Microsporophylls		Megasporophylls
↓↓		↓↓
Microsporangia		Megasporangia (ovules)
↓	←*Reduction*→	↓
Microspores		Megaspores
↓		↓
Male gametophyte (Pollen-grain)		Female gametophyte (Endosperm)
↓		↓
Vestigial antheridium		Archegonium
↓		↓
Generative cell		
↓		↓
Sperms	*Fertilization*	Egg

↘ ↙

Oösperm
↓↓
Embryo
↓↓
New Cycad plant
(Sporophyte)

364. Distribution.—The cycads and their relatives are all tropical or subtropical. Four genera (*Microcycas*, *Zamia*, *Ceratozamia*, *Dioön*) occur in the western hemisphere, with the chief center of distribution in Mexico; and five genera (*Cycas*, *Bowenia*, *Macrozamia*, *Encephalartos*, and *Stangeria*) in the eastern hemisphere, with

FIG. 303*a*.—Wilhelm Hofmeister (1824–1877). His comparative studies of the history of development of mosses, vascular cryptogams, and seed-bearing plants, disclosed the fact of an alternation of generations throughout those forms, and afforded the basis for a correct interpretation of the genetic relationship of the great groups of plants.

the chief center of distribution for the first three in Queensland, Australia. *Encephalartos* and *Stangeria* are confined to Africa.

CHAPTER XXVI

SEED-BEARING PLANTS (Continued)

GYMNOSPERMS

LIFE HISTORY OF THE PINE

Description of the Tree

365. The Trunk.—Everyone is so familiar with the general features of pine trees as to render a detailed description unnecessary here. The main stem or *trunk* is normally a straight vertical shaft, that may be traced from the ground to the apex of the tree (Fig. 304). Such a trunk is called *excurrent*, in contrast to the opposite type which may be traced for only a short distance from the ground, to a point where it divides into the main branches or *limbs*. The latter type of trunk is termed *deliquescent* (Fig. 305).

The excurrent trunk results from the fact that the main stem, as well as the lateral branches, always has a *terminal bud*, which carries the trunk upward from year to year. Trees may continue to increase in height each season, until they have reached the limit for the given species. Many factors may, of course, modify the height, among which is the limit of height to which the species can raise sap. Some species of pine attain a height of 160 feet.

366. Branching.—At first glance pine trees appear to bear their main branches in circles or *whorls*, but closer

FIG. 304.—Grove of pines showing excurrent trunks.

observation discloses the fact that these are really *pseudo-whorls*, since the branches do not emerge at precisely the same level on the trunk, as in true whorls. Both because they are older, and because they receive less light, the

FIG. 305.—Elm tree (*Ulmus americana*), showing deliquescent trunk.

lower branches are longer, and the gradual decrease in length from below upward, combined with the excurrent habit of the trunk, gives the tree a pyramidal outline when it grows free in the open. This shape is modified by mutual shading and crowding, resulting in natural pruning, when trees grow close together in the forest.

367. Long and Short Branches.—The pines, like several other groups of plants, bear two distinct kinds of branches —long branches, and short branches. The short branches are often called "spur-shoots." Long branches, in addition to being longer and larger, commonly bear *only* scale-like leaves, while the spur-shoots bear the foliage-leaves (Fig. 308). In certain cases *juvenile forms* of long branches are recognized, which bear foliage-leaves as an exception to the general rule.

368. Leaves.—The long, needle-like leaves of the pine are familiar to everyone. They occur on the spur-shoots in groups or *fascicles* of one, two, three, or five, according to the species. The spur-shoots are borne in the axils of the scale-like leaves of the long shoots (Fig. 307). The base of the leaf cluster is sheathed by the thin membranous scales of the terminal bud of the spur. When there are two leaves in a fascicle they are semi-circular in cross-section, the adjacent faces being flattened as a result of their contact in the bud; when there are three or more they are triangular in cross-section. The white pine (*Pinus Strobus*), and its nearest relatives, have five leaves to a fascicle, the pitch-pine (*P. rigida*), and its nearest relatives, bear the leaves in threes, the scrub-pines and the European pine (*P. sylvestris*), in twos.

369. Leaf-fall.—The duration of the leaves varies with the species and the locality from two to ten years. As a result there are always green leaves on the tree, whence the term "evergreen." That the leaves are shed may be easily determined by examining the ground under any pine tree. The duration of the leaves is also easily ascertained by observing the oldest annual growth still bearing spur-shoots. When the leaves are shed the entire spur-shoot falls away.

Reproduction

370. Staminate Cones.—Most of the cone-bearing trees (Coniferæ) are monœcious, *i.e.*, bear both microspores and megaspores on the same tree. The staminate cones appear in the spring, usually in May in the northern states,

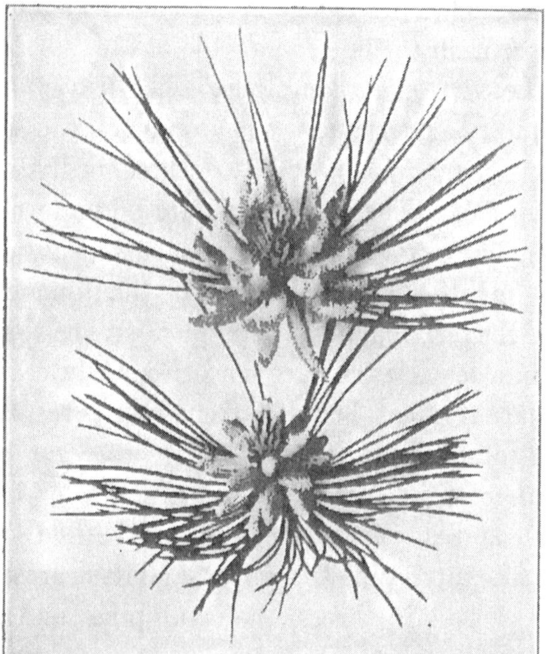

FIG. 306.—Staminate cones of the Austrian pine (*Pinus austriaca*). Below, before shedding pollen; above, after shedding.

and persist for only a few weeks. They are borne in clusters on the long branches on the current year's growth, and occupy the lateral position of spur-shoots; they are never terminal (Fig. 306). They are, in reality, modified branches, consisting of the main axis, bearing the scales (microsporophylls, or *stamens*) arranged in spirals. On the underside of the microsporophyll is the spore-case, containing the microspores. The staminate cones pass the winter inside the bud, and during this period the sporangia contain only spore-mother-cells. The tetrad-division of

FIG. 307.—Scotch pine (*Pinus sylvestris*). Showing carpotropism of carpellate cones. Young cones at the left; cones one year old at the right. (Cf. Figs. 308 and 309.)

the spore-mother-cells, occurs early in the spring, the exact time varying with the species, the locality, and the character of the season, but the young microspores are usually all formed by the first of May. On either side of the main body of the microspore is a tiny air-sac which gives the spore great buoyancy in the air (Fig. 313).

371. Carpellate Cones.—One or more young carpellate cones appear *near the tip* of the new growth in early spring (Figs. 307–309), and are noticeable at that time

FIG. 308.—Scotch pine (*Pinus sylvestris*). Branch bearing carpellate cones, one, two, and three years old. (Cf. Figs. 307 and 309.)

from their delicate tint of red. They terminate short, lateral, axillary branches. Like the staminate cones, the carpellate cones are branches, modified for the purpose of reproduction. The central axis bears lateral scales (Figs. 309 and 310), but the homology of these scales is difficult to determine, and is still a matter of debate. There are

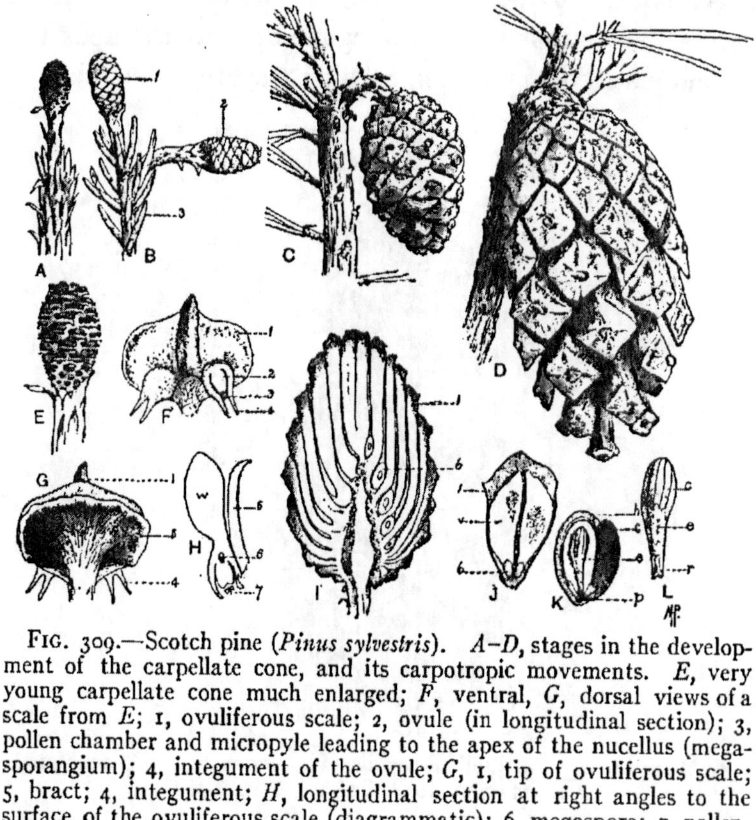

FIG. 309.—Scotch pine (*Pinus sylvestris*). *A–D*, stages in the development of the carpellate cone, and its carpotropic movements. *E*, very young carpellate cone much enlarged; *F*, ventral, *G*, dorsal views of a scale from *E*; 1, ovuliferous scale; 2, ovule (in longitudinal section); 3, pollen chamber and micropyle leading to the apex of the nucellus (megasporangium); 4, integument of the ovule; *G*, 1, tip of ovuliferous scale; 5, bract; 4, integument; *H*, longitudinal section at right angles to the surface of the ovuliferous scale (diagrammatic); 6, megaspore; 7, pollen-chamber; *I*, longitudinal section of a mature cone; 6, ovule; *J*, scale from a mature cone; 6, seed; *w*, wing of seed; *K*, dissection of mature seed; *h*, hard seed coat; *c*, dry membraneous remains of the nucellus, here folded back to show the endosperm and embryo; *e*, embryo; *p*, remains of nucellus; *L*, embryo; *c*, cotyledons; *e*, hypocotyl; *r*, root-end.

good reasons for considering that they are not simple sporophylls, but are of a more complex character.

Each scale comprises a bract and an *ovuliferous* (ovule-bearing) *scale* (Fig. 309). It is probable (but not certain) that the ovuliferous scale represents two sporophylls fused together.

372. Megasporangia.—As in *Cycas*, the megasporangium is an ovule, comprising a nucellus (sporangium proper), surrounded by an integument. At the apex the integument does not come quite together, so that a

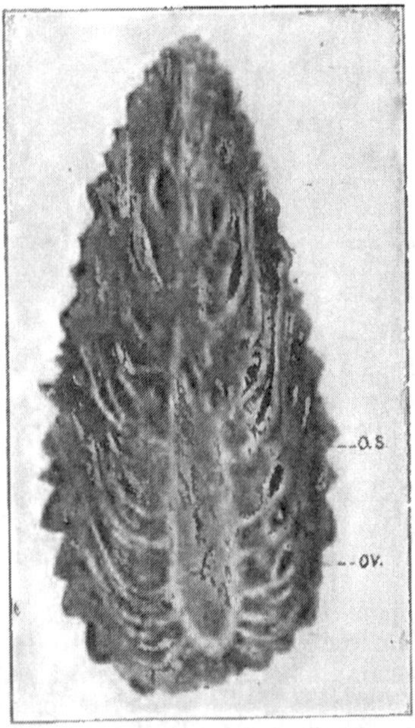

FIG. 310.—Median longitudinal section of a pine cone. *o.s*, ovuliferous scale; *ov*, ovule at the base of a scale.

tiny opening or pore (the *micropyle*) is left. The micropyle leads to the *pollen-chamber* below (Figs. 309 and 311). The megaspores are more backward in development than the microspores, the spore-mother-cell not appearing until June. Reduction by two divisions gives rise to either three or four megaspores in a row, but only the basal one ever germinates; the others become disorganized and furnish nourishment for the one that germinates.

373. Female Gametophyte.—During the first season the megaspore (Fig. 311) enlarges somewhat, and its nucleus divides several times, forming free nuclei. In this condition it remains until the next season, when the formation of the gametophyte is carried to completion. As the gametophyte develops it feeds on the nucellus, which is entirely consumed except for a thin membrane, which

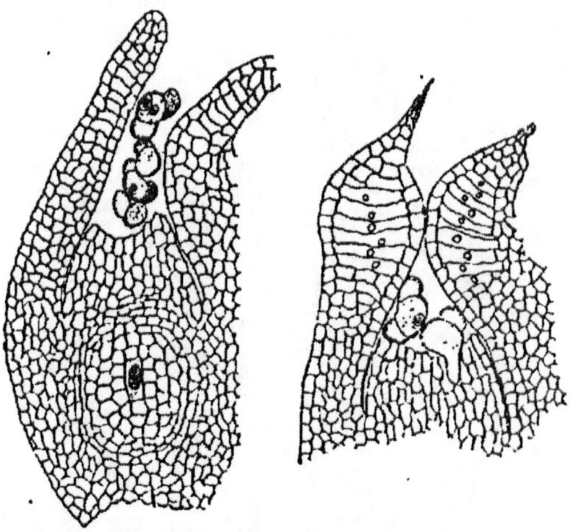

FIG. 311.—White pine (*Pinus Strobus*). At left, megasporangium with megaspore in the center; above, pollen grains in the micropyle and pollen chamber. At right, pollen grains beginning to germinate; the cells of the integument have enlarged and closed the micropyle. (After Margaret C. Ferguson.)

adheres to the surface of the gametophyte or endosperm, and a cap of tissue at the tip of the gametophyte (Figs. 309, K, and 312).[1] The archegonia, two to five in number, at the micropylar end of the gametophyte, are mature by the last of May or forepart of June, in the northern states. In *Pinus* the neck of the archegonium is very much re-

[1] In the seeds of some of the higher plants the tissue of the nucellus becomes filled with nourishment stored for the use of the developing embryo, during germination. It is then called *perisperm*.

duced, consisting usually, in the white pine, of only four cells, all in the same plane; the number of these cells is somewhat variable. No neck-canal cells are formed; only the egg, and the ventral canal-cell (the sister-cell of the egg) which disorganizes early (Fig. 312).

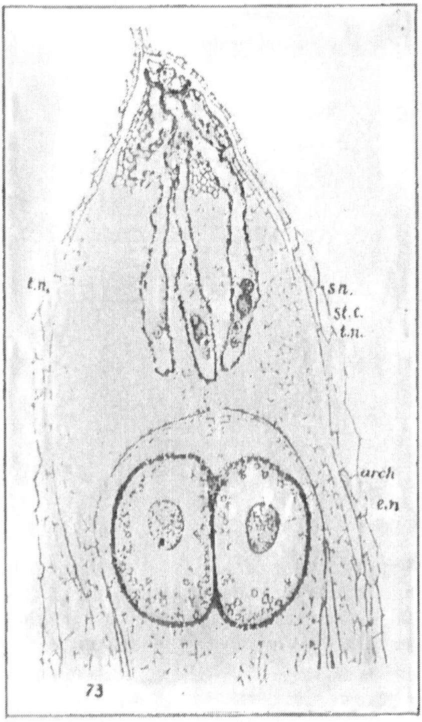

FIG. 312.—White pine (*Pinus Strobus*). Vertical section through the upper part of an ovule, shortly before fertilization. *s.n*, sperm-nuclei; *st.c*, stalk-cell; *t.n*, tube-nucleus; *arch*, archegonium; *e.n*, egg-nucleus. (After Margaret C. Ferguson.)

374. Male Gametophyte.—The germination of the microspore consists chiefly of a series of cell-divisions, all within the wall of the microspore. The first three divisions result in the formation of four cells, namely, two *prothallial cells*, one *mother-cell of the antheridium*, and a larger cell, the *tube-cell*, composing the larger portion of what is now the mature male gametophyte or pollen-grain. Commonly one of the two prothallial cells disintegrates, so that only one is visible (Fig. 313). Thus it is seen that the vegetative portion of the male gametophyte is reduced to nearly its lowest terms—only one or two cells of no known function; the antheridium is also represented only by its mother-cell. At this stage pollination occurs.

375. Distribution of Pollen.—In all cone-bearing trees pollination is accomplished by the wind. At about the

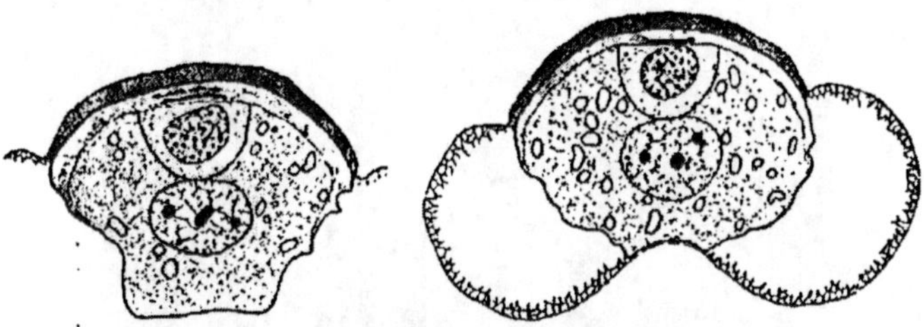

FIG. 313.—The white pine (*Pinus Strobus*). Sections through mature pollen grains; at the left the remnants of two prothallial cells can be seen, while at the right all signs of the first cell have disappeared. Pollen collected June 9, 1898. × about 600. (After Margaret C. Ferguson.)

time the pollen-grain is mature the axes of the carpellate cones elongate, thus separating the scales from each other (Fig. 309, *E*). At the same period the axes of the staminate cones elongate, separating the anthers from each other (Fig. 306). The sporangial walls now become opened by a longitudinal slit, and the least jarring of the branch is sufficient to shake out the dry pollen-grains, which appear in countless millions as a fine yellow dust, the "pollen."

376. Abundance of Pollen.—The pollen is so abundant that it forms a really dense cloud that is easily seen in a photograph of a tree shedding its pollen (Fig. 314). The pollen-grains are, of course, blown hither and thither with every breeze, and millions of them never reach a carpellate cone. The writer once found an accumulation of pine pollen in a desk drawer that had remained constantly closed (but in the vicinity of a pine tree) during the season of pollination. A microscopic examination of

FIG. 314.—Shedding of pollen from a young pine tree. Note the cloud of pollen at the left, caused by shaking the tree.

dust from ledges, indoors and out, at the pollen season, will usually disclose one or more pollen-grains of pines and other species.

377. Pollen and Coal-formation.—A microscopic examination of muck from the bottom of almost any inland lake will disclose the fact that it contains millions of pollen-grains of various cone-bearing trees, and spores of

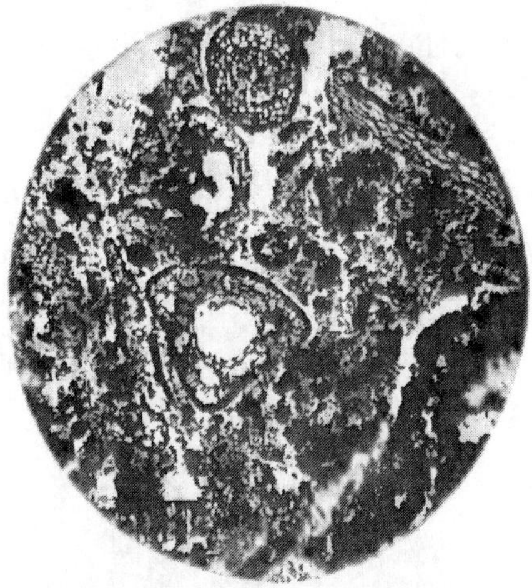

FIG. 315.—The organization of shallow water accumulations in a lake of the present geological epoch, showing remains of roots, leaves, etc. Near the center of the figure may be seen a cross-section of the triangular needle of a white pine. (Cf. Figs. 316 and 317.) (After E. C. Jeffrey.)

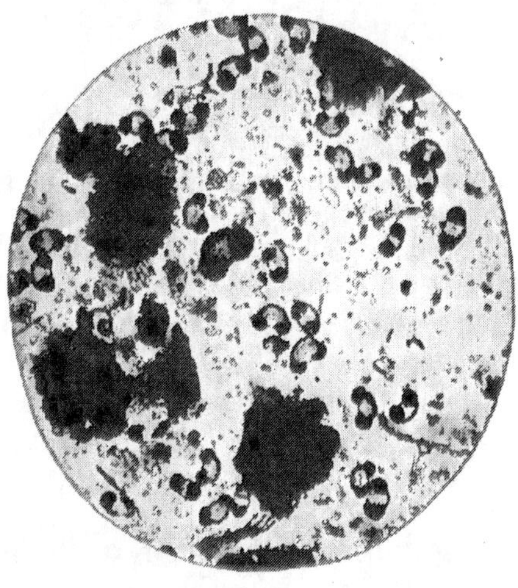

FIG. 316.—Fine muck from the bottom of a pond, as seen under the compound microscope, showing the presence of pollen grains of pine, spruce, and fir. (Cf. Figs. 315 and 317.) (After E. C. Jeffrey.)

horsetails, and other cryptogams (Figs. 315 and 316). It is instructive in this connection to recall recent careful studies of the structure of coal as seen in transparent sections by the aid of the microscope. These sections, prepared by Professor Jeffrey, reveal the remarkable fact that the soft, or bituminous, coals contain carbonized remains of innumerable spores of the plants which constituted the dominant vegetation during the geological

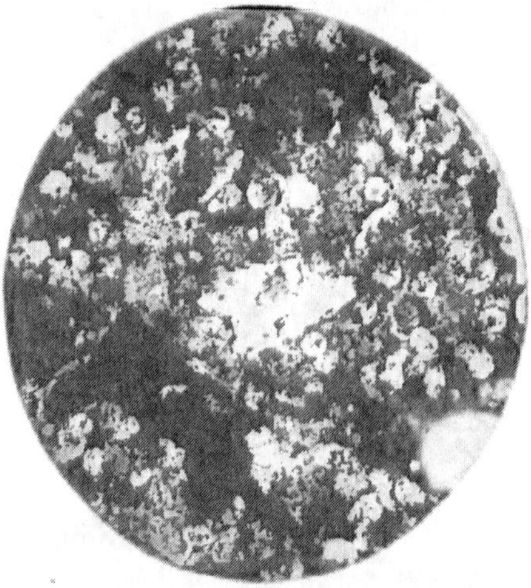

FIG. 317.—Photomicrograph of a thin section of cannel coal from Kentucky, formed under open-water conditions, *i.e.*, of the muck at the bottom of ancient lakes or lagoons. The light, roundish bodies are spores. (Cf. Figs. 315 and 316.) (After E. C. Jeffrey.)

period (Carboniferous), when coal was being formed (Fig. 317). Such studies necessitate a radical change in our earlier conception as to the conditions and method of coal-formation.

These facts also illustrate how the study of what might, at first thought, seem insignificant, impractical, or unimportant, and not closely related to our daily lives, may, at any time, furnish the key to unlock the mystery of some very important fundamental fact or scientific principle.

The formation of pollen in such abundance is one of the numerous instances of the "factor of safety" in plant organization; and the necessity for it is recognized at once when one considers the small chance that any given pollen-grain will reach the pollen-chamber of an ovule.

378. Pollination.—Some of the pollen-grains, of course reach the carpellate cones, which are usually situated higher up on the tree and higher up on the individual shoots, than are the staminate cones. This location is an advantage, because the light pollen-grains, specially buoyant because of their two air-sacs, readily float upward. Those that reach the carpellate cones, fall between the ovuliferous scales, and settle down to the bases of the scales. Some of them get caught in the sticky fluid that fills the pollen-chamber at this time, and as the fluid dries up the grains are drawn close down to the tip of the nucellus (Fig. 311). Here, as always, the deposit of pollen on the surface where it is to germinate is called *pollination*. Pollination in *Pinus* occurs in late May or early June, depending on the species, the locality, and the nature of the season.

379. Nodding of the Cone.—Soon after pollination the stalk of the carpellate cone, in most species, changes its relation to gravity, becoming *negatively* geotropic. One side grows more rapidly than the others, thus causing the cone to nod and hang pendant (Figs. 307 and 308). This position it retains throughout the remainder of its life.

380. Germination of the Pollen-grain.—Very soon after pollination, the tube-cell begins to develop a pollen-tube, which secretes an enzyme that dissolves the cell-walls and contents of the nucellar tissue, thus facilitating the passage of the delicate tube. The dissolved contents nourish the growing tube, which at first serves as a haustorium to absorb the nourishment. Thus the male (as well as the female) gametophyte, lives as a parasite upon the tissue of the sporophyte.

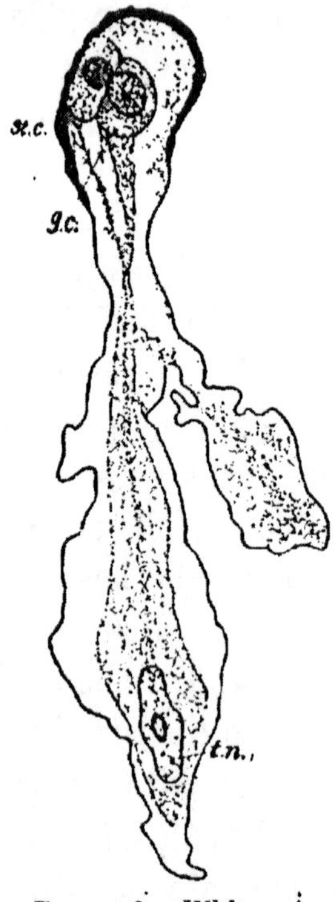

FIG. 318.—White pine (*Pinus Strobus*). Germinating pollen tube on Jan. 4, 1899. *st.c*, stalk-cell; *g.c*, generative cell; *t.n*, tube-nucleus. × about 236. (After Margaret C. Ferguson.)

Soon after the pollen-tube has begun to form, the tube-nucleus moves down toward the tip, where it remains, presiding over the subsequent growth of the tube (Fig. 318). At about this time, also, the antheridial mother-cell divides, forming a *wall-cell*[1] and a *generative cell.* In this condition the first winter is passed. After pollination the carpellate scales, by growth, are brought close together, and secrete a very sticky, resinous substance, all of which very completely excludes any water from between the scales. The cone then increases greatly in size (Fig. 309).

381. Fertilization.—Early in the following spring (May–June), the generative cell, after passing into the pollen-tube, divides to form two *sperm-cells*, and the pollen-tube continues its growth toward the archegonia. By this time (June) the egg lies mature within, and completely

[1] Also commonly called "*stalk-cell.*"

filling, the venter of the archegonium. The pollen-tube passes between the neck-cells of the archegonium, but does not ordinarily enter the venter. The apex of the tube is ruptured, probably by internal osmotic pressure, and its entire contents are emptied into the cytoplasm of the egg. One of the sperm-nuclei unites with the egg-nucleus (June of the second season), and fertilization is accomplished (Fig. 319).

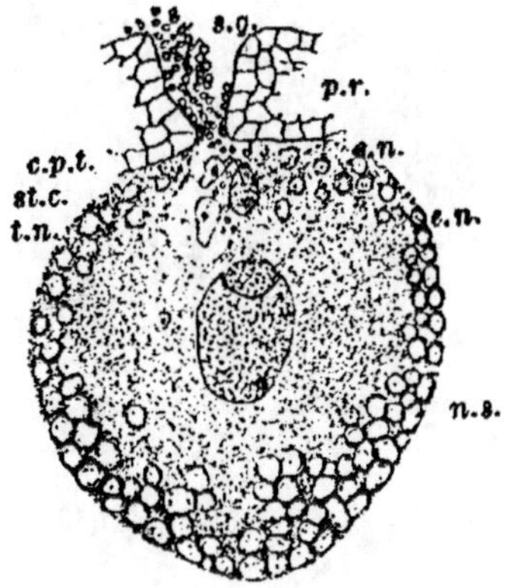

FIG. 319.—White pine (*Pinus Strobus*). Longitudinal section through an archegonium at the time of fertilization. Above the fusing nuclei are various other elements emptied into the egg from the pollen-tube. Collected June 21, 1898. × about 62. *s.g*, starch grains; *p.r*, prothallium; *c.p.t*, cytoplasm from pollen-tube; *st.c*, stalk-cell; *t.n*, tube-nucleus; *s.n*, sperm-nucleus; *e.n*, egg-nucleus; *n.s*, nutritive spheres. (After Margaret C. Ferguson.)

382. Formation of the Seed.—After fertilization the oösperm begins at once to develop, giving rise to three distinct structures; the pro-embryo, the suspensor, and the embryo-sporophyte. During the early divisions of the fertilized egg the male and female chromatins can be clearly distinguished (Fig. 320). At the same time the adjacent tissues of the ovule become transformed. A portion of the prothallus or gametophyte nourishes the developing embryo, but the large bulk of it becomes stored as *endosperm* around the embryo. The remains of the nucellus persist as a thin membrane surrounding the endosperm (as mentioned above), the integument of the ovule develops into the *seed-coat*, and from the integument there also develops a long, thin, membranous wing.

383. Seed-dispersal.—From the above description we learn that it takes about a year and a half to make a pine seed. When the seeds are mature, the scales of the car-

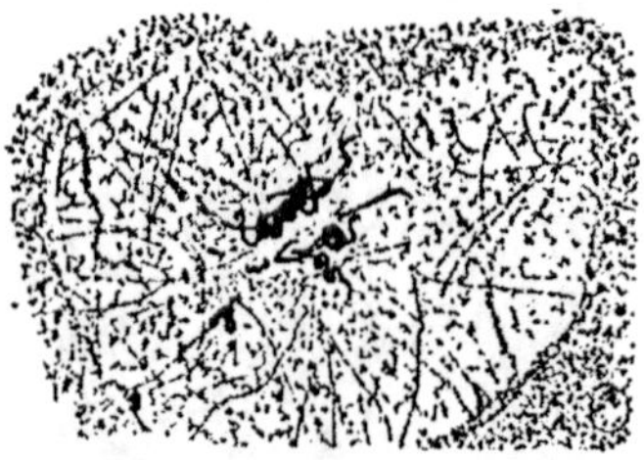

FIG. 320.—White pine (*Pinus Strobus*). Late prophase in the first nuclear division of the fertilized egg. The nuclear membrane has disappeared, and the chromatin from both egg and sperm may still be distinguished. × about 236. (After Margaret C. Ferguson.)

pellate cone, which have now become large and woody, spread apart (Figs. 308 and 309, *D*), and thus permit the loose seeds to fall out. By means of the membranous wing, the seeds are easily dispersed by the wind.

384. Germination of the Seed.—The seeds usually do not germinate until the spring after they are dispersed, or two years after pollination. Under suitable conditions of environment the hypocotyl elongates, forming an arch, and drawing the cotyledons out of the ground, while the tap-root develops from the opposite end. By the straightening of the arch the green cotyledons are lifted into the air and light, the hypocotyl elongates, the root-system begins to develop, and thus the seedling sporophyte becomes established as an independent plant.

OUTLINE OF LIFE HISTORY OF PINUS

The pine tree
(Sporophyte)

↓↓	↓↓
Carpellate cone (Modified branch)	Staminate cone (Modified branch)
↓↓	↓↓
Ovuliferous scale (Homology obscure)	Stamens (Microsporophylls)
↓↓	↓↓
Ovule (Megasporangium)	Anthers (Microsporangia)
↓↓	↓↓
Megaspore-mother-cell	Microspore-mother-cell
↓ ←—— *Reduction*	——→ ↓
Megaspore	Microspore
↓	↓
Embryo-sac (Female gametophyte)	Pollen-grain (Male gametophyte)
↓	↓
Archegonium	(Antheridial cell)
↓	↓
Egg	Sperm

Fertilization

Oösperm
↓↓
Embryo (In a seed)
(Zygote)
↓↓
Embryo-rests
↓↓
Germination of seed
↓↓
Mature sporophyte (The pine tree)

385. Comparison with Lower Forms.—It will be specially instructive, at this point, for the student to make a careful comparison of the life history of *Pinus* with the lower forms, such as *Cycas*, *Selaginella*, *Lycopodium*, *Equisetum*, and a true fern, noting especially the relative importance, in the ascending scale, of gametophyte and sporophyte, and the evidences which point to a possible mode of origin of the vegetative body of the sporophyte. A fundamental question, still being debated by botanists, is whether, in racial history, the vegetative (sterile) tissue appeared first, and the sporogenous (fertile) tissue later,

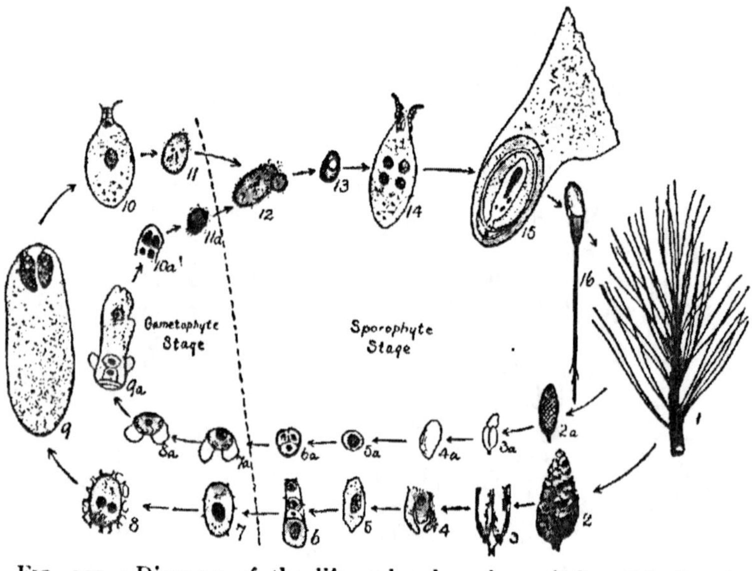

FIG. 321.—Diagram of the life-cycle of a pine. (After Schaffner.)

or whether the fertile tissue appeared first. The question may be put as follows: Is the cone (strobilus) the older structure in the development of the race, and are the vegetative parts to be regarded as developed from it by progressive *sterilization?* It is better that this question be merely stated here, as one of the larger, fundamental problems of botany, and that the pleasure of discussing it be reserved for the teacher and students together, in connection with a later chapter. (Cf., also, p. 379.)

CHAPTER XXVII

SEED-BEARING PLANTS (Continued)

LIFE HISTORY OF AN ANGIOSPERM

386. Variations in Life Histories.—In the groups previously studied there is a marked uniformity or similarity in the life histories, making it comparatively simple, once one has the key, to interpret the structures involved. Even as we pass from one group to the next, homologies are detected without serious difficulty. Under various more or less transparent disguises, we have been able to trace such structures as the sporophyll, spore-case, microspore and male gametophyte, megaspore and female gametophyte, and, in the latter, the archegonium, egg, and embryo. But studies of the highest group of plants, the Angiosperms, soon lead us into difficulties not readily overcome. It is not difficult to detect the sporophylls, spore-cases, megaspores and microspores; but, just as among the Gymnosperms the antheridium had disappeared as a distinct, fully developed organ, so among the Angiosperms the archegonium has disappeared, and certain new structures have made their appearance. Thus it is not possible to choose from the Angiosperms any actual plant whose life history, in detail, is typical of the entire group. For external features any one of several plants might be chosen to illustrate the floral organs commonly met with. The life history of the yellow adder's-tongue, or dog's-tooth violet, illustrates the essential points for Angiosperms.

387. Dog's-Tooth Violet.[1]—The dog's-tooth violet (*Erythronium americanum*) belongs to the order which includes

FIG. 322.—Dog's-tooth violet (*Erythronium americanum*). Stages of deveopment from the seed. 1–5 show the stage of development in each of five successive years. Full explanation in the text. 6, Bulb showing a surface bud (the sprout has been destroyed). (After F. H. Blodgett.)

the lilies (Liliales), and its structure is quite typical of that order (Fig. 322). Its stem is a small, underground, scaly bulb, giving rise to numerous roots. From the upper

[1] The dog's-tooth violet is really not a violet at all, the common name, as frequently, having no regard to botanical relationships. John Burroughs has suggested that "fawn-lily" would be a much more appropriate name. But common names of plants and animals are, fortunately, not easily changed.

surface of the stem arise two smooth leaves, with a shiny, but mottled surface, and acute apex. The petioles sheathe the base of a flower-stalk (*scape*), which also arises from the upper surface of the bulb. At the tip of the flower-stalk is the solitary flower.

388. Blossoming.—Early in the spring the flower-stalk begins to elongate rapidly until it has developed into a long, slender, unbranched stem, the *scape*, bearing at its tip the flower-bud, raised several inches above the ground, and soon expanding into a flower. During the formation of the flower-bud, *in the preceding autumn*, the outer surfaces of the floral envelopes grew more rapidly than the inner surface, thus causing the formation of the bud. The opening of the bud is caused largely by the more rapid growth of the inner surfaces of the floral envelopes.

389. Structure of the Flower.—In *Erythronium* (or any liliaceous plant; cf. Fig. 323) we may recognize all the parts of a complete flower, as follows:

1. An outer circle of three *sepals*, together constituting the *calyx*.

2. An inner circle of three *petals*, alternating with the sepals, and together constituting the *corolla*. The sepals and petals in *Erythronium* look very much alike, but each petal has a nectary, or gland secreting nectar, at its base. The calyx and corolla together constitute the *perianth*.

3. Two inner circles of microsporophylls, the *stamens*, three in each circle, one opposite each sepal, and one opposite each petal. All the stamens, taken together constitute the *androecium*.*

*In *Erythronium* three of the six stamens are frequently noticeably shorter than the other three, and mature their pollen later. This is exceptional in the Lily family, to which *Erythronium* belongs.

Each stamen consists of a slender stalk, the *filament*, bearing at its tip two microsporangia (*pollen-sacs*), united to form the *anther*. In the pollen-sacs are numerous microspores, which finally develop into *pollen-grains*.

FIG. 323.—Wood lily (*Lilium philadelphicum*).

A central organ, the *pistil*, composed of three megasporophylls (*carpels*) united, and enclosing the megasporangia (*ovules*). All the pistils taken together (one or more) constitute the *gynoecium*.

The pistil consists of three distinct regions as follows:

(*a*) The enlarged basal part, enclosing the ovules, and hence called the *ovary*.

(*b*) A slender upward prolongation of the ovary,

called the *style*. Through the center of the style extends a tiny canal, so that the style is hollow. The walls of this canal, in *Erythronium*, are lined with a glandular layer of cells forming the *conducting tissue*, which serves to nourish the pollen-tubes (Fig. 324). An expansion of this tissue is exposed at the tip of the style, forming the *stigma*, or surface for the reception of the pollen-grains in pollination. The conducting tissue extends continuously from the stigma down through the style to the *placenta*, or point of attachment of the ovules.

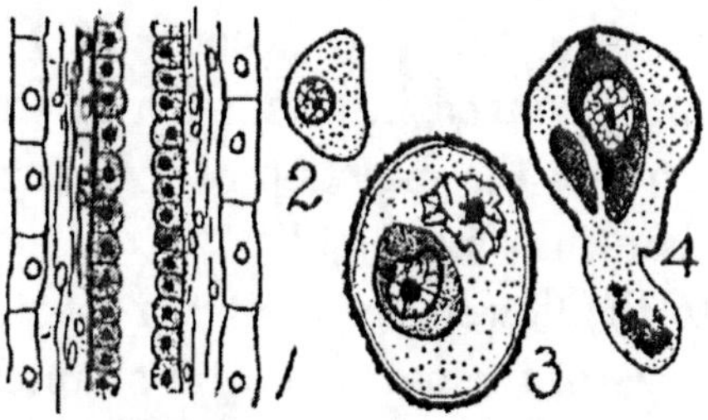

FIG. 324.—*Erythronium americanum*. 1, longitudinal section of hollow style, showing glandular cells of the conducting tissue lining the canal; 2, microspore; 3, young pollen grain (male gametophyte), showing generative nucleus and tube nucleus; 4, pollen-grain germinating. 1 and 4 are from *E. albidum*. (After J. H. Schaffner.)

In many plants the style is not hollow, and the conducting tissue completely fills the center. The *stigmatic surface* secretes a sticky substance by which the pollen-grains are held fast. In some species of plants this surface is covered with tiny hairs, by which the pollen-grains are held until they germinate.

390. Pollination.—The flower of *Erythronium* stands out in sharp contrast to that of the gymnosperms, in two respects, namely, the occurrence of both stamens and carpels in the same flower, and the possession of a conspicuous, colored perianth. The significance of the perianth can be understood only in connection with pollination. It will be recalled that in the gymnosperms the pollen is transferred by wind, but in *Erythronium* this transfer is accomplished by means of insects. The perianth, conspicuous to us by its petals, appears to attract certain insects. Whether this is accomplished by color, or by odor, or by some other means not clearly demonstrated, is not absolutely known. It is generally believed to be by color, but certain experiments seem to disprove this theory. Be that as it may, we know that the development of a conspicuous perianth appeared in the same geological age (Cretaceous) as did the more highly developed, winged insects, such as the butterflies and moths. In fact the insects probably appeared somewhat earlier than the "flowers."

Attracted to the flowers by whatever means, the insect finds, at the bases of the petals, nectar secreted by glands. While feeding on the nectar the back of the insect becomes dusted over with pollen from the anthers. When he flies to another flower some of this pollen is rubbed off on to its stigma, thus accomplishing pollination.

391. The Male Gametophyte.—The young pollen-grain has already been recognized as a microspore. In some species it develops into a male gametophyte before pollination, in other cases not until afterward. In either case the gametophyte is very greatly reduced. The mature pollen-grain of the milkweed, for example, is a mature gametophyte, having the sperm-cells formed at about the time the flower-buds open. In *Erythronium* the generative cell, formed between December 1 and April 1, does not divide to form the sperm-cells until after pollination, and after the pollen-tube has begun to form (Fig. 324).

392. The Female Gametophyte.—Megaspores are probably not formed in tetrads by two divisions of a megaspore-mother-cell, but the ancestral-cell of the female

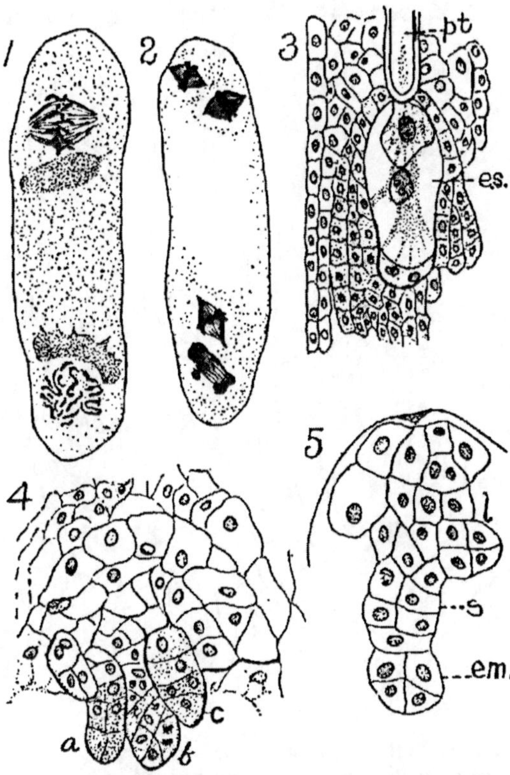

FIG. 325.—Dog's-tooth violet (*Erythronium*). 1, embryo-sac, binucleate stage, the two nuclei dividing; 2, four nucleate stage; 3, mature embryo-sac (*es*); the pollen-tube (*p.t*) has reached the egg-apparatus and fertilization has just taken place; the male and female nuclei are both visible in the fertilized egg. The synergids are not shown; 4, polyembryony; four embryos have developed from the embryogenous tissue, one embryo at the left of *a* not shaded; 5, longitudinal section of an embryo (*em*); *s*, suspensor; 1, 2, and 5, *E. albidum* (after Schaffner); 3 and 4, *E. americanum* (after Jeffrey). Only one of the multiple embryos persists.

gametophyte (*archesporial cell*) functions directly as a megaspore, without division. In very early spring the megaspore begins to germinate, increasing in size, and its nucleus undergoing divisions, forming, in succession, a two-celled, four-celled, and eight-celled embryo-sac (Figs. 325 and 326). Three of these cells pass to one end of the sac, opposite the micropyle, and are known

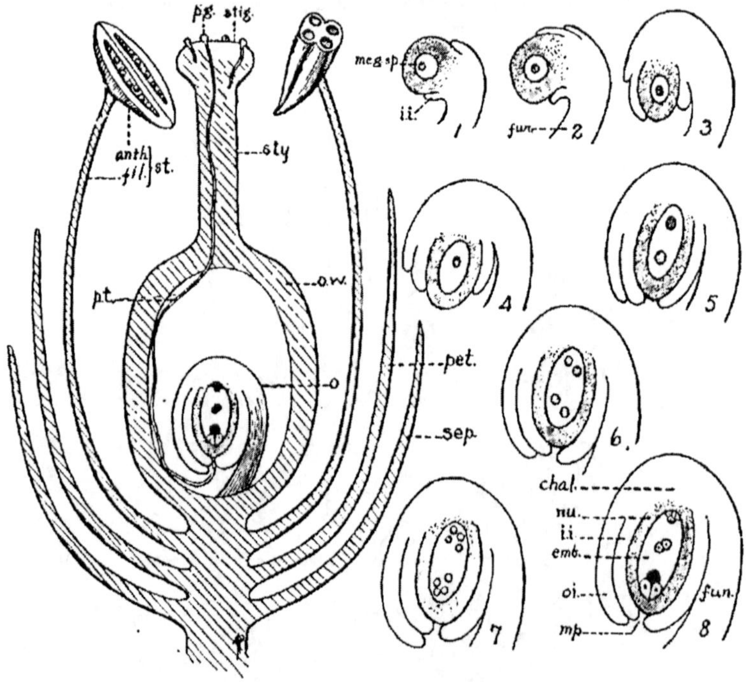

FIG. 326.—At the left, diagram of the anatomy of an angiospermous flower shortly after pollination; *anth.*, anther; *fil.*, filament; *st.*, stamen; *stig.*, stigma; *p.g.*, pollen grains germinating; *sty.*, style; *pt.*, pollen tube; *o.w.*, ovary wall; *o.*, ovule, containing embryo-sac; *pet.*, petal; *sep.*, sepal. 1–8, Stages in the development of the female gametophyte (embryo-sac); *meg.sp.*, megaspore-mother-cell; *i.i.*, inner integument; *o.i.*, outer integument; *fun.*, funiculus; *chal.*, chalaza; *nu.*, nucellus (megasporangium); *emb.*, embryo-sac. All diagrammatic.

as the *antipodal cells*, or antipodals, while two of them meet in the center and fuse, forming the *endosperm-nucleus*. The remaining three pass to the end near the micropyle, where one of them becomes organized as the *egg-cell;* the others are called *synergids* (helpers) (Cf. Fig. 326).

393. Fertilization and Formation of Embryo.—After pollination the pollen-grain, stimulated by the sticky substance secreted by the stigma, begins to develop a pollen-tube, which passes down the canal that extends through the style from stigma to placenta, nourished by the specialized cells that line the inner surface of the

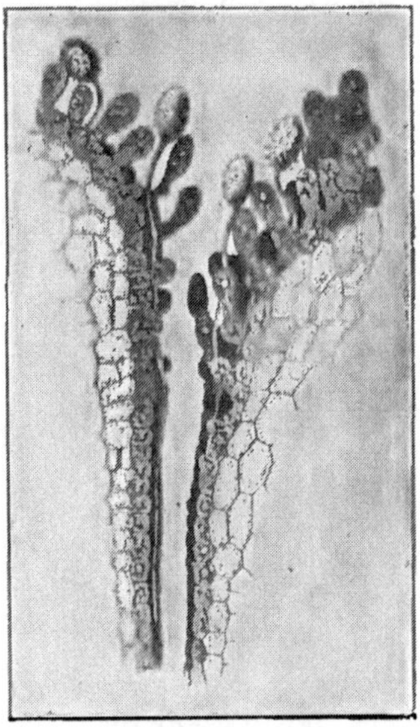

FIG. 327.—*Lilium Martagon.* Longitudinal section of the stigma and upper part of the style. The pollen-grains, caught on the papillæ of the stigma, have germinated, and the pollen-tubes are growing down along the walls of the style-canal, nourished by the specialized cells that line it. (After Dodel-Port.)

canal (Cf. Figs. 324 and 327). When the tip of the tube has passed through the micropyle and into the embryo-sac, the sperm-cells, formed during the growth of the tube, pass out into the protoplasm of the embryo-sac, and one of them fuses with the egg-cell, thereby accomplishing fertilization (Fig. 328. Cf. Fig. 325). In some cases the embryonic tissue that arises from the fertilized egg gives rise to as many as four embryos (Fig. 325), but usually only one of them develops.

394. Formation of the Seed.—While the fertilized egg is developing into the embryo, the endosperm-nucleus

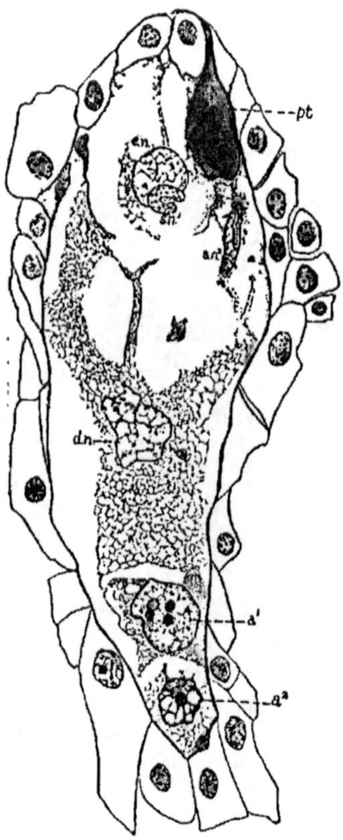

FIG. 328.—*Lilium canadense.* Embryo-sac at the time of fertilization; a^1, a^2, antipodal cells; *dn.*, endosperm-nucleus; *pt.*, remains of pollen-tube; *e.n.*, egg-nucleus; *s.n.*[1], sperm-nucleus, fusing with the egg-nucleus; *s.n.*[2], second sperm-nucleus, which may later fuse with the endosperm-nucleus, thereby accomplishing *double fertilization.* (Redrawn from camera lucida drawing by O. E. White.)

is undergoing successive, rapid divisions, which finally result in the formation of an abundance of starchy endosperm, surrounding the embryo, and serving to nourish it when the seed germinates.[1] At the same time the integuments of the ovule develop into a hard, horny seed-coat. This kind of seed-coat is characteristic of the Liliaceæ.

395. Germination of the Seed.—The seeds are mature by about June, and lie on the ground dormant until the following April, when they germinate. Both ends of the embryo elongate, absorbing all the endosperm for nourishment. By about the time that older plants are blossoming, the young seedling has reached the stage shown in Fig. 322, 2. At one side, near the end of the hypocotyl, there develops a root, and the tip becomes enlarged into a bulb by the storage of starch, manufactured by the green, cylindrical seed-leaf. Within this bulb the first bud (*plumule*) develops, the seed-leaf withers, and the young seedling remains in this condition during the following winter.

396. Formation of Flower Bulb.—In the spring of the second year several *runners* develop from the first-formed or *plumule-bulb*, and at their tips bulbs also form, called *runner-bulbs*. From each of the runner-bulbs, three more runners, with bulbs, are produced, and one of these bulbs, under favorable conditions, produces a flowering plant. It takes at least four years to produce a bulb that will develop a flowering plant.

"The following table illustrates the number of plants of different ages during each of five years, supposing that five seeds from each fruit ripen and survive the cycle, and provided that all fourth year bulbs produce flowers."[2]

[1] It will be instructive for the class to discuss the origin and mode of formation of the starch in the endosperm.

[2] Quotation and table from Frederick H. Blodgett, Bull. Torrey Club 27:307–308. 1900.

1st year	2d year	3d year	4th year	5th year
5 seeds	5 seeds 5 plumule-bulbs	5 seeds 5 plumule-bulbs 5 yearlings	5 seeds 5 plumule-bulbs 5 yearlings 15 two years old	5 seeds 5 plumule-bulbs 5 yearlings 15 two years old 45 flowers

397. Annual Bulbs.—At the base of an old flowering bulb, and in the axil of one of the bud-scales, there de-

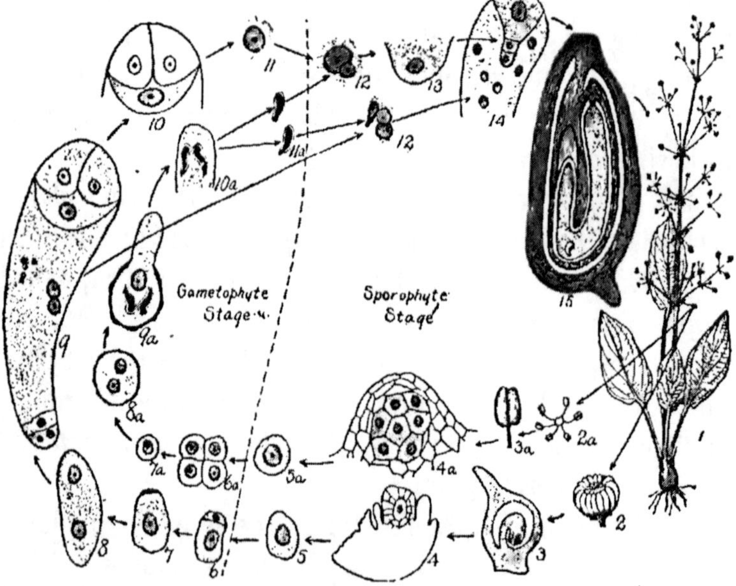

FIG. 329.—Diagram of life-cycle of an angiosperm (*Alisma Plantago-aquatica*). 9, female gametophyte (embryo-sac); 8*a* and 9*a*, male gametophyte (pollen-grain). (After J. H. Schaffner.)

velops each year an annual bulb, which attains full size about April, and begins in May to form the bud for the leaves and flowers of next spring.

If one digs up a bulb in the fall, he will find the flower perfectly formed, and ready to be raised above the ground the following spring. All the parts of the flower, at this period, are white, on account of having been formed in entire darkness; and they are also quite brittle.

When the buds resume their growth the second spring they push up through the ground quickly, and with considerable force. The pointed end of the sprout is covered by a mass of hard tissue, which protects the more delicate cells below from injury. The well-protected tip, and the growth-force, enable the sprout to pierce even small twigs. This has given rise to the striking name of "vegetable awl."

As soon as the sprout is well above the surface of the ground the flower bud becomes free from the parts that enclose it, and expands into the nodding blossom; pollination is accomplished, and the life-cycle begins again.

The life cycle of another angiosperm, the water-plantain (*Alisma Plantago-aquatica*), is indicated in Fig. 329.

CHAPTER XXVIII

SEED-BEARING PLANTS (Continued)

ANGIOSPERMS

398. Essentials of a Flower.—Reduced to its lowest terms, a flower is a branch bearing sporophylls. The

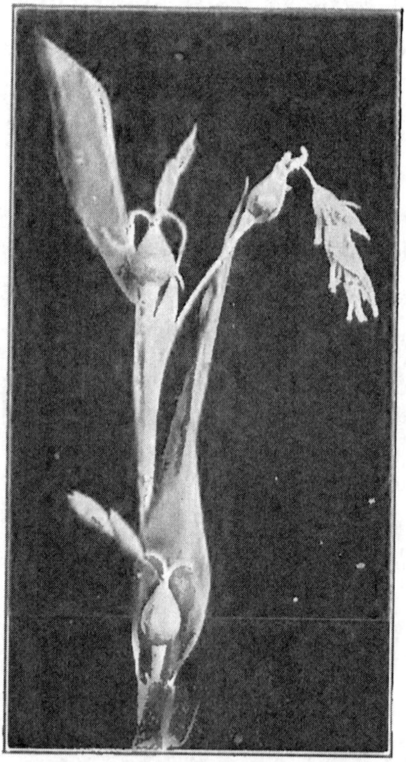

FIG. 330.—Inflorescences of Job's tears (*Coix lacrima-Jobi*), one of the Gramineæ.

latter may be microsporophylls only, as in the staminate cone of *Pinus* (Fig. 306), which is thus seen to be, in reality, a flower; or they may be megasporophylls. In the latter case they may occur on the main stem, as in *Cycas* (Fig. 291), or grouped on a specialized branch, forming a cone, as in *Macrozamia* (Fig. 289).[1]

399. Perfect and Imperfect Flowers.—A flower having stamens but no carpels, or carpels but no stamens is

FIG. 331.—Flowers of a rex begonia; staminate above; pistillate below; one of the latter with the perianth removed to show the ovary and stigmas. (Photo by Elsie M. Kittredge.)

unable, by itself, to produce seed, and is hence called an *imperfect* flower (Figs. 331–333). A species in which the imperfect flowers occur on separate plants is *diœcious*.

[1] Whether the carpellate cone of *Pinus* is a flower or a cluster of flowers (inflorescence), has long been debated. There is strong evidence for considering it a cluster of flowers, since the individual scales are probably not simple sporophylls. (Cf., p. 419.)

Such is the case in the willow, hop, ailanthus and, of course, the cycads. When the staminate and pistillate flowers occur on the same plant, either on the same branch or axis, as in cat-tail, "Job's tears," begonia, *et cetera* (Figs.

FIG. 332.—Inflorescences of the birch (*Betula sp.*). Below, the staminate flowers in large, pendant catkins; above, the pistillate catkins, erect.

330–332, 375) or on separate branches, as in Indian corn, arrow-leaf, and others (Fig. 333), the species is *monœcious*.

Since stamens and pistils are necessary to the formation of seeds they are called the *essential organs* of the flower. A flower like the tulip, rose, water-arum, or buttercup (Fig. 345), having both kinds of essential organs, is a *perfect* flower.

400. Complete Flowers.—In the majority of Angiosperms the flower, in addition to the essential organs,

FIG. 333.—Arrow-leaf (*Sagittaria*). At the left, branches with staminate flowers only; in the middle, branches with pistillate flowers only; at the right, pistillate branch, bearing fruit.

possesses a calyx or a corolla, or both. Flowers possessing both kinds of floral envelopes and both kinds of essential organs are called *complete.*

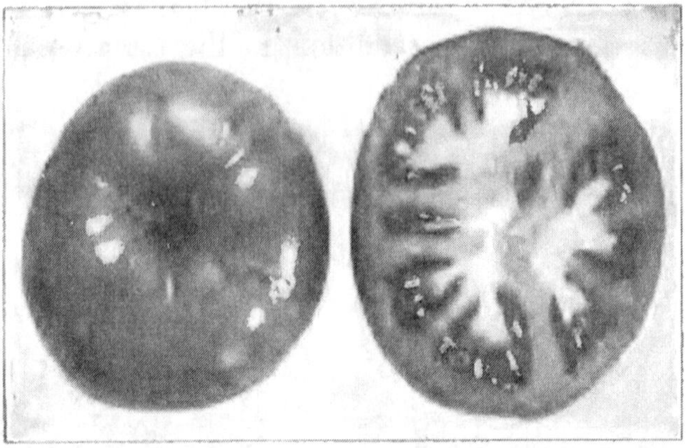

FIG. 334.—Fruit of the tomato (*Lycopersicum esculentum*). A berry, showing seeds (ripened ovules) attached to the placentas, and inclosed in the tissue of the ripened ovary (*i.e.*, angiospermous).

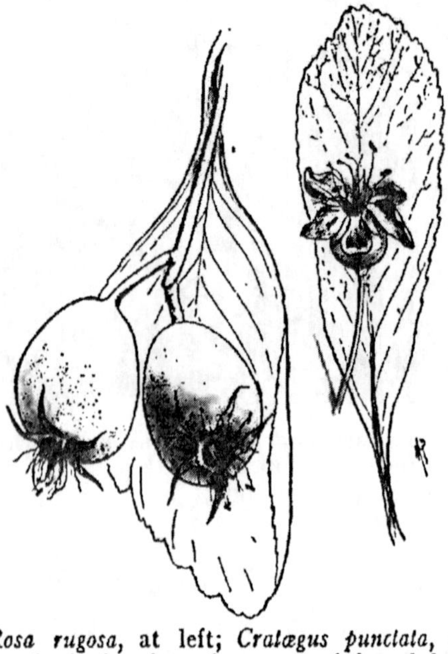

FIG. 335.—*Rosa rugosa*, at left; *Cratægus punctata*, at right. The fruit is composed of the ripened ovary, reinforced by the enlarged receptacle.

401. Essentials of a Fruit.—In the Gymnosperms we found the seeds unprotected on the surface of the megasporophyll or carpel; but in the Angiosperms the ovules are produced in a closed ovary composed of one or more carpels (Fig. 334). As the ovules ripen into seeds the carpels and surrounding parts ripen into the *fruit.* In some cases the fruit consists only of the ripened ovary (Fig. 334) while in other cases it may comprise the enlarged calyx and receptacle also (Fig. 335).

402. Immediate Effect of Pollen.—The effect of the germinating pollen in stimulating the growth of the ovary and adjacent tissues is a very interesting phenomenon. A portion of the edible part of the fruit of apples is calyx, which has developed into fleshy tissue as a result of the stimulus of the pollen; in the case of pears the receptacle and end of the peduncle become fleshy and form a part of the fruit; most of the strawberry fruit is the common receptacle of the small flowers, stimulated to a fleshy development by the growth of the pollen on the stigmas; in the watermelon, orange, tomato, and many other plants, it is the ovary alone that is thus stimulated.

The immediate effect of pollen is often greatly increased by cross-pollination. This is strikingly shown in the blueberries (*Vaccinium*), as shown in Fig. 336. The two twigs "grew in equally good situations on the same bush, contained the same number of flowers, all pollinated by hand with equal care, and the fruits were pollinated on the same day. The only difference in treatment was that the pollen used on the left-hand twig came from other flowers on the same bush, while the pollen for the right-hand twig was taken from another bush."

FIG. 336.—Effect of self-pollination in the blueberry (*Vaccinium corymbosum*), as compared with cross-pollination. These two twigs, both natural size, were in equally good situations on the same bush, contained the same number of flowers, all pollinated by hand at the same time with equal care, and the fruits were photographed on the same day. The only difference in treatment was that the pollen used on the left-hand twig came from other flowers on the same bush, while the pollen for the right-hand twig was taken from another bush. The cross-pollinated flowers produced a full cluster of handsome fruit. The self-pollinated flowers produced no ripe fruit, all the fruit that set remaining small and green and later dropping off, until at the time the photograph was taken only two such imperfect fruits remained. A plantation made up wholly from cuttings from a single bush would produce little or no fruit. At least two original propagation stocks are necessary. (After Coville. Courtesy of the U. S. Dept. Agric.)

403. Essentials of a Seed.—In the cycads and pines we have seen accomplished the first step necessary for the production of a true seed, namely, the retention within the sporangium of the megaspore and the female gametophyte to which it gives rise. The final step was the formation of an embryo, *which usually rests* before proceeding to develop into an adult sporophyte. With few exceptions, *the distinctive feature of a seed is a resting embryo.* The embryo may or may not be surrounded by nourish-

FIG. 337.—John Ray (1628–1705). An early and noted English botanist. First to distinguish monocotyledons from dicotyledons.

ment stored in the form of endosperm. In the absence of endosperm, as for example in the bean seed, the nourishment is stored in the cells of the embryo itself, having been absorbed while the embryo was forming. Enclosing the other parts of a seed is the *seed-coat* which may be derived from one integument (as in *Pinus*), or from two integuments organically united. These features are illustrated in Fig. 83.

404. Monocotyledons and Dicotyledons.—Except in rare cases, all plant-embryos possess either one or more "seed-leaves," or cotyledons, and on this basis Ray (1628–1705), the noted English botanist, divided the class of Angiosperms into two large sub-classes—*mono-*

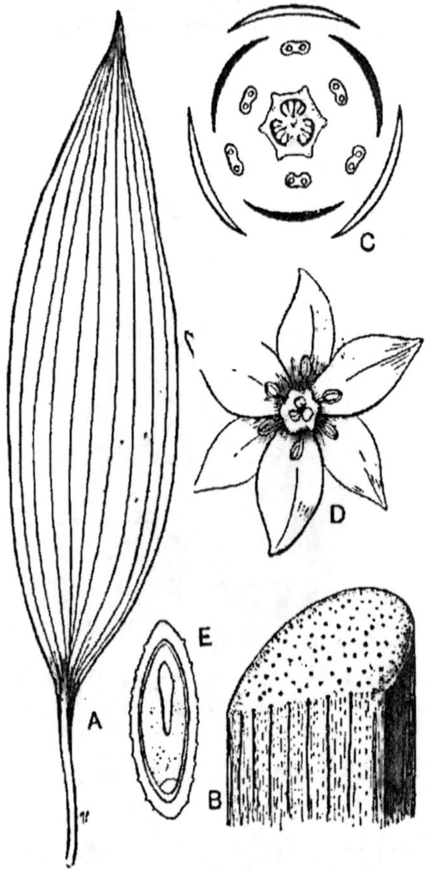

FIG. 338.—Morphology of typical monocotyledonous plant. *A*, leaf, parallel-veined; *B*, portion of stem, showing irregular distribution of vascular bundles; *C*, ground plan of flower (the parts in 3's); *D*, top view of flower; *E*, seed, showing monocotyledonous embryo.

cotyledons and *dicotyledons*.[1] These two groups are distinguished by other characters which are quite con-

[1] Plants like *Pinus* having more than two cotyledons are *polycotyledons*.

stantly associated with the possession of one or two cotyledons. Thus, in monocotyledons the leaves are, with rare exceptions, parallel-veined, and the growth of the stem is endogenous; while in dicotyledons the leaves are

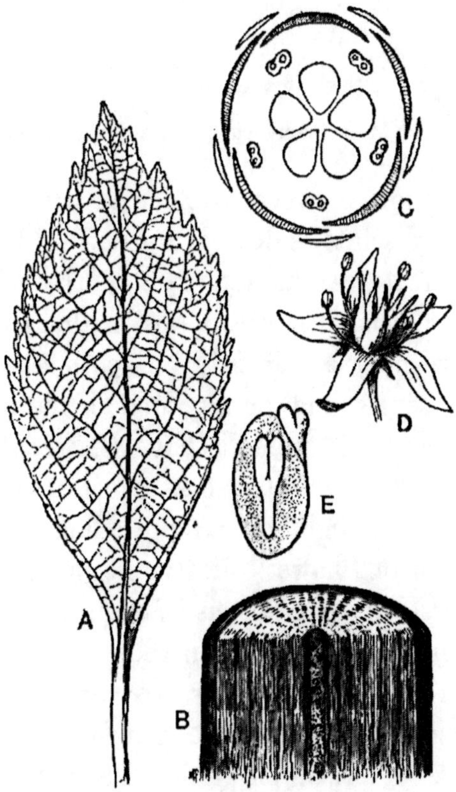

FIG. 339.—Morphology of a typical dicotyledonous plant. *A*, leaf, pinnately-netted veined; *B*, portion of stem, showing concentric layers of wood; *C*, ground-plan of flower (the parts in 5's); *D*, perspective of flower; *E*, longitudinal section of seed, showing dicotyledonous embryo.

usually net-veined, and the stem exogenous. In monocotyledons, also, the parts of the flower usually occur in *threes* (as in *Erythronium*), or in *sixes*, never in fives, while in dicotyledons the parts are typically in *fours* or *fives*. These characters are illustrated diagrammatically in Figs. 338 and 339.

405. Groups of Dicotyledons.—There are two main groups of dicotyledons, based on the fusion or non-fusion of the parts of the calyx or corolla, as follows:

Dicotyledons	Archichlamydeæ	Apetalæ
		Polypetalæ
	Metachlamydeæ	Sympetalæ (Gamopetalæ)

The distinction between Archichlamydeæ and Sympetalæ is not absolute, since each group contains plants having some features characteristic of the other. The Apetalæ, as the name suggests, are without corolla (in some cases without either calyx or corolla); the Polypetalæ have sepals and petals (one or both) entirely distinct; while the Sympetalæ have the sepals and the petals wholly or partly united so as to form a tubular calyx or corolla. In the light of our preceding study of the fruiting branch or "flower" of Gymnosperms, it will be readily understood that flowers of simple structure are presumably more primitive than those of more complex structure. The simplest flower we can imagine is an apetalous staminate flower of one stamen; or an apetalous pistillate flower of one simple pistil. Polypetalous flowers are more highly organized than apetalous, and may therefore be less primitive; sympetalous flowers are more complex or more highly organized and are therefore less primitive than either Apetalæ or Polypetalæ.

The following examples will serve to illustrate 15 of the more common or more familiar families of Dicotyledons, out of a total of over 250.

ARCHICHLAMYDEÆ

Apetalæ

406. Willow Family (Salicaceæ).—This family comprises both the willows (*Salix*) and the poplars (*Populus*). There are about 20 species of poplar in North America. The willows, in North America, comprise over 30 species,

Fig. 340.—Inflorescence of a willow (*Salix discolor*). At the left pistillate, at the right staminate catkins.

trees and shrubs, and are specially common in moist situations. Several species are cultivated to furnish twigs for basket-making. The weeping willow (*Salix babylonica*), an object of peculiar beauty along streams and lakeshores, owes its pendulous or "weeping" character to its failure to develop sufficient mechanical tissue (wood) in its smaller branches to hold them erect.

All willows are diœcious. The imperfect, apetalous flowers occur crowded together on scaly spikes called *catkins* (Fig. 340). Each scale bears one flower in its axil. The staminate flowers consist usually of two (sometimes

FIG. 341.—Willow (*Salix*). Leafy branch, bearing two pistillate catkins. Staminate flower above, at the left; pistillate flower below, at the right. (After Britton and Brown.)

three to ten) stamens (Fig. 341). In some species the stamens are united. When the flower buds open, early in spring, the numerous hairs on the scales or filaments (one or both) give the soft, fur-like appearance, which suggested the name "pussy-willow." As in the pines, pollination is accomplished by the wind.

407. Lizard's-tail Family (Saururaceæ).—The lizard's tail (*Saururus cernuus*), closely related to the willows, has apetalous but perfect flowers, borne sessile on a moderately long, common axis, called a *spike* (Figs. 342 and 343). There are three to five more or less united ovaries. The plant is commonly found in swamps and marshes.

FIG. 342.—Lizard's-tail (*Saururus cernuus*).

POLYPETALÆ

408. Crowfoot Family (Ranunculaceæ).—The Latin name *Ranunculus* (little frog) was applied to the buttercups by the ancient Roman naturalist Pliny, because they are common in wet places where frogs abound. The name of the family is derived from this generic name, but the family comprises about 35 genera, 28 of which occur in

Eastern North America. The yellow water-crowfoot (*Ranunculus delphinifolius*) is one of the commoner of the 40 to 50 North American species. It is found at the bor-

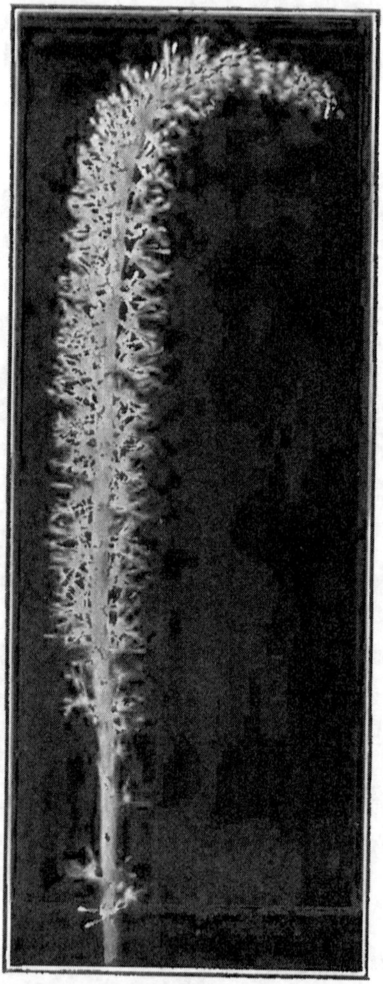

FIG. 343.—Lizard's-tail (*Saururus cernuus*). Inflorescence, about natural size.

ders of quiet water, and the submerged leaves are filiformly dissected, in marked contrast to those borne in the air.

The bright shining, yellow petals vary in number from five to eight, and are much longer than the sepals; each has a little scale at its base concealing a nectar-gland. The simple pistils (*carpels*) are grouped in a round head, surrounded by the numerous stamens (Figs. 344 and 345).

FIG. 344.—Plant of a buttercup (*Ranunculus sp.*).

409. Spiral and Cyclic Arrangement.—It will be recalled that in the lower type of flower, characteristic of the Gymnosperms, the sporophylls are arranged in spirals on the flower axis. A study of the flower in Angiosperms discloses a tendency for the flower parts to occur in circles; the higher the plant in the system of classification the more completely is the cyclic arrangement realized. In the Crowfoot family there are some species, especially of *Ranunculus*, in which the sepals and petals are in circles, while the stamens and pistils are in spirals—a more primitive feature.

410. Petalody of Bracts.—It is also common in certain species of this family (notably in the genera *Trollius* and

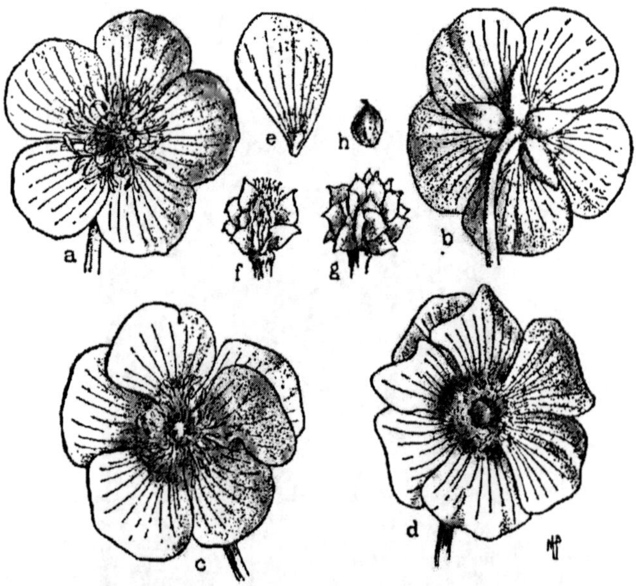

FIG. 345.—Flower of a buttercup (*Ranunculus sp.*); *a*, *b*, normal, showing 5 petals; *c*, *d*, petalody of stamens; *e*, petal with nectary at its base; *f–h*, ripened ovaries.

Anemone) for the green foliage-like *bracts* below the perianth to assume the characters of sepals, and even of petals, so that frequently one can hardly say whether a given segment of the perianth is a true petal, or a transformed bract. By the *petalody of the bracts* the flower appears to be "double."

411. Coalescence of Petals.—It frequently occurs in flowers of Ranunculaceæ (and in other normally polypetalous families also) that the initial stages or *primordia* of two or more petals become wholly or partly fused or coalesced, thus reducing the number of separate members of the corolla (Fig. 346). Sometimes coalescence and petalody of stamens will occur in the same specimen, so that a flower that would normally have five petals may have six or eight, or more, some of which have coalesced, as is indicated by the two or more points at the tip.

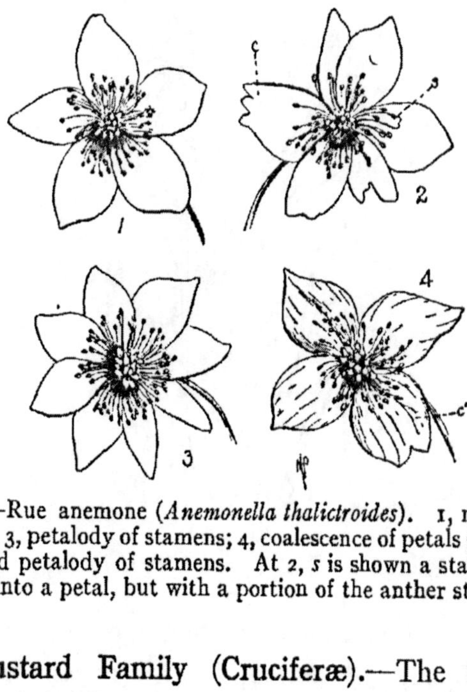

FIG. 346.—Rue anemone (*Anemonella thalictroides*). 1, normal flower with 5 petals; 3, petalody of stamens; 4, coalescence of petals (c^1); 2, coalescence (c), and petalody of stamens. At 2, s is shown a stamen partially transformed into a petal, but with a portion of the anther still remaining.

412. Mustard Family (Cruciferæ).—The flowers of the mustard family are mostly characterized by having the four narrow petals opening out at an angle of 90° from each other, forming a Greek cross (Fig. 347), whence the family name, Cruciferæ. This character of the corolla also appears in rare instances in other families (*e.g.*, some Rubiaceæ), whose corolla is then said to be "cruciferous." The fruit, a *silique*, is also one of the ear-marks of the family. The mustard family contains many valuable economic plants, such as the white and black mustard, radish, cabbage, turnip, kohlrabi, and brussels sprouts.

413. Rose Family (Rosaceæ).—One of the common wild roses (*Rosa carolina*) illustrates a type of flower structure more advanced in several ways than that of *Ranunculus*. The flowers, with rare exceptions, have

FIG. 347.—Black mustard (*Brassica nigra*).

sepals and petals which are borne on the margin of a well-developed *hypanthium*, formed by the enlargement of the *torus*, at the extremity of the peduncle. The numerous stamens are always inserted on the sepals (*adnation* of parts), and the pistils vary from one to many. In marked contrast to the numerous horticultural varieties of the rose, the wild roses are single; that is, they have one circle of petals (usually five). The "doubling" of the cultivated varieties is caused by the replacement of stamens by petal-like organs (Fig. 346). Not that stamens are "transformed into petals," as is often stated, but that petal-like organs appear at the points where stamens normally occur in the wild form. In other words, the supernumerary petals are homologous with stamens.

FIG. 348.—Petalody of stamens in a cultivated rose. *a*, indicates the remains of anthers on petal-like organs that have replaced stamens.

This homology is made clear by transitional forms, showing all gradations between true stamens and normal petals (Figs. 348 and 349).

By comparing the methods of doubling the flower in the buttercup and the rose, we see that double flowers may be produced by either (or both) of two methods, often referred to, respectively, as "petalody of bracts" and "petalody of stamens." The causes of these variations are not known.

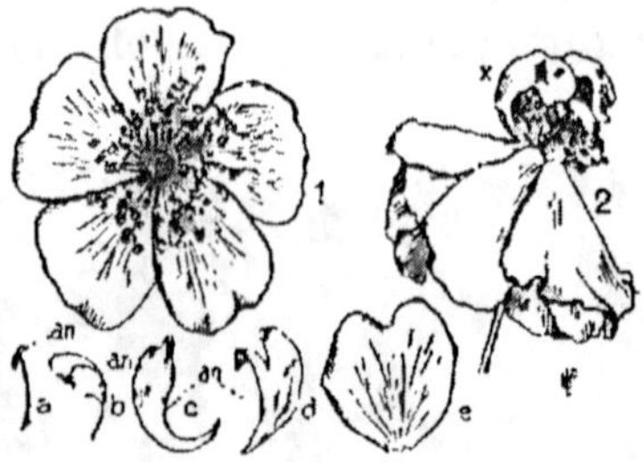

FIG. 349.—Wild rose. A "single" flower showing incipient doubling by the replacement of stamens by petals. Below, a series of transitional forms from stamen to fully formed petal; *an.*, anther, or remnant of anther.

FIG. 350.—Perennial pea (*Lathyrus latifolius*).

414. Leguminoseæ.—The legume family is the largest, and one of the most widely distributed of all the Archichlamydeæ, and includes three sub-families, as follows:

1. *Papilionoideæ*, containing such commonly recognized plants as the peas, beans, lentils, clovers, peanuts,

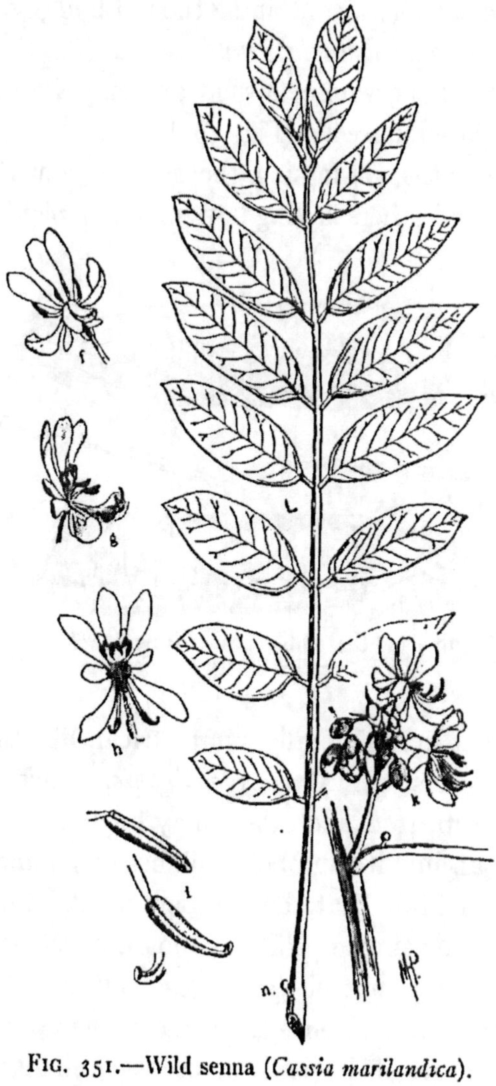

FIG. 351.—Wild senna (*Cassia marilandica*).

lupines, lead-plant (*Amorpha*), locust or false-acacia (*Robinia*), wistaria, and others, all of which have the peculiarly modified corolla called *papilionaceous*, from its fancied resemblance to a butterfly (Fig. 350).

2. *Cæsalpinioideæ*, containing the red-bud (*Cercis*), true or honey-locust (*Gleditsia*), wild senna (*Cassia marilandica*), and others, whose flowers are only imperfectly or not at all papilionaceous (Fig. 351).

3. *Mimosoideæ*, containing the acacias, sensitive plants (*Mimosa*), and others having flowers with a *regular* corolla.

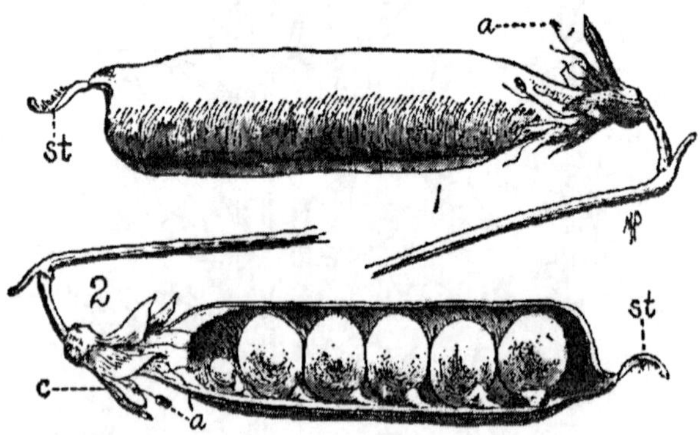

FIG. 352.—Legume of the edible pea (*Pisum sativum*). *a*, anther; *c*, calyx; *st*, stigma.

Flowers that are bilaterally symmetrical, like the papilionaceous flowers, are called *zygomorphic.* Such flowers as the buttercup, rose, and others may be divided into equal halves by an infinite number of planes of symmetry.

The one feature that characterizes all three of the subfamilies[1] is the simple pistil, composed of one carpel, and enlarging greatly in fruit (as in peas and beans) to form a *legume* (Fig. 352); whence the name of the family.

The structure of the papilionaceous corolla is illustrated in Fig. 350. The upper and largest petal, stands erect,

[1] By some authors each group, designated above as a sub-family, is considered as a separate family.

forming the standard, the two lateral petals are the "wings;" while the two lower petals adhere along their adjacent edges to form the keel. In these flowers there are usually ten stamens (rarely five), which commonly occur in two groups or "brotherhoods" (*diadelphous*), nine in one group with their filaments united into a tube, cleft on the upper side, the other standing alone above the cleft.

FIG. 353.—Alsike, or Alsatian clover (*Trifolium hybridum*). Inflorescences, showing carpotropic movements of the flowers after pollination by an insect. At the extreme left, flowers in bud, the outermost ones just beginning to open; next to the last, at the right, only one flower remaining erect on account of not having yet been pollinated; at the extreme right, every flower pollinated, turned down, and withering.

Pollination is usually accomplished in this family by means of insects which visit the flowers for the nectar secreted by glands. In the case of white clover and alsike, each flower of the head, when pollinated, turns down, and the corolla becomes brown (Fig. 353). This change has been interpreted by some as a sign to the insects that the nectar has been taken, and therefore that another visit would not be profitable. Other students regard this as questionable.

Since, as shown by examining a bud, the flowers of the clover head mature from the circumference toward the center (centripetally), the outer flowers are the first to be visited, and hence the first to bend down (Fig. 353).[1] Many of the papilionaceous legumes are self-pollinated. This is true of the "sweet pea" as a rule, but not without exceptions.

The fact that the legumes furnish so many kinds of food and fodder plants, and that the organisms causing the tubercles on their roots (pp. 317–318) are an important source of the nitrogen necessary for successful agriculture, renders this family one of the most important of all the economic plants, possibly exceeded only by the grass family.

415. Evening-primrose Family (Onagraceæ).—The evening-primroses have recently come into very great prominence on account of the fact that they have been extensively used for the experimental study of evolution. A knowledge of their structure has, therefore become increasingly important. The flowers are perfect and symmetrical, with the parts usually in fours. The ovary is one- to six- (usually four-) chambered, and the calyx tube adheres to the walls. The stamens are inserted commonly on the summit of the calyx tube. In the evening-primrose itself (*Œnothera*[2]), the pollen-grains are held together by delicate threads that resemble a cobweb. The seedling usually forms a rosette the first year, and thus passes the winter (Fig. 354). The follow-

[1] Often one will find a solitary, unpollinated flower left standing, and in some localities these are sought by children as "old-maid clovers."

[2] Called also *Onagra*.

ing season an erect stem is sent up which bears the flowers and fruit (Fig. 400).

416. Parsley Family (Umbelliferæ).—The most highly organized family of the Archichlamydeæ is that to which the common parsley belongs. In this family the calyx-

FIG. 354.—Rosette of the evening-primrose (*Œnothera biennis*).

tube adheres throughout its length to the wall of the ovary, and the five petals and stamens are inserted on a disk at the base of the two styles (Fig. 355). The relatively small flowers are, with rare exceptions, borne in clusters known as *umbels*. The characteristics of an umbel are that the numerous flower-stalks are of such relative lengths as to bring all the flowers to substantially the same plane (Fig. 356), and that the outer flower buds open first; in other words the *anthesis* is centripetal. Some of the

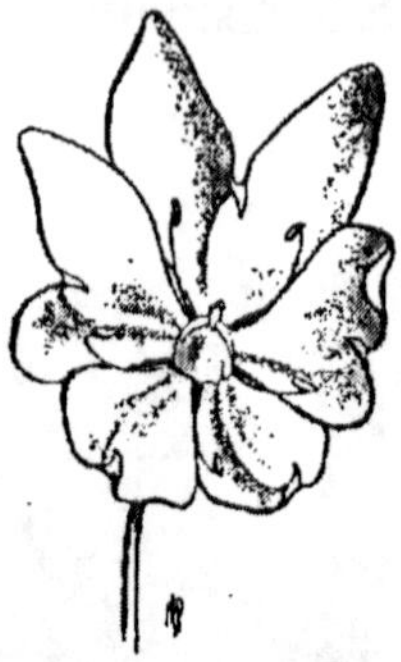

FIG. 355.—*Heracleum lanatum* (Parsley family). Individual flower from the margin of an umbel.

FIG. 356.—A compound umbel of cow parsnip (*Heracleum lanatum*).

genera of this family (*e.g.*, caraway, parsley, parsnips, carrots) are edible, while, as often happens in other families also, some of their near relatives (*e.g.*, the water-hemlock, *Cicuta*) are very poisonous.

CHAPTER XXIX

SEED-BEARING PLANTS (Continued)

METACHLAMYDEÆ (Sympetalæ)

417. Coalescence.—We have seen above that genera normally having polypetalous flowers frequently furnish examples of the more or less complete fusion or coalescence of the petals. In certain entire families this fusion of different members of the same circle of floral organs becomes the rule, giving rise to an entire group, the *Sympetalæ*, based upon this character. Only a few of these families can be cited in illustration.

418. Heath Family (Ericaceæ).—The heath family in North America is composed chiefly of shrubs, though a few, as, for example, Indian pipe (*Monotropa*) are herbs;[1] some of the tropical genera are trees. The beautiful rhododendrons, azaleas, and laurels, trailing arbutus (first harbinger of spring in the northern states), the aromatic wintergreen, and the well-known huckleberries (*Gaylussacia*), and blueberries (*Vaccinium*) belong here.

The structure of an Ericaceous flower may be illustrated by the common mountain laurel (*Kalmia latifolia*), of the eastern states (Figs. 357 and 358). The sepals are united below, but parted above; the sympetalous corolla

[1] By some authors the large heath family is separated into a number of smaller families, *e.g.*, Monotropaceæ, Ericaceæ, Vacciniaceæ. In Monotropaceæ, Clethraceæ, and Pyrolaceæ, and a few of the true heaths (Ericaceæ), the corolla is polypetalous.

FIG. 357.—Mountain laurel (*Kalmia latifolia*). Note the anthers resting in the depressions of the sympetalous corolla. (Photo by Elsie M. Kittredge.)

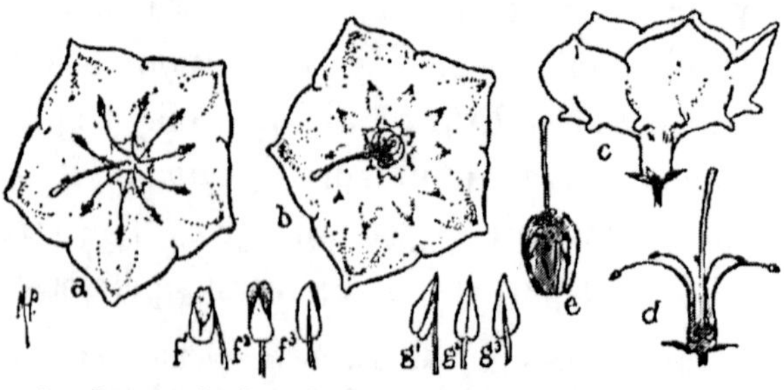

FIG. 358.—Mountain laurel (*Kalmia latifolia*). *a*, stamens in their original position, with the anthers in the pouches; *b*, stamens inflexed (detail at *e*); *c*, side view; *d*, essential organs; *f* and *g*, stamens.

is five-lobed having the shape of a broad, shallow bell. Its coloration[1] as viewed *en masse* on the bush, gave rise to the common name "calico bush," popular in certain locali-

FIG. 359.—Common milkweed, *Asclepias syriaca*. (Photo by Elsie M. Kittredge.)

ties. The corolla has ten pouches, each of which contains one anther borne on a recurved filament. When an insect alights on the flower the anthers become loosened

[1] Coloration = color pattern.

from the pouches, and snap over in, toward the center, thus dusting the insect with pollen, which is then transferred to the stigma of the next flower visited by the insect.

The corpse-plant, or Indian-pipe (*Monotropa uniflora*), is of interest because, although belonging in a sympetalous

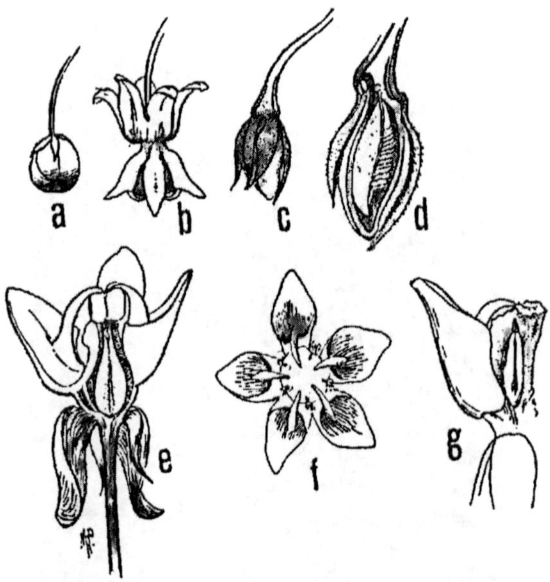

FIG. 360.—Milkweed (*Asclepias sp.*). *a*, flower-bud; *b*, flower; *c*, very young pod; *d*, older pod in section, showing seeds; *e*, section of flower; *f*, top view of flower, showing the 5 *hoods* of the crown, each with a *horn* incurving to the stigma; between the horns are the cleft glands (shown enlarged at *g*), to which the pollinia are attached.

family, it is polypetalous, and further because, living entirely as a saprophyte (or, possibly, as a root-parasite), it has entirely lost the power to make chlorophyll, and hence the power of photosynthesis (Fig. 230, p. 323).

419. Milkweed Family (Asclepiadaceæ).—The milkweeds[1] present a most curious and interesting modifica-

[1] So called because they contain a milky juice or *latex*.

tion of flower-structure (Fig. 359). The deeply five-parted and reflexed corolla bears a crown of five "hooded" bodies, in each of which there arises a pointed, incurved "horn" (Fig. 360). *The anthers are more or less united around the stigma*, and each cell contains a waxy, pear-shaped pollen-mass (*pollinium*). The pollinia of adjacent anthers adhere in pairs to cleft glands that grow one on each of the five angles of the stigma. As bees climb over the flowers in search of nectar in the bottom of the hoods, their legs are drawn through tiny slits, and catch the cleft gland

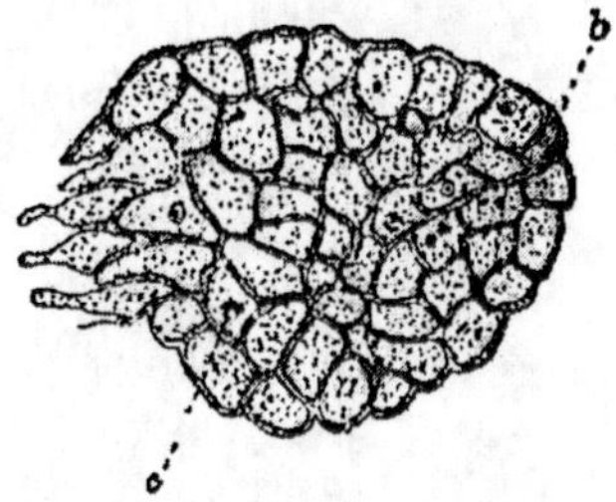

FIG. 361.—Milkweed (*Asclepias*). Pollen-mass (*pollinium*), showing germination.

when pulled out. Often the gland cannot be loosened, and the legs of the insects are pulled off and left attached to the flower. When the insect visits another flower the pollen-masses (which by this time have twisted and folded together) become inserted into the stigmatic chamber of the second flower, where they germinate, sending out numerous pollen-tubes (Fig. 361). On account of the complicated nature of this process, pollination often fails, so that only a small percentage of the very numerous flowers produces seed. After fertilization, the carpels increase enormously in size, and ripen into a pod, filled with a large quantity of flat, thin seeds, each of which bears a tuft of long silky hairs, whence one of the common names, "silk weed." These hairs facilitate the distribution of the seeds by the wind (Fig. 362).

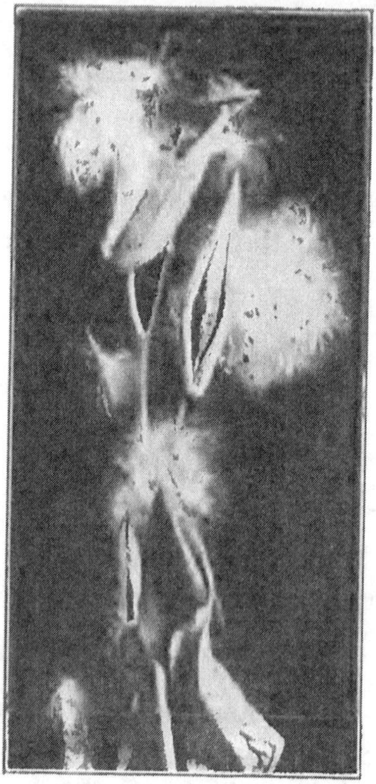

FIG. 362.—A milkweed (*Asclepias syriaca*), with tufted seeds scattering from the dehiscing pods. (Photo by Elsie M. Kittredge.)

420. Convolvulus Family (Convolvulaceæ).—The features of this family are well illustrated by the genus from which it gets its name, *Convolvulus*, or bind-weed. The five-lobed corolla is bell-shaped, all the parts of the flower are in fives, and the pistil two-celled. Most genera of the family are trailing or (as the name indicates) twining vines (Fig. 363).

421. Mint Family (Labiatæ).—The Mint family is characterized by a square stem, opposite leaves, a tubular calyx, caused by the coalescence of the five sepals, a highly modified corolla having two lips or *labia* (singular *labium*, whence the family name), and leaves containing many

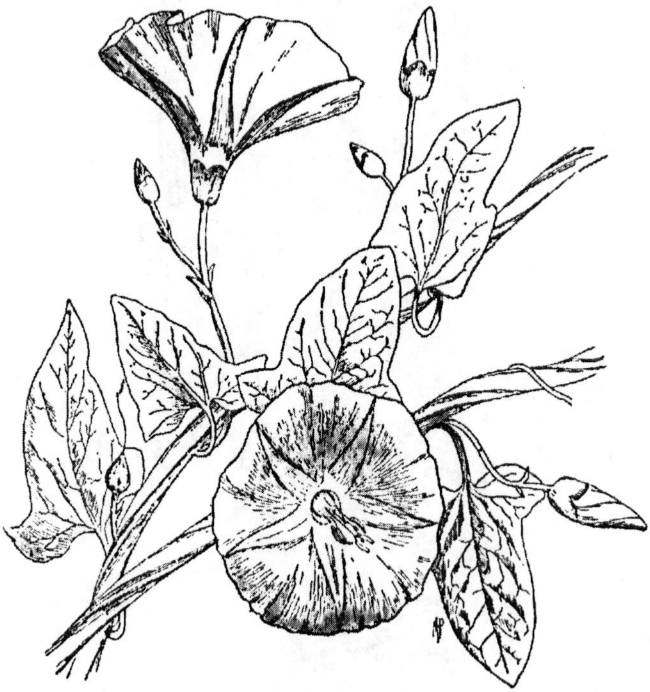

FIG. 363.—Bindweed (*Convolvulus arvensis*).

small glands that secrete a volatile oil, which gives the characteristic odor and taste to all the plants of the family. The upper lip results from the fusion of two petals, the lower lip by the fusion of three. Everyone is familiar with one or more of these features, as embodied in the various mints, pennyroyal, horehound, catnip, sage, savory, thyme, hyssop, wild marjoram, and other condiments and drugs. The features of the flower are illustrated in Fig. 364.

422. Nightshade Family (Solanaceæ).—The Nightshade family is of interest chiefly because it contains

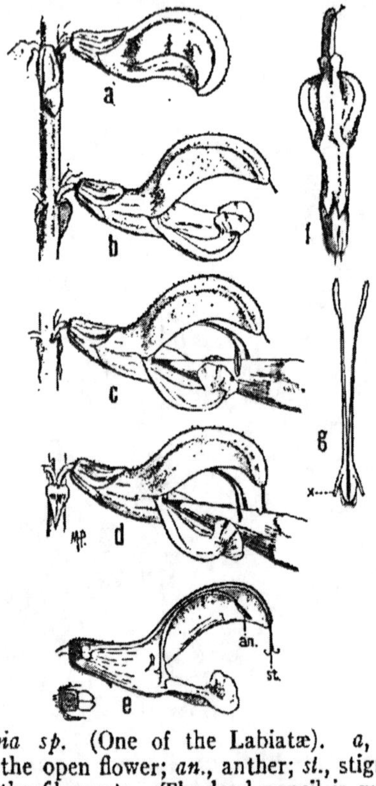

FIG. 364.—*Salvia sp.* (One of the Labiatæ). *a*, flower bud; *b–f*, various views of the open flower; *an.*, anther; *st.*, stigma; *x*, projections near the base of the filaments. The lead pencil is made to imitate an insect visiting the flower for pollen. By pressure at the base of the filaments, the anthers are brought into contact with the surface of the pencil, which thus becomes covered with pollen. When the next flower is visited the stigma, having then bent down and spread apart, receives the pollen from the other flower. Thus is accomplished cross-pollination. In *b*, before the visit of the insect, the stigmatic surfaces are still in contact, so that pollination is not possible.

several genera of very great economic importance, *viz.*: potato (*Solanum tuberosum*), tobacco (*Nicotiana Tabacum*), tomato (*Lycopersicum esculentum*), and several medicinal herbs, such as belladonna, henbane, capsicum, and others. Most of the genera are tropical. The bitter-sweet (*Solanum Dulcamara*[1]) may serve to illustrate the family (Fig. 365). This is a perennial, climbing vine, having the parts of the flower (including the stamens) in fives

FIG. 365.—Nightshade, or bittersweet (*Solanum Dulcamara*).

and the fruit a two-celled *berry* with many seeds (*e.g.*, the tomato, Fig. 334). The corolla is wheel-shaped and five-parted, and the anthers converge to form a tube around the single style. The anthers discharge the pollen through a pore or "chink" at the tip.

423. Figwort Family (**Scrophulariaceæ**).—The "butter-and-eggs," or "toadflax" (*Linaria vulgaris*), will serve to illustrate the figworts (Fig. 366). The stamens are inserted

[1] The staff-tree or waxwork (*Celastrus scandens*), of the Staff-tree family, Celastraceæ, is also called "bitter sweet" in certain localities.

on the tube of the irregular, two-lipped corolla, which bears a well-developed *spur* at the base (Fig. 367). Not infrequently abnormal flowers are found with five spurs,

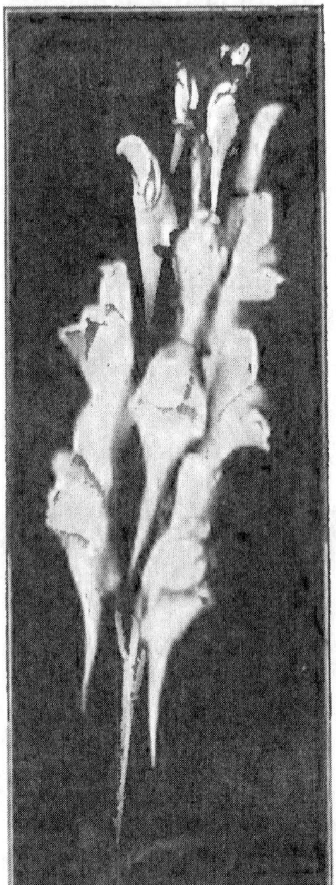

FIG. 366.—The toad-flax, or butter-and-eggs (*Linaria vulgaris*).

or with none, and other attendant modifications of the corolla (Figs. 368 and 369). Such flowers are called *pelories*, since they are thought to be variations indicating the character of the ancestral form from which they are believed to be derived. The method of pollination in normal flowers is illustrated in Fig. 370.

424. Composite Family (Compositæ).—The composites represent the highest development of dicotyledons. The flowers are borne on a common receptacle in a compact

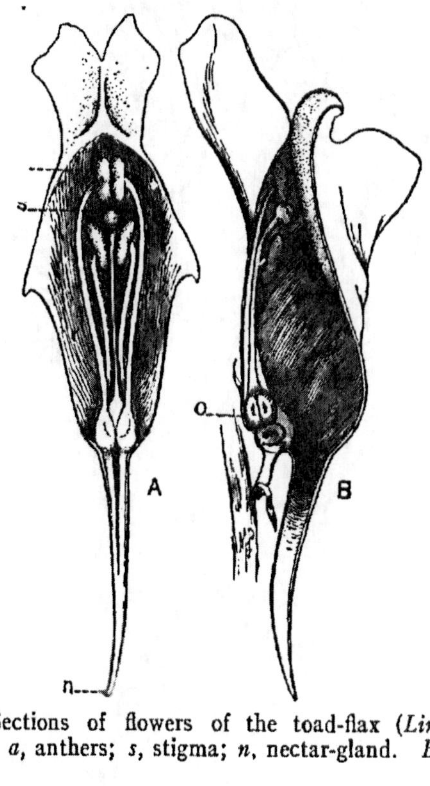

FIG. 367.—Sections of flowers of the toad-flax (*Linaria vulgaris*). *A*, front view; *a*, anthers; *s*, stigma; *n*, nectar-gland. *B*, side view; *o*, ovary.

"head," giving the appearance, not so much of an inflorescence as of a compound flower, whence the family name, assigned by early botanists, who did not understand the morphology of the head.

The heads are surrounded by a circle of bracts, called an *involucre*. The bracts which often occur on the receptacle among the flowers are called *chaff*. The family is composed of two series: I. Tubulifloræ, with all the perfect

FIG. 368.—Toad-flax (*Linaria vulgaris*). Inflorescence, showing normal (spurred) flowers, and several abnormal flowers without spurs.

flowers tubular, as in the daisy; II. Liguliforæ, with no tubular flowers, but all the flowers having a strap-shaped

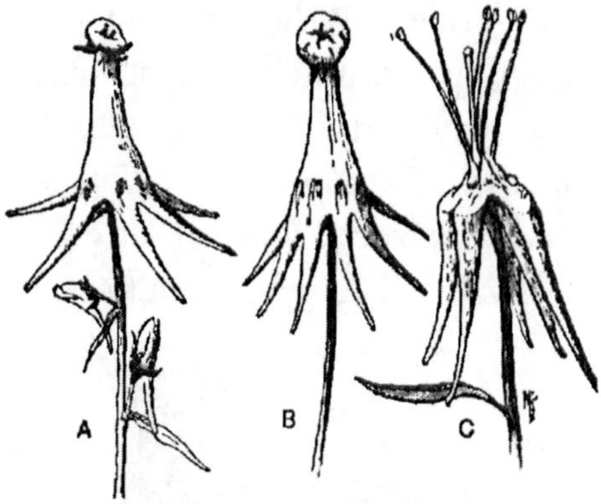

FIG. 369.—Toad-flax (*Linaria vulgaris*). Abnormal flowers (pelories), having five or more spurs. Normal, one-spurred buds are shown in *A*.

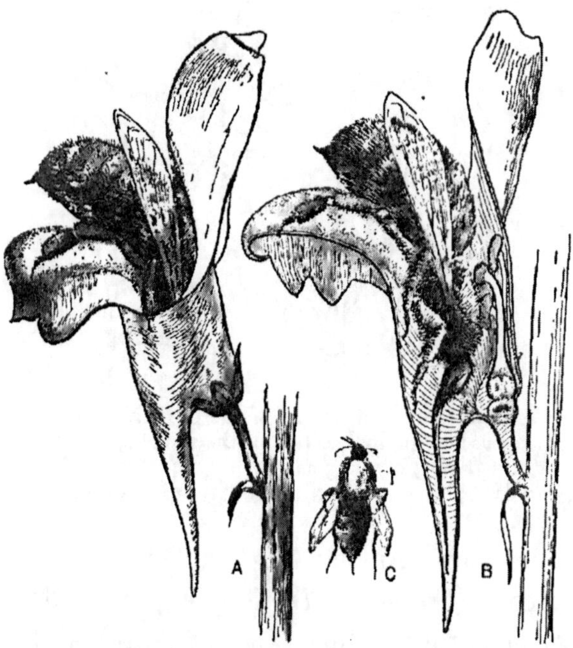

FIG. 370.—Toad-flax (*Linaria vulgaris*). Flowers being visited by an insect for nectar. *B*, longitudinal section, showing the insect's proboscis extended down the spur toward the nectar-gland; *C*, insect with a mass of pollen (*p*), rubbed off from anthers onto the dorsal hairs of the thorax, during successive visits.

(*ligulate*) corolla, formed by the fusion of the five petals, as indicated by the five notches at the end (Fig. 372). The tubulifloræ may have both tubular and ligulate flowers, as in boneset (*Eupatorium perfoliatum*) or in white daisy (*Chrysanthemum leucanthemum*), or only tubular, as in the burdock (*Arctium*, Fig. 371), or in the Canada thistle

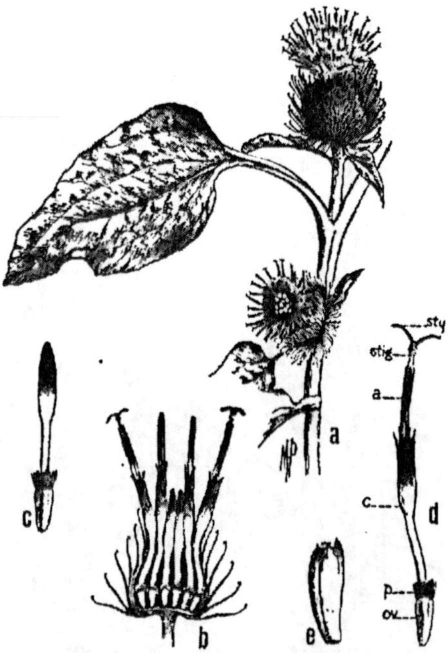

FIG. 371.—Inflorescence and flowers of the burdock (*Arctium minus*). *a*, Inflorescences; *b*, longitudinal section of the same; *c*, bud of individual flower; *d*, mature flower; *sty*, stigma; *stig*, style; *a*, ring of syngenesius anthers; *c*, corolla; *p*, pappus (calyx); *ov*, ovary; *e*, mature seed.

(*Cirsium arvense*). Among the liguliforæ may be mentioned chicory (*Cichorium Intybus*, Fig. 372), dandelion (*Taraxacum*), garden lettuce (*Lactuca sativa*), and others, all of which possess a milky juice, or *latex*. The five stamens (rarely four) are inserted on the corolla, and have their anthers united in a tube (*syngenesious*) around the style.

The calyx tube is united to the one-celled ovary, and its upper free part, or *limb*, is differentiated into hairs (*pappus*), scales, teeth, or is merely cup-shaped, or in some

FIG. 372.—Chicory (*Cichorium Intybus*). *A*, portion of flowering branch; *B*, basal leaf (runcinate-pinnatifid); *C*, median longitudinal section through a head, showing the insertion of the flowers; *D*, individual flower; *E*, fruit (ripened ovary), showing the persistent pappus (calyx) of short scales.

species entirely wanting. When the fruit is ripe, the pappus aids in its dissemination by the wind.

While the style is growing up through the tube of anthers the stigmatic surfaces are in contact with each other, and thus protected from becoming pollinated with the flower's own pollen. As the styles emerge above the anthers their two tips spread apart and roll back, exposing the infacing

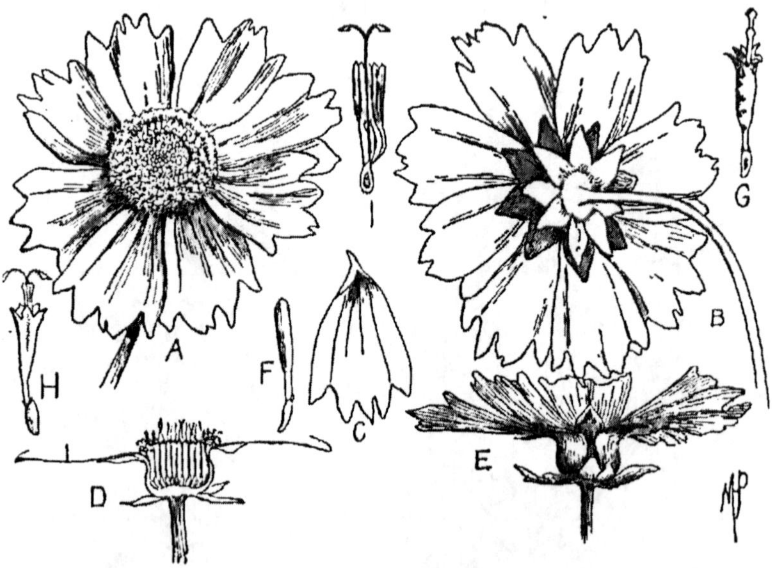

FIG. 373.—A composite (*Coreopsis sp.*). *A, B, E*, views of the inflorescence or head; *C*, a ray-flower; *D*, section through the head; *F*, a disc-flower in bud; *G*, disc-flower just opened; *H*, older disc-flower, the stigmas reflexed; *I*, disc-flower with corolla removed.

stigmatic surfaces so that they may receive pollen brought by insects from other flowers (Fig. 373).[1]

[1] The family Compositæ, as recognized above, including two series, Tubulifloræ and Liguliforæ, is restricted by some authors so as to include only plants having florets with tubular or both tubular and ligulate corollas in the head. Such plants as the chicory, dandelion, and lettuce, having only ligulate corollas, comprise the family Cichoriaceæ. Cichoriaceæ and Compositæ (in this restricted sense) have syngenesious anthers. Plants whose florets have tubular corollas only (sometimes none), but anthers *not truly syngenesious*, comprise the Ambrosiaseæ, including the rag-weeds, cockle-bur, marsh-elder (*Iva*), and *Gærtneria*.

CHAPTER XXX

SEED-BEARING PLANTS (Concluded)

MONOCOTYLEDONS

425. General Characters.—The monocotyledons are, in almost every respect, of simpler structure than the dicotyledons. As the name indicates, the embryo has only one cotyledon; the parts of the flower are usually in threes or sixes, but never in fives, as in dicotyledons; the leaves are, with rare exceptions, parallel-veined, and the early ones are always alternate on the stem. A cross-section of the stem shows that the fibro-vascular bundles are not arranged in a circle about a central pith (exogenous type), but are distributed irregularly throughout the parenchyma (endogenous). There is no layer of perennial cambium, and consequently no cylinders of wood and bark are formed each growing season, as in the dicotyledons. The general characters of the group are illustrated diagrammatically in Fig. 338.

426. Relation to Dicotyledons.—A comparison of the monocotyledons with the more highly developed dicotyledons raises at once the question as to whether the former are the more ancient forms from which the dicotyledons have been evolved, or whether dicotyledons are the more primitive, in order of development, and the monocotyledons derived from them by reduction and simplification. There is evidence on both sides of this question, which will be considered again later on (page 608). In treating of the dicotyledons first, however, we have tacitly assumed

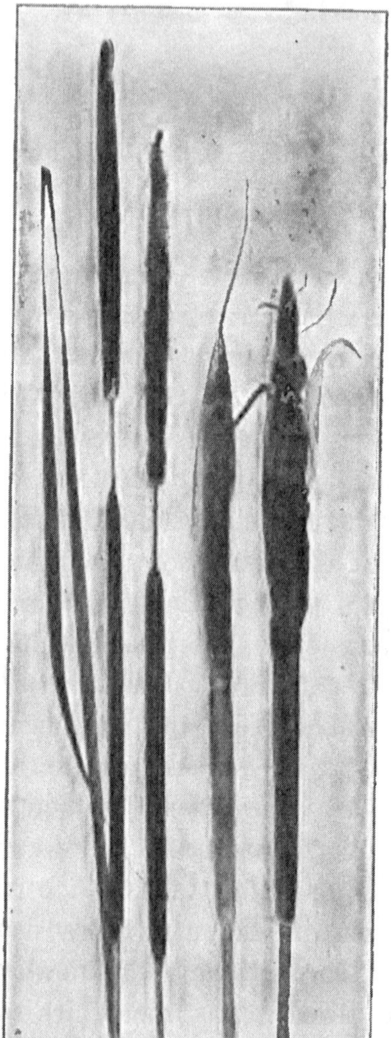

FIG. 374.—Cat-tails. *Typha angustifolia* at left; *Typha latifolia* at right. Staminate flowers above; pistillate flowers below.

that they are the older forms, from which the monocotyledons have been derived.

TYPES OF MONOCOTYLEDONS

427. Cat-tail Family (Typhaceae).—The cat-tails are one of the most primitively organized family of Angiosperms. They grow in groups or *associations* in swamps and wet places, and are conspicuous by their tall, upright and grass-like leaves, and by the inflorescences or "cat-tails" in late summer and fall (Fig. 374). The monœcious

FIG. 375.—Staminate flower of the broad-leaved cat-tail (*Typha latifolia*). (Cf. Fig. 376.)

flowers are borne on a fleshy axis or spadix, the pistillate below, and the staminate above near the tip. The flowers have neither calyx nor corolla (Figs. 375 and 376), and the one-celled ovary contains but one ovule. The embryo is surrounded by abundant endosperm, often called *albumen*. The copious brown down of the fruit is composed of club-shaped hairs on the *stipe*, or stalk-like support of the pistil.

428. Water-plantain Family (Alismaceæ).—The *type genus*[1] of the water-plantain family is the water-plantain

[1] The type genus of a family is the genus from which the family name often is derived, and usually (though not always) embodies in a striking way the characters which distinguish the family.

(*Alisma Plantago-aquatica*). Like the cat-tails, the water-plantains are marsh herbs (Fig. 377), with flowers either perfect, monœcious or diœcious; in *Alisma* they are perfect, with usually six stamens. The three sepals are *persistent*, but the three white petals are *deciduous* (*i.e.*, falling

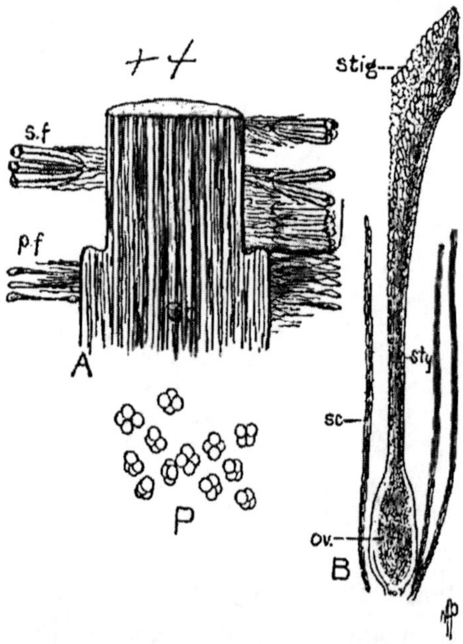

FIG. 376.—Cat-tail (*Typha latifolia*). *A*, longitudinal section of portion of inflorescence; *Sp*, spadix; *p.f.*, pistillate flowers; *s.f.*, staminate flowers. *B*, pistillate flower, greatly magnified; *ov*, ovary; *sty*, style; *stig.*, stigma; *sc*, sterile hair; *P*, pollen grains, in characteristic groups of four each. (Cf. Fig. 375.)

away early). The numerous ovaries are borne in a circle on a flattened receptacle. The possession of calyx and corolla, together with other features, mark the family as more highly organized than the cat-tails.

429. Grass Family (Gramineæ).—The grasses constitute one of the largest, one of the most important economically, and one of the most difficult taxonomically, of all the plant families. Here belong the "grains" (wheat, rice, oats, barley, rye, corn, and others) which furnish the most important vegetable foods of the entire human race. The commercial grains have been cultivated so long by man

FIG. 377.—Water plantain (*Alisma Plantago-aquatica*).

that their origin is shrouded in mystery, antedating, as it does, the dawn of written history. Except the bamboos, which are shrubs or trees, the grasses are all herbaceous.

The chief characteristics of the family are that the fruit is always a *grain* or *caryopsis*.[1] The seed invariably con-

[1] A one-seeded, seed-like fruit, with the wall of the ovary (*pericarp*) united closely (*adnate*) to the seed within.

tains endosperm, with the embryo located at one side (Figs. 378 and 83). The cotyledon (*scutellum*) serves to secrete enzymes that digest the endosperm, and then

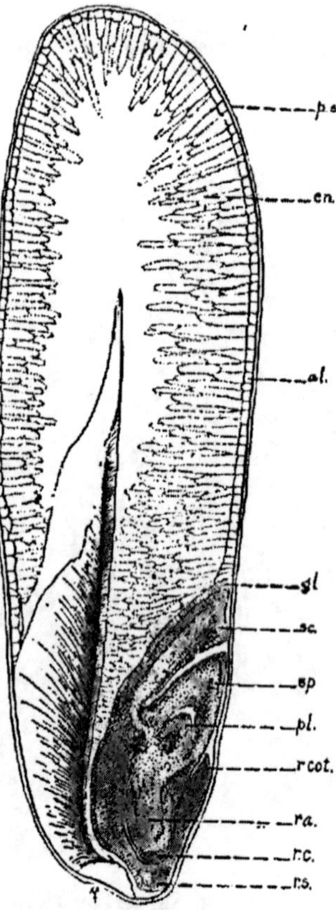

FIG. 378.–Longitudinal section of a grain of wheat (*Triticum vulgare*). *p.s.c.*, pericarp and seed-coats (united); *en*, endosperm; *al*, aleurone layer; *gl*, glandular layer of the scutellum; *sc*, scutellum; *sp*, sheath of plumule (*coleoptile*); *pl*, plumule; *r.cot.*, rudimentary cotyledon; *ra*, radicle; *rc*, root-cap; *r.s.*, root-sheath (*coleorhiza*). (From microscopical preparation of E. W. Olive.)

absorb the digested food by osmosis (Fig. 62). The cylindrical stems are jointed and usually hollow (except at the joints). The leaves are usually long, slender, and parallel-veined. The flowers are arranged in *spikelets*, and the spikelets in spikes (Fig. 379), racemes, or panicles[1] (Fig. 380). The leafy parts of the flower-clusters are modified as dry scales called *glumes*. When grain is thrashed the glumes constitute the so-called "chaff." There is no perianth.

430. Palm Family (Palmaceæ).—The palms are mostly tropical and subtropical. With certain exceptions (*e.g.*, *Calamus*—rattan), the stem or caudex is normally unbranched, varies in height with the species, and in most species bears all the foliage near the tip (Figs. 381 and 382). Frequently the old leaves, or their petioles or bases only, remain attached to the trunk. The leaves, though not morphologically compound, usually have their blades cleft or divided as they mature. The flowers are complete, with three sepals and petals, three to six stamens, and pistil of three carpels. They are monœcious, diœcious, or perfect, according to the species.

FIG. 379.—*Nazia racemosa* (L.) Kuntze. Terminal spike with one-flowered spikelets. (After Britton and Brown.)

The flowers, intermingled with bracts, occur on a more or less fleshy spadix, often much branched, and enclosed in a large spathe. The inflorescence may be axial (lateral), or terminal. When terminal the plant usually dies after the fruit has matured.

[1] A *spike* is "a form of simple inflorescence with the flowers sessile or nearly so upon a more or less elongated common axis." A *panicle* is "a loose, irregularly compound inflorescence with pedicellate flowers." A *raceme* is "a simple inflorescence of pediceled flowers upon a common, more or less elongated axis."

No species of palm has ever been found in both the eastern and western hemisphere, except when introduced artificially. Many of the palms have great commercial value, such as the date palm, cocoanut palm (Fig. 383), fan palm, vegetable-ivory palm (whose endosperm is hard and white like ivory), and the oil palm. In the tropics the leaves of various species are used to make thatched

Fig. 380.—Johnson-grass (*Sorghum halpense*). Spikelets in a panicle. (After Britton and Brown.)

roofs, and the trunks are often used for fence posts and porch pillars.

431. Arum Family (Araceæ).—The arum family is well illustrated by the "skunk cabbage" (*Symplocarpus fœtidus*) (Figs. 384 and 385).[1] The flower has no petals, but four sepals, and four stamens—one opposite each sepal. The ovary contains only one suspended ovule. The compound globular fruit is composed of the spongy spadix, greatly enlarged, bearing the coalesced ovaries, with the spherical seeds just underneath the surface.

[1] Called by some authors, *Spathyema fœtida.*

The roughness of the surface is caused by the persistence of the styles and the fleshy sepals.

The family is divided into several sub-families on the basis of various structural differences, such as phyllotaxy, venation of leaves, presence or absence of milky juice, presence or absence of perianth, and others.

FIG. 381.—Cocoanut palms along the beach. Philippine Islands. (Photo from Bureau of Science, Manila.)

432. Orchid Family (Orchidaceæ).—The Orchidaceæ are the most highly developed of all monocotyledons. No flower surpasses the orchids in beauty of color-pattern, endless diversity of unusual forms, and wonderful mechanisms that secure cross-pollination by insects. As in the papilionaceous flower, the flower of orchids is bilaterally symmetrical (*zygomorphic*), with (usually) three sepals resembling in texture the three petals (Fig.

386). One of the petals, *the lip*, presents a greater variety of form in the various species than do the other petals. At its base is the *column*, composed of the style, with which are fused the one (or sometimes only two) stamens (Fig. 387). Except in the lady's slipper (*Cypripedium*), and its

FIG. 382.—Sabal palmetto. (In the right distance a barragona palm). Cuba.

nearest relatives, the pollen adheres in masses or pollinia, as in the milk-weed. The stalked pollinia adhere to visiting insects, sometimes to their eyes, and are thus transferred from one flower to another.[1]

[1] For details of the wonderful contrivances for cross-pollination, the student should consult some larger treatise, such as Darwin's "Cross-fertilization of Orchids."

FIG. 383.—Germinating cocoanuts; the one seeded fruit of the cocoanut palm. (From Bull. Agricole du Congo Belge, 1910.)

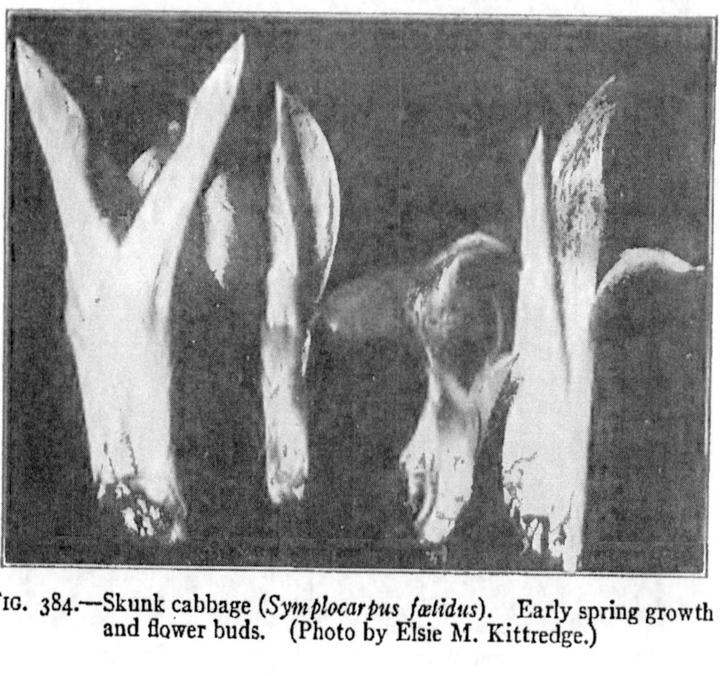

FIG. 384.—Skunk cabbage (*Symplocarpus fœtidus*). Early spring growth and flower buds. (Photo by Elsie M. Kittredge.)

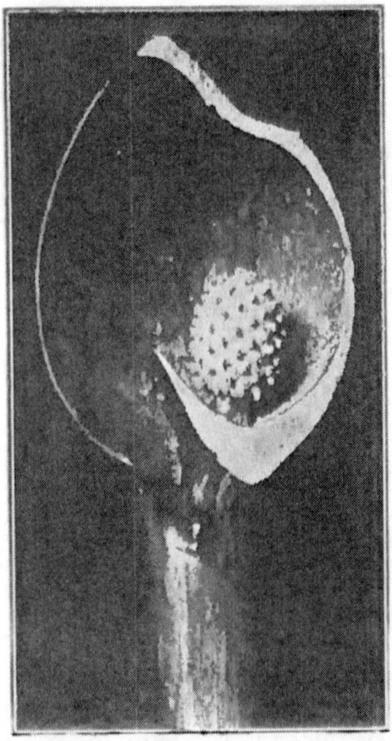

FIG. 385.—Skunk cabbage (*Symplocarpus fœtidus*). Inflorescence, with portion of the fleshy spathe removed, showing the perfect flowers covering the globose spadix. (Photo by Elsie M. Kittredge.)

FIG. 386.—Flower of an orchid (*Catleya sp.*). (Cf. Fig. 387.)

Of about 24,000 known species of monocotyledons, over one-fourth are orchids. The number of individuals, however, of any given species is small, as compared, for

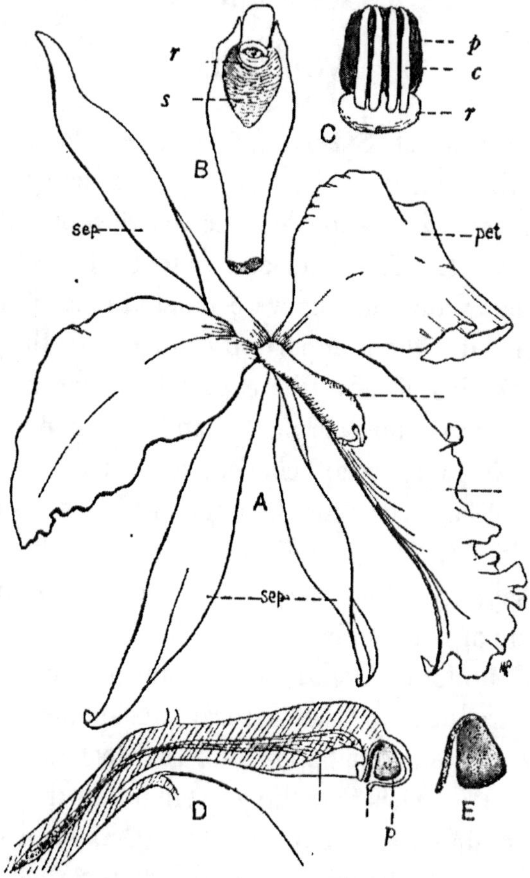

FIG. 387.—Floral organs of an orchid (*Cattleya sp.*). *A*, the entire flower; *sep*, sepal; *pet*, petal; *B*, column, showing *s*, stigma and *r*, the rostellum (beak), with the small glands at the tip; to the glands are attached the four strap-shaped caudicles of the pollinia; *C*, pollinia, with the four caudicles; below, the gland; *D*, longitudinal section of the column; *p*, pollinium; *E*, the same, enlarged. (Cf. Fig. 386.)

example, with the grasses. The most highly modified forms are tropical, and are seen in temperate regions only in plant-houses.

CHAPTER XXXI

EVOLUTION

433. Doctrine of Special Creation.—In the time of Linnæus, the "father of botany," men believed that the seven "days" of creation left the world substantially as we now find it. The stars and planets, mountains and oceans, plants and animals were created once and for all, and continued without important change until the present. In the beginning, as now, there were the same oceans and hills, the same kinds of plants, and the same kinds of animals. Nor, it was believed, are any fundamental changes now in progress. Creation was not continuous; it took place within a brief period (seven "days"), and then ceased; after that the Creator merely watched over the objects of his handiwork.

434. Meaning of Evolution.—Evolution means gradual change. Applied to the natural world the theory of evolution is the direct opposite of the doctrine of special creation. It teaches that things were not in the beginning as we now find them, but that there has been constant though gradual change. Creation is regarded, not as having taken place once and for all, but as being a continuous process operating from the beginning without ceasing—and still in progress.

435. The Course of Evolution.—The theory teaches that the gradual changes have been from relatively simple conditions to those more complex. The complication has been two-fold: (1) simple individuals, whether mountains, rivers, planets, animals, or plants, have become more complex (*e.g.*, compare the structure of *Pleurococcus*, a simple spherical cell, with that of the fern); (2) the relation between living things, and between them and their surroundings has become more complex (*e.g.*, compare a unicellular bacterium, with its relatively simple life relations, with the clover plant, highly organized, and related to water, air, soil, light, temperature, gravity, bacteria (in its roots), and insects (for cross-pollination).

Most of the steps of evolution have been *progressive*, toward higher organization, greater perfection of parts, increased efficiency of function, as, for example, from algæ to angiosperms; but not all the steps have been in this direction. Some of the steps have been *regressive*, toward simpler organization, less perfection of parts, decreased efficiency of function, as, for example, from green algae to the alga-like fungi (Phycomycetes), from independence to parasitism (dodder), or to saprophytism (Indian pipe and bread-mold).

436. Inorganic Evolution.—The process of evolution is not confined to living things, but, as indicated above, applies to all nature. Even the chemical elements are now believed to have been produced by evolutionary changes, and to be even now in process of evolution. This is one of the results of the recently discovered phenomenon of radioactivity, which is essentially the transformation of the atoms of one chemical element into those of another. Fossil remains of marine animals and plants, found imbedded in the rocks on mountain summits, indicate, without possibility of reasonable doubt, that what is now mountain top was formerly ocean bottom. The mountain has come to be, by a series of gradual changes. Rivers and valleys are constantly changing so that the present landscape is the result of evolutionary processes; climates have changed, as we know from the fact that fossil remains of tropical plants are now found in the rocks in arctic regions; even the stars and planets, like our own earth, are coming gradually into being, undergoing changes of surface and interior condition, and ceasing to exist. *Nothing is constant except constant change.* The main problem of astronomy is to ascertain and record, in order, the evolutionary changes that have resulted in the present system of suns and planets. The main problem of geology is to ascertain and record, in order, the evolutionary steps that have resulted in the present condition of the earth.

437. Organic Evolution.—Developmental changes in living things constitute organic evolution. Such changes are manifested in the development of an individual from a spore or an egg. The development of a mature individual is *ontogeny*. The development of a group of related forms (genera, families, orders, etc.) is *phylogeny*. The chief problem of biology is to ascertain and record, in order, the evolutionary changes that have resulted in the appearance of life and the present condition of living things.

The major problem of botany is to record, in order, the evolutionary steps that have culminated in the present condition of the plant world.

Organic evolution means that, after the first appearance of life, all living things, plant or animal, have been derived from preëxisting living things, in other words, that the present method of formation of living things, by the reproduction of organisms already existing, has always been the method—"*Omne vivum ex ovo*" (all life from an egg), "*omne vivum e vivo*" (all life from preëxisting life).

438. Method of Evolution.—To recognize that evolution is the method of creation still leaves unanswered the important question as to the method of evolution. By what process was the gradual development of the living world accomplished? Various hypotheses have been elaborated in answer to this question. We can here only briefly outline three of the most important ones.

FIG. 388.—Louis Agassiz. (From Ballard's "Three Kingdoms.")

1. *Agassiz's Hypothesis.*—The great teacher and student of nature, Louis Agassiz, believed that the vast array of plant and animal species, past and present, had no material

connection, but only a mental one; that is, they merely reflected the succession of ideas as they developed in the mind of the Creator, but were not genetically related to each other. "We must . . . look to some cause outside of Nature, corresponding in kind to the intelligence of man, though so different in degree, for all the phenomena connected with the existence of animals in their wild state . . . . Breeds among animals are the work of man: Species were created by God."[1]

But to state that species were created by God does not satisfy the legitimate curiosity of the scientific man. What he wishes to know is: *By what method* was creation accomplished? God might have worked in various ways. Now, the study of Nature has never revealed to us but one method by which living things originate, and that is *by descent from preëxisting parents.* Agassiz's hypothesis contradicts this. All oaks now-a-days are derived by descent from preëxisting oaks, but the first oak, according to the doctrine of special creation, was created by supernatural means; it had no ancestors. The chief objection to the acceptance of this hypothesis is that the more profoundly and accurately we study living things, the more obvious it becomes that truth lies in another direction.

2. *Lamarck's Hypothesis.*—The noted French naturalist, Lamarck, taught that all living things have been derived from preëxisting forms; that the effects of use and disuse caused changes in bodily structure; that these changes were inherited and accentuated from generation to generation; that, being of use, those individuals possessing the changes in greatest perfection survived while others per-

[1] Agassiz, L. "Methods of Study in Natural History," Boston, 1893, pp. 146, 147.

ished; and that the derivation of new species is thus accounted for in a simple and logical manner. By continual reaching for tender leaves on high branches, the long neck of the giraffe was gradually produced, the slight gain in length in one generation being transmitted by inheritance to the next, and so on.

The main thesis of Lamarck, as stated by himself, is as follows:

"In animals and plants, whenever the conditions of habitat, exposure, climate, nutrition, mode of life, *et cetera*, are modified, the characters of size, shape, relations between parts, coloration, consistency, and, in animals, agility and industry, are modified proportionately."

As illustrating the direct effect of environment on organisms, Lamarck chose a plant, the water-buttercup (*Ranunculus aquatilis*), which may grow in marshy places, or immersed in water. When immersed, the leaves are all finely divided, but when not immersed, they are merely lobed.

While plants are more passive, and are affected by their surroundings directly, through changes in nutrition, light, gravity, and so on, animals react to environmental changes in a more positive and less passive manner. Thus, in the words of Lamarck:[1]

"Important changes in conditions bring about important changes in the animals' needs, and changes in their needs bring about changes in their actions. If the new needs become constant or durable, the animals acquire new habits. . . . Whenever new conditions, becoming constant, impart new habits, to a race of animals . . . these habitual actions lead to the use of a certain part in

[1] Translated from his *Philosophie Zoologique*, vol. I, pp. 227, 223, 224, 248.

preference to another, or to the total disuse of a part which is now useless. . . . The lack of use of an organ, made constant by acquired habits, weakens it gradually until it degenerates or even disappears entirely." Thus, "it is part of the plan of organization of reptiles, as well as of other vertebrates, that they have four legs attached to their skeleton . . . but snakes acquired the habit of gliding over the ground and concealing themselves in the grass; owing to their repeated efforts to elongate themselves, in order to pass through narrow spaces, their bodies have acquired a considerable length, not commensurate with their width. Under the circumstances, legs would serve no purpose and, consequently, would not be used, long legs would interfere with the snakes' desire for gliding, and short ones could not move their bodies, for they can only have four of them. Continued lack of use of the legs in snakes caused them to disappear, although they were really included in the plan of organization of those animals."

On the other hand, "the frequent use of an organ, made constant by habit, increases the faculties of that organ, develops it and causes it to acquire a size and strength it does not possess in animals which exercise less. A bird, driven through want to water, to find the prey on which it feeds, will separate its toes whenever it strikes the water or wishes to displace itself on its surface. The skin uniting the bases of the toes acquires, through the repeated separating of the toes, the habit of stretching; and in this way the broad membrane between the toes of ducks and geese has acquired the appearance we observe to-day."

If such modifications are acquired by both sexes they are transmitted by heredity from generation to generation.

One of the weaknesses in Lamarck's hypothesis appears in his illustration of the snake. If we should grant that inheritance of the effects of disuse of the legs might possibly explain their absence in snakes, still it would not explain the *origin* of the snake's *desire to glide.* That is, of course, as much a characteristic of the snake as the absence of legs.

Other arguments against the validity of Lamarckism are: first, that no one has ever been able to prove, by experiment or otherwise, that the effects of use (the so-called

FIG. 388*a*.—Jean Baptiste Lamarck (1744–1829).

"acquired characters") are inheritable, while innumerable facts indicate that they are not; second, the hypothesis could apply only to the animal kingdom, since plants in general have no nervous and muscular activities like those of animals. A hypothesis of organic evolution, to be valid, must apply equally to both plants and animals.

3. *Darwin's Hypothesis.*—This will be outlined in the next chapter.

CHAPTER XXXII

DARWINISM

439. Charles Darwin.—The question of the method of evolution continued to be debated, with no satisfactory solution in sight, until 1859,[1] when Charles Darwin published the greatest book of the nineteenth century, and one of the greatest in the world's history, the *Origin of Species.*[2] This book was the result of over 20 years of careful observation and thought. It consisted of the elaboration of two principal theories: (1) that evolution is the method of creation; (2) that natural selection is the method of evolution.

440. Early Antagonism to Evolution.—The conception that evolution (as distinguished from periodic, *supernatural* interventions of the Deity) is the method of creation was arrived at independently by Darwin, but was not new with him. As we have just seen, it was proposed by Lamarck. Greek philosophers 2,000 years previously had suggested the idea; but it had never won the general acceptance of the educated world, partly because it was feared to be anti-religious, partly because it was never substantiated by sufficiently convincing evidence, and partly because of the antagonism of a few men of great

[1] This date should be memorized. It is one of the most important in the whole history of human thought.

[2] The full title of the book was, "The Origin of Species by Natural Selection, or the Preservation of Favored Races in the Struggle for Life."

influence in the world of intellect. Men preferred to follow a leader, more or less blindly, rather than take the

FIG. 389.—Charles Darwin. The publication of his "*Origin of Species*," in 1859, revolutionized human thought, and gave direction to all scientific and philosophic thinking from that time to the present.

pains to examine the voluminous evidence for themselves, and accept the logical conclusion without prejudice or fear, wherever it might lead them, or however much it might contradict all their prejudice and preconceived notions. But truth will always, in the end, command recognition and acceptance, and there is almost no scientific man, now-a-days, who does not regard evolution as axiomatic. It is one of the most basic of all conceptions, not only in the natural and the physical sciences, but also in history, sociology, philosophy, and religion; it has, indeed, completely revolutionized every department of human thought.

441. Darwinism.—It is the second of the above mentioned theories, *i.e.*, natural selection, that constitutes the essence of Darwinism. The theory is based upon five fundamental facts, which are matters of observation, and may be verified by anyone, as follows:

1. *Inheritance.*—Characteristics possessed by parents tend to reappear in the next or in succeeding generations. We are all familiar with the fact that children commonly resemble one or both parents or a grandparent, or great grandparent in some characteristic. From this we infer that something has been inherited from the ancestor which causes resemblance in one or more characters—physical or mental.

2. *Variation.*—But the expression of the inheritance is seldom, if ever, perfect. Eyes are a little less or a little more brown; stature is never just the same; one-half the face may resemble a given ancestor more than another; petals may be *more or less* red or blue; no two oranges taste exactly alike; no two maple leaves are of precisely the same shape. There is inheritance, but inheritance is usually expressed with modifications or variations of the ancestral type.

3. *Fitness for Environment.*—It is common knowledge that living things must be adjusted to their environment. Poor adjustment means sickness or weakness; complete or nearly complete lack of adjustment means death. Water-lilies, for example, cannot live in the desert, cacti cannot live in salt marshes; cocoanuts cannot be grown except in subtropical or tropical climates, edelweiss will not grow in the tropics. This is because these various kinds of plants are so organized that they cannot adjust themselves to external conditions, beyond certain more or less definite limits or extremes. A cactus is fit to live in the desert because it is protected by its structure against excessive loss of water, and has special provision for storing up water that may be used in time of drought. Deciduous trees are fitted to live in temperate regions, partly because their deciduous habit, and their formation of scaly buds enables them to withstand the drought of winter. Negroes live without discomfort under the tropical sun because they are protected by the black pigment in their skin. And so, in countless ways, we might illustrate the fact that all living things, in order to flourish, must be adjusted to their surroundings.

4. *Struggle for Existence.*—The clue to the method of evolution first dawned upon Darwin in 1838, while reading Malthus on "Population." Malthus emphasized the fact that the number of human beings in the world increased in geometrical ratio (by multiplication), while the food supply increased much less rapidly by arithmetical ratio (by addition). Therefore, argued Malthus, the time will soon be reached when there will not be food enough for all; men will then struggle for actual existence, and only the fittest (*i.e.*, the strongest, the fleetest, the most clever or

cunning) will survive. In pondering this hypothesis Darwin at once saw its larger application.[1] There are always more progeny produced by a plant or an animal than there is room and food for, should they all survive. Darwin showed that the descendants of a single pair of elephants (one of the slowest breeders of all animals) would, if all that were born survived, reach the enormous number of 19,000,000 in from 740 to 750 years.[2] But the total number of elephants in the world does not appreciably increase: evidently many must perish for every one that lives. There must therefore be an intense *struggle for existence.* Darwin[3] gives the following illustration:

"Seedlings, also, are destroyed in vast numbers by various enemies; for instance, on a piece of ground 3 feet long and 2 wide, dug and cleared, and where there could be no choking from other plants, I marked all the seedlings of our native weeds as they came up, and out of 357 no less than 295 were destroyed, chiefly by slugs and insects. If turf which has long been mown, and the case would be the same with turf closely browsed by quadrupeds, be let to grow, the more vigorous plants gradually

[1] "In October 1838," says Darwin, "that is, 15 months after I had begun my systematic inquiry, I happened to read for amusement 'Malthus on Population,' and being well prepared to appreciate the struggle for existence which everywhere goes on from long-continued observation of the habits of animals and plants, it at once struck me that under these circumstances favorable variations would tend to be preserved, and unfavorable ones to be destroyed. The result of this would be the formation of new species. Here then I had at last got a theory by which to work."

[2] One pair of elephants produces an average of only one baby elephant in 10 years, and the breeding period is confined to from about the 30th to the 90th year. For illustrations of the prolific nature of plants, see paragraph 173, pp. 190–191.

[3] "Origin of Species" (New York, 1902 edition), pp. 83, 84.

kill the less vigorous, though fully grown plants; thus out of 20 species growing on a little plot of mown turf (3 feet by 4) nine species perished, from the other species being allowed to grow up freely."

"Struggle for Existence" Used in a Large Sense.—"I should premise," said Darwin, "that I use this term in a large and metaphorical sense including dependence of one being on another, and including (which is more important) not only the life of the individual, but success in leaving progeny. Two canine animals, in a time of dearth, may be truly said to struggle with each other which shall get food and live. But a plant on the edge of a desert is said to struggle for life against the drought, though more properly it should be said to be dependent on the moisture. A plant which annually produces a thousand seeds, of which only one on an average comes to maturity, may be more truly said to struggle with the plants of the same and other kinds which already clothe the ground. The mistletoe is dependent on the apple and a few other trees, but can only in a far-fetched sense be said to struggle with these trees, for, if too many of these parasites grow on the same tree, it languishes and dies. But several seedling mistletoes, growing close together on the same branch, may more truly be said to struggle with each other. As the mistletoe is disseminated by birds, its existence depends on them; and it may metamorphically be said to struggle with other fruit-bearing plants, in tempting the birds to devour and thus disseminate its seeds. In these several senses, which pass into each other, I use for convenience sake the general term of Struggle for Existence."

5. *Survival of the Fittest.*—In this struggle for existence only those best suited to their environment will survive.

The dandelion from the seed that germinates first secures the best light; the one that sends down the longest and most vigorous root-system, that produces the largest, most rapidly growing leaves will survive, and will tend to transmit its vigorous qualities to its progeny. Less vigorous or less "fit" individuals perish. To this phenomenon Herbert Spencer applied the phrase, "survival of the fittest." Darwin called it "natural selection," because it was analogous to the artificial selection of favored types by breeders of plants and animals. It will be readily seen, however, that the process in nature is not so much a selection of the fittest, as a *rejection* of the unfit; the unfit are eliminated, while the fit survive. It has been suggested that "natural rejection" would be a better name than "natural selection." "Variations neither useful nor injurious," said Darwin, "would not be affected by natural selection."

442. Difficulties and Objections.—The publication of Darwin's "Origin of Species" aroused at once a storm of opposition. Theologians opposed the theory because they thought it eliminated God. Especially bitter antagonism was aroused by Darwin's suggestion that, by means of his theory "much light will be thrown on the origin of man and his history." The unthinking and the careless thinkers accused Darwin of teaching that man is descended from monkeys. Neither of these accusations, however, was true. Darwinism neither eliminates God, nor does it teach that monkeys are the ancestors of men.

By slow degrees, however, men began to give more careful and unprejudiced attention to the new theory, and not to pass adverse judgment upon it until they were sure they understood it. "A celebrated author and divine has written to me," says Darwin, "that he has gradually learnt to see that it is just as noble a conception of the Deity to believe that He created a few original forms capable of self-development into other and needful forms, as to believe that He required a fresh act of creation to supply the voids caused by the action of His laws."

And in closing his epoch-making book, Darwin called attention to the fact that, in the light of evolution, all phases of natural science possess more interest and more grandeur.

"When we no longer look at an organic being as a savage looks at a ship, as something wholly beyond his comprehension; when we regard every production of nature as one which has had a long history; when we contemplate every complex structure and instinct as the summing up of many contrivances, each useful to the possessor, in the same way as any great mechanical invention is the summing up of the labour, the experience, the reason, and even the blunders of numerous workmen; when we thus view each organic being, how far more interesting—I speak from experience—does the study of natural history become!"

"It is interesting to contemplate a tangled bank, clothed with many plants of many kinds, with birds singing on the bushes, with various insects flitting about, and with worms crawling through the damp earth, and to reflect that these elaborately constructed forms, so different from each other, and dependent upon each other in so complex a manner, have all been produced by laws acting around us. These laws, taken in the largest sense, being Growth with Reproduction; Inheritance which is almost implied by reproduction; Variability from the indirect and direct action of the conditions of life, and from use and disuse;

a Ratio of Increase so high as to lead to a Struggle for Life, and as a consequence to Natural Selection, entailing Divergence of Character and the Extinction of less-improved forms. Thus, from the war of nature, from famine and death, the most exalted object which we are capable of conceiving, namely, the production of the higher animals, directly follows. There is grandeur in this view of life, with its several powers having been originally breathed by the Creator into a few forms or into one; and that, whilst this planet has gone cycling on according to the fixed law of gravity, from so simple a beginning endless forms most beautiful and most wonderful have been, and are being evolved."

443. Objections from Scientists.—Objections to Darwin's theory were also brought forward by scientific men—partly from prejudice, but chiefly because they demanded (and rightly) more evidence, especially on certain points which seemed at variance with the theory. For example, they said, no one has ever observed a new species develop from another; this ought to be possible if evolution by natural selection is now in progress. The absence of "connecting links," or transitional forms between two related species was noted; the presence of apparently useless characters (of which there are plenty in both animals and plants) was not accounted for; and the geologists and astronomers claimed that the time required for evolution to produce the organic world as we now behold it is longer than the age of the earth as understood from geological and astronomical evidence.

There is not space here to summarize the answers to all these objections. Suffice it to say that scientific investigation since Darwin's time has given us reasonably satisfactory answers to most of them, so that now practically no scientific man doubts the essential truth of evolution; it is the corner stone of all recent science, the foundation of all modern thought.

444. The Modern Problem.—But Darwinism left us with a very large and very fundamental problem unsolved. Upon what materials does natural selection act in the formation of species? Obviously the "fittest" survives, but *what is the origin of the fittest?* This problem Darwinism did not solve. The solution of it is one of the most fundamental and important tasks now being undertaken by biologists. The most effective attack is by the method of *experimental evolution*, which forms the subject of the next chapter.

CHAPTER XXXIII

EXPERIMENTAL EVOLUTION

445. A New Method of Study.—Previous to Darwin's time the study of plants and animals, was carried on chiefly by observations in the field. The science was largely descriptive—a record of what men had observed under conditions over which they did not endeavor to exercise any control; it was accurately named "Natural History"—a description of Nature. But Darwin and a few of his contemporaries, especially among botanists, began to make observations under conditions which they determined and largely regulated. In this way the problems were simplified, observation became more accurate, and the endeavor was made to assign the probable *causes* of the observed phenomena. With the introduction of this experimental method, science began to make rapid strides, and, more than ever before, facts began to be, not only recorded, but interpreted and explained.

446. Hugo de Vries.—The director of the Botanic Garden in Amsterdam, Holland, Hugo de Vries, was among the first to demonstrate that the method of experiment may be applied to the study of evolution. His plan was to secure seed of a given species from a plant which he believed to be *pure* with reference to a given character, that is, not contaminated or mixed by being cross-pollinated with another variety or species. The characters of the parent plant were carefully noted and recorded by photographs and written descriptions, and by preserving dried and pressed herbarium specimens. The plants of the second generation were carefully guarded from being cross-pollinated, and thus "pure" seed were secured for a third generation. This was continued often for 25 or 30 generations of the plant, requiring as many years when a

FIG. 390.—Hugo de Vries. His pioneer studies of osmosis resulted in fundamental contributions to our knowledge of that subject; his mutation-theory is one of the most important contributions to the study of evolution since Darwin.

species produced only one crop of seed a year. Very careful records and preserved specimens were kept of the plants of each generation, and accurate comparisons were made to see if any individuals showed a tendency to vary widely from their parents in any significant way, such as showing entirely new characters, not expressed in the parents, or failing to manifest one or more of the characters of the parent.

447. Two Kinds of Variation.—One of the first results of de Vries's painstaking work was the demonstration of what he believed to be a fundamental difference between two distinct kinds of variation—*continuous* (or fluctuating) and *discontinuous* (or saltative, *i.e.*, leaping).

448. Continuous Variation.—Continuous variation is *quantitative*—a case merely of more or less. It deals with *averages*. Some flowers on a red-flowered plant may be lighter or darker red, but, in a series of generations, the average of a large number in each generation does not vary, and the departure from the average never exceeds certain limits. The flowers of a given species may have a certain characteristic odor, but the odor may be stronger in some flowers than in others, or in some individual plants than in others. The plants grown from a handful of beans of the same variety may vary in height *within limits*, but the *average* height of a large number will not vary in successive generations, and will be characteristic of the species or variety. In other words, *continuous or fluctuating variation is variation about a mean.* It may be illustrated by the bob of a swinging pendulum, which continually fluctuates within definite limits about the mean position assumed when the pendulum is at rest (Fig. 396).

All plants and animals manifest fluctuating variation in all their characters (Fig. 391), and such variations are largely, if not entirely, dependent upon the environment. A slight change in the kind of food elements supplied, or in the amount of water or sunlight available will make the leaves or petals a deeper or a paler color. Rich soil, favoring a more abundant food supply, will cause a greater average growth than poor soil, but unless the seed for future generations is selected from the tallest plants, and the richness of the soil is maintained, the plants will *revert* to their normal, lower average of height. In other words, the average height of the plants of any given variety is a constant (unvarying) character, except that it may be

FIG. 391.—Branch of *Brachychiton diversifolium*, illustrating fluctuating or continuous variation in the shape of the leaves on one plant.

temporarily altered by careful selection of seeds from the tallest or shortest individuals, or by choosing the largest or the smallest seeds from any given plant, or by making the soil richer or poorer. When the selection ceases, and the soil is maintained at average fertility, the characteristic *average* height of the plants is restored.

449. Illustrations of Continuous Variation.—In a quart of beans, for example, there are no two seeds of precisely the same proportion or size; some are longer, some shorter. De Vries describes[1] an experiment in which about 450 beans were chosen from a quantity purchased in the market, and the lengths of the individuals measured. The length varied from 8 to 16 millimeters, and in the following proportions:

Millimeters	8	9	10	11	12	13	14	15	16
Number of beans	1	2	23	108	167	106	33	7	1

The beans were then placed in a glass jar divided into nine compartments, all the beans of the same length in the same compartment. When this was done it was found that the beans were so grouped that the tops of the columns in the various compartments followed a curve, known as Quételet's[2] curve (Fig. 392).

This curve may be plotted by erecting vertical lines (*ordinates*) at intervals of 1 millimeter on a horizontal line or base, the height of each vertical line being proportionate to the *number* of beans having the length indicated in figures at its base. This curve shows the *frequency* of occurrence of seeds of any given dimension between the two limits or extremes, and is therefore often referred to as a *curve of frequency*. It should be noted that, in the case illustrated, the greatest frequency (indicated by the highest point of the curve) very nearly coincides with the *average* dimension; in other words, *the more any given character*

[1] De Vries. "The Mutation Theory," vol. 2, p. 47, Chicago, 1909.

[2] So named from its discoverer, Quételet (Ket-lay). As de Vries states: "For a more exact demonstration a correction would be necessary, since obviously the larger beans fill up their compartment more than a similar number of small ones."

departs from the average for that character, the less frequent is its occurrence.

In another experiment, ears of corn, harvested from the same crop, were measured and found to vary in length from 4½ inches to 9 inches; the largest number of ears (20) were 7 inches long. The greater the departure from this length, in either direction, the fewer the individuals; for the lengths 4 inches and

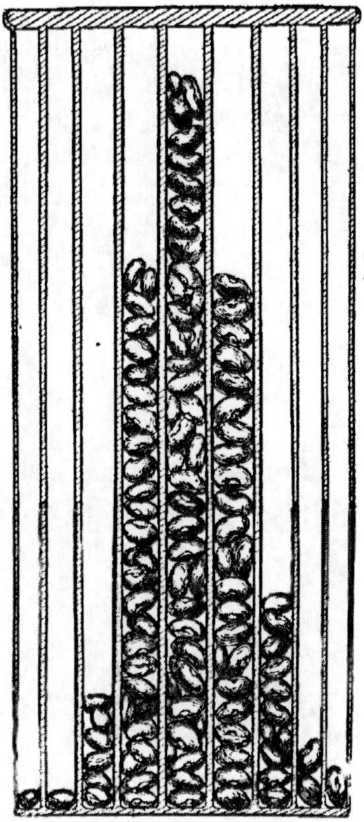

FIG. 392.—Demonstration of Quételet's law of fluctuating variability in the length of seeds of the common bean (*Phaseolus vulgaris*). Description in the text. (Redrawn from de Vries.)

FIG. 393.—Curve of fluctuating variation (Quételet's curve), formed by arranging 82 ears of corn in ten piles, according to the length of the ears. The extremes were 4.5 and 9 inches. The ears were taken from unselected material from a field of corn. (After Blakeslee.)

FIG. 394.—Photograph of beans rolling down an inclined plane and accumulating at the base in compartments, which are closed in front by glass. The exposure was long enough to cause the moving beans to appear as caterpillar-like objects hopping along the board. If we assume that the irregularity of shape of the beans is such that each may make jumps either toward the right or toward the left in rolling down the board, the laws of chance lead us to expect that in very few cases will these jumps be all in the same direction, as indicated by the few beans collected in the compartments at the extreme right and left. Rather the beans will tend to jump in both right and left directions, the most probable condition being that in which the beans make an equal number of jumps to the right and to the left, as shown by the large number accumulated in the central compartment. If the board be tilted to one side, the curve of beans would be altered by this one-sided influence. In like fashion, a series of factors—either of environment or of heredity—if acting equally in both favorable and unfavorable directions, will cause a collection of ears of corn to assume a similar variability curve, when classified according to their relative size. Such curves, called Quételet's curves, are used by biometricians in classifying and studying variations in plants and animals. (Photo by A. F. Blakeslee. Legend slightly modified from Journal of Heredity, June, 1916.)

9 inches the frequency was zero. When the ears were arranged in piles according to their length, the tops of the piles indicated the curve of frequency (Fig. 393).

The curve of frequency indicates the quantitative distribution of any character or quality when its occurrence is dependent largely upon chance. This is strikingly illustrated by the grouping of bean seeds rolled down a smooth inclined plane, and collected in receptacles at the bottom (Fig. 394). The seeds are started rolling midway between the edges of the plane; the chances are about equal for some of the seeds to fall into the outside compartments, but the odds are vastly in favor of their landing at or near the center. Thus they group themselves so that the tops of the piles form a curve of chance variation. When the result is influenced in one direction more than in another the crest of the curve will be nearer one extreme than the other, and the curve is to that extent *skew*. The curve of bean seeds in Fig. 394 is slightly skew toward the right-hand extreme. Suggest one or more reasons why.

450. Fluctuating Variation and Inheritance.—When the ancestry is not mixed or hybrid the curve of frequency of any character in one generation ordinarily tends to recur in successive generations of descendants,[1] providing the environment remains essentially the same.

451. Discontinuous Variation.—Long before Darwin, students of plants and animals had observed a different kind of variation than continuous—one which was not quantitative but *qualitative*, resulting in the expression of new characters, or of *a new curve of frequency;* that is, in fluctuation about a new mean. Plants from *some* of the

[1] The behavior of hybrid descendants is a special case described in Chapter XXXVII.

seeds of a red-flowered specimen bear flowers, not that vary from deeper to paler red, but that suddenly, at one step, have become pure white; one or more seeds from an odorless plant may give rise to individuals whose flowers are sweet-scented; or *vice versa*, odorless specimens may spring at one leap, not by gradual minute changes, from those that

FIG. 395.—Leaves of varieties of the Boston fern (*Nephrolepis*), showing (from left to right) progressive branching of the pinnæ and pinnules, and illustrating so-called "orthogenetic saltation." (After R. C. Benedict.)

are fragrant; *in one generation* the factors controlling height are so altered that, in successive generations, the average of height may change by either more or less, so that the heights of the individuals *fluctuate about a new mean.* In other words, we recognize a second type of variation—not the fluctuation of *individuals* about an unchanging mean, but *the appearance of a new mean,* about which the given character in individuals may fluctuate.

When discontinuous variation proceeds along a definite line through several successive generations, each step being an intensification of the preceding one, it is designated "*orthogenetic saltation*" (Fig. 395).

451. Illustration of the Pendulum.—The difference between discontinuous and fluctuating variation may be

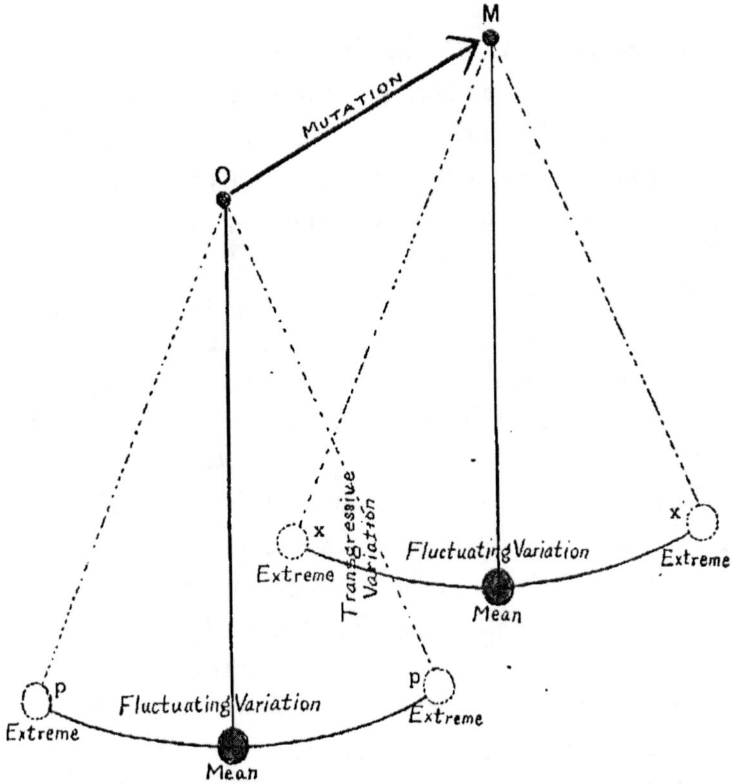

FIG. 396.—Diagram to illustrate the difference between fluctuating variation and mutation; *O*, original point of suspension; *M*, new point of suspension after the mutation has occurred.

aptly illustrated by a swinging pendulum (Fig. 396). The vertical position, assumed when at rest, is the mean of all positions that may be assumed as the pendulum swings;

the oscillation about this mean illustrates continuous or fluctuating variation.

But we may conceive that the point of suspension of the pendulum changes, as shown in the figure. The pendulum continues to oscillate, but now about a new mean position; *a new character has been introduced*, with its own fluctuations of more or less.

453. Mutations.—Darwin, as well as others before and after him, recognized both kinds of variation, but de Vries was the first to work out in detail the hypothesis that *discontinuous variations furnish the material for natural selection*. Discontinuous variations he called *mutations;* plants which give rise to or "throw" them are said to *mutate*. A plant that arises by mutation is an *elementary species*, or *mutant;* and the theory that mutations (and not fluctuations) explain the origin of the fittest, and supply the materials upon which natural selection operates in the formation of new species, de Vries called *the mutation theory.*

454. Examples of Mutation.—The kohlrabi, cauliflower, and other horticultural varieties of the wild cliff-cabbage (Fig. 397), are believed to be mutants, and to have arisen, not by the prolonged selection of fluctuating variations, but at one step—in one generation—as "sports" of the wild *Brassica oleracea.* Strawberry plants without runners, green dahlias and green roses, the common seedless bananas of the markets, the Shirley poppies, pitcher-leaved ash trees, Pierson's variety of the Boston fern, 5-9- "leaved" clovers (Fig. 398), white black-birds (and other albinos, including albino men), moss-roses, thornless cacti and thornless honey-locusts, red sunflowers, composites with tubular corollas in the ray-flowers (Fig. 399), and the innumerable white flowered varieties of colored

FIG. 397.—Horticultural varieties of the wild cabbage. *A*, wild cliff-cabbage, hypothetical ancestor of the numerous modern horticultural forms; *B*, broccoli (leaves and flowers both used); *C*, kale; *D*, kohlrabi; *E*, brussels sprouts (lateral buds used); *F*, common cabbage (a highly developed terminal bud); *G*, cauliflower (flower-buds used). (Redrawn from various sources.)

flowered species, are all illustrations of mutation. Frequently the mutative change occurs in a lateral bud, producing a "bud-sport" (Fig. 400). Such was the origin of the seedless navel orange from the seed-bearing orange.

FIG. 398.—Clover leaves with three to nine leaflets, illustrating a tendency to mutate. The normal clover leaf is a pinnately compound leaf with three leaflets. Plants with leaves having five to nine leaflets constitute a "half-race," *i.e.* the normal character is active, the anomaly semi-latent. (Photo by the author; specimens from cultures of G. H. Shull.)

455. The Evening-primrose.—In 1886 de Vries began to search for a species that was in a mutating condition, believing that any given species is at some periods in its history more labile or changeable than at other periods. After a long search he found in an abandoned potato field at Hilversum, near Amsterdam, a large number of plants of Lamarck's evening-primrose (*Œnothera Lamarckiana*) (Fig. 401.)

"That I really had hit upon a plant in a mutable period became evident from the discovery, which I made a year later, of two perfectly definite forms which were immediately recognizable as two new elementary species. One of them was a short-styled form: *O. brevistylis*, which at first seemed to be exclusively male, but later proved to have the power, at least in the case of several individuals,

FIG. 399.—Yellow daisy, or cone-flower (*Rudbeckia sp.*), showing variations of the character of mutations in the ray- and disc-flowers. At *d* the normally ligulate corollas are tubular; at *f* they have all aborted, except two; at *h* many of the normally tubular disc-flowers have become ligulate, making a nearly "double flower." (Photo by E. M. Kittredge.)

of developing small capsules with a few fertile seeds. The other was a smooth-leaved form with much prettier foliage than *O. Lamarckiana*, and remarkable for the fact that some of its petals are smaller than those of the parent type, and lack the emarginate form which gives the petals of

Lamarckiana their cordate character. I call this form *O. lævifolia.*"

"When I first discovered them (1887) they were represented by very few individuals. Moreover each form occupied a particular spot on the field. *O. brevistylis* occurred quite close to the base from which the Œnothera

Fig. 400.—A plant of the evening-primrose (*Œnothera biennis*) which, by "bud sporting," has given rise (at the left) to a branch having the characters of another species.

had spread; *O. lævifolia* on the other hand, in a small group of 10 to 12 plants, some of which were flowering whilst others consisted only of radical leaves, in a part of the field which had not up to that time been occupied by *O. Lamarckiana.* The impression produced was that all these plants had come from the seeds of a single mutant. Since that time, both the new forms have more or less spread over the field" (*de Vries*).

Another mutant of *Œ. Lamarckiana* was called by de Vries *Œnothera gigas* (Fig. 402). The cell-nuclei of this mutant have twice as many chromosomes as the parent form.

FIG. 401.—Lamarck's evening-primrose (*Œnothera Lamarckiana*). A mutating species. (After de Vries.)

456. The Test of a Mutation.—The deciding test as to whether a given new form, arising without crossing from a form that has bred true for at least two generations, is really a mutant or merely a fluctuating variant, is to see if it breeds true to seed for the new character or characters. If it does it is a mutant; otherwise it is not. It is clear, therefore, that the only way the problem can be followed out is by experiment—hence the term *experimental evolu-*

tion. The great contribution of de Vries is that he demonstrated that evolution may be studied by the method of experimentation. The next step for him to take after discovering the two forms that he supposed to be mutants, was to breed them in carefully guarded, pedigreed cultures

FIG. 402.—Giant evening-primrose *Œnothera gigas*, a mutant from *Œnothera Lamarckiana*, originated in 1895. (Cf. Fig. 401.) (After de Vries.)

in his garden, and also to breed the parent form, *Œnothera Lamarckiana*, and see if he could observe the two forms above mentioned, or other mutants, arise from seed produced without crossing with any other species.

The entire story of this classical series of experiments is too long to be told here. Suffice it to say that de Vries did observe numerous other aberrant forms arise, and also found that they bred true (except for additional mutations) when propagated by seed for over 25 years—that is, they were true mutations.

457. Relation of Mutation Theory to Darwinism.—The mutation theory is not intended by de Vries to supplant the theory of natural selection, but to demonstrate that the materials upon which selection acts *in the formation of new species* are mutations, and mutations only—never fluctuating or individual variations. In the second place the mutation theory explains away numerous objections to natural selection. It shows how characters that are never of vital importance[1]—*i.e.*, matters of actual life or death—to a species may arise and be perpetuated. Without mutation this is difficult to explain,[2] and yet many, if not most, of the characteristics by which different species are distinguished from each other are of this kind—not, so far as we can see, absolutely essential to the life of the species. Mutation also offers a method by which evolutionary changes may take place within a much shorter time-period than was demanded by the natural selection of fluctuations.

Incidentally, the mutation theory clearly shows that the absence of "connecting links" between species is no argument against evolution, but is, on the contrary, just what we might expect to find.

458. Value of the Mutation Theory.—As stated above, the elaboration of the mutation theory has furnished the

[1] As required by Darwin's theory. See quotation on p. 516.

[2] Other explanations have been offered. For example, sometimes two characters appear to be always associated, so that the presence of one involves the presence of the other; as a mane and maleness in the lion, dicotyledony and exogeny in Angiosperms.

biological world with a new method of study. It has demonstrated that the method of evolution may be studied by experimentation, and this demonstration is, probably, de Vries's greatest service to science. The mutation theory should also be of great service to breeders. It has helped to establish plant and animal breeding on a more scientific basis, has pointed the way to correct methods where men were formerly groping in the dark, and has showed that results of commercial value do not require a life time, but may be obtained within two or three seasons. By the application of modern methods it has been possible, within a few seasons, to obtain new strains of oats yielding as much as 14 bushels per acre more than the variety from which they were derived, and to produce new strains of corn not only giving a larger yield, but maturing nearly two weeks earlier than the parent variety.

459. Classification.—Mere information is not science. A "book of facts" is not a scientific treatise, for it is composed of bits of unrelated information, presented on some artificial basis of sequence, as for example, alphabetically. Scientific knowledge, in addition to being as accurate as possible, is characterized by having an orderly arrangement in one's mind, and this order is based on a logical, fundamental relationship between the facts and ideas. Only by such an arrangement of our ideas are we able to understand their relation to each other, their relative importance, and their real significance. Classification, therefore, is essential to all science. The very existence and use of such words as oaks, maples, roses, indicate that men have grouped or classified their ideas of certain plants (*e.g.*, red oaks, white oaks, black oaks, bur oaks, live oaks, etc.), and have thereby recognized that certain kinds resemble each other closely enough to be placed in one group with a group-name. All the common names of plants indicate the recognition of classes—a classification.

FIG. 403.—Linnæus, the great classifier (1707–1778). He is wearing a sprig of the twin-flower (*Linnæa borealis*), one of his favorite flowers, and named after him by his friend, Gronovius. He is regarded as the father of modern systematic botany.

460. Evolution and Classification.—Without the guiding idea of evolution classification would be arbitrary and artificial. Linnæus classified plants on the basis of the number of stamens they possessed, thus placing in one group plants now known to be wholly unrelated, except that they have a chance similarity in the number of stamens. In like manner we may group together plants with red flowers, blue flowers, or pink flowers, as is often done in "popular" guides to the wild flowers. This has its value, but it tells us really nothing about the significant relationship between plants, does not help clear up our own ideas, does not show the gaps in our knowledge and tell us where to search for new facts to fill up the gaps. Evolution, by showing that plants are all related to each other by descent, just as are the members of a large family of persons, discloses to us the only true basis of classification—the plan that endeavors to arrange all plants so as to show their descent and their relationship to each other. Without evolution there might be any number of arbitrary systems; on the basis of evolution there can, in the end, be but one true system, which all students must accept, because it will be a true record of what has actually occurred in the history of development of the plant or animal worlds. In other words, *if our knowledge should ever become sufficiently complete and exact, the classification of plants would give a summary—a bird's eye view—of the course of evolution and the history of development. To approximate this end is one of the largest problems of botany.*

CHAPTER XXXIV

HEREDITY

461. Importance of the Study.—1. *To Pure Science.*—No knowledge is more fundamental than a correct understanding of the laws of heredity. Its fundamental importance to pure science becomes evident at once when we consider that, since evolution has been accomplished by the descent of one organism from another, there have been one or more unbroken lines of inheritance from the dawn of plant life to the present. Hence, until we know the laws of heredity, we cannot fully understand expression, reproduction, development, variation, sex, or evolution.

2. *To Applied Science.*—Correct ideas concerning heredity are absolutely essential to such phases of applied science as animal and plant breeding. In the light of such knowledge the breeder can avoid making useless experiments, and can accomplish desired results more quickly, more cheaply, and with greater certainty of success.

3. *To Man.*—A correct knowledge of the principles of heredity is vital to mankind; no knowledge is more so. To realize this, we have only to reflect that our own characters are very largely the result of inheritance from our ancestors; and not only our characters, but our physical characteristics, our vigor of mind and body, our capacity for education, our susceptibility to disease, and often the actual existence of some disease within our bodies or minds.

462. Heredity Reduced to Its Lowest Terms.—We may study heredity under the very simplest conditions in the descent of one-celled organisms, such as *Pleurococcus.* This plant, as we learned in Chapter XVIII, is a globule of protoplasm, containing chlorophyll, and surrounded by a cellulose cell-wall. But why is it globular, why does it contain chlorophyll, why has it a cell-wall of cellulose? Why is it not elliptical, why is it not red instead of green, why does it have a cell-wall, instead of existing naked like the plasmodium of a slime-mold, why is its cell-wall of cellulose, rather than of lignin or chitin?

The short answer is, because its ancestors, for ages and ages, have possessed the characteristics which now characterize *Pleurococcus* plants. But that only puts the question back an indefinite number of generations. The real reason is, because the *Pleurococcus* protoplasm possesses a physical and chemical constitution—or in other words a mechanism—that, under normal external conditions, manufactures green pigment instead of red, cellulose instead of lignin, or any other substance, at the surface, and makes the cell-wall of even resistance to the osmotic pressure within, thus producing a sphere and not an ellipsoid, or filament, or any other shape.

463. What is Inheritance?—When the *Pleurococcus* cell divides, this wonderful, invisible mechanism—the certain definite physical and chemical constitution—is transmitted to each of the daughter-cells; each, in other words, receives *Pleurococcus* protoplasm. *This protoplasm, with its definite organization, constitutes the inheritance.* The daughter-cells do not inherit a spherical shape (as is evident from Fig. 183), but a definite kind of protoplasm, cell-sap of certain osmotic properties, and surface cellulose of even elasticity, so that, in surroundings uniform on all sides, a spherical shape must finally result. The shape is an *expression of the inheritance* for the given environment. *Under different external conditions the expression might be different; but the inheritance would be the same.* The chlorophyll in the daughter-cells, immediately after cell-division, is a direct inheritance, but the chlorophyll subsequently manufactured, and the green color which it gives to the plant, are not inherited; they are expressions of the inheritance—which in this instance is a chloroplastid that reproduces itself by division, and manufactures chlorophyll in the presence of sunlight. Under abnormal external conditions the mechanism may not act, or may act abnormally, so that yellow pigment appears instead of green—or in darkness no pigment at all. In either case the inheritance is the same, but the expression varies. A modern writer has defined inheritance as *all that an organism has to start with.* It is the protoplasmic substance, with all its potentialities, passed on from parent to offspring.

464. Inheritance Versus Expression.—In the light of this information, obtained by a study of the lowly *Pleurococcus*, we are able to understand that what we inherit from our parents or grandparents, is not a certain shape of nose, a certain characteristic gait, a musical or mathematical bent of mind, a quick temper, but *a substance* (protoplasm) possessing a very delicate, intricate, and characteristic constitution or mechanism. Under certain conditions this inheritance may so express itself as to cause resemblance in some physical or mental trait; or it may find a quite different expression, as when parents of medium height have tall children, or parents musically inclined have children that do not care for music; or sweet-peas having white flowers only, produce, when crossed, peas having colored flowers. Or again, not all that is inherited may be expressed; this is illustrated when children resemble, not their parents, but their grandparents. Here the parents transmitted an inheritance which, in them, found no expression. A remarkable illustration of inheritance without expression is seen in the case of the alternation of generations (pages 181–183) The initial protoplasm of the sporophyte is all inherited through the fertilized egg from the gametophytes, but most of the gametophytic characters do not appear in the sporophyte, nor do the typically sporophytic characters find expression in the gametophyte.[1]

465. Inheritance Versus Heredity.—As stated above, *the inheritance is that which is actually transmitted* from parent to offspring. The fern-spore, for example, is the inheritance of the fern gametophyte from the sporophyte. *Heredity is the genetic relationship that exists between successive generations of organisms.* The *relation* between two brothers and their parents is similar—it is one of heredity; their inheritance may be quite different.

466. Inheritance and Reproduction.—Inheritance is, of course, inseparably linked with reproduction and may be studied in connection with the three following types:

1. *In vegetative propagation*[2] the new plant, as noted in Chapter XVII, is obviously only a portion of the vegetative tissue of the parent plant, isolated and growing independently by itself. The separation of the propagating piece from the parent is often (though not always) mechan-

[1] The chlorophyll, of course, is an exception. But the osmotic strength of the cell-sap is a different expression in gametophyte and sporophyte, otherwise the young sporophyte could not live parasitically upon the gametophyte.

[2] *E.g.*, by means of tubers, cuttings and "slips," bulbs and bulbils, gemmæ, "runners," scions, etc.

ical and artificial. The protoplasm remains unaltered by the act of separation, reduction divisions are not involved, and the inheritance, except in bud-variations, is unaffected by the change. This is evident in those cases where the

FIG. 404.—Graft of tomato (*Lycopersicum esculentum*) on tobacco (*Nicotiana tabacum*). On the tomato are grafted *Solanum nigrum*, *S. integrifolium*, and *Physalis alkekengi*. *Cf.* Fig. 243. (Graft made by Mr. M. Free.)

isolated piece is grafted upon another plant; the specific or varietal characteristics of the scion are seldom, if ever, affected by the stock. Thus, in the experiment illustrated in Fig. 404, a tomato stem was grafted upon a tobacco plant, and upon the tomato were grafted three other species—*Solanum nigrum*, *Solanum integrifolium*, and *Physalis alkekengi*. Each species was apparently not in the least altered by this drastic change in the conditions of its life.

2. *In asexual reproduction by spores* the situation is quite similar to that in vegetative propagation, but in certain cases there is abundant opportunity for the protoplasm to become more or less altered during the complicated changes that accompany nuclear division. This is especially the case in the reduction divisions preceding spore-formation in the sporophytes of higher plants, especially when the plant is a hybrid; and in spore-formation *in the sporangia produced from the zygospore* of some of the filamentous fungi, like *Mucor Mucedo*. In the latter case the nuclear divisions, some time preceding spore-production, result in separating out the female (+) and male (−) strains, so that the spores in a given sporangium are unlike as to sex—some being female (+), some male (−). This will be discussed more fully in the next chapter. Such changes result merely in distributing the heritable units (*genes*) of the mother-cell unequally to the daughter-cells, but introducing nothing new; they may, however, result in the complete loss of one or more heritable units, or in the formation of a new one, not existent in the parent. In the latter two cases we recognize a mutation. No hard and fast line can be drawn between the various kinds of asexual reproduction; there are various degrees of transition between reproduction by spores, gemmæ, bulbs and tubers, and the artificially severed buds and scions used in grafting and "slipping."

3. *In sexual reproduction* there intervene between par-

ents and offspring, not only the complicated reduction divisions involved in the formation of the gametes, but also the *nuclear and cell-fusions* accomplished by the union of the egg and sperm in fertilization. Both processes—the formation of the gametes, and their fusion—offer almost unlimited opportunities for alterations of the protoplasm—especially that of the nucleus. This method of reproduction, therefore, has the very greatest interest and importance for the study of heredity. In the fertilized egg[1] are united the inheritances from two parents—from two distinct lines of ancestry—protoplasms (germ-plasms) with two entirely different histories extending back into the past, no one knows how far. How will these two inheritances affect each other when they intermingle in the fertilized egg? Will one tend to inhibit or check certain characteristics or functions of the other; will they evenly blend, so as to produce an expression intermediate between that of the parents; or may entirely new substances be formed or new combinations take place, resulting in an entirely new expression in the offspring?

467. Methods of Study.—To endeavor to answer the questions just asked is as fascinating an occupation as it is important, and the answers are significant for man, as well as for plants. It is indeed, a fortunate thing that principles ascertained by studying plants apply equally to man and other animals, since plants are so much easier to handle in experimental investigations.

We may go about the answering of these questions in either of two ways. We may gather large numbers of statistics to measure and analyze (*statistical or biometrical*

[1] The fertilized egg (as Thomson has pointed out) *is* the inheritance, and becomes, in the mature individual, the inheritor.

method), or we may employ the *experimental method.* The method of *biometry* enables us to deal with a larger number of individuals, but the material studied is usually a mixed population, whose history is only imperfectly known, the conditions are more complex, and little if at all under control. By the experimental method it is not necessary to deal with such large numbers; we may choose carefully pedigreed material about the history of which we have more or less accurate knowledge, and we may greatly simplify and control the conditions under which we make our observations. The largest advance toward the solution of the problems of inheritance has been made by the experimental method, in the form first employed successfully by Gregor Mendel. This method will be briefly explained in the next chapter.

CHAPTER XXXV

EXPERIMENTAL STUDY OF HEREDITY

468. Gregor Mendel.—Two of the most important contributions ever made to biological science, namely,

FIG. 405.—Gregor Mendel, at the age of 40. His theory of alternate inheritance (Mendelism), based largely on experiments with the garden pea, is the most important and most fruitful contribution ever made to the study of inheritance.

Mendel's laws of heredity, and his method of investigating them, were made by a teacher who studied plants as a pastime because he loved to do it. This man was Gregor

Mendel, a monk in the monastery at Brünn, Austria, where he finally became abbott. In order to understand his work clearly the student should examine carefully the structure of the edible or garden pea, the chief plant with which Mendel worked.

469. Mendel's Problem.—It was a favorite study of Mendel's to *hybridize* (*i.e.*, cross-pollinate) plants of different species and varieties, and observe the behavior of the resulting *hybrids* in successive generations. The problem which he endeavored to solve was the law or laws "governing the formation and development of hybrids,"[1] with special reference to the laws according to which various characters of parents appear in their offspring.

470. Mendel's Method.—He recognized that, in order to solve the problem, attention must be given to at least three points, as follows:

1. "To determine the number of different forms under which the offspring of hybrids appear."
2. "To arrange these forms with certainty according to their generations."
3. "To ascertain accurately their statistical relations," that is, to express the results quantitatively.

No previous student had recognized the fundamental importance of these requirements.

471. Choice of Material.—Mendel realized that the success of any experiment depends upon choosing the most suitable material with which to experiment. He laid down the requirements as follows:

[1] All the quotations in this chapter are from an English translation of Mendel's original paper. His form of expression has been preserved as far as possible, even when the "quotes" are omitted.

1. "The experimental plants must necessarily possess constant *differentiating characters*."[1]

2. "The hybrids of such plants must, during the flowering period, be protected from the influence of all foreign pollen, or be easily capable of such protection."

3. "The hybrids and their offspring should suffer no marked disturbance in their fertility in the successive generations."

Mendel also called attention to the advantage of choosing plants which, like the peas, are easy to cultivate in the open ground and in pots, and which have a relatively short period of growth.

472. Characters Chosen for Observation.—"Each pair of differentiating characters [have been thought to] unite in the hybrid to form a new character, which in the progeny of the hybrid is usually variable. *The object of the experiment was to observe these variations in the case of each pair of differentiating characters, and to deduce the law according to which they appear in successive generations.* The experiment resolves itself therefore into just as many separate experiments as there are constantly differentiating characters presented in the experimental plants." The following were the characters chosen for observation:

1. The difference in the shape of the ripe seeds (round and smooth *vs.* angular and wrinkled).

[1] Differentiating characters are those in respect to which the two species or varieties to be crossed differ. The possession of chlorophyll by the leaves of peas, for example, is a *common character*. "Common characters are transmitted unchanged to the hybrids and their progeny." The color of the corolla (for example, white in one species and purple in the other) is a *differentiating character*, serving to differentiate or distinguish one species from another.

2. The difference in the color of the cotyledons (pale or bright yellow, or orange *vs.* light or dark green).

3. The difference in the color of the seed-coat (white *vs.* gray, gray-brown, leather-brown, with or without violet spotting, etc.).

FIG. 406.—Method of protecting flowers from foreign pollen by paper bags, in plant-breeding experiments. (After O. E. White.)

4. The difference in the form of the ripe pods (deeply constricted between the seeds and more or less wrinkled, or the opposite).

5. The difference in the color of the unripe pods (light or dark green *vs.* vivid yellow).

6. The difference in the position of the flowers (*i.e.*, axial *vs.* terminal).

7. The difference in the length of the stem (the extremes chosen were "talls" 6 to 7 feet, and "dwarfs" ¾ feet to 1½ feet in height).

473. Artificial Hybridizing.—The edible pea is commonly self-fertilized; therefore, to make crosses it is necessary carefully to remove the stamens of one flower before the anthers have begun to shed their pollen, and then place pollen from another flower on the stigma. The flowers must then be carefully guarded, *e.g.*, by tying paper bags over them (Fig. 406), to prevent other pollen being deposited by insects or otherwise. In this way the experimenter knows just what characteristics enter into the hybrid. Careful record is kept of all data, and plants produced in this way, with ancestral characters noted and recorded, are called *pedigreed*. Plantings of such plants are called *pedigreed cultures*.

In many species, in "making the cross" (*i.e.*, doing the cross-pollinating) great care must be taken to avoid contamination from foreign pollen, of which the air may be full.[1] The fingers and all instruments are usually rinsed in alcohol before each operation, to insure killing any foreign pollen that might be present. Numerous other precautions are also taken.

When the hybrid plants are mature, careful observations of whatever character is under observation are made and recorded. Whenever possible the observation should be quantitative.

474. Mendel's Discoveries.—We may illustrate Mendel's results in a simple manner by choosing, as the pair of contrasted characters, smooth and wrinkled seeds of the pea. Removing all the stamens from flowers of a variety having smooth seeds, he pollinated those flowers with pollen from a plant bearing wrinkled seeds.

It should now be kept clearly in mind just what the inheritance of the fertilized egg is in such a case. From the pistillate plant the inheritance, contributed by the egg-cell, included the protoplasmic properties (whatever they may be) which, when free to produce their effect, cause smooth seeds; from the staminate parent the inheritance, contributed by the sperm-cell, included the protoplasmic properties, which, when free to act, cause wrinkled seeds.

1. *Law of Dominance.*—What Mendel actually found

[1] See p. 423, paragraph 376.

by his experiments was that, in such a cross, all the seeds of the hybrid plants are smooth. The inheritance was "smooth" and "wrinkled," but the expression was of only one type—smooth. A character thus expressed,

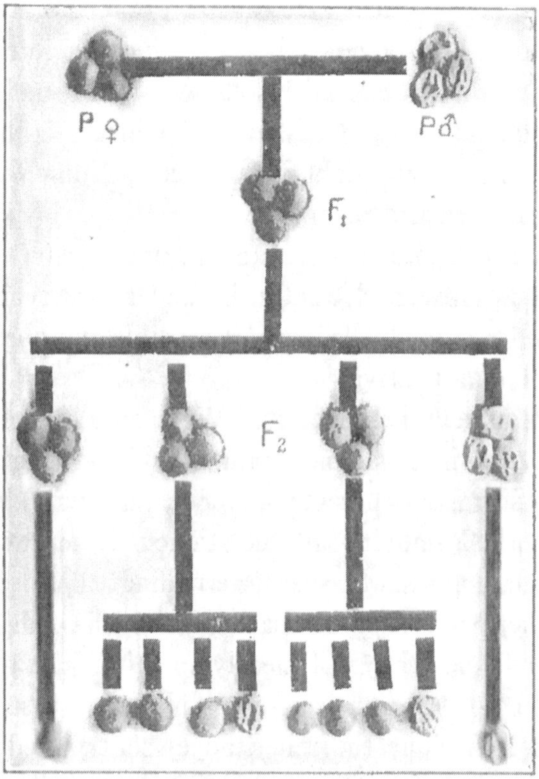

Fig. 407.—Mendelian segregation in the edible pea (*Pisum sativum*). Full explanation in the text. (Cf., Fig. 408.)

to the exclusion of another, in the first filial (F_1) generation Mendel called *dominant*, and the phenomenon he called *dominance;* the other character is *recessive.* From such observations Mendel formulated the law of dominance, as follows: *When pairs of contrasting characters are combined in a cross, one character behaves as a dominant over the other, which is recessive.*

By similar experiments Mendel found that, in the cotyledons, yellow is dominant over green, tallness over dwarfness, axial flowers over terminal, and so on. Such pairs of contrasting characters are called *allelomorphs*.

2. *Law of Segregation.*—But what will happen if the first filial (F_1) generation is inbred or self-pollinated. Its inheritance included factors that make for both "smooth" and "wrinkled," but the expression was all of one kind only. The experiment was made, and Mendel found that the second filial (F_2) generation included plants, part of which possessed only smooth seeds, while the others had only wrinkled seeds (Fig. 407). "Transitional forms were not observed in any experiment." This illustrates in a striking way the difference between inheritance and expression.

475. Ratio of Segregation.—But now we come to that feature of Mendel's experiments which, perhaps more than anything else, made them superior to all others that had preceded. He carefully *counted* the number of plants bearing each kind of seed, and found that the number of smooth-seeded plants was to those with wrinkled seeds as 3 : 1.

476. Theory of Purity of Gametes.—When the wrinkled seeds (one-fourth of the total crop) were sown they all bred true to wrinkledness—their descendants of the F_3 generation bearing only wrinkled seeds. The expression was alike in every case. The gametes that united to produce these plants were therefore considered pure *for "wrinkledness;"* that is, it was inferred that they did not carry any inheritance tending to produce smoothness of seed.

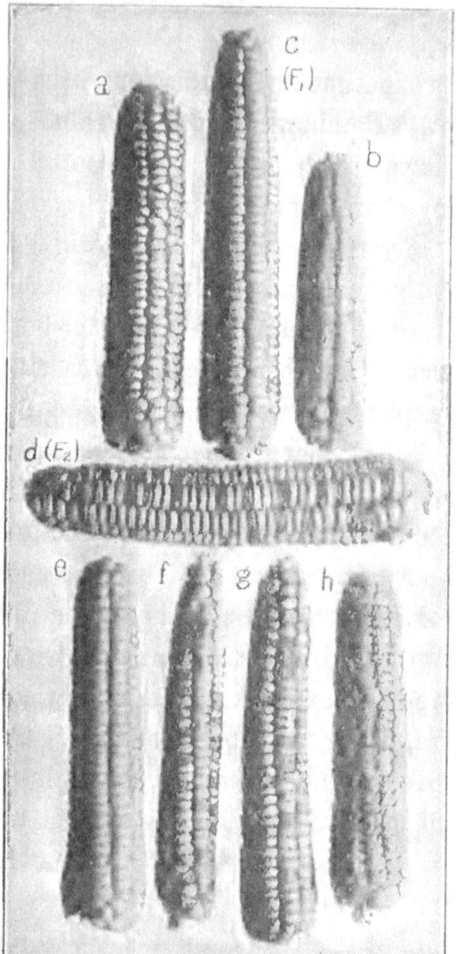

FIG. 408.—Mendelian segregation in maize. *a*, the starchy parent; *b*, the sweet parent; *C*, the first hybrid (F_1) generation, produced by crossing *a* and *b*, showing the dominance of starchiness; *d*, the second hybrid (F_2) generation, showing the segregation of starchiness and sweetness with the ratio of three starchy to one sweet (wrinkled) grain. Lower row, daughters of *d; e*, *f*, and *g* resulted from planting starchy grains. One ear in three is pure starchy, the other two mixed; *h*, result of planting sweet (wrinkled) seeds. They are pure recessives, and the ear is pure sweet. (After East.) (Cf. Fig. 407.)

477. Not All Dominants Alike.—But when the seeds of the F_2 plants, having only smooth seeds, were sown it was found that *the dominants were not alike*, except in external appearance. The seeds, though all appeared smooth, carried different inheritances. One-third of them (*i.e.*, one-fourth of all the seed produced by the F_2 generation) bred true to smoothness, being therefore pure, or homozygous, *for smoothness;* the other two-thirds of the dominants (*i.e.*, one-half of all the seed produced) again segregated in the ratio of 3:1—one-fourth wrinkled and three-fourths smooth, showing that they were *heterozygous;* that is, that they still carried inheritance from both the wrinkled and smooth-seeded grandparents.

If we designate the first parental generation by P, the dominant character (whatever it may be) by D, and the recessive character by R, then the facts above described may be diagrammed as follows:

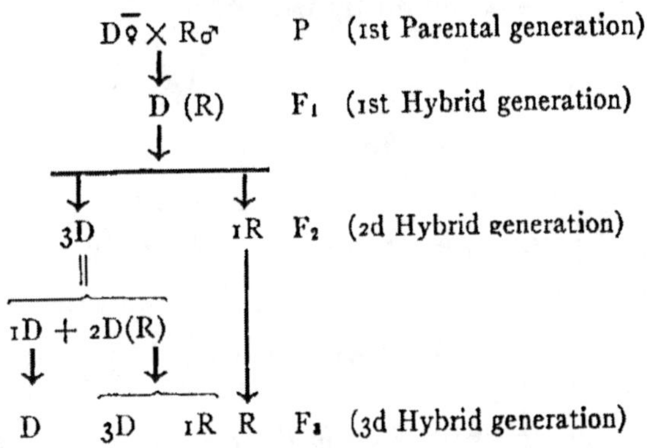

478. Significance of the Mendelian Ratio.—The ratio 3 : 1 or, as it appears on analysis, 1 : 2 : 1, is the ratio that one might expect, or that might be predicted, on the basis of chance. Students of algebra will recognize in it the essence of the familiar square of $a + b$, namely, $a^2 + 2ab + b^2$, where a and b each equal 1. In the plants the multiplication of inheritances (produced in fertilization) was as follows:

$$\text{eggs } (s + w) \times \text{sperms } (s + w) = ss + 2sw + ww$$

where w = wrinkling and s = absence of wrinkling, *i.e.*, smoothness.

479. Theory of Purity of Gametes.—The above ratio is what we would expect if half of the egg-cells and half of the sperm-cells in a heterozygous plant (one of the F_1 generation), carried only character-units or determiners[1] that make for smoothness; the other half only those factors that make for wrinkling, giving s and w egg-cells, and s and w sperm-cells *in equal numbers*. Therefore, in pollination the chances would be equal that an s-egg would be fertilized with either an s-sperm or a w-sperm, giving $(s + w) \times (s + w) = ss + 2sw + ww$. Since s is dominant over w the product should be written:

$$ss + s(w) + s(w) + ww$$

giving *in external appearances* $3s + 1w$. Since the result actually observed is what it would be *if* the gametes were thus "pure" *for smoothness and wrinkling*, Mendel concluded that they really are, and moreover that each *character* behaves as a unit, appearing and disappearing in its entirety.

480. Character-units versus Unit-characters.—As just stated, Mendel held that the various visible characters of his plants (dwarfness, for example) behaved as units,

[1] The substance or condition (protoplasmic constitution), whatever it is, in the germ-cells that corresponds to any given character of the plant is variously referred to by the terms *factor*, *determiner*, *gene* (= producer), *character-unit*, and others. These terms are essentially synonyms.

either appearing in their fullness, or not appearing at all. From more careful observations we know that such is not the case. A blossom may, for example, be more or less pink, an odor more or less strong, dwarfs are not all the same height, but fluctuate around a mean. We conclude therefore that characters do not behave as units, and that the conception of "unit-characters" is erroneous. The evidence does, however, seem to justify the conclusion that the factor or factors, whatever they may be,[1] that are causally related to the given character do behave as units. We may therefore designate them as *character-units.* They are commonly known as *genes.* Quite probably, in many if not all cases, more than one gene or character-unit is involved in the production of any given character.

481. Applications of Mendel's Law.—Over 100 pairs of structural and color characters have been found, in plant breeding, to behave more or less closely in accordance with the Mendelian conception. In peas alone over 20 pairs of characters are expressed in successive generations, in accordance with this law. Among the more striking results which are explainable upon Mendelian theory are the following:

1. Mottled beans have been produced in the F_1 generation by crossing two varieties, neither of which had mottled seeds. Vaiious types appeared in the F_2 generation.

2. Jet black beans have appeared in the F_1 generation from a cross between two varieties, one of which had pure white seeds, the other light yellow. Various shades and colors appeared in the F_2 generation.

3. In one case three distinct varieties of beans, breeding

[1] Substance or condition, we know not what, within the germ-cells.

true to white seeds (when selfed[1]), were crossed with the same variety of red bean. In the F_1 generation each cross gave a different color—one blue, another black, and the third brown. A varied assortment of colors appeared in each case in the F_2 generations.

4. Two varieties of sweet peas, each breeding true to white flowers, when crossed gave, in the F_1 generation, nothing but purple-flowered offspring, resembling the wild sweet pea. A medley of white, pink, purple, and red-flowered plants appeared in the F_2 generation. Numerous other cases might be cited, all of which would have been unsolvable riddles except in the light of Mendelism.

482. Inheritance and Environment.—Emphasis should be laid on the fact that the behavior of any plant, and the characters it manifests, are the result of the combined influence of inheritance and environment. A bean seedling is green, not merely because it has inherited chloroplastids, but because it develops in sunlight; without sunlight the green color could not come into expression. If we vary any factor of environment (temperature, moisture, illumination, food) the expression of the inheritance may be altered, just as truly as though the inheritance were changed. *The characteristics expressed by any plant (or animal) are the result of the combined action of inheritance and environment.* It is of fundamental importance to a man, not only to be "well-born" (*eugenics*), but also to be "well-placed" (*euthenics*).

483. Johannsen's Conception of Heredity.—The conception that inheritance, as previously noted, is not the transmission of external characters from parent to offspring, but the reappearance, in successive generations,

[1] The pollination of a flower with its own pollen, or with pollen from another flower of the same plant, is called *selfing*.

of the same organization of the protoplasm with reference to its character-units, was first developed by Johannsen, of Copenhagen, Denmark, who proposed the term "genes." "The sum total of all the 'genes' in a gamete or zygote," is a *genotype*. *Inheritance is the recurrence, in successive generations, of the same genotypical constitution of the protoplasm.* Johannsen does not attempt to explain the nature of the genes, "but that the notion 'gene' covers a reality is evident from Mendelism."

This conception of heredity is diametrically opposed to the older and popular conception, but is much more closely in accord with the facts revealed by recent studies of plant and animal breeding.[1]

484. Value of Mendel's Discoveries.—The discoveries that, in inheritance, certain characters are dominant over certain others; that a given inheritance (*e.g.*, conditions associated with seed-color, odor, eye-color, stature, musical ability, insanity, tendency to some disease) may be carried and transmitted to offspring by an adult who gives no outward signs of carrying the inheritance; that, under certain conditions of breeding, some characters (the recessive ones), whether good or bad, may become permanently lost; that dominant characteristics are certain to appear in *some* of the offspring—all of these truths, learned by the study of a common garden vegetable, will be recognized at once as of enormous importance to the breeders of plants and animals, and above all to mankind, in connection with our own heredity. They point the way to the explanation of such enigmas as the proverbial bad sons of pious preachers, spendthrift children

[1] A discussion of Johannsen's very fruitful method of "pure line" breeding belongs to more advanced studies.

of thrifty parents, talented offspring of mediocre parents, blue-eyed children of brown-eyed parents,[1] and so on.

485. Increased Vigor from Crossing.—Experiments with pedigreed cultures have disclosed a principle of the utmost practical importance for the plant breeder. A careful analysis of a field of Indian corn (*Zea Mays*) has disclosed the fact that any given variety is very complex, being heterozygous for many characters; in other words any horticultural variety is a composite of numerous elementary species, and is therefore heterozygous for most of its characters. When pollination is allowed to take place in the corn field without interference by man, both crossing and selfing occur. As a result the yield, in bushels per acre, remains about stationary, or gradually becomes less and the variety changes and deteriorates by the segregation and recombination of the numerous elementary species that compose it.

By artificial self-pollination for several generations (*e.g.*, five or more) less complex strains result, which are homo-

[1] If both parents have blue eyes the children can never have brown eyes; if one parent has brown eyes and one blue, the children may be both blue- and brown-eyed, or all brown-eyed, for brown eye-color in man is dominant over blue color. When both parents have brown eyes, part of the children may have blue eyes and part of them brown, or they may all be brown-eyed. As used here, the term "brown eyes" means all eyes having brown pigment, whether in small spots (gray eyes), or traces (hazel eyes), or generally distributed (brown, or sometimes black, eyes). The term "blue eyes" designates only those cases in which brown pigment is entirely lacking.

FIG. 409.—*Zea Mays.* In the experiment, the results of which are here illustrated, nine strains of Indian corn were selected according to the number of rows of kernels on the cob, varying from 8 to 24 rows. These were pollinated by hand each year, with mixed pollen, in such manner that self-pollination was entirely prevented. An average ear of each strain is shown in the first row above. In the second row is shown an average ear of each strain after self-fertilization for five generations. Note the resulting decrease in the number of rows, lack of filling out of the ears, and other marks of inferiority. The last row shows the remarkable and immediate increase of vigor resulting in the F_1 generation of hybrids between various pairs of the selfed strains. (Photo supplied by G. H. Shull.)

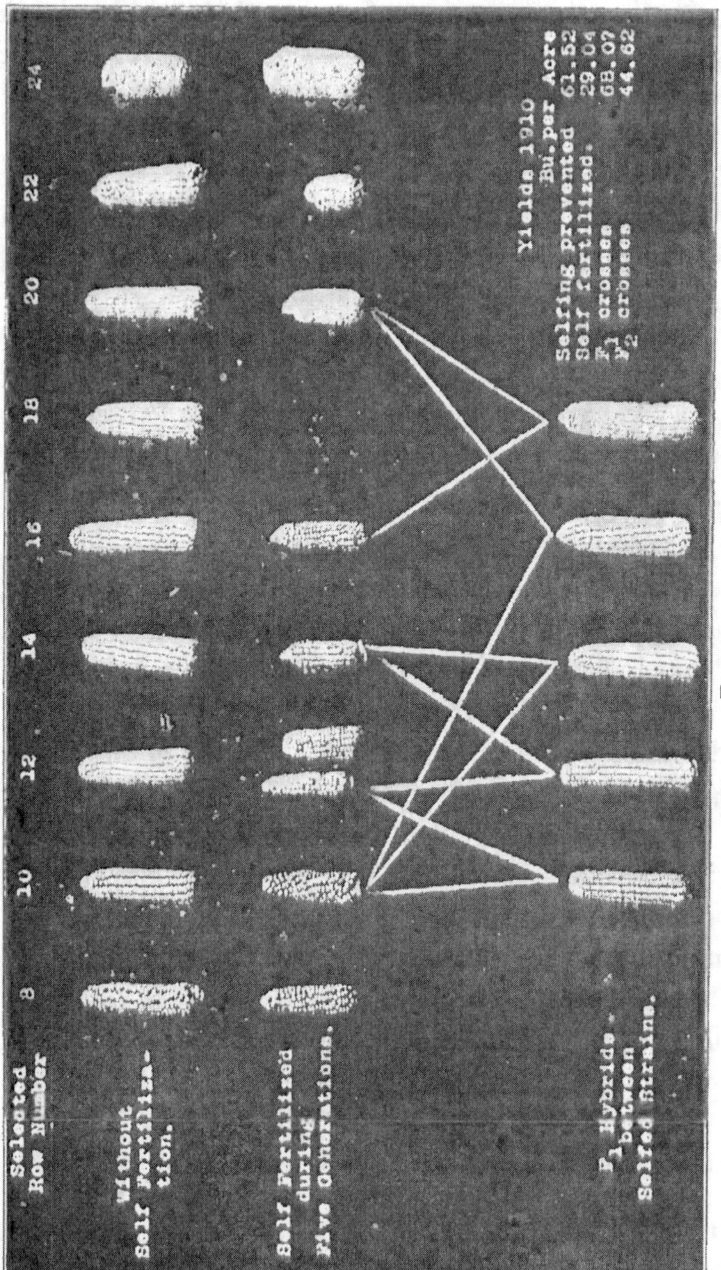
Selected Row Number
8
10
12
14
16
18
20
22
24
Without Self Fertilization.
Self Fertilized during Five Generations.
F_1 Hybrids between Selfed Strains.
Yields 1910 Bu. per Acre
Selfing prevented 61.52
Self fertilized. 29.04
F_1 crosses 68.07
F_2 crosses 44.62

FIG. 409.

zygous for one or more characters, and the yield per acre may thus become greatly reduced.[1] If now, two of these simplified strains, homozygous for many characters, and having a low yield per acre, are crossed, there results an F_1 hybrid progeny that is heterozygous for all of these characters. This heterozygosity is correlated with a greatly increased vigor; the plants are much larger, and the yield per acre is enormously increased (Fig. 409). Thus in one experiment of this kind the average yield of the heterozygous horticultural variety was 61.25 bushels per acre. After self-fertilization for several generations the yield became reduced to 29.04 bushels per acre; but in the F_1 generation of a cross between two of these self-fertilized strains the yield per acre rose at once to 68.07 bushels. In the F_2 generation the yield again fell to 44.62 bushels. From this, and numerous other experiments, it is found that the biggest corn crop is to be obtained by finding the strains that will produce the largest yield when crossed, and thus using for seed the grains of the first-generation hybrids each year.

486. Unsolved Problems.—Like all truly great contributions to science, Mendel's discoveries have raised more questions than they have answered. Therein lies, in part, their great value. So, also, the most important effect of Darwin's work was that it set men to asking questions. The history of botany, as of all natural science since 1859, is chiefly the attempts of men to answer the questions raised by Darwin, or stimulated in their own minds by his books. So with Mendel and de Vries;

[1] If a high-yielding strain was separated out by selection, the yield would of course be increased above the average of the mixed field.

biological science, since 1900, has been largely occupied in trying to answer the questions raised by these men.

What are these questions? There is not space here even to ask them all, much less to endeavor to answer them even briefly; but they include the following large problems:

1. *What is the mechanism of inheritance?* In other words, by what arrangement and interaction of atoms and molecules is it made possible that the peculiar tone of one's voice, the color of a rose, the odor of a carnation, the evenness (or otherwise) of one's disposition, may be transmitted from one generation to another? How may it be transmitted *through* one generation, without causing any external expression, and reappear in the second generation removed? Is the cytoplasm the carrier, or the chromatin, or both combined, or neither? Is the transfer accomplished by little particles (*pangens*), as de Vries contends, or by chondriosomes, or otherwise? We do not know.

2. *How may dominance be explained?* Why is tallness dominant over dwarfness, brown eye-color over blue, any one character over any other? We have not the faintest idea.

3. *Are acquired characters inherited?* In other words, do characteristics acquired after birth by the body or mind of the parent, either by its own activity or as a result of the immediate effects of environment, influence the germ-cells so as to alter the inheritance which they transmit? Some say yes, others say no; others say, only in part. There seems to be evidence both ways. We can arrive at the correct answer only by careful experimentation, that is, by asking questions of nature.

4. *Can the inheritance of a strain be artificially altered?* This is a question of the very first importance. If the inheritance could be so altered the marvels that breeders might perform would be greatly increased. A blue rose (the despair of all plant breeders) might possibly be produced by sufficiently careful and extended experimenting; disease and undesirable traits of character might be eliminated from certain tainted family strains by artificial treatment. On the other hand, by an unfortunate combination of circumstances, most undesirable and regrettable results might be experimentally produced. The experiment has been made of exposing the ovaries of flowers to the rays of radium, and of injecting them with various chemical substances, with an idea of altering the physical or chemical nature of the egg-cells, and thus altering the inheritance. The results of such experiments, so far tried, need to be further confirmed before we can say with certainty that the result sought has been accomplished.

487. Eugenics.—Students of biology have been quick to recognize the fact that, if we correctly understand the laws of heredity, we are in a position to apply them, not only to plants and the lower animals, but to mankind. *The application of the laws of heredity in a way to produce a healthier and more efficient race of men constitutes the practice of eugenics.*[1] The underlying principles of eugenics are of course, very largely those of heredity. Eugenics is the *applied science* based upon the *pure science* of heredity. The main problem of eugenics is how to eliminate human beings with a tendency to any physical or mental weakness, making for poverty, misery,

[1] Eugenics is from two Greek words meaning *well born*.

ignorance, and crime; and how to increase the number of individuals physically, mentally, and morally more robust and sound; and withal how, if possible, to raise the standard of all desirable human traits. A careful study of heredity and eugenics will make possible a much more intelligent and efficient program for charity work and social betterment.

488. Investigations Since Mendel.—It must be remembered that Mendel's most valued contribution was not the observations which he made and recorded concerning the garden pea, nor the hypotheses which he advanced on the basis of those observations, but this *method of procedure*, whereby he elevated the study of heredity to the rank of an exact science. As in the case of all hypotheses, the task for science is to subject them to the most searching tests, to see if they invariably agree with facts, and may be accepted as in all probability embodying the actual truth—may be elevated to the rank of theories. The testing of Mendelism has been occupying all the best talents of many investigators since the rediscovery of Mendel's publication, about 1900. Many biologists are still skeptical, others reject the hypotheses, and still others believe they contain the germ of truth, but must be more or less modified. *Whether they prove to be erroneous or true is not so important, but it is important for us to know which is the case.* True or not, they, like nearly all working hypotheses (natural selection, mutation, nebular hypothesis, atomic hypothesis in chemistry, etc.) are rendering, or have rendered, a priceless service to science by pointing the way to further study, which enriches our knowledge of the living world, including ourselves, and therefore increases the intelligence with which we may order our own conduct and lives. If the study of plants had rendered no other service to mankind than this contribution of an effective method of ascertaining the laws of heredity, it would have amply justified all the arduous labor that men have devoted to it for 2,000 years.[1]

[1] Only one of the simplest cases worked out by Mendel is summarized in this chapter. A more thorough study of his experimental results and theories must be reserved for a more advanced course.

CHAPTER XXXVI

THE EVOLUTION OF PLANTS

489. The Problem Stated.—If we knew the entire history of development of the plant world, we could arrange all plants now living, and that have lived, so as to show their genetic relation to each other. The problem is illustrated on a small scale by various related cultivated plants, all known to be derived from a common wild ancestor. Cabbage and its relatives are a case in point. The botanical relatives of the cabbage include such forms as kohlrabi, brussels-sprouts, collards, kale, broccoli, and cauliflower (Fig. 397). All of these garden vegetables are believed to have been derived from the common wild cliff-cabbage (*Brassica oleracea*) of Europe and Asia, by selecting mutations in various directions, *e.g.*, excessive development of the stem in kohlrabi, of the terminal bud in cabbages, of the lateral buds in brussel's sprouts, of the flower buds in cauliflower. Or, to refer to de Vries's studies in experimental evolution, where the course of descent was actually observed, we may arrange the forms of Lamarck's evening-primrose so as to show their known derivation.

The general problem, therefore, is to establish the genetic relationship of all known plants, living and fossil. Since the Angiosperms stand at the top of the series, the problem resolves itself largely into ascertaining the *phylogeny*, or line of ancestry, of that group.

490. Methods of Study.—In the solution of this problem two methods of attack may be employed: (1) That of observation and comparison of structure, followed by classification, and inference; (2) that of experiment. The use of experiment is indicated in Chapters XXXIII and XXXV. By this means we may learn something of the relationship of different groups having living representatives; but it chiefly serves to throw light on the *method* of evolution. The *course* of evolution is best ascertained by the observation and comparison of plant structures.

491. Sources of Evidence.—There are four main sources of evidence as to the course of evolution:

1. *Comparative anatomy of living forms.*
2. *Comparative life histories of living forms.*
3. *Structure of fossil forms.*
4. *Geological succession of fossil forms.*

Studies along these four different lines have resulted in some conflict of evidence, but on the whole the evidence from the various sources all points to the same broad conclusions. Conflict or contradication is in most cases the result of insufficient evidence from one or more sources.

492. Evidence from Comparative Anatomy.—Comparative study of structure has led to the conclusion that, in its broadest aspects, the course of plant evolution has been from the simple to the complex; that such simple organisms as *Pleurococcus*, and other green algæ, preceded more complex forms like the liverworts; that Bryophytes appeared before ferns, and they in turn before the modern Gymnosperms and Angiosperms.

A difficulty of accepting this conclusion as final is the possibility that, at certain points, the course of evolution may have been retrograde. For example it is generally accepted that the filamentous, alga-like fungi were derived from green algæ by retrograde evolution (degeneration). Were the plants with one seed-leaf (monocotyledons) derived from those with two (dicotyledons) by retrograde evolution, or were the dicotyledons derived from the monocotyledons by progressive evolution? Evidence, recently ascertained by studies of structure and development, points to the conclusion, that, although monocotyledony seems the simpler, more primitive condition, it is really a later phenomenon, the monocotyledons being derived from the dictoyledons by simplification.[1] Again, a careful student of fossil plants has recently been led to state that, "it is beginning to appear more probable that the Higher Cryptogams (ferns and fern allies) are a more ancient and primitive group than the Bryophytes, which would seem to owe their origin to reduction from some higher type."[2] In view of this diversity of opinion, we learn at once that great caution must be used in interpreting the evidence—that we must not "jump at conclusions."

493. Results of the Method of Comparative Anatomy.—By their study of comparative anatomy and morphology, botanists have been led to propose the following arrangement of plant groups as representing *the general course* of their evolution (Table V):

From what has already been said, however, it should be understood that such a table represents, not the line of evolutionary advance, but the paths travelled by plants in the course of their development. For example, it implies that dicotyledons were derived from monocotyledons,

[1] See paragraph 519, Chapter XXXVIII.

[2] Scott, D. H. "The Evolution of Plants," p. 18.

TABLE V.—SEQUENCE OF PLANT GROUPS, BASED ON THE MORPHOLOGY OF LIVING FORMS

Thallophytes (no archegonia)	Algæ—having chlorophyll.
	Fungi—no chlorophyll.
Archegoniates (archegonia, but no seeds)	Bryophytes—no vascular system.
	Pteridophytes, Calamophytes, Lepidophytes — vascular system.
Spermatophytes (seeds)	Gymnosperms—no closed ovary.
	Angiosperms—closed ovary (pistil).
	Monocotyledons—one seed-leaf.
	Dicotyledons—two seed-leaves.

pteridophytes from bryophytes—hypotheses which, from other trustworthy evidence, as stated above. now seem untenable.

Again, the table suggests that Angiosperms were derived from Gymnosperms, and therefore appeared late in the history of plant life; but the study of fossil plants shows that they appeared in the geological past, and were dominant in the Tertiary period, as now. We are led, therefore, to proceed with caution in drawing inferences based only upon a comparative study of the structure of forms now living.

494. Evidence from Life Histories.—In the study of the life history (ontogeny) of any higher sporophyte, we find that vegetative (sterile) tissues develop first. On the basis of this fact it has been inferred that all reproductive organs (stamens, carpels, sporophylls) arose by a modification of vegetative organs. Other facts, however, lead to the directly opposite conclusion.

495. Evidence from Comparative Ontogeny.—In Chapters XVI and XXIII attention is called to the fact that the most primitive sporophytes of the lower liverworts consist almost entirely of "fertile" (*i.e.*, reproductive) cells, and that the relative amount of vegetative or sterile tissue gradually increases (as we pass to more highly organized forms) by a *progressive sterilization* of fertile tissue. This progressive sterilization accompanied a change in the habitat of plants from water to dry land.

496. Consequences of an Amphibious Habit of Life.—The life history of the fern affords a concrete illustration. The gametophyte is semi-aquatic in habit, and the method of fertilization is purely aquatic, the sperm being unable to reach the egg except by swimming through free water. But, when the fertilized egg began to develop as a land plant, the chances of fertilization by a sperm swimming in free water became increasingly remote. The perpetuation of the species, and the multiplication of individuals could be insured only by the formation of a large number of reproductive bodies (spores), capable of distribution by wind in dry conditions, and each able to reproduce its kind independently, without fusion with another reproductive body. The larger the number of such spores, the greater the chances of perpetuation of the given species.

497. Consequence of Enormous Spore-production.—But the formation of a large number of spores requires a vigorous plant body to supply them with an abundance of water and nourishment, and to lift them up into the air where they would stand a better chance of distribution when dry. This is accomplished by the sporophyte,[1] producing an abundance of broad, green leaves for food-

[1] "The fern, as we normally see it, is an organism with, so to speak, one foot in the water, the other on the land." Bower, F. O., "The Origin of a Land Flora," p. 82.

manufacture, and of roots for absorption of water and minerals in large quantities. From this point of view, the plant body of the sporophyte is regarded as produced by the progressive sterilization of tissues originally reproductive. After the formation of a vigorous plant body then spores, produced in special regions (sporangia), could be nourished in enormous numbers.

498. Origin of Vegetative Organs.—On the basis of the theory just outlined, we are to regard foliage-leaves and branches, either as *new formations*, developed (by "*enation*") on some primitive reproductive axis like a strobilus or cone, or else as produced by the sterilization of parts originally fertile, *i.e.*, modifications of reproductive tissues. The sporophyte, as we have already seen,[1] has become increasingly well developed and *increasingly independent*, while the gametophyte has become increasingly simple and *increasingly dependent*. The evolution of plants has proceeded by the progressive development of the sporophyte, and the gradual but steady regression of the gametophyte.

499. Steps in the Evolution of the Sporophyte.—The possible steps in the evolution of the sporophyte may be tabulated as follows:[2]

1. Sterilization of fertile tissue.
2. Localization of spore-production in sporangia.
3. Origination of lateral organs (leaves), and of roots.
4. Development of heterospory.
5. Introduction of fertilization by the pollen-tube (*siphonogamy*).
6. Assumption of the seed-habit.

[1] Chapter XXIII.

[2] Following F. O. Bower.

500. Another Hypothesis of Alternation of Generations.—Some of the facts of paleobotany support the hypothesis that the modern sporophyte has not been gradually developed from a simple structure like the moss sporogonium (derived, in turn, by progressive sterilization), but that the gametophytic and sporophytic stages were at the first vegetatively or somatically equivalent, except for chromosome number (as is the case now, for example, with *Dictoyota*[1] and *Polysiphonia*); and that, in the course of evolution, the sexual phase became more, and the asexual phase less, important in certain forms (*e.g.*, mosses), and the asexual phase more, and the sexual phase less, important in other forms (*e.g.*, ferns). This is the hypothesis of *homologous alternation*, as opposed to that of *antithetic alternation.*[2] The structural differences in the two generations are, on the basis of this hypothesis, considered as due almost, if not entirely, to differences in environment, the main factor being the gradual transition from aquatic to dry-land surroundings. Where the environment is uniform and the same for both generations, as for *Dictyota*, the gametophyte and sporophyte are identical in external organs and general appearance (Fig. 177). In any event the hypothesis postulates a homology between the various organs of the two generations, however much these parts may differ in external appearance as a result of individual variation and environmental influence.

501. Lang's Ontogenetic Hypothesis.—Viewing the matter from the standpoint of individual development (ontogeny), Lang has developed the *ontogenetic hypothesis*

[1] See Chapter XVII.
[2] See Chapter XIV.

of alternation. From this point of view two alternatives are recognized:

1. Either the fertilized egg and the haploid spore are potentially unlike, and will *therefore* produce unlike plant bodies, even under essentially similar environment, or

2. Fertilized eggs and spores are potentially alike, but produce unlike plant bodies *as the result of the difference in the environment in which they develop.*

The ontogenetic school accepts the latter alternative as a working hypothesis, and regards the gametophytic and sporophytic generations as essentially homologous. The degree of homology which can actually be traced in the vegetative structure of the two generations may vary from substantial identity, as in *Dictyota*, to such wide divergence that the tracing of homologies is quite out of the question. In testing this hypothesis a *crucial experiment* would be to obtain a gametophyte by artificially bringing a fertilized egg to mature development outside of the archegonium and under the environment in which the spores normally develop; or to obtain a sporophyte by causing a spore to develop within the tissue of a gametophyte, as the fertilized egg normally does.

502. Hypothetical Ancestral Tree.—From a comparative study of both living and fossil forms some botanists have been led to infer the common derivation of Filicales, Equisetales, and Lycopodiales from the Hepaticæ, and probably through some form belonging to the Anthocerotales somewhat as shown in the following ancestral "tree" (Fig. 410). It should be clearly understood that this tree does not illustrate known facts, but only the hypotheses which have been tentatively proposed by careful students on the basis of known facts.

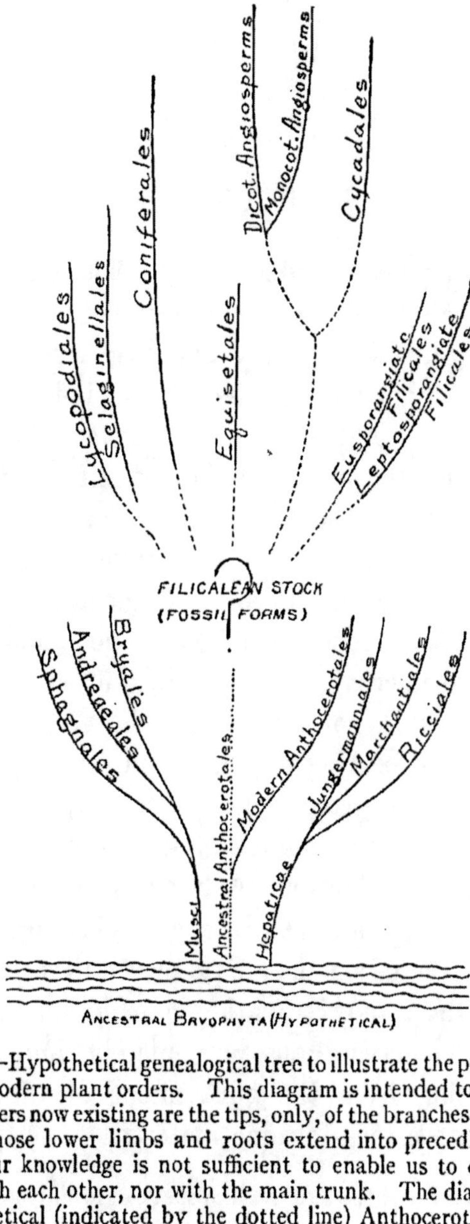

FIG. 410.—Hypothetical genealogical tree to illustrate the probable affinities of the modern plant orders. This diagram is intended to indicate that the plant orders now existing are the tips, only, of the branches of a genealogical tree, whose lower limbs and roots extend into preceding geological periods. Our knowledge is not sufficient to enable us to connect these branches with each other, nor with the main trunk. The diagram teaches that hypothetical (indicated by the dotted line) Anthocerotales gave rise to a now fossil Filicalean stock, from which have been derived all the modern orders above the mosses and liverworts.

CHAPTER XXXVII

PALEOBOTANY

503. The Scope of Paleobotany.—The study of fossil plants, though of course a phase of botany, constitutes a science by itself, not only covering a special subject matter, but having its own methods (technique), and possessing a large literature. It is called *paleobotany*. One cannot pursue this study without a knowledge of the anatomy and morphology of living forms. This is necessary in order to interpret the meaning of plant fossils, which often occur only in small fragments of the entire plant. Moreover, one must have a good knowledge of at least the elements of geology, since fossils are found in rocks. One must not only know the geological age to which the fossil-bearing rock he studies belongs, but also something of the geological processes by which fossils, and even the rocks themselves, are formed.

504. What is a Fossil?—A fossil is any remains of a plant or animal that lived in a geological age preceding the present; these remains are preserved in rocks.[1] There are two methods of preservation, namely, *incrustation* and *petrifaction*. Incrustations are merely impressions or casts resulting from the encasement of the organ or organism in the rock-forming material. The tissue itself

[1] By an extension of the term we also speak of fossil footprints of animals, fossil ripple marks, *et cetera*. The word fossil is derived from the Latin *fodere* (to dig), and originally signified anything dug up.

either decayed or became carbonized, leaving only the impression of its surface features. The well-known "fossil fern-leaves," found in coal mines are of this nature. The tissues of the plant were transformed into coal, leaving the impression or cast on the adjacent shale. The first stage in this process may often be observed in the autumn, when impressions of recently fallen leaves are made on the surface of wet mud. Obviously from such fossils we can learn nothing of internal structure.

Petrifactions are formed by the gradual replacement of the organic tissue by mineral matter, usually carbonate of lime ($CaCO_3$) or silicic acid (H_4SiO_4). In this process the tissues become soaked with a saturated solution of the given mineral, which is gradually deposited from solution, and takes the place of the original organic matter. By this means the most minute details of microscopic structure are preserved, even in some cases the nuclei and other cell-contents.

505. Conditions of Fossil-formation.—In order to understand how fossils come to be formed, we must picture to ourselves certain geological processes now in operation—the initial stages of rock-formation. Rocks are of two kinds, *igneous* and *sedimentary*. Igneous rocks result from the cooling of molten lava poured out on the surface or injected into crevices by volcanic action. Such rocks never contain fossils, as the intense heat necessary to melt the rock destroys all trace of organic matter.

Sedimentary rocks are formed by the deposit under water of the sediment formed by weathering and erosion, and transported by streams. This deposit may occur along the flood-plains or at the mouths of streams empty-

FIG. 411.—Bean Pond, near Wanakena, an extreme type of Adirondack bog. The lifeless, open-water zone, the dwarf heath-shrub, and the surrounding dwarfed black spruce are shown. At the pond margin, borings show over twenty-four feet of brown peat. This becomes shallower toward the margins of the basin, being about eight feet deep under the black spruce, one hundred yards to right of pond in the figure. (Photo by H. P. Baker. Legend quoted from W. L. Bray.) (Cf. Fig. 412.)

ing into inland lakes or into the ocean. In addition to rock-sediment eroded from the surface of the land, streams

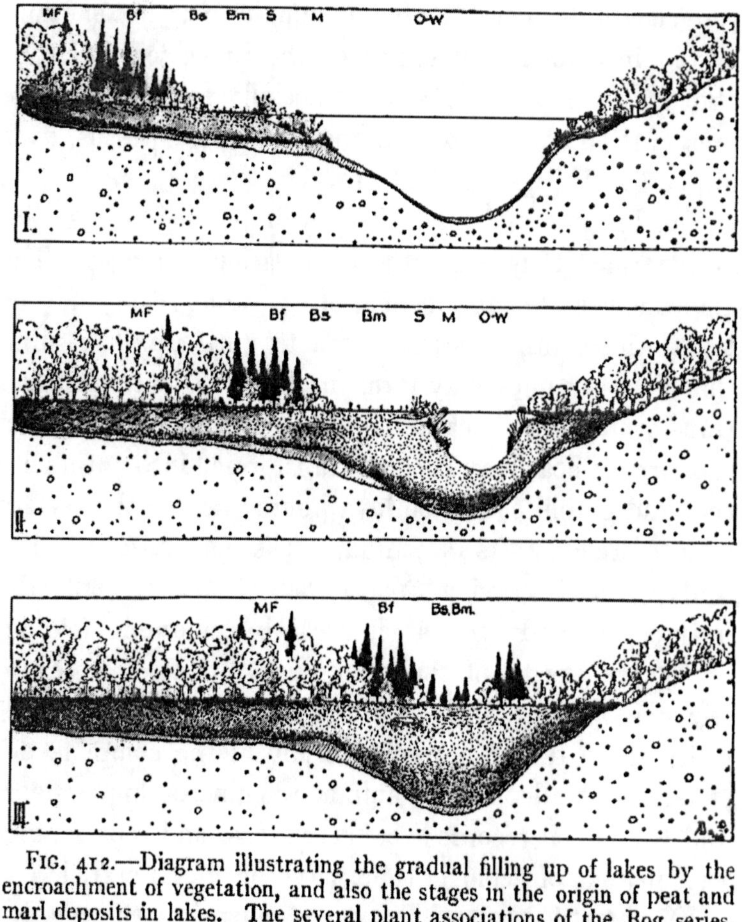

FIG. 412.—Diagram illustrating the gradual filling up of lakes by the encroachment of vegetation, and also the stages in the origin of peat and marl deposits in lakes. The several plant associations of the Bog series, displacing one another, belong to the following major groups: (1) O. W., open water succession; (2) *M.*, marginal succession; (3) *S.*, shore succession; (4) *B.*, bog succession, comprising the bog-meadow (*Bm*), bog-shrub (*Bs*) and bog-forest (*Bf*); and (5) *M. F.*, mesophytic forest succession (Cf. Fig. 411.)

also transport quantities of plant (and animals) fragments, leaves, stems, pieces of bark, fruit, flowers, pollen and spores, roots, and even entire plants. These naturally become buried in the mud and sediment wherever deposition takes place, and when the deposit becomes converted into rock the organic remains may become converted into fossils by either of the processes described above. Swampy regions are especially favorable to the preservation of plant and animal remains as fossils, as is illustrated in Figs. 411 and 412.

506. Metamorphism.—After sedimentary rocks are once formed they are subject to various changes. The amorphous carbonate of lime, of limestone rocks, may be transformed into crystals of calcite until *marble* results; thin flakes of mica may form in clay rock in thin sheets, transforming the rock into *slate;* vegetable deposits in the form of peat may become transformed into anthracite coal and graphite; molten lava poured out on the surface or into crevices of sedimentary rocks may fuse the adjacent material, causing *contact metamorphism;* while the heat engendered over larger areas by mountain folding, or by the weight of superincumbent strata[1] may cause *regional metamorphism.* Obviously such changes, especially those caused by heat, result in the complete destruction of all plant or animal remains or impressions, and thus fossil records over large areas, and representing vast periods of geologic time, have been obliterated.

507. Stratification of Rocks.—Changes in the relative level of sea and land have occurred many times in the geological past, so that submerged areas of sedimentation in one period have become areas of dry land, undergoing erosion in another; and *vice versa,* areas of erosion have become areas of sedimentation. As a result of this,

[1] Some rocks are buried under more than 40,000 feet of strata, and the temperature increases approximately 1°F. for every 50 to 60 feet of depth.

rocks occur in layers,[1] the deeper lying layers (with exceptions readily explained by geologists) being older than those above, or nearer the surface. Moreover, as a result of a second submersion following elevation and erosion, subsequent layers were often deposited with an *unconformity* on the weathered and eroded surface underneath.

By the presence of fossil imprints of rain drops, footprints, ripple marks, and mud cracks, and by the character of the plant and animal fossils which they contain, we know that most sedimentary rocks were deposited in shallow water, not far from the shore line. But since these same rocks may have a thickness of thousands of feet we know the area of sedimentation must have been slowly sinking while the sediment was being deposited. As a result of the enormous pressure of the overlying material, of the deposit of cementing substances from solution, and of other causes, the sedimentary deposits became, in time, converted into solid rock.

508. Classification of Rock Strata.—By a study of the fossils which the rocks contain, geologists have been able to classify the various strata according to their age. As a result of the period of erosion, indicated by unconformity, the transition from the stratum of one age to that of another is often abrupt, the fossils in successive periods being quite characteristic of the given stratum or period. In other cases, as for example between the Silurian and Devonian in New York State, there is no unconformity, and this renders it more difficult to decide just where the plane of division lies. The names and order of occurrence of the known rock strata are given in

[1] Several layers form a *stratum* or *bed*.

the following table, the older rocks being at the bottom, the most recently formed at the top.

TABLE VI.—TABLE OF GEOLOGICAL TIME

Era		Period
Cenozoic	Quaternary	Holocene (recent, or the present) Pleistocene (ice age)
	Tertiary	Pliocene Miocene Oligocene Eocene
Mesozoic	Secondary	Upper Cretaceous Lower Cretaceous (Comanchean) Jurassic Triassic
Paleozoic	Primary	Permian Upper Carboniferous (Pennsylvanian) Lower Carboniferous (Mississippian) Devonian Silurian Ordovician Cambrian
Archean		Huronian Laurentian

509. Paleogeography.—By changes in the relative level of the land and sea, above referred to, rocks containing fossils may be elevated as dry land, and frequently as mountains, so that remains of marine organisms, as well as of others, are often found at high elevations. In some cases forests near the seashore have been submerged,

FIG. 413.—Fossil tree stumps in a carboniferous forest, Victoria Park, Glasgow. (Cf. Fig. 414.) (After Seward.)

FIG. 414.—Part of a submerged forest as seen at low tide on the Cheshire coast of England. (Cf. Fig. 413.) (After Seward.)

and covered over with sediment, then elevated again as dry land, so that subsequent excavations have revealed the fossilized trunks and stumps (Figs. 413 and 414). Thus it is seen that, by a study of fossils, we may not only learn of their structure and thus fill in many of the gaps in the evolutionary sequence left by a study of forms now living, but we may also learn of the distribution of plants and animals in previous geological ages—in other words, we have the basis for a science of fossil geography or *paleogeography*.

510. Plant Migrations.—With the development of Paleogeography, a clearer conception of the location and changes of the continental areas of the past is gradually being gained. As a consequence, plant geography is a subject of increasing interest to the paleobotanist. Moreover, geology, the fossil record, and the present zonal grouping of plants indicate that, in the past, the polar areas, once tropic or sub-tropic, must have been fruitful in new species.[1] High mountains or plateaus are also suggested as homes of plastic races. In the tropics environments are more nearly static, and, it is reasonable to suppose; less likely to cause variation. It is known that, once established, many species move most readily along the geologic formation which supplies the exact soil constituents, the rate of movement often being rapid. Flotation of seeds is also a factor. The facts here briefly cited rest on the observations of a large number of invesitgators, extending over more than a century.

511. Distribution of Plants in Time.—In addition to the distribution of plants in space (plant geography), the

[1] Owing to the precession of the equinoxes these areas undergo an extreme variation in the length of winter and summer of 37 days every 12,934 years.

problem of their distribution in geologic time is one of absorbing interest and importance. The following table indicates the known distribution of the various plant groups from the earliest geologic time to the present.

TABLE VII.—DISTRIBUTION OF PLANTS IN GEOLOGIC TIME[1]

Division		Subdivision, class, or order	Range	Common name or example
IV. Spermatophyta Cycadophyta	Angiospermæ	Dicotyledones	Comanchean to present	Oaks
		Monocotyledones	Comanchean to present	Grasses
	Gymnospermæ	Gnetales	(Fossil record scant)	Ephedra
		Coniferales	Permian to present	Pines
		Ginkgoales	Permian to present	Ginkgo
		Cordaitales	Devonian to Permian	Cordaites
		Cycadales	Permian to present	Cycads
		Cycadofilicales	Devonian to Jurassic	Neuropteris
III. Lepidophyta Calamophyta Pteridophyta		Lycopodiales	Devonian to present	Club mosses
		Equisitales	Devonian to present	Horsetails
		Sphenophyllales	Devonian to Permian	Sphenophyllum
		Filicales	Devonian to present	Ferns
II. Bryophyta		Musci	Tertiary to present	Mosses
		Hepaticæ	Tertiary to present	Liverworts
I. Thallophyta		Fungi	Silurian to present	Fungi
		Algæ	Pre-Cambrian to present	Seaweeds
		Diatomeæ	Jurassic to present	Diatoms
		Schizophyta	Pennsylvanian to present	Bacteria
		Myxomycetæ	(Fossil record lacking)	Slime-molds

[1] Modified from Shimer.

512. Gaps in the Fossil Record.—In the *Origin of Species* Darwin called attention to the paltry display of fossils in our museums, as evidence of how little we really know of the plant and animal life of past ages. "The number, both of specimens and of species, preserved in our museums," says Darwin, "is absolutely as nothing compared with the number of generations which must have passed away during a single formation." The meagerness of the record is, of course, due in part to the relatively small area explored in proportion to the whole; but there are other reasons much more serious, because they represent opportunities lost forever. Among them are metamorphosis, explained above, and the fact that many of the organisms of the past were composed wholly or partly of soft tissues, which were entirely destroyed, by decay or otherwise, in the process of rock-formation. Such plants, for example, as *Spirogyra* and many other algæ, the fleshy fungi, and, among animals, jelly-fish, earthworms, and others, would form fossils only under exceptionally favorable circumstances, if at all.

But there is an even more effective cause of obliteration of the fossil record in the long-continued erosion and denudation represented by unconformity in the rock strata. In many cases only a small proportion now remains of the thickness of a rock stratum originally deposited, and all traces of the plant and animal life that may have existed on the denuded area have thus been obliterated forever. These blank intervals between successive periods were of vast duration.

"I look at the geological record," said Darwin, "as a history of the world imperfectly kept, and written in a changing dialect; of this history we possess the last volume alone, relating only to two or three countries. Of this volume, only here and there a short chapter has been preserved; and of each page, only here and there a few lines. Each word of the slowly changing language, more or less different in the successive chapters, may represent the forms of life, which are entombed in our consecutive formations, and which falsely appear to have been abruptly introduced."[1] These views have received added emphasis from the recent development of Paleogeography.

513. Factors of Extinction.—The question may naturally arise, "Why did the species common in previous geological ages die out, giving place to newer forms?" The answer is found in the facts of struggle for existence and survival of the fittest. In the words of the great American botanist, Asa Gray, species may continue only "while the external conditions of their being or well-being continue." The struggle may be with other organisms or with the physical conditions of the environment. Among the more important factors of extinction, may be mentioned the following:

1. *Struggle with other plants for adequate space.* This is illustrated in a simple way by the crowding out of cultivated plants by weeds in a garden. By more rapid germination and growth, and by other "weedy" characteristics, the weeds get the start of the cultivated plants, occupying all available space, and choking them out.

2. *Attacks of disease-causing parasites, e.g.*, chestnut trees by a parasitic fungus, elm trees by the elm tree beetle.

3. *Changes of environment too great or too rapid to permit of readjustment.* Plants are plastic organisms, and can adapt or readjust themselves to considerable environmental change, but there are limits of speed and amount of change beyond which readjustment is not possible, and the plant must consequently perish. If such changes

[1] Darwin, C. "Origin of Species," New York, 1902, vol. 2, p. 88.

involve the entire area of distribution of the species concerned, the species will, obviously, become extinct. The following seven factors are specific instances of this.

4. *Diminished water supply.* Aquatic plants may be destroyed by the draining of a pond or lake; hydrophytic forms by the drying up of a swamp. Sometimes forms suited to conditions of moderate water supply (*hydrophytes*) are destroyed by the conversion of wide areas into desert regions, as has doubtless occurred. If such changes are gradual, resting spores (*e.g.*, *Spirogyra*), winter buds (*e.g.*, *Utricularia*, and eel-grass), and seeds readily transported by wind (*e.g.*, cat-tail) enable the species to become reëstablished in a new location, but not so when the changes are too abrupt, or cover too wide an area.

5. *Temperature changes*, when too abrupt, too extreme, or too long continued. When the continental ice-sheet advanced southward during the glacial period, many forms, adapted only to temperate conditions, became extinct. Fossils of extinct tropical plants are found in Greenland, which is now undergoing a glacial period.

6. *Volcanic eruptions*, such, for example, as those of Mount Pelee, which occurred in 1902, on the island of Martinique, W. I., often destroy all signs of life over a radius of many miles. In the states of Washington, Oregon, and Idaho floods of molten lava, covering thousands of square miles, have been poured out over the surface, forming a wide plateau. It is almost certain that many species of plants and animals have become extinct by such agencies. Not only the lava, but poisonous gases that fill the air during volcanic eruptions, are fatal to plant life.

7. *Encroachment of salt water* in coastal regions, caused

by changes in the level of the land, resulting in the killing of fresh-water vegetation.

8. *Disturbance of symbiotic relationships.* The interrelationships of organisms are very complex, affording innumerable opportunities for extinction by a disturbance of adjustments. Shade-loving forms in a forest may perish by the destruction of those affording the shade; obligate parasites may perish from the destruction of the necessary host; plants dependent upon certain insects for cross-pollination may perish on account of the extinction of the necessary insects.

9. *Diminution of carbon dioxide in the atmosphere.* There are reasons for thinking that in certain past ages the atmosphere was richer than now in carbon dioxide, and that that condition was favorable to the development of certain vegetatively vigorous species which cannot live in an atmosphere like the present, having a smaller percentage of carbon.

10. *Denudation of the land surface.* In the course of ages even lofty mountains are planed down by erosion, and the arctic and sub-arctic species of the high altitudes thus undergo extinction. Furthermore, erosion may be coupled with general subsidence. In fact, not only do geologists now recognize numerous old mountain "roots," such for example as the Adirondack region of New York State, but there are also abundant evidences of periodic emergence and subsidence of areas of continental extent, quite throughout geologic time. The climatic and other environmental disturbances accompanying such changes would inevitably result in the extinction of certain species. (See also ¶505.)

CHAPTER XXXVIII

THE EVOLUTION OF PLANTS (Concluded)

514. Evidences from Fossil Plants.—The study of fossil plant remains has greatly enlarged our knowledge of the course of plant evolution, filling in gaps derived from the study of living forms, and affording new facts, not disclosed by the study of plants now living. Like the study of comparative anatomy and life histories, paleobotany teaches us that there has been a gradual evolutionary progress from the simple to the more complex, but it has also disclosed the fact that some of the complex forms are much more ancient than had been inferred from the study of living plants only.

515. Discovery of Seed-bearing Ferns.—For example, remains of seed-bearing plants, quite as highly organized as those of to-day, are found far back in the earliest fossil-bearing strata of the Paleozoic. Great forest types existed as early as the Devonian. Later in the Carboniferous occur many seed-bearing ferns. These have been called *Cycadofilicales* (cycadaceous ferns), or, by some, *Pteridosperms*. Recent studies have disclosed the fact that most of the fossil plants from the Carboniferous coal-bearing strata, formerly thought to be ferns, are not even cryptogams, but are these fern-like seed-bearing plants. The best known pteridosperm is *Lyginodendron oldhamium* (Fig. 415), first described from fossil leaves, in 1829, as a tree-fern, under the name *Sphenopteris Hoeninghausi.*

After investigations extending over nearly 90 years, "we are now in position to draw a fairly complete picture of the plant as it must have appeared when living.

"It was in effect a little tree-fern, with long, slender,

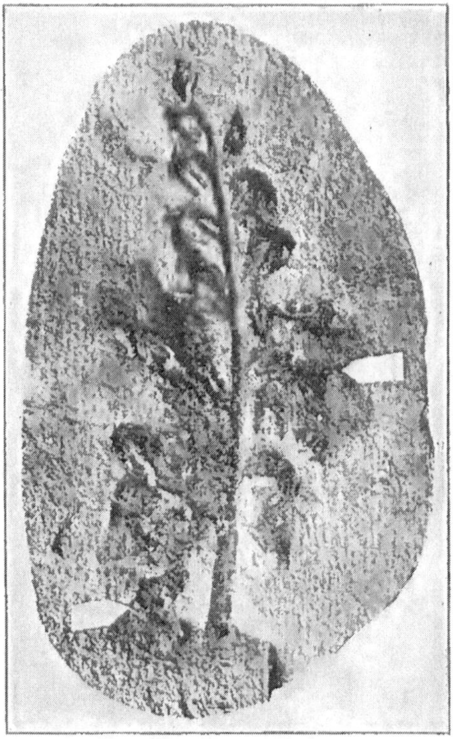

FIG. 415.—*Lyginodendron oldhamium.* Pinna of a microsporophyll, found in an ironstone nodule. Before its identity was established this specimen was named *Crossotheca Hoeninghausi.* The somewhat pellate fertile pinules on the ultimate branches, bear each a fringe of microsporangia about 3 mm. long. The appearance has been likened to that of a fringed epaulet. (After Scott, from a photo by Kidston.)

sometimes branched, stem, 4 centimeters or less in diameter, and provided with spines by means of which it probably climbed on its neighbors. The foliage was disposed spirally and consisted of relatively very large, finely divided fronds with small, thick pinnules with revolute margins, suggesting a xerophytic or halophytic habitat. The stem in the lower portion gave rise to numbers of slender roots, some of which appear to have been aerial in their origin. These grew downward and often branched where they entered the soil.

FIG. 416.—Young leaf of the Cycad, *Bowenia serrulata.* Comparison of this with a leaf of the fern *Angiopteris* (Fig. 417) shows how difficult it might be to decide from a fossil leaf whether the plant was a cycad or a fern. (Cf., also, Fig. 420.)

"The stems, roots, and petioles, and even the pinnules, have been found [calcified] and so beautifully preserved that their entire structure can be made out with certainty. Without going into a technical description of these organs, it may be said that the stem when young, and before secondary growth has begun, has a very strong resemblance to the stem of [the fern] *Osmunda*, but when more mature certain cycadean characters appear to predominate."[1]

FIG. 417.—Leaf of a fern (*Angiopteris evecta*). (Cf. Fig. 416.)

Its foliage and other characters closely resemble some of our modern tree-ferns (Cf. Figs. 416 and 417) but more careful study of the calcified specimens of much beauty

[1] Knowlton, F. H. *American Fern Journal*, 5:85. 1915.

found in the English "coal balls"[1] has disclosed both the microsporophylls, bearing pollen-sacs, and the megasporophylls, bearing, not merely megasporangia, but *true seeds*. The ovule has a *pollen-chamber*, like the cycads, except that it projects a bit through the micropyle, and, strange as it may seem, fossil pollen-grains have been discovered, well preserved within this chamber. The seeds, about ¼ inch long, have been described as resembling little acorns, en-

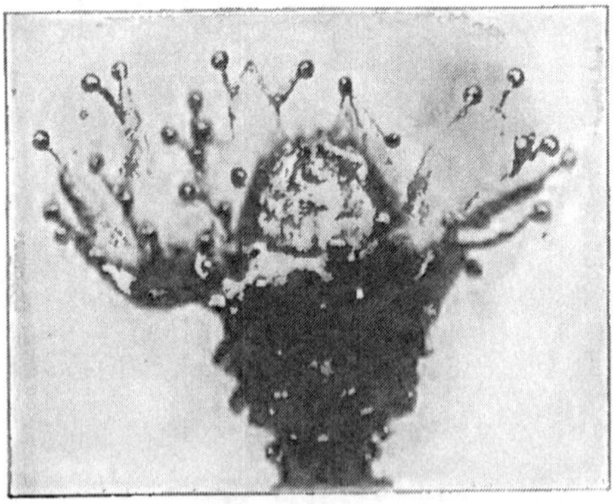

FIG. 418.—Restoration of a seed of *Lyginodendron oldhamium* (*Lagenostema Lomaxi*), from a model by H. E. Smedley. (After Scott.)

closed like hazelnuts in smaller glandular cupules (Fig. 418). They are similar to those of the cycads, except that they are not known to have organized an embryo with cotyledons and caulicle. Instead, the tissues of the female gametophyte only are so far found, retained within

[1] Coal balls are "concretions of the carbonates of lime and magnesia which formed around certain masses of the peaty vegetation as centers and, through inclosing and interpenetrating them, preserved them from the peculiar processes of decay which converted the rest of the vegetation into coal. In them the mineral matter slowly replaced the vegetable matter, molecule by molecule, thus preserving the cellular structure to a remarkable degree. Such balls are especially frequent in the coal of certain parts of England (Lancashire and Yorkshire)."

the megasporangium, which is enclosed in the integument. In this connection it is of interest to note that the seeds of some modern plants (*e.g.*, orchids) do not possess differentiated embryos, but whether this is a primitive or a reduced character is not certain. The pollen was formed in spindle-shaped pollen-sacs, having two chambers and borne in clusters of four to six on the under side of little oval discs from 2 to 3 millimeters long. These structures

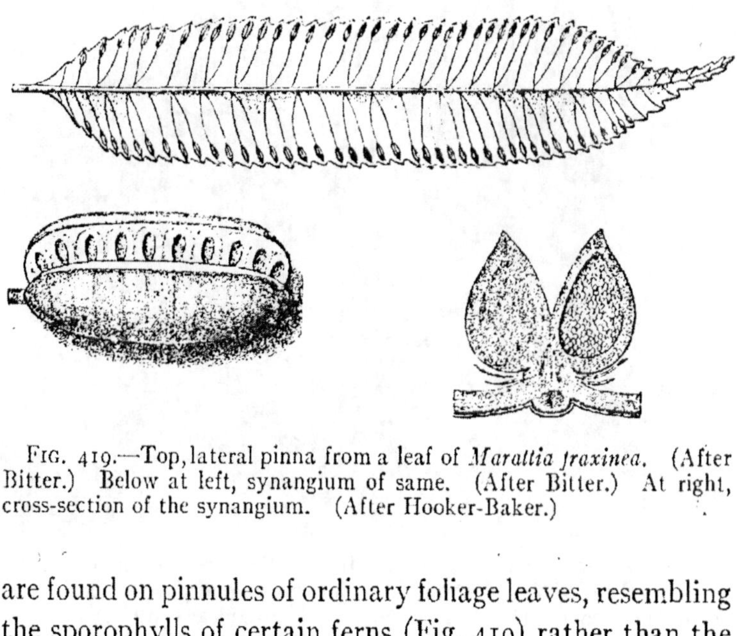

FIG. 419.—Top, lateral pinna from a leaf of *Marattia fraxinea.* (After Bitter.) Below at left, synangium of same. (After Bitter.) At right, cross-section of the synangium. (After Hooker-Baker.)

are found on pinnules of ordinary foliage leaves, resembling the sporophylls of certain ferns (Fig. 419) rather than the stamens of modern flowers.

The discovery of the seed-bearing character of the fern-like plants of the Paleozoic was predicted by Wieland, of Yale University, nearly two years before it was made by Oliver and Scott. It is now believed that seed-bearing plants of the pteridosperm type were nearly as numerous in the Paleozoic as were the cryptogams.

516. Significance of the "Pteridosperms."—The close resemblance of the pteridosperms to ferns, on the one hand, and to modern cycads on the other, justifies the conclusion that they represent a "connecting link" between the true ferns and the cycads, and that the modern cycads have descended from the same ancestry as the modern ferns, each developing along somewhat different lines.

FIG. 420.—*Stangeria paradoxa* Moore. Specimen from the cycad house at the New York Botanical Garden, bearing, at the apex of the stem a carpellate cone. (Photo from New York Botanical Garden.)

It was in recognition of their vegetative resemblances that the Pteridosperms were first called (by Potonié) Cycadofilices, now *Cycadofilicales*. Van Tieghem tersely described them as "phanerogams without flowers."

517. A Modern Fern-like Cycad.—One of the modern cycads (*Stangeria paradoxa*)[1] is of much interest in this

[1] *Stangeria paradoxa* Moore = *Stangeria eriopus* (Kunze) Nash.

connection. So closely does it resemble a certain fern (*Lomaria*) that the botanist Kunze, who first described it when it was brought from Natal to the botanic garden at Chelsea, England, supposed it was a fern, and named it *Lomaria eriopus*. The specimen possessed no fruit, which would have helped to identify it. Its leaves, with circinate vernation, have a pinnately compound blade, and leaflets with pinnate dichotomous venation. Two or three years later another botanist, examining it more closely, pronounced it a "fern-like Zamia or a Zamia-like fern." These facts show how puzzling the specimen was, and how closely a plant may resemble both a cycadophyte and a fern. In a sense this plant may be called a living fossil. Specimens have since come into flower in botanic gardens, and the typical cycadaceous cones (Fig. 420) leave no doubt that the plant is a true cycadophyte.

518. Derivation of New Types.—Attention should here again be called to the fact that the theory of evolution does not teach that one given species becomes transformed into another, but simply that new species are descended from older forms which may or may not continue to exist. It is not supposed, for example, that ferns developed into cycads, and cycads into higher gymnosperms, but that there has been an unbroken line of descent (possibly more than one) in the plant kingdom; that closely related forms (like ferns and cycads) have descended from a common ancestral type which may or may not now be found. We must not, in other words, expect necessarily to find in fossil forms the direct ancestors of those now living, although a study of their structure is of the greatest value in enabling us to understand the genetic relationships of the great groups of plants.

519. Ancestors of the Angiosperms.—Just as the Cycadofilicales indicate the ancestry of the cycads, so fossil types of Cycadophyta have been discovered which are interpreted by some paleobotanists as ancestors of the modern angiosperms. Other investigators, however, dissent from this view and consider that we have not yet

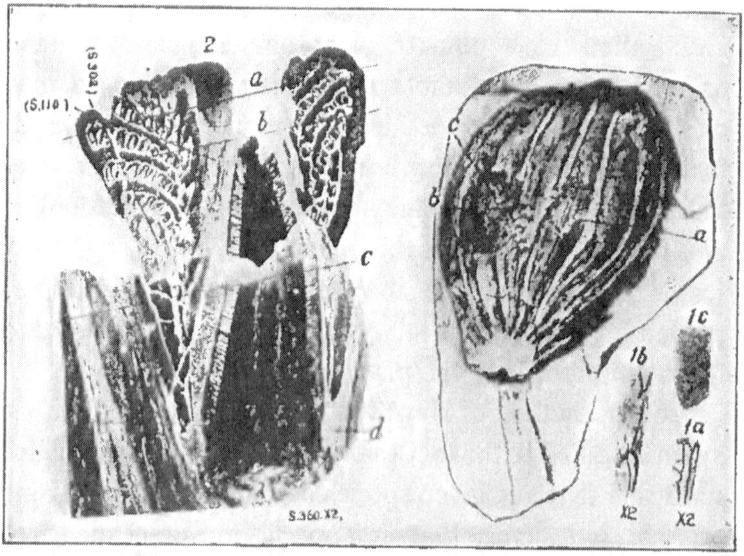

FIG. 421.—To the left, *Cycadeoidea dacotensis* Macbride. Longitudinal section of a silicified specimen of a bisporangiate cone (unexpanded flower), so taken that the pinnules of the microsporophylls on both sides of the central axis, or receptacle, are successively cut throughout their entire length. The lines indicate the planes of various sections through the cone, published in Wieland's "American Fossil Cycads." To the right *Cycadocephalus Sewardi* Nathorst. Microsporangiate cone, natural size, preserved as an impression on a flat slab. From a fossil-bearing bed of the Trias, at Bjuf, Southern Sweden. (Left figure from Wieland, right figure from Nathorst.)

sufficient knowledge of fossil forms to be justified in designating the ancestors of the Angiosperms. This difference of opinion is largely due to the meagerness of the available evidence. As one writer has stated it, "A trayful of flowers may be all the record of the Pteridosperms from the Devonian on. The gaps in the evidence are always enormous."

Although the Cycadophyta are now a very insignificant element in the earth's flora; in the Mesozoic period they form about one-third of the recovered vegetation of the land. One order, the Bennettitales, then had a cosmo-

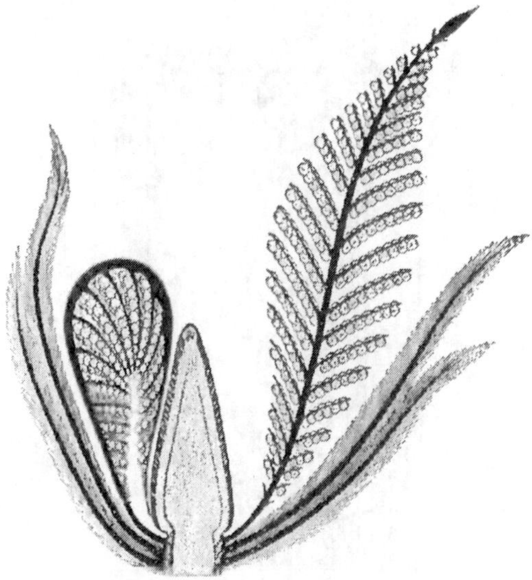

FIG. 422.—*Cycadeoidea dacotensis.* Semi-diagrammatic sketch of a flower (bisporangiate cone), cut longitudinally; one sporophyll folded, and one (at the right) arbitrarily expanded. At the center is the apical, cone-shaped receptacle, invested by a zone of short-stalked ovules and interseminal scales. The pinnules of the sporophylls bear the compound sporangia (*Synangia*). Exterior to the flower are several hairy bracts. About three-fourths natural size. (After Wieland.)

politan distribution and seemingly was as important as the Dicotyledons are now. Over 30 species of the petrified stems have been found in the Mesozoic terrains of the United States, the Black Hills of South Dakota alone yielding a score. The Isle of Portland forms were called

Cycadeoidea by the celebrated geologist Buckland. The name of the order is derived from the genus-name, *Bennettites*.[1] Other forms, usually found as casts, are called *Williamsonia*, still others are known mainly as genera founded on leaf imprints.

520. Cycadeoidea.—In most of its purely vegetative characters, such as the anatomy of the stem and the

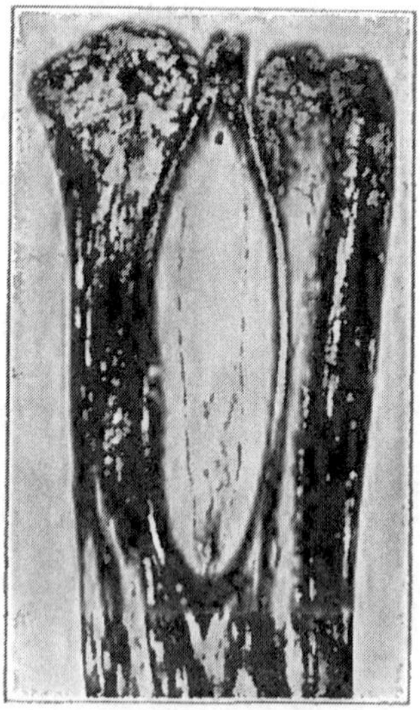

FIG. 423.—*Cycadeoidea dacotensis* (?). Photomicrograph of a young seed (× 15), showing a sterile scale on either side. Between them projects the entire length of the tube through which the micropyle extends. The partially collapsed nucellus is distinctly shown in the center. (After Wieland.)

structure of the leaves, *Cycadeoidea* resembled modern cycads, but its reproductive branches were characteristically lateral, which is one of the most fundamental characteristics of the higher seed-bearing plants of to-day. Only two modern cycads (*Macrozamia* and *Bowenia*) have lateral seed-bearing cones (Fig. 289).[2] Various

[1] *Cycadeoidea* Buckland = *Bennettites* Carruthers.

[2] The staminate cones of *Zamia* are lateral.

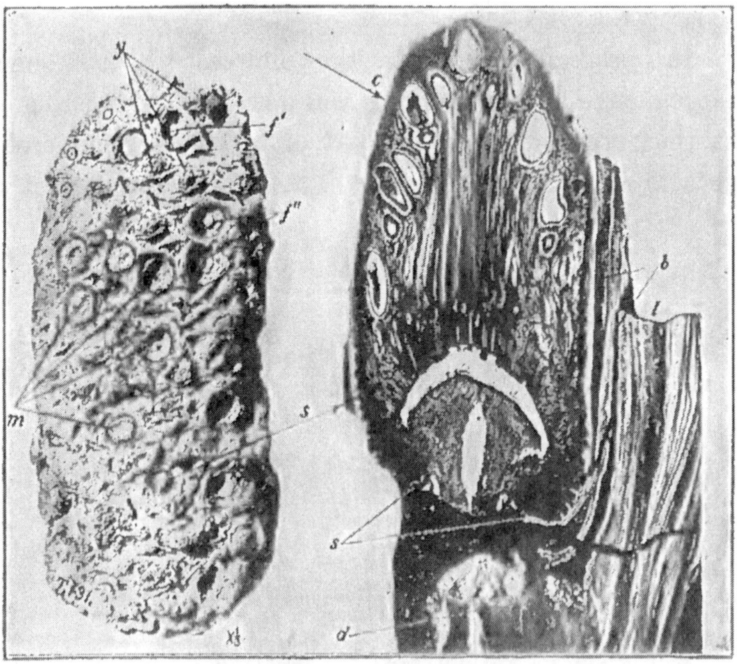

FIG. 424.—*Cycadoidea Wielandi.* At left, a finely preserved trunk bearing many ovulate cones with seeds approaching maturity, and a lesser number of either young or abortive cones. *f'*, Receptacle of a shed or non-preserved cone with surrounding bracts yet present; *f''*, two cones broken away during erosion, with a portion of the basal infertile pedicel yet remaining; *m*, four cones eroded down to the surface of the armor, in this instance about or a little beneath the level of the lowermost seeds; *y*, three of the dozen or more very young cones, in some cases known to be simply ovulate and to be regarded as having aborted or else as belonging to a later and sparser series of fructifications than the seed-bearing cones present, the latter unquestionably representing the culminant fruit-producing period in the life of this cycad; *s* (over lower arrow), the ovulate strobilus shown at right in its natural position, this photograph having been made before the cone was cut out by a cylindrical drill. × about 1⁄4; at right, longitudinal section of the small ovulate strobilus cut from its natural position on the trunk as denoted by the arrow *s*, in photograph 1. *c* (upper arrow), seed with dicotyledonous embryo preserved, cotyledons being similarly present in the lowermost seed on the left-hand side of the strobilus; *s*, traces of hypogynous staminate disk; *b*, bracts; *l*, leaf bases. × about ¼. (After Wieland.)

structural characters of *Cycadeoidea* are shown in Figs. 421–427.

In *Cycadeoidea dacotensis* the "flower," which in some specimens was 5 inches long, was a strobilus, consisting of a thick axis on the lower part of which were numerous bracts arranged in spirals. The bracts surrounded a

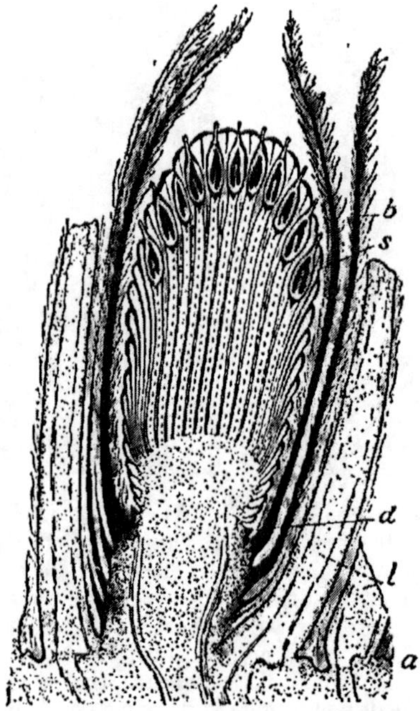

FIG. 425.—*Cycadeoidea Wielandi.* Longitudinal section through the axis of a female inflorescence, or cone. *l*, old leaf-base; *d*, insertion of disc; *s*, erect seed, borne at summit of seed-pedicle inserted on convex receptacle; *b*, hair-covered bract. (After Wieland.)

campanula of about 20 stamens. Each stamen was, in reality, a pinnately compound sporophyll, about 4 inches long, rolled in toward the center of the flower, and bearing two rows of compound microsporangia (pollen-sacs) on each leaflet. They thus closely resembled the sporophyll of a fern.

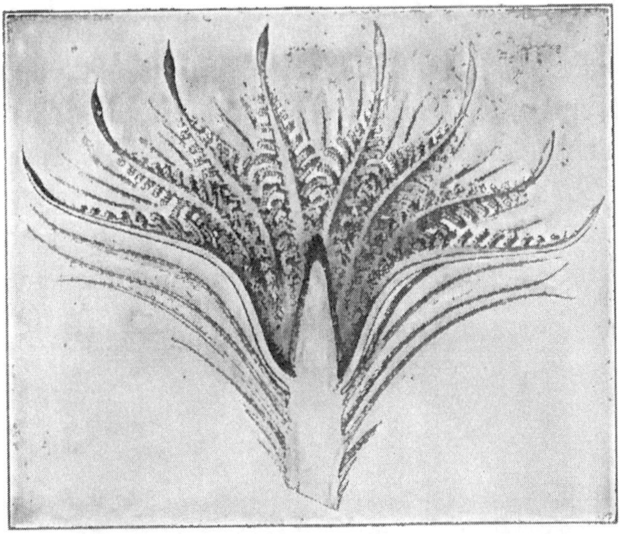

FIG. 426.—*Cycadeoidea ingens.* Restoration of an expanded bisporangiate cone, or flower, in nearly longitudinal section. Restored from a silicified fossil. (After Wieland.)

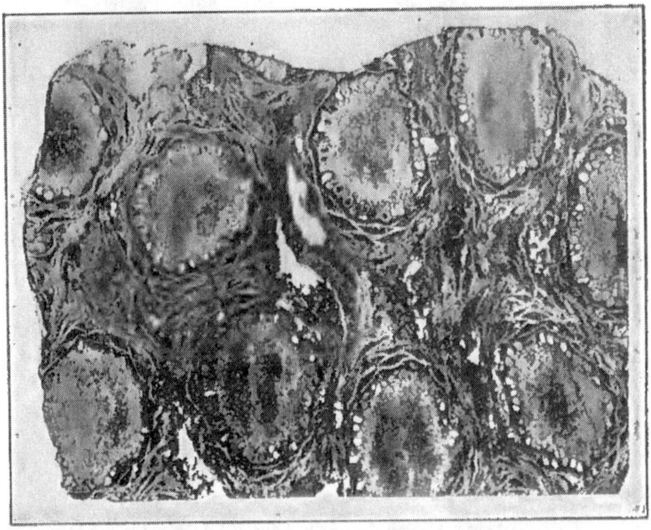

FIG. 427.—*Cycadeoidea Dartoni.* Tangential section through outer tissues of the (fossilized) trunk, showing the very numerous seed-cones. The seeds are very small (the illustration being natural size), and nearly every one has a dicotyledonous embryo. There were over 500 such cones on the original stem. (After a photograph loaned by Prof. Wieland.)

The axis of the flower terminated in a cone-shaped receptacle, bearing the stalked ovules, and numerous sterile scales (Figs. 424 and 425). The mature seeds often contain the well-preserved fossil embryos, with *two cotyledons* which quite fill out the nucellus, and show that there was little or *no endosperm.* These are characters never found in the lowest group of modern seed-

FIG. 428.—Flower of magnolia. (Cf. Fig. 429.)

bearing plants (the Gymnosperms), but only in the highest group of Angiosperms, the Dicotyledons. In fact, the French paleobotanist, Saporta, called some of the Cycadeoids, *Proangiosperms.*

521. Relation of Cycadeoidea to Modern Angiosperms. —The question of the ancestry of the Angiosperms is the most important problem of paleobotany. Although the Bennettitales possess many of the primitive anatomical features that characterize the Cycadofilicales, their development of a bisporangiate strobilus with two set of sporophylls, related to one another as they are in the flower of the Angiosperms. indicates a genetic relationship to that group, as does also the fact that the seeds, enclosed in a fruit, possess a dicotyledonous embryo, without endosperm. In other features the Bennettitales are unlike the Angiosperms; the ovules, for example, are enclosed by sterile scales, instead of by the carpels on which they are borne, and the protrusion of the pollen-chamber through the micropyle signifies the gymnospermous type of fertilization.

FIG. 429.—Magnolia. Flower with perianth removed, showing the compound pistil, and four of the stamens. Most of the stamens have been removed. Note their spiral arrangement as shown by the scars at the points of attachment. (Cf. Fig. 428.)

These and other comparisons indicate that the Bennettitales were essentially Gymnosperms having certain Angiospermous characters, and therefore, while they are not to be considered as the ancestors of the Angiosperms, it is probable that they and the modern dicotyledons are both descended from a common branch of the ancestral tree. Among modern plants, the flower of the magnolias most closely resembles that of *Cycadeoidea* in the spiral arrangement of its stamens and pistils (Figs. 428 and 429.). How much significance should be attached to that fact has been disputed by students of morphology.

The gap between the stamen of *Cycadeoidea* and the type characteristic of modern Angiosperms is partially bridged by the genus *Williamsonia* (which has simple *vs.* pinnately compound stamens), and by another genus, *Wielandiella*, both older genera than *Cycadeoidea*. From this it has been inferred that the Bennettitales are a lateral branch, further removed than their ancestors from the direct evolutionary stock of the Angiosperms.

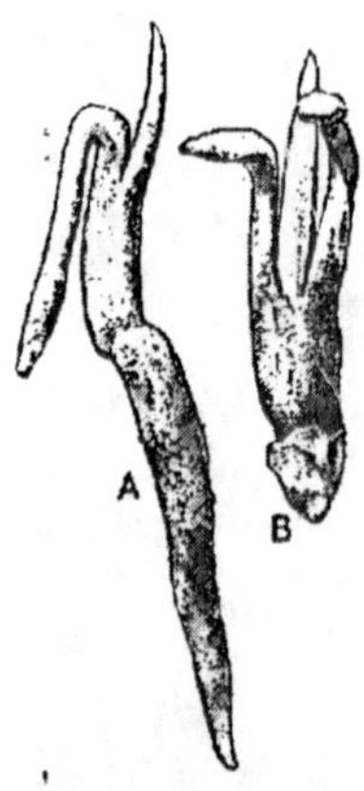

FIG. 430.—*Agapanthus umbellatus.* *A*, monocotyledonous embryo; *B*, dicotyledonous embryo. (Redrawn from photo by W. J. G. Land.)

522. Origin of Monocotyledons.—If the earliest Angiosperms were dicotyledons, as seems to be the case, the monocotyledons were probably derived from the dicotyledons by a process of simplification. Much light has been thrown on this question by a study of the development of the embryos (*embryogeny*) of certain plants. The case of *Agapanthus umbellatus* L'Hèr. (Fig. 430), a South African plant of the Lily family, may be taken as illustrating the nature of the evidence derived from embryogeny. The sequence of events is as follows.[1] As the massive proembryo enlarges, the root-end elongates, thus remaining narrow and pointed; while the shoot-end widens, becoming relatively broad and flattish. At this broad and flat end the peripheral cells remain in a state of more active division than do the central cells, and form what is known as the *cotyledonary zone.* In this zone two

[1] The above description closely follows Coulter and Land (1914).

more active points (*primordia*) appear and begin to develop. Soon the whole zone is involved in more rapid growth, resulting in a ring or tube, but with the primordia still evident. The cotyledonary zone continues its growth until a tube of considerable length is developed, leaving the apex of the proembryo depressed. At this stage either one of two things may occur. As the cotyledonary zone continues to grow, the two primordia on the rim of the tube may continue to develop equally, forming two cotyledons; or one of the primordia may cease to grow, resulting in an embryo of only one cotyledon; in other words, the entire cotyledonary zone may develop under the guidance of only one growing point. One cotyledon is not eliminated, but the whole growth is diverted into one cotyledon. There thus develops what appears to be an "open sheath" and a "terminal" cotyledon.

In other words, monocotyledony is not the result of the fusion of two cotyledons, nor of the suppression of one; but is simply the continuation of one growing point on the cotyledonary ring, rather than a division of the growth between two growing points. In a similar way, polycotyledony is the appearance and continued development of more than two growing points on the cotyledonous ring. The rudimentary second cotyledon of a "monocotyledonous" grass-embryo (wheat) is shown in Fig. 378, (p. 494).

523. Ancestors of the Gymnosperms.—As far back as Devonian time, preceding the great coal period (Carboniferous), fossils have been found of a plant, *Cordaites* (of the order Cordaitales), common in that period, and having characters which indicate that it stands in the ancestral line of our modern conifers—that it and the conifers had a common ancestry.

The leaves of *Cordaites* resembled those of the Kauri pines (*Agathis*) of the southern hemisphere (Fig. 431), or the leaflets of *Zamia*. They varied from a decimeter to over a meter in length. The male cones resembled those of the still living *Ginkgo*, each stamen having from four to six microsporangia (pollen-sacs) on a stalk. The female

FIG. 431.—Branch, with cones, of the Kauri pine (*Agathis australis*). (From Gardener's Chronicle.)

cones resembled the male in general appearance, and the seeds resembled those of the Cycadofilicales (Fig. 423). The plant itself was a slender tree, some forms of which attained a height of over 100 feet. *The Cordaitales formed the world's first great forests.* They represent a wide departure from the Cryptogams, and must be considered as true seed-bearing plants. They were closely related to the *Ginkgo*—another living fossil, ranking next below the modern cone-bearing trees. We thus ascend from the ferns to the conifers by a series of transitional forms as follows (reading from the bottom, up):

6. Coniferales (modern cone-bearing trees).
5. Ginkgoales (primitive gymnosperms).
4. Cordaitales (transitional conifers).
3. Cycadales (true cycads).
2. Cycadofilicales (cycad-like ferns).
1. Filicales (true ferns).

524. Relation of the Above Groups.—It must not be inferred that the above groups were derived one from the other by descent from lower to higher. They should be interpreted rather as samples remaining to show us, not the steps, but *the kinds* of steps through which the plant kingdom has passed in developing the more highly organized, modern cone-bearing trees from more primitive forms like the ferns. As stated above, it is doubtful if the actual transitional forms have been preserved, so that the entire history of development can probably never be written.

525. A Late Paleozoic Landscape.—Fig. 432 illustrates the kind of landscape that must have been common in the latter part of the Paleozoic era along sluggish streams in certain regions such as Texas and New Mexico. Of the primitive vertebrates then abounding, only a few larger types are shown. The dragon-flies of that time are known to have had a spread of wing amounting, in some cases, to as much as 2 feet. In the foreground, at the left, are representatives of the Cycadofilicales, some of them bushy, and others resembling our modern tree ferns. At the right are dense thickets of Calamites, the ancient representatives of our modern scouring rushes (*Equisetum*).

FIG. 432.

In the background, at the left, are the unbranched Sigillarias, and the branched Lepidodendrons. The Cordaitales, which formed the Devonian forests, were not yet extinct, but none is shown in the figure. Other forms, ancestors of our modern conifers and angiosperms, must be imagined as hidden in the recesses of the forest.

526. Significance of the Fossil Record.—Before the brilliant discoveries in fossil botany, just outlined, were made, there had been (as stated in Chapter XXXVI) a general tendency among botanists to consider the comparatively simple moss-plants as an older type than the fern, and that either they or their close relatives were the ancestors of Pteridophytes. As outlined in the same chapter, the sporogonium of the moss was regarded as representing the form from which, by elaboration of vegetative tissues and organs, the sporophyte of the fern was derived. This view was clearly expressed in 1884 by the noted botanist Nägeli, who considered that the sporophyte of Pteridophytes was derived from a moss-like sporogonium by the development of leafy branches.

FIG. 432.—Restoration of a scene along a sluggish creek in Texas and New Mexico during the late Carboniferous (Upper Pennsylvania) and early Permian times. The lowlands of this period doubtless swarmed with reptiles such as shown in the picture, and with other animals, now extinct. Some specimens of the giant "dragon-flies" had a spread of wings of two feet. The fern-like trees and the bushy plants in the foreground are Cycadofilicales. To the right of the water are wide stretches of the huge scouring rush (*Calamites*); on the left bank of the stream are the unbranched *Sigillarias* (still as prominent as earlier in the coal period), and on higher ground to the left the branched *Lepidodendrons*. One must view this scene as one of many such landscapes, with ever-varying detail, along streams and inlets. *Cordaites*, which in later Devonian time made the first great forests of which there is record, is still present, though not shown. So, too, there are hidden in the recesses of the forest the forerunners of the modern coniferous types, as well as other forms destined to give rise to the angiosperms. (Landscape from Williston, adapted from Neumayr.)

A consideration of the fossil record, however, makes it difficult to accept this hypothesis. Not only do we find, in the fossil forms described above, sporophytes that do not bear the remotest resemblance to the moss-sporogonium, but fossil mosses and liverworts have never been positively identified in either the Palaeozoic or the Mesozoic rocks, while the same rocks are rich in fossils of such advanced forms as the broad-leaved sporophytes of the Cycadofilicales and Cycadophytes. We must not, however, hastily conclude, from this lack of evidence, that mosses and liverworts did not exist in those early ages. Quite likely they were present when the Paleozoic rocks were being deposited, though doubtless not represented by the same genera, or at least not by the same species, as are now living.

527. Summary of Results.—From what has been said, in this and in Chapter XXXVI, we recognize that *the method of evolution is to be ascertained chiefly by experiment*—by studying *living plants* in action; but *the course of evolution chiefly by the study of comparative morphology, with special attention to fossil forms.* Other points are necessary to complete the history of the evolution of plants; the above paragraphs give only the barest outline of the problem, for the entire history is much too long and much too difficult to be treated here. To summarize; the facts now known have led some investigators to infer:

1. The origin of Angiosperms from Cycadophyta (pro-angiosperms).
2. The origin of Cycadophyta from Cycadofilicales.
3. The origin of Cycadofilicales from Primofilices.
4. The origin of Filicales from Primofilices.

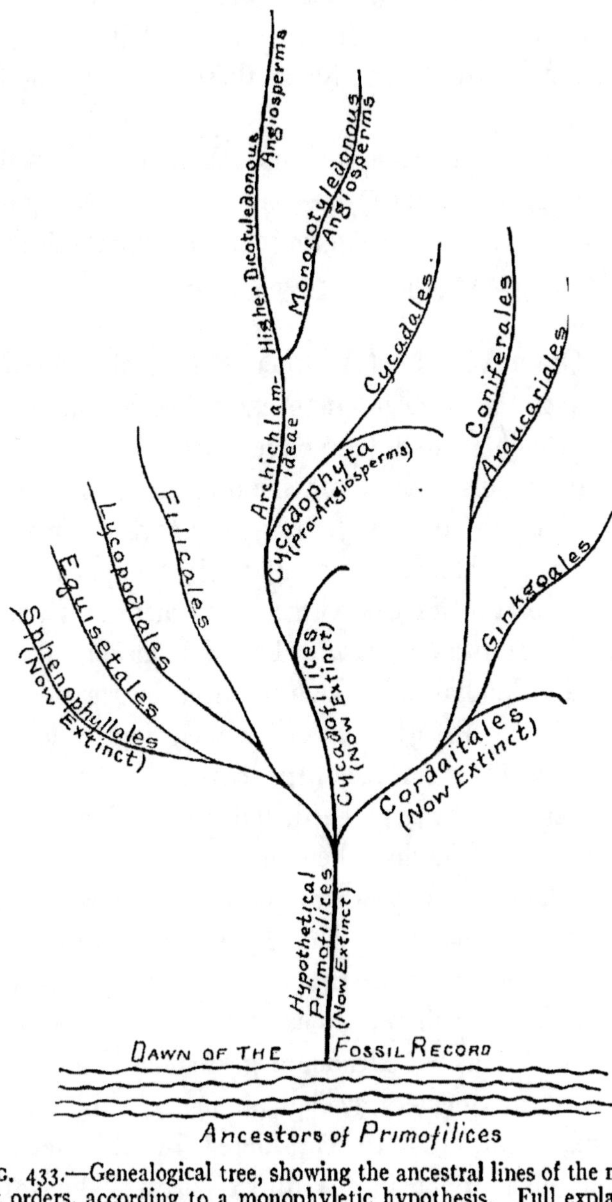

Fig. 433.—Genealogical tree, showing the ancestral lines of the modern plant orders, according to a monophyletic hypothesis. Full explanation in the text. (Cf. Fig. 434.)

5. The origin of Cordaitales from Primofilices.[1]
6. The origin of Coniferales from Cordaitales.

An ancestral tree embodying these views is shown in Fig. 433.

What was the origin of the Primofilices? Here, as often in every science, we have to acknowledge that we do not know; the group is a hypothetical one, and some investigators doubt its actual existence altogether.

528. Other Views.—(*a*) Other and equally competent students of the problem take exception to one or more of the six points tabulated above. Not all of their views can here be discussed, but mention may be made of that first elaborated by Jeffrey, of Harvard University. According to this view vascular plants appear at the beginning of the fossil record as two distinct series, the *Lycopsida* and *Pteropsida*. The Lycopsida, like the modern Lycopodiales, are characterized by the possession of small leaves (a primitve character), and by few sporangia on the *upper* surface of the leaves. The Pteropsida, by contrast, are distinguished, like the modern Filicales, by large leaves, having the numerous sporangia on the lower surface. The two groups also have well-marked anatomical differences. The Lycopsida reached their greatest development in the Paleozoic period, and now appear to be on their way to extinction. The Pteropsida, on the other hand, although possessing many representatives in former geological ages, still maintain their full vigor, and are considered by this school of paleobotanists to be in the direct ancestral line of our

[1] The term *Primofilices*, not .. :herto used in this text, refers to a hypothetical, primitive fern stock.

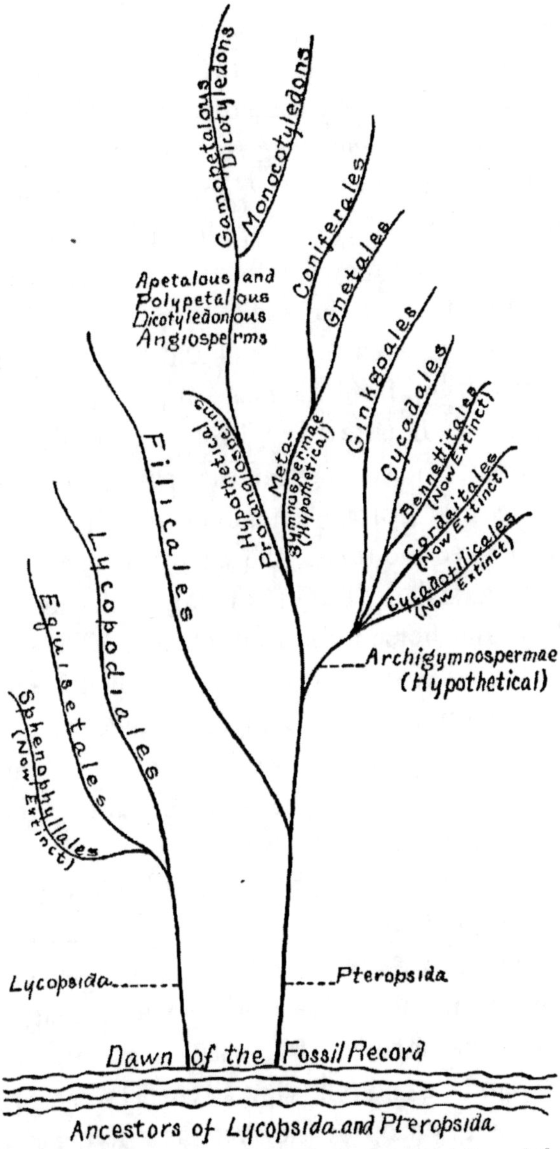

FIG. 434.—Genealogical tree, showing the ancestral line of the modern plant orders according to a polyphyletic hypothesis. Full explanation in the text. (Cf. Fig. 433.)

modern vascular plants, substantially as indicated in Fig. 434.[1]

(*b*) Greater precaution in drawing conclusions from the few known facts has led still other students of fossil plants to refrain from endeavoring to connect up the ancestral lines, claiming that while they may converge, indicating a common ancestry of the known forms in the geologic past, on the other hand they may not unite, or at least may not all converge toward the same ancestral type. In other words, it is suggested that fossil and modern plants had a *polygenetic* origin from the stage of primitive protoplasm. Such views are illustrated in Table VII (p. 619).

It is seen from this diagram that our modern ferns have a long ancestral history, extending from the present back to early Palaeozoic times; the same is true of our modern cycads, maidenhair tree (Ginkgo), club-mosses (Lycopodiales), and horse-tails (Equisetales). The Coniferales may be traced back into the upper Carboniferous period, while the most highly developed of modern plants, the Angiosperms, appear to have come into existence as late as about the middle of the Mesozoic era, perchance as recently as 20 million years ago.

"The construction of a pedigree of the Vegetable Kingdom is a pious desire, which will certainly not be realized in our time; all we can hope to do is to make some very small contributions to the work. Yet we may at least gather up some fragments from past chapters in the history of plants, and extend our view beyond the narrow limits of the present epoch, for the flora now living is after all

[1] Scott restricts the name Lycopsida to the Lycopodiales, and proposes a third group, Sphenopsida, including the Equisetales, Pseudoborniales, Sphenophyllales, and Psilotales.

nothing but one particular stage in the evolution of the Vegetable Kingdom."[1]

TABLE VIII

Ascendancy	Periods	Persistence and relationship of great groups
VII. Reign of Angiosperms	Tertiary Cretaceous Comanchian	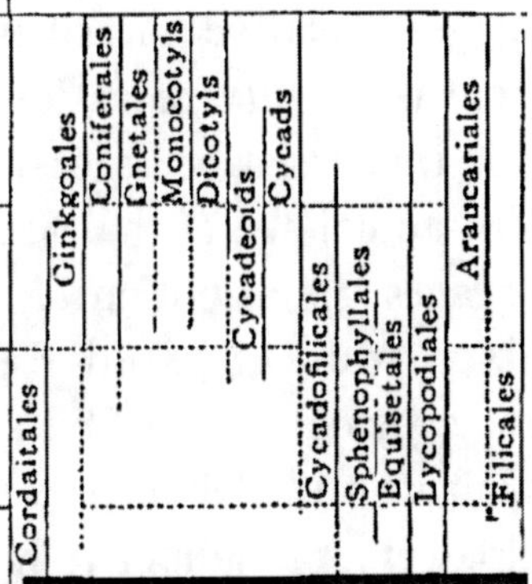
VI. Reign of Pro-angiosperms	Jurassic Triassic Permian	
V. Reign of Acrogens (Higher Equisetes. Lycopods, etc.)	Pennsylvanian Mississippian	
IV. Reign of Gymnosperms	Devonian	
III. Reign of Early Land Plants	Silurian Ordovician	5. Actual Fossil Land Plant record begins 4. Primofilices—Early Equisetes 3. Basal Plant Complex with variety of species
II. Reign of Algæ	Cambrian Precambrian (Proterozoic)	2. Differentiation of Dry Land and Aquatic Plants (Fossil Algæ abundant)
I. Reign of Primitive Life (Hypothetical)	Old Precambrian (Archeozoic)	(Fossil Algæ begin) 1. Primitive Protoplasm and Unicellular Life

In the above table (after Wieland), the groups are to be considered as arranged on an unrolled cylinder, projected from a hemisphere; thus the phyletic lines are to be pictured as converging above toward the pole, and the Cordaitales as coming between the Ginkgoales and Filicales, to both of which they are related.

529. The Element of Geological Time.—How many years has it taken for the evolution of the higher Angiosperms—that is, from the dawn of the fossil record in the

[1] Scott, D. H. "Studies in Fossil Botany," p. 3.

Silurian period to the present? No one knows. From a study of the thickness of rock strata, and a knowledge of the probable time required for the depositing of those strata as sediment on the floor of the ancient oceans, and their elevation and denudation to their present condition by weathering and erosion, geologists have been able to suggest relative measures of geologic time. Paleozoic time is *long*, twice as long as Mesozoic time, and Mesozoic time must be at least twice as long as Cenozoic time. The actual age of the earth is, however, a problem which engages the attention of physicists as well as geologists. Sixty years ago Lord Kelvin gave a mean estimate of 100,000,000 years. With this estimate the geologists, Walcott and Geikie, have nearly concurred; but since the discovery of radium it has been estimated that certain carboniferous iron ores have an age of 140,000,000 years.

Figures of such magnitude convey but little meaning to our minds; they are too large for us to grasp their real value. "Therefore," as Darwin has said, "a man should examine for himself the great piles of superimposed strata, and watch the rivulets bringing down mud, and the waves wearing away the sea-cliffs, in order to comprehend something about the duration of past time, the monuments of which we see all around us."

530. The Essence of Science.—A careful reading of this book will have led the student to realize that the unsolved problems of botany are more numerous and quite as interesting as those we have solved. The essence of science is the endeavor to ascertain by the best method that which is most worth knowing.

APPENDIX

THE GREAT GROUPS OF PLANTS

Division	Subdivision	Class	Order
I. Thallophyta	A. Algæ	1. Cyanophyceæ	
		2. Chlorophyceæ	
		3. Phæophyceæ	
		4. Rhodophyceæ	
	B. Fungi	1. Myxomycetes	
		2. Schizomycetes (Bacteria)	
		3. Phycomycetes	
		4. Ascomycetes	
		5. Basidiomycetes	
		6. Fungi imperfecti (life histories imperfectly known)	
II. Bryophyta		1. Hepaticæ	Ricciales
			Marchantiales
			Jungermanniales
			Anthocerotales
		2. Musci	Andreales
			Sphagnales
			Bryales
III. Pteridophyta		1. Eusporangiatæ	Ophioglossales
			Marratiales
			Isoetales
		2. Leptosporangiatæ	Filicales
			Marsiliales
IV. Calamophyta		1. Sphenophyllineæ	Sphenophyllales
		2. Equisetineæ	Equisetales
		3. Calamarineæ	Calamarales
V. Lepidophyta		1. Lycopodineæ	Lycopodiales
		2. Lepidodendrineæ	Selaginellales
			Lepidodendrales
VI. Cycadophyta		1. Cycadofilicineæ	Cycadofilicales
		2. Cycadineæ	Cycadales
		3. Bennettitineæ	Bennettitales
		4. Cordaitineæ	Cordaitales
			Ginkgoales
			Gnetales

- VII. Spermatophyta
  - A. Gymnospermæ
    - 1. Pinoideæ.........
      - Coniferales
      - Taxales
  - B. Angiospermæ
    - 1. Monocotyledoneæ
      - Pandanales
      - Naidales
      - Graminales
      - Arales
      - Xyridales
      - Liliales
      - Scitamnales
      - Orchidales
    - 2. Dicotyledoneæ.....32 Orders, including
      - (a) Archichlamydeæ Apetalæ Polypetalæ
        - Salicales
        - Polygonales
        - Ranunculales
        - Rosales
        - Violales
        - Myrtales
        - Umbellales
      - (b) Metachlamydeæ Sympetalæ (= Gamopetalæ)
        - Ericales
        - Polemoniales
        - Plantaginales
        - Rubiales
        - Campanulales

INDEX

N

S